The Boston Terrier Handbook

BY

LINDA WHITWAM

ISBN- 13: 978-1540485908

Copyright

Contributing Authors

PAMELA H. PRESTON

AND

JO DALTON

Acknowledgements

My sincere thanks to the Boston Terrier breeders as well as owners and canine experts who have generously contributed their time and expertise to this book. Their knowledge and love of their Bostons shines through and without them, this book would not have been possible.

Special thanks to (in alphabetical order): Anne and Bill Connor, Emily Little, Gwion Williams, IDOG International, Jo Dalton, Lindsey Scanlon, Lisa Williams, Lynda Montgomery, Michelle Courtney-Kaye, Susan Maxwell, Pamela H. Preston, and Dr Sara Skiwski.

TABLE OF CONTENTS

1. Meet the Boston Terrier

Of all the nicknames given to different dog breeds, the Boston Terrier's is perhaps the best: 'The American Gentleman'.

The Boston, as owners like to call him, has the distinction of being the first breed to have been developed and registered in the United States of America. In a reversal of trend at the beginning of the 20th century, Boston Terriers were bred in America and later exported to Europe.

And a gentleman he surely is, not only in looks, but also in temperament. The Boston Terrier earned his nickname through his striking black and white markings, which create a 'tuxedo' effect, with a white chest and dark body. Add to that the intelligent expression, compact body, muscular physique and sleek, short coat and it's no wonder that he's most often described as 'dapper.' This certainly is one good-looking dog.

And if you're out and about with your Boston, you may well find that he's a people magnet.

For 30 years in the first half of the 20th century, the Boston was either ranked Number One or Two in America and, after falling out of favour, the breed is enjoying something of a renaissance. It is currently ranked just outside the top 20 in the US, and numbers are rising in the UK.

Although originally bred from fighting dogs, today's Boston is highly affectionate, lively and non-aggressive. The breed has a reputation for gentleness - even empathy - as well as an ability to get on well with children, and is a popular choice for families.

Add to that the fact that the Boston is adaptable, easy to groom and exercise, he is a small, manageable size and suitable for apartment life, old people and families, and you can see why he ticks so many boxes for so many people.

The Boston is in the Non Sporting Group in the US and Utility Group in the UK. He has been bred as a companion dog and that is what he excels at. He loves to be with his people, is extremely affectionate and will keep you amused with his antics and sense of fun. This is a breed that can have an independent streak, but underneath is a huge heart from a loyal companion that is only too eager to please you.

The American Kennel Club describes the Boston as: "Friendly, bright, amusing, and adaptable." The Breed Standard states: "The expression indicates a high degree of intelligence...The dog conveys an impression of determination, strength and activity, with style of a high order; carriage easy and graceful."

The Kennel Club (UK) says: "The Boston is the smallest of the Bull breed, i.e. containing Bulldog blood... The colour pattern of white on legs, chest, collar and head make the Boston a very 'Dandy' dog and the term 'Boston marked' is sometimes applied to other breeds with similar colour patterns, e.g. Mantle Great Danes."

Temperament

Your Boston Terrier's character will depend largely on two things. The first is his temperament, which he inherits - and presumably one of the reasons why you have chosen a Boston. What many owners do not realise is that as well as being born with those distinctive coat markings, big eyes, muscular physique and other trademark physical features, your dog has also inherited his temperament from his parents and ancestors.

Good breeders select their breeding stock based not only on appearance, but also on what sort of disposition their dams and sires (breeding females and males) have. And that's another reason to take your time to find a good, responsible breeder.

The Boston Terrier Club of America (BTCA) is the parent breed club, and says: "Boston Terriers are special dogs that can do special things. They are highly intelligent and learn quickly.

"They enjoy showing off in the conformation ring and do very well in Obedience, therapy work, and performance events (Agility, Flyball and even Weight-Pulling!). Bostons excel in many roles. A Boston Terrier can be a child's rough and tumble best buddy, or a senior citizen's soul mate and confidante. Most of all they excel at being your 'best friend!'

"However, they are not for everyone. Bostons require a lot of time and attention. They are, and have been bred to be, companions. They will languish without human contact. They are not 'outside' dogs.

"Boston Terriers are very active dogs that love to play. Without some basic training, they may jump on you and maybe even give little nips while playing. Some Bostons have been given up for adoption or dropped off the local dog pound for these very reasons. Boston Terriers can also be prone to some health problems, many of which require expensive veterinary attention.

"We are NOT trying to discourage you from having a Boston. We just want people to be aware, as we have helped to rescue and place a few of these wonderful little creatures and do not want to end up needing to 'rescue' any more. Please buy ONLY from a reputable breeder that has health clearances on their dogs."

The second factor affecting character is environment - or how you rear and treat your dog. In other words, it's a combination of **Nature and Nurture**. The first few months in a dog's life are so important. Once he has left the litter, your puppy takes his lead from you as he learns to react to the world around him. And one essential aspect of nurture is socialisation.

Even though the Boston is an affectionate and non-aggressive breed, it is essential to spend time introducing your dog to other dogs and humans, as well as loud noises and traffic and other new things, from an early age. A dog comfortable in his surroundings without fear or anxieties is less likely to display unwanted behaviour. Through your guidance and good socialisation, your Boston learns whom he can trust, whether to be afraid - which in turn may cause an aggressive or fearful reaction - how much he can get away with, and so on.

Typical Boston Traits

To say all dogs of the same breed are alike would be akin to saying that all Americans are optimistic and friendly and all Brits are polite and reserved. It is, of course, a huge generalisation. There are grumpy, unfriendly Americans or rude in-your-face Brits. However, it is also true to say that being friendly and optimistic are general American traits, as is being polite in Britain.

It's the same with the Boston Terrier. Each individual dog has his or her unique character, but there are certain traits that are common within the breed. Also, the Boston is one of the 'Bully breeds' - in other words, it originated from the Bulldog - and all Bully breeds share certain characteristics, which can include a single-mindedness! So here are some typical Boston Terrier traits:

- They are very loving, loyal and enjoy spending time with their owners

- They make unparalleled companion dogs, provided you can give them the time they need

- They are adaptable to your lifestyle and when raised properly, they are very affectionate without being needy

- Without sufficient training and socialisation, they can sometimes become attention-seeking, or possessive of toys, you or their food

- Despite their muscular appearance, Bostons are not aggressive dogs - they love cuddling up

- They often have a comical personality and do funny, illogical things - it's hard to work out what's going on in their heads sometimes

- While energy levels vary from one dog to another, the breed is regarded as having medium exercise requirements - all Bostons need some daily exercise, preferably out of the garden or yard

- They have been bred to live indoors, not outdoors, and are a suitable choice if you live in an apartment

🐾 They are known for being good with babies and children - although, like any dog, they should be supervised until the child is old enough to look after herself

🐾 They were bred as companion dogs, it's in their genes that they do not like being alone for many hours on end, and they may suffer from separation anxiety if left alone for long periods when not used to it

🐾 Boston Terriers LOVE to chew, especially when young or bored

🐾 They can be quite sensitive emotionally, picking up on the mood in the household, and can also sulk if you tell them off - they do not respond well to shouting or harsh treatment

🐾 Generally, Boston Terriers do not bark a lot - they may bark when somebody comes to the door, then greet them like an old friend, so they do not make good guard dogs

🐾 Bostons are highly food motivated - which means you have to monitor their food and treats to stop them putting on weight; however, on the plus side, food is a very strong motivator when training

🐾 Bostons are smart dogs and, as well as burning off physical energy, they need to channel their intelligence - they enjoy games and puzzles

🐾 They are often not one-man dogs, being friendly with everybody - they have big hearts and will respond to anyone who shows them kindness – or food

🐾 Like all brachycephalic (flat-faced) breeds, they overheat easily and benefit from air conditioning in hot climates - they are sensitive to temperature fluctuations and are also sensitive to cold conditions, so benefit from a coat or sweater on cold days

🐾 They are often good with other dogs and cats, especially if introduced at an early age

🐾 They have short easy-to-groom coats and don't shed a lot

🐾 **With vigilance and consistency,** the Boston Terrier can generally be easily housetrained - but without those two key factors, they can take a lot longer

🐾 Bostons are very gassy...if you are easily embarrassed, a less windy breed might be more suitable!

🐾 Bostons - especially poorly bred ones - can be prone to eye, joint, breathing or other health issues, which can rack up expensive vets' bills

If we haven't managed to put you off, then read on and learn more about this unique breed and how to fulfil your part of the bargain by taking good care of these affectionate and bubbly little dogs.

Is the Boston the Right Dog for Me?

If you haven't got your dog yet and you answer YES to the next set of questions, then the Boston Terrier could be just the dog for you:

1. Are you looking for a companion dog?

2. Do you want a dog that is suitable for children or old people?

3. Are you prepared to put in the time to train and housetrain your dog - even if your pup is a bit wilful?

4. Does everyone in your house like Boston Terriers?

5. Are you around a lot of the time - or can you make arrangements for someone to help with your dog when you are not there?

6. Can you afford a puppy from health-tested parents and the cost of annual or monthly pet insurance? Medical issues could well run into thousands of dollars or pounds - and, even then, not all conditions may be covered by insurance.

7. Are you prepared to exercise your dog? The Boston is a muscular, active dog and needs more exercise than some other small 'Bully breeds,' such as the French Bulldog. Playing indoor or outdoor games and running round the yard or garden are great forms of exercise, but you should be prepared to take your dog out for at least one daily walk.

....

What the Experts Say

You can read any number of websites and books about Boston Terriers, but the best way to find out what a breed is truly like is to speak to those in the know. It's not very practical for you to contact lots of breeders and owners to interrogate them about their Bostons, but here's some good news – we've done it for you!

We asked our contributors to describe the typical Boston temperament and what first attracted them to the breed. This is what they had to say:

"I like their level of intelligence, loyalty, size and the beautiful look of them. When it's play time they are ready to play, when it's time to rest, they are ready to snuggle. They are just the perfect all-round family or one-person dog. They are loving and people-friendly, they will let you know if anyone is at the door - and they are fearless. Bostons are very social animals; they love attention and love to give attention. I have eight grandchildren who love to play with the puppies - when they are old enough - and so do their friends."

One UK Kennel Club Assured breeder who switched to Bostons after breeding French Bulldogs said: "Bostons are an amazing breed, I adore them. If you have young children they fit in with family life so easily. One of my dogs, Clover, has really a special bond with my son. They are very affectionate, active and want to learn and I find them easy to train. The French Bulldog tends to take over, whereas the Boston is more adaptable. They can have health issues - but not like Frenchies; Bostons are generally healthier."

"They are a small compact breed with an alert and humorous nature. They are highly intelligent and playful; however, their energy levels are manageable. They are loyal and eager to please. In my experience (UK), females tend to be more eager to please, with higher energy levels and are more attentive to the owner, while males tend to be more laid back and docile. They are by far easier to train - especially when compared to the temperament of a Pug. The most appealing thing about Bostons is their temperament - they are highly affectionate and alert."

"I was most attracted to the Boston's intelligence, character/personality, and size. They are very easy to train, are wonderful (and funny) companions, and are compact enough to travel easily with you. Bostons have an ideal temperament (especially when well-bred by a reputable breeder who takes early socialisation into consideration). They are outgoing, confident, active, silly, easy-going, friendly, and smart."

"Boston Terriers are intelligent, enthusiastic, affectionate and playful. They get along well with other pets, dogs, and children. They have strong, friendly personalities, but can range in temperament from those that are eager to please their master to those that are more stubborn. Both types can be easily trained, given a patient and assertive owner. Some Boston Terriers are very cuddly, while others are more independent.

"They are generally very happy little dogs, but they do require a great deal of human contact and hate being left on their own. They can be very persistent when they want your attention, often poking and prodding you or even sitting on the object that they think is preventing you from giving them the attention that they want! They love to play, especially with toys that they can shake and throw around.

"Many Bostons tend to be enthusiastic and excitable, though affectionate and good humoured too, so they are better off with an owner who has a sense of humour and doesn't mind being bounced on and licked a lot. Their boisterous nature needs a firm hand and they can quickly become unruly and bored if not properly trained and stimulated."

One new UK owner said: "The most appealing characteristics of the Boston are the cheeky, sulky look, and the mischievous and comical personality that keeps me smiling to myself all day long. Grooming is minimal and they are very clean and do not smell, due to the short coat. I have a three-year-old Border Terrier and my five-month-old Boston runs rings around her. She is the alpha: bossy, alert and very much in charge and, to my surprise, my Border is quite happy to let her be!

"The Boston is a very good early warning alarm system, very alert hearing and protective of her territory, but also very friendly and non-aggressive. My Boston loves the outdoors, sunbathing, playing ball and is very sociable with other dogs. Bostons are a people puller and I do get strangers coming up and chatting. They are well liked and loved by many, but due to the price tag can be a target to be stolen - so beware and keep a close eye on them."

From a UK breeder: "We bred British Bulldogs for 42 years but downsized to Bostons 10 years ago. We were attracted to their friendly temperament and smart appearance. They have a friendly, happy, outgoing character and are good with people and other dogs. They are very intelligent and quick to learn where food is on offer."

One US breeder of 20 years' standing said: "The Boston Terrier was our choice as it was such a versatile breed, ready for anything and its sleek wash-and-wear coat was great for travel care as well as its size. They are the perfect companion for young or old, ready for that hike in the woods or to curl up on a pillow to snuggle! They have the perfect temperament for an active or laid back family; they are affectionate, but can keep up in a tussle with bigger dogs. They are fearless and affectionate - the best of both worlds!

"The Boston Terrier is a breed that loves to be around people. Although I don't feel any dog should be 'left in the backyard' alone without attention, the Boston really likes to be part of the family. They are willing to be a couch potato and also ready for that long hike or a day on the river. This is truly a really versatile little dog. They are very loving and natural little clowns that will keep you laughing for hours. They are very intelligent, fun and easy to train."

A British breeder added: "The variety in size and the striking markings first caught my eye about Bostons - and I absolutely love the head that the Boston Terrier has. They make great family pets, they are great with people, children and other dogs. Speaking from experience, I have always found males more affectionate and quicker to housetrain. I have also found a male to be more protective of his owner and territory. Not in an aggressive manner, more of an alert to let strangers know that he is the guard dog of the house."

"They are nicknamed 'the American Gentleman' and they are exactly that."

We then asked breeders and owners to sum up Bostons up in a few words:

- ❧ "Intelligent, loving, loyal and fun"
- ❧ "Lively, intelligent, determined, strong-willed"
- ❧ "Outgoing without being shy or hyper"
- ❧ "Happy hooligan!"
- ❧ "Happy, fun and loving"
- ❧ "Affectionate, humorous, intelligent, active"
- ❧ "The PERFECT devoted companion"

Read on to learn more about this unique breed and how to fulfil your part of the bargain by taking good care of these highly affectionate and fun-loving little dogs.

2. History of the Boston Terrier

Unlike almost all the other 188 breeds registered with the American Kennel Club, the Boston Terrier was not imported from foreign shores; the breed was developed in the United States of America.

The Boston's Ancestors

Although the exact origins of the Boston are unclear, it is generally agreed that the modern Boston can trace its roots back to a dog with Bulldog and Terrier heritage known as **Hooper's Judge** and owned in the 1870s by Mr Robert C. Hooper of Boston. According to the Boston Terrier Club UK, opinions differ as to whether Judge was imported from England by Hooper or by a Mr William O'Brien who then sold him to Hooper.

What is clear is that the Boston Terrier as we know it today originated in America, and this new breed was later exported back to the UK. This was a reversal of trend; the normal direction of travel for many leading purebred dogs in the early 20th century was west from Europe to dog fanciers in the USA.

Unsurprisingly, the first people to write about Boston Terriers were Americans, and they were extremely proud that the breed was created in America - and not imported from "The other side" as they called Britain!

Hooper's Judge was a mix of English Bulldog, of the day and the now-extinct English White Terrier (pictured), with probably a hint of other breeds such as the French Bulldog. The Bulldog and Terrier cross eventually became known as the Bull Terrier.

In his 1922 '*The Complete Book of the Dog,*' author Leighton Roberts explains why there was a big interest in crossing the English Bulldog with various Terriers: "In the first quarter of the nineteenth century attention was being directed to the improvement of Terriers generally, and new types were sought for.

"They were alert, agile little dogs, excellent for work in the country; but the extravagant Corinthians of the time - the young gamesters who patronized the prize-ring and the cock-pit - desired to have a dog who should do something more than kill rats, or unearth the fox, or bolt the otter: which accomplishments afforded no amusement to the Town.

"They wanted a dog combining all the dash and gameness of the Terrier with the heart and courage and fighting instinct of the Bulldog. Wherefore the Terrier and the Bulldog were crossed. A large type of Terrier was chosen, and this would be the smooth-coated Black-and-tan, or the early English White Terrier; but probably both were used indifferently, and for a considerable period. The result gave the young bucks what they required; a dog that was at once a determined vermin killer and an intrepid fighter, upon whose skill in the pit wagers might with confidence be laid."

It is interesting to note the foundations of the Boston's temperament were being laid even at this early stage. The early Bulldogs' aggressive instincts were bred out (today's Bulldog is a gentle soul), and "dash and gameness" and "heart and courage" could describe many of today's Boston Terriers.

Working Terriers have existed in the UK for over 200 years. In the late 18th and 19th centuries they were popular with working men and women. These dogs were small, cheap to feed, they kept the vermin down around the home, and hunted small animals. Terriers have always been quite variable in terms of size and shape, with dogs ranging in size from 10 to 15 inches, and with both drop ears and prick ears, smooth, broken and rough coats.

With the birth of official dog shows in the 1860s, breed fanciers raced to name and 'improve' every type of dog they could find – and Terriers were top of the list. In the rush to create and claim new breeds, competing groups sometimes came up with different names for the same type of dog, and it was common for entirely fictional breed histories to be cobbled together as part of a campaign to declare a new breed – not to mention creating a ripple of personal fame and fortune for a dog's originator!

Around this time the English White Terrier was developed by a handful of breeders keen to claim a new breed from prick-eared white working Terriers that later gave rise to Jack Russells, Parson Russells, Sealyhams and Fox Terriers. There were problems with this claim as both drop-eared and prick-eared puppies were often born in the same litter.

The breed never gained widespread popularity and a further nail in the English White Terrier's coffin occurred in 1898 when a law was passed banning ear cropping. This barbaric practice was originally done to stop the ears of fighting dogs being ripped off. The procedure was not performed until the dog was seven to 10 months of age, when the poor animal would be sedated with chloroform and strapped down while its ears were cut with a pair of scissors.

Within just 30 years the English White Terrier had slipped into extinction – but not before its blood had intermingled with that of the English Bulldog to help create the modern Bull Terrier and – sometime later in America - the Boston Terrier and the Rat Terrier.

This book (The Boston Terrier Handbook) stresses the importance of genetics and DNA testing when selecting a puppy, and it is interesting to note how far back genetics can affect a breed. Deafness is an issue that even today affects some Boston Terriers with a coat containing a lot of white. This link between deafness and white coat was noted as early as the 19th century.

When describing the breed standard for Bull Terriers in his 1894 book *'A History and Description of the Modern Dogs of Great Britain and Ireland (The Terriers),'* Victorian English dog breeder and writer Rawdon Briggs Lee stated: "Colour pure white for show purposes; but for ordinary purposes a patched dog, i.e. one with fawn or brindled marks, need not be discarded, nor need fawn or fallow or brindled dogs. The latter are even hardier than the whites, which, on account of their colour, or because they are cropped, are often quite deaf."

In his 1910 book *'The Boston Terrier And All About It. A Practical, Scientific, And Up To Date Guide To The Breeding Of The American Dog,'* early breeder and writer Edward Axtell (pictured) explains how he deliberately interbred a hardy female Boston Terrier with her healthy father as an 'experiment.' The result was that all four puppies in the litter were born deaf. He added: "As we have never had a case of deafness in our kennels before or since, we attribute this solely to inbreeding."

In the early days there was a huge difference in the size of dogs classed as Bull Terriers - from 4lb to 55lb! Describing the ferocity of the early Bull Terriers, Lee says: "There is little or no doubt that the original bull Terrier was a cross between an ordinary kind of terrier and a bulldog....He has been bred for fighting or for killing rats, and long before the era of canine exhibitions, some of the rougher so-called sporting men in London and in the Midlands, of which Birmingham may be taken as the metropolis, had strains of more or less celebrity.

"The dogs that fought with Wombwell's lions were bull terriers and not bull dogs, as stated in the journals of that day, and the fighting dogs of that time and now (for this brutal sport is still followed in many places) were and are bull Terriers."

This was before the days of Breed Standards, and it is not clear if the dogs involved in the famous lion baitings of 1825 Warwick (pictured) were a type of Bulldog or Bull Terrier, but certainly a 'fight' between three dogs and a lion did take place, organised by a promoter called Wombwell.

The event, held on July 26th, involved three Bulldog or Bull Terrier types and a lion named Nero in an enclosure at the Old Factory Yard near Warwick. The dogs were fallow coloured – reddish brown – and were named Captain, Tiger and Turk. Spectators paid a small fortune to watch the sorry spectacle. The dogs were incredibly brave, they rushed at Nero, "pinning" him by the nose and face. Although the gentle-natured lion repeatedly roared with pain and fended off the dogs with his paws, he refused to bite them.

After two dogs were maimed, Turk, the lightest of the three, showed much courage: "Poor Turk was then taken away by the dog-keepers, grievously mangled but still alive and seized the lion, for at least the twentieth time, the very same moment that he was released from under him."

The public were outraged at the promotion of such baiting spectacles. The matter was raised in Parliament and Wombwell's lion baits were the last to be staged in the UK.

Lee mentions a famous 13lb Bull Terrier called Jacko, owned by a Jeremy Shaw of London. The dog died in 1869, but not before he had become famous in dog circles for killing 60 rats in two minutes 40 seconds and 1,000 rats in less than 100 minutes. All told he won 200 'matches' around the country.

Lee himself owned a 30lb fawn Bull Terrier with a black muzzle called Sam. He writes: "For a long time he was my constant companion, and became an adept at hunting rats by the riverside, a capital rabbiter, and as good a retriever as most dogs. He would perform sundry tricks, find money hidden away, and could be sent back a mile for anything - glove, a stick - that had been left behind.

"He would take part in a game at cricket, and fielded the ball so expeditiously that on more than one occasion Sam and I played single wicket matches against a couple of opponents, and as a rule came out successfully. On his father's side he came of a fighting stock, and as he grew older he developed a love for a "turn-up" with any passing canines, which caused me to part with him. He was the death of about a couple of dogs, but otherwise he was the gentlest of the gentle; our cat kittened in his kennel, and with one little shaggy dog longing to be a friend he struck up a great friendship."

In the early and mid-1800s Bull Terriers were often a mixture of colour, such as brindle, fallow, fawn, black and tan or 'smut,' often with white patches. Other dogs were mainly white with black patches over the body, eye or ear – as can be seen from Victorian photographs.

It wasn't until conformation dog shows became hugely popular in Britain in the late 1800s and early 1900s that the 'milky white' Bull Terrier became the dog of choice for the show ring and elsewhere.

(Pictured is 1904 show champion Bull Terrier Greenhill Duchess).

The Boston Terrier's other main ancestor, the Bulldog, has a long and bloodthirsty history and was first known about in 1631, during the reign of Charles I, when an Englishman called Prestwich Eaton wrote to a friend from Spain in London requesting: "A good Mastive (Mastiff) dog, a case of liquor and I beg you to get for me some good Bulldogs."

The Bulldog was extremely athletic and powerful, bred for the cruel sport of bull baiting. The following description given by the French Advocate Mission, who lived in England during the late 1600s, is taken from *Chambers Book of Days':* "After a coming Bull-baiting had been advertised, the bull, decorated with flowers or coloured ribbons would be paraded round the streets of the town, and the dog that pulled off the favours in the subsequent baiting would be especially cheered by the spectators. The parade ended, the bull, with a rope tied round the root of his horns, would be fastened to a stake with an iron ring in it, situated in the centre of the ring."

The dogs would then be goaded to set upon the tethered bull. Previously, the bulls had been allowed to move freely within an enclosed area.

The new tethered method of bull-baiting suited a medium sized, active dog of moderately low stature with well laid-back nose and a protruding underjaw. From early writers' descriptions, we know that the Bulldog had a short muzzle, a massive head and a broad mouth. The big, heavy head and powerful jaws gave the dogs a vice-like grip on the bull, as well as helping to prevent the enraged beast from shaking the dog around and breaking its back.

The protruding underjaw enabled the dog to grasp the bull and get him a firmer hold. This thick and strong lower jaw gave the mouth the appearance of curving upwards across the middle of the face.

The top of the nose inclined backwards to allow free passage of air into the nostrils while still holding on to the bull with its powerful jaws. The rope – or fold of skin across the face - channelled the blood away from the Bulldog's eyes.

During bull-baiting, the dog would

flatten itself to the ground, creeping as close to the bull as possible, then dart out and try to bite the bull on the nose or head. As the dog darted at the bull, the beast would try to catch the dog with his head and horns and throw it into the air. Most of these fearless dogs were so tenacious that they would hold on to the bitter end and be tossed off rather than let go as the bulls swung them around violently in the air. A great many dogs were killed, more were badly maimed and some held so fast that by the bull swinging them, their teeth were often broken out. Often, men were tossed as well as the dogs.

England wasn't the only country to host the bloodthirsty spectacle of bull-baiting. In the 18th century it was also one of America's favourite pastimes. The journal of the American Revolution states that in 1774 the cruel blood sport of bull-baiting had crossed the Atlantic along with other customs and was still practised long after the American Revolution ended.

According to Jennie Holliman's *American Sports 1785-1835*: "British troops stationed in America during the Revolution and until 1783 played a part in establishing certain English sports in the States, an impetus being given to bull baiting and cockfighting during this time.

"...For the purpose of the sport, dogs of undisputed pedigree were kept, usually bull dogs. Many butchers kept dogs and buffaloes for animal baiting. The wildest and fiercest bulls of the neighborhood were selected for a bull bait."

"Large crowds of spectators gathered behind a circular enclosure as a chained bull would face off against six to eight bull dogs, which oftentimes were immediately killed," Holliman explains. In his July 28, 1774, *New-York Gazetteer*, printer James Rivington published a bull-baiting advertisement for John Cornell. Apparently the blood sport had such a draw that a whole "season" of weekly bull-baiting matches was scheduled.

However, the Bulldog's early role in America was not limited to sport. In mid-17th century New York, they were used as a part of a city-wide round-up effort led by Richard Nicolls, the first English colonial governor of New York province. Because cornering and leading wild bulls was dangerous, Bulldogs were trained to seize a bull by its nose long enough for a rope to be secured around the animal's neck.

Like dog fighting, bull baiting continued to be legal in Great Britain until 1835 when the Cruelty to Animals Act was passed in Parliament outlawing 'Blood Sport.' And, if it had not been for some keen enthusiasts, the Bulldog might have died out completely after the ban. But interest remained among a number of working class men who began carefully breeding Bulldogs with attention to their trademark physical features, while at the same time breeding out the dog's aggressive nature.

They organised small evening shows in public houses, where their dogs paraded on the sanded floors of tap rooms. The landlord usually provided the prizes, though sometimes the working men themselves clubbed together to contribute a handsome silver collar or similar prize.

At this time, the Bulldog was far more of a functional dog than today's descendant. It had longer legs, neck and tail, a longer muzzle and was sleeker, more athletic in build. *Crib and Rosa* (pictured) is an 1817 painting by Samuel Raven that depicts two famous Old English Bulldogs. Both dogs had deep chests, extremely well-defined muscle tone, roach backs and low tails. These two dogs were considered the ideal. (Note how athletic they are compared with today's Bulldog, which has been bred to exaggerate certain features).

Once dog shows started in 1860, a new line of 'Toy Bulldogs' began to be exhibited. At the same time, lace workers from Nottingham in England no longer had work at home due to the Industrial Revolution. Many left and settled in Normandy, France, taking their dogs, including many miniature Bulldogs with them. These dogs sparked a craze, and English breeders sent over Bulldogs that they considered to be too small, or with faults such as pricked ears.

A decade or two later, there were few miniature Bulldogs left in England, such was their popularity in France. These dogs were highly fashionable and sought after by everyone from society ladies to Parisian prostitutes! They also became popular with creative types such as artists, writers and fashion designers. The small Bulldog type gradually became thought of as a breed, and received a name, the Bouledogue Francais - or French Bulldog. (Incidentally, in France "dogue" means Mastiff or Molosser).

The prototype Boston Terriers were also developed from smaller, less aggressive examples of Bulldogs, crossed with Bull Terriers. French Bulldogs - as they came to be known - may have been used to reduce the size of the Boston Terrier, and many of the early Bostons had more of the shape of the Bulldog than today. Whereas the modern Bulldog has undoubtedly got stockier and less athletic over the decades, today's Boston is lighter in body and leg than his ancestors.

BOSTON TERRIER   FRENCH BULLDOG

A common question today is "What is the difference between a French Bulldog and a Boston Terrier?" We can see from this brief history that the Frenchie was bred as a miniature Bulldog, while the Boston has much more Terrier in his make-up. This also accounts for some of the differences in temperament between the two breeds.

....

Birth of a New Breed

As you've read, the 1800s was a period of great experimentation among dog fanciers. Throughout the century, Bulldog types were crossed with Terrier types, which eventually led to the Bull Terrier and laid the foundation for the Boston Terrier.

Bostonian Robert C. Hooper was an admirer of these English Bulldog and Terrier crosses that were popular with the working classes in the UK. The dogs were very intelligent and inherited the many good features from both breeds, being both good ratters and fighters.

'The Boston Terrier', written by Dr J. Varnum Mott (pictured) and published in 1906, was probably one of, if not THE, first book ever written about the breed. The following excerpt was written by the expert of the day, Mr Dwight Baldwin: "About twenty-five, now thirty-five, years ago (around 1870) Mr. Robert C. Hooper of Boston came into possession of a dog named Judge.

This dog, which he purchased of Mr. William O'Brien of the same city, was undoubtedly imported from the other side. Judge, commonly known as Hooper's Judge, was destined to be the ancestor of almost all the true modern Boston Terriers.

"He was a cross between an English Bulldog and an English Terrier, leaning in type rather more toward the Bulldog. He was a strongly built, high-stationed dog of about thirty-two pounds weight. In color he was a dark brindle, with a white stripe in the face. His head was square and blocky, and he resembled the present Boston Terrier in that he was nearly even mouthed."

(Author's note: I presume 'even mouthed' meant that the dog had two almost symmetrical jaws, unlike the original Bulldog, which had a large protruding lower jaw).

"Judge was bred to Burnett's Gyp (or Kate). Gyp was a white bitch, owned by Mr. Edward Burnett of Southboro. She was of about twenty pounds weight, had a fine three-quarter tail and was quite low stationed. She was of stocky build, showing considerable strength in her make-up. Her head was good, being short and blocky. From Judge and Gyp descended Wells' Eph. This dog was of strong build and, like his dam, was low stationed. His weight was about twenty-eight pounds. He was of a dark brindle color, with even white markings, and, like Judge, was nearly even mouthed."

"From Vells' Eph and Tobin's Kate came Barnard's Tom (pictured), the first dog in this line to rejoice in a screw tail. Tom was a dark brindle dog, with a white blaze on the side of his face, white collar, white chest and white feet. His weight was about twenty-two pounds. This dog was a great improvement over his sire and grandsire, being the first to show that fine quality that is present in a good specimen of the modern Boston Terrier. Tom was undoubtedly the best Boston Terrier of his day, and was naturally much used in the stud. He proved very prepotent, much more so than his litter brother, Atkinson's Toby. The latter was also dark brindle and white, but differed from Tom in being evenly marked. His tail was not as good, being of full length."

It wasn't just the screw tail that was changing the look of the Boston Terrier, gradually breeders began producing smaller, lighter dogs with a specific look that differed from the earlier heavy Bulldog-type Bostons.

One of the best early accounts of this new breed comes from Edward Axtell, who was also proprietor of St Botolph Kennels, Cliftondale, Massachusetts, in his book *'The Boston Terrier And All About It. A Practical, Scientific, And Up To Date Guide To The Breeding Of The American Dog:'* "On my last visit to England I found that quite a number of dogs have been bred in this way, viz., a first cross between the bull and Terrier, especially in the neighborhood of Birmingham in the middle of England; but these dogs are no more like the Boston Terrier than an ass is like a thoroughbred horse."

He then goes on to write about Hooper's dog: "Judge was a dark brindle, with a white stripe in face, nearly even mouthed, weighing about thirty-two pounds, and approximating more to the bull than the Terrier side. He was mated to a white, stocky built, three-quarter tail, low stationed bitch, named Gyp (or Kate), owned by Mr. Edward Burnett of Southboro.

"Like Judge, she possessed a good, short, blocky head. It may not be out of place to state here that some few years ago, on paying a visit to Mr. Burnett at Deerfoot Farm, Southboro, he told me that in the early days he possessed thirteen white Boston Terrier dogs that used to accompany him in his walks about the farm, and woe to any kind of vermin or vagrant curs that showed themselves."

He then refers to the famous dog of the day, Barnard's Tom: "I shall never forget the first visit I made to Barnard's stable to see him. To my mind he possessed a certain type, style and quality such as I had never seen before, but which stamped him as the first real Boston Terrier, as the dog is today understood. I was never tired of going to see him and his brother, Atkinson's Toby.

"Tom was mated to a dark brindle bitch, evenly marked, weighing twenty pounds. She had a good, short, blocky head, and a three-quarter tail, and known as Kelley's Nell. The result of this mating was a dog destined to make Boston Terrier history, and to my mind the most famous Boston Terrier born, judged by results. He was known as 'Mike,' commonly called 'Barnard's Mike.' He was a rather light brindle and white, even mouthed, short tailed dog, weighing about twenty-five pounds, very typical, but what impressed me was his large, full eye, the first I had ever seen, and which we see so often occurring in his descendants.

"I owned a grandson of his named "Gus", 48136, who was almost a reproduction of him, with eyes fully as large. Unfortunately he jumped out of a third-story window in my kennels and permanently ended his usefulness." Pictured is one of Hooper's Judge's direct descendants and noted stud dog, Hall's Max. (Note the long tail).

According to Axtell, as well as the sons and daughters of Hooper's Judge and Barnard's Tom, several smaller dogs of indeterminate breeding were imported to America to reduce the size of the Boston Terrier. The breed was slowly changing, in appearance and temperament, and there were many variations within litters.

He adds: "The dog is in no sense a fighting dog. While he is plucky, as might be expected from his ancestry, he is not quarrelsome. The present Boston Terrier, as he is now known (his name some fifteen years ago having been changed from the Boston Bull), is a result of inbreeding of the most careless or happy-go-lucky sort, and as a consequence, even after a lapse of thirty-five years, he continues to present himself as representing several distinct types - so that we often have an example of the English Bull, the true type of Boston Terrier and a pronounced Terrier in the same litter, despite the utmost care in breeding."

The Boston Terrier Club

In 1890, Charles F. Leland invited several other men in the Boston area who shared an interest in the dog known as the Round-Headed Bull and Terrier to form a club to improve the breed. The Club was originally called the American Bull Terrier Club. The dog had been shown for the first time at the New England Kennel Club show, held in Boston in April, 1888.

In 1891, owners began keeping breeding records and were strongly discouraged from crossing their dogs with other breeds. The same year the breeders applied for their dogs to be recognised by the American Kennel Club and included in the Stud Book, as the AKC would not give their dogs places in the Bull Terrier classes at Bench Shows. The AKC agreed to accept the club, but would not register members' dogs in its Stud Book.

According to Varnum Mott: "They (the AKC) also made a suggestion, which was subsequently adopted, that as the dog was not a Bull Terrier, and as he was then bred exclusively in Boston, a better name would be the Boston Terrier Club. In 1893, the A. K. C. were convinced of the merits of the breed and formally acknowledged the same by admitting the Club to membership and giving their dog a place in the Official Stud Book."

So, it took a couple of years, but the AKC eventually accepted the Boston Terrier, making it the first US breed to be recognised. The Boston also claimed the distinction of being the first Non-Sporting dog to be bred in the US. While many breeds were developed for their usefulness in the field or the hunt, early Boston breeders were keen to breed a small, attractive dog with an appealing personality – with the show ring, not the field, firmly in their sights. And the popularity of this dapper little all-American dog spread like wildfire.

The new Boston Terrier Club began organising an annual conformation show, which soon became "the largest and greatest of one breed fixtures," in the country as new clubs sprang up all around America.

Pictured are some early American show champions and stud dogs

The first Breed Standard of 1891 stated: "The general appearance of the Boston Terrier is that of a smooth, short-coated, compactly-built dog of medium station.

"The head should indicate a high degree of intelligence, and should be in proportion to the dog's size; the body rather short and well-knit, the limbs strong and finely turned, no feature being so prominent that the dog appears badly proportioned. The dog conveys an impression of determination, strength and activity. Style of a high order, and carriage easy and graceful."

From this description it is clear that the new Boston Terrier had moved far from its heavy, pit fighting ancestors. Edward Axtell continues: "If one takes the pains to analyze the standard he will be impressed by the perfect co-relation of harmony of all parts of the dog, from the tip of his broad, even muzzle, to the end of his short screw tail. Nothing incongruous in its makeup presents itself, but a graceful, symmetrical style characterizes the dog, and I firmly believe that any change whatever would be a detriment."

"It is a breed, the only breed, that is distinctively American and consequently there is no importing from England. This fact has done much to keep this breed from falling into the hands of the English professional handlers, who, with one exception, pay no attention to the variety. As it has been impossible to import winners, it has been necessary for someone to breed them and while there are some who still follow the buying game so popular in other breeds, the vast majority of the Boston fancy are breeding their show stock. The success that has attended the efforts of the Boston Terrier men and women along these lines shows very plainly that it is possible to breed good dogs in America and the fanciers devoted to other varieties will do well to take the hint."

This wasn't strictly true, as several small dogs were imported to reduce the size of the Boston Terrier, including a six pound dog from Scotland, bluish and white in colour with a three-quarter straight tail. Another was the 14lb 'Jack Reede dog', "evenly marked, reddish brindle and white, rather rough in coat."

In the early days, the colour of the Boston Terriers varied greatly. The 1891 Breed Standard stated that the colour should be: "Any color, brindle, evenly marked with white, strongly preferred." This was updated in the revised 1914 Standard to: "Color: Brindle with white markings." The present day AKC Breed Standard states: "Color and Markings: Brindle, seal, or black with white markings. Brindle is preferred only if all other qualities are equal. (Note: Seal Defined. Seal appears black except it has a red cast when viewed in the sun or bright light). Disqualify - Solid black, solid brindle or solid seal without required white markings. Any color not described in the standard."

Axtell says that, due to the youth of the breed, it was initially impossible to breed to type, with litters producing puppies of various shape and size – some taking more after the Bulldog, while others had more Terrier attributes. This uncertainty had the advantage of making the breed more accessible to all levels of society. It enabled both large scale and hobby breeders to produce good dogs and successfully take part in shows – something that was not always the case with other, more established, breeds, where a handful of large scale breeders often dominated.

(Photo 1900-1910).

When the carriage drivers of the Beacon Hill rich set and other working men began breeding these new dogs, prices dropped. And whereas many top purebred dogs – even at the beginning of the 20th century - could fetch a three-figure sum, suddenly the Boston became not only desirable, but also affordable, to people from all walks of life. Boston Terriers became "the rage of the day." They were not just popular with men of all classes, but became a favourite with ladies and working women as well. For three decades at the beginning of the 20th century they were either ranked one or two in the most popular dogs in the USA. At the turn of that century, they were also the majority breed at nine out of every 10 Bench Shows, according to Axtell:

"There are more people devoted to the breeding and showing of the "American" dog than any other two breeds put together, with the possible exception of Setters and Pointers, who, while they are largely supported in the western part of the country where game abounds, are not very extensively bred in the East. As a show dog, however, the Boston is without a peer and never has a breed so largely predominated the entries as at present this is doing."

In just a little over a third of a century, the debonair Boston Terrier established himself as a firm favourite in America. In 1910 Axtell wrote: "Who and what is this little dog that has forced his way by leaps and bounds from Boston town to the uttermost parts of this grand country, from the broad Atlantic to the Golden Gate, and from the Canadian border to the Gulf of Mexico? Nay, not content with this, but has overrun the imaginary borders north and south until he is fast becoming as great a favorite on the other side (England!) as here, and who promises in the near future, unless all signs fail, to cross all oceans, and extend his conquests wherever man is found that can appreciate beauty and fidelity in man's best friend.

"What passports does he present that he should be entitled to the recognition that he has everywhere accorded him? A dog that has in 35 years or less so thoroughly established himself in the affections of the great body of the American people, so that his friends offer no apology whatever in calling him the American dog, must possess peculiar qualities that endear him to all classes and conditions of men, and I firmly believe that when all the fads for which his native city is so well known have died a natural death, he will be in the early bloom of youth.

"Yea, in the illimitable future, when the historian McCauley's New Zealander is lamenting over the ruins of that marvelous city of London, he will be accompanied by a Boston Terrier, who will doubtless be intelligent enough to share his grief. In reply to the query as to who and what he is, it will be readily recalled that on the birth of possibly the greatest poet the world has ever seen it was stated:

"The force of nature could no further go,

To make a third, she joined the other two."

And this applies with equal force to the production of the Boston Terrier. The two old standard breeds of world-wide reputation, the English Bulldog and the bull Terrier, had to be joined to make a third which we believe to be the peer of either, and the superior of both."

(Pictured around 1916 with his beloved Bostons Spot and Fleck is a young Gerald Ford, who went on to become the 38th President of the United States. George wasn't the only US President to have a penchant for Boston; the 29th incumbent Warren G. Harding (1921-23) had a Boston named Hub).

"There are several features that are characteristic of the dog that tend to its universal popularity - its attractive shape, style and size, its winning disposition, and its beautiful color and markings. From the Bulldog he inherits a sweet, charming personality, quiet, restful demeanor, and an intense love of his master and home. He does not possess the restless, roving disposition which characterizes so many members of the Terrier tribe, nor will he be found quarreling with other dogs.

"From the bull Terrier side he inherits a lively mood, the quality of taking care of himself if attacked by another dog, and of his owner, too, if necessary, the propensity to be a great destroyer of all kinds of vermin if properly trained, and an ideal watch dog at night. No wonder he is popular, he deserves to be."

"The celebrated Dr. Johnson once remarked that few children live to fulfil the promise of their youth. Our little aristocrat of the dog world has more than done so. May his shadow never grow less!"

One fearless little dog was Sergeant Stubby, (July 21, 1916–March 16, 1926), that has been described as the most decorated war dog of World War I and the only dog to be nominated for rank and then promoted to Sergeant through combat. This claim has no official documentary evidence, but was recognised in an exhibition at the Smithsonian Institution.

Stubby was the official mascot of the 102nd Infantry Regiment (United States), assigned to the 26th (Yankee) Division. He served for 18 months and participated in 17 battles on the Western Front.

He saved his regiment from surprise mustard gas attacks, found and comforted the wounded, and once caught a German soldier by the seat of his pants, holding him there until American soldiers found him! Back home, Stubby's exploits were front page news in major newspapers, which described him as either a Boston Terrier or a Bull Terrier.

....

Today's Dog

Boston University made the Boston Terrier its mascot in 1922, and the breed has also made its way into other local events as well, including the Boston Calling Music Festival. The breed became the state dog of Massachusetts in 1979, and continues to be a symbol of the Bay State.

And the Boston Terrier has continued to be a firm favourite with not only Americans, but also in Europe. At the time of writing - late 2016 - the breed is gaining in popularity in the UK (following a huge surge in numbers of French Bulldogs and Pugs), with over 2,000 pedigrees being registered in the previous 12 months. In the US, the Boston is currently making something of a comeback and is currently just outside the top 20 most popular dogs.

The stylish lines and appealing expression of the Boston Terrier have led to the breed starring in TV commercials and appearing in numerous advertising brochures. Celebrity owners include actors Leonardo DiCaprio, Ben Stiller, Jake Gyllenhaal, Rose McGowan, and supermodel Christy Turlington. The modern well-bred Boston Terrier is intelligent with a cheerful personality. Not only does he make an excellent companion and show dog, but the breed is also making a mark in other areas, such as Fly Ball, agility trials, and as therapy and service dogs.

One accolade that has so far escaped the breed is the coveted title of Best in Show at The Westminster Kennel Club Show.

However, in describing the perfect modern Boston Terrier, The Westminster Kennel Club helps to explain why this attractive little dog was and still is so popular:

"Today's Boston carries a clean cut square head, large, soft, dark eyes and moves in perfect rhythm, each step indicating grace and power. Intelligence, alertness and a loving disposition makes him an ideal companion, a dog well-suited to the city dweller and the suburbanite. His great style and loving disposition have rightly earned the nickname, 'The American Gentleman.'"

© 2016 Linda Whitwam

No part of this history may be reproduced without the express permission of the author

....

Sources:

Chest of Books http://chestofbooks.com

Chambers Book of Days, 1864, by Robert Chambers

A History and Description of the Modern Dogs of Great Britain and Ireland (The Terriers), 1894, by Rawdon B. Lee

The Boston Terrier, 1906, by J. Varnum Mott, MD

The Boston Terrier And All About It. A Practical, Scientific, And Up To Date Guide To The Breeding Of The American Dog, 1910, by Edward Axtell

The Complete Book of the Dog, 1922, by Leighton Robert

American Sports 1785-1835, 1931, by Jennie Holliman

Wikipedia https://en.wikipedia.org/wiki/Boston_Terrier

The Boston Terrier Club of Scotland http://www.btcos.co.uk

3. The Breed Standard

The **breed standard** is what makes a Boston Terrier a Boston Terrier, a Great Dane a Great Dane and a Chihuahua a Chihuahua. It is a blueprint not only for the appearance of each breed, but also for character and temperament, how the dog moves and what colours are acceptable. In other words, it ensures that the Boston Terrier looks like a Boston Terrier and is "fit for function."

The breed standard is laid down by the breed societies. In the UK it's the Kennel Club, and in the USA it's the AKC (American Kennel Club) that keeps the register of pedigree (purebred) dogs. Dogs entered in conformation shows run under Kennel Club and AKC rules are judged against this ideal list of attributes. Breeders approved by the Kennel Clubs agree to produce puppies in line with the breed standard and maintain certain welfare conditions.

In the UK, the Boston is listed in the Utility Group, while it is a member of the Non-Sporting Group in the USA.

Kennel Club registered and Assured Breeders select only the best dogs for reproduction, based on factors such as the health, looks, temperament and the character of the parents and their ancestors. They do not simply take any available male and female and allow them to randomly breed.

The same is true of AKC Breeders of Merit, who are "AKC Breeders who are dedicated to breeding beautiful purebred dogs whose appearance, temperament, and ability are true to their breed. These breeders are the heart of AKC."

They also aim to reduce or eradicate genetic illnesses. In the case of Bostons, these include eye, breathing and joint problems. The Kennel Clubs in the UK, North America and Europe all have lists of breeders. If you have not yet got a puppy, this is a good place to start looking for one. Visit the Kennel Club website in your country for details of approved breeders.

A breed standard is an essential factor in maintaining the look and temperament of any breed. But in the past, breeders of some types of dog have concentrated too closely on the appearance of the animal without paying enough attention to soundness and health.

In response, the Kennel Club set up Breed Watch, which serves as an 'early warning system' to identify points of concern for individual breeds. In the UK the Boston Terrier is listed in Category 1, with Category 1 being the breeds with no major points of concern and Category 3 being: "Breeds where some dogs have visible conditions or exaggerations that can cause pain or discomfort."

Despite being in the best Category, Bostons are bred from a fairly small gene pool, compared with some other breeds. The average COI (Coefficient of Inbreeding) for Boston Terriers in the UK is 11.3%, which is relatively high. The downside of a smaller gene pool means that, along with all the good genes, there is a higher chance of genetic ailments being passed on to puppies.

UFAW (Universities Federation for Animal Welfare) says: "Essentially, COI measures the common ancestors of dam and sire, and indicates the probability of how genetically similar they are. There are consequences to being genetically similar, some good, some bad. The fact that dogs within individual breeds are so genetically similar is what makes them that breed - and why, if you breed any Labrador to any other Labrador, the puppies will look recognisably like Labradors."

It goes on to explain why a high COI can be a problem: "Inbreeding will help cement 'good' traits but there's a danger of it also cementing bad ones. In particular, it can cause the rapid build-up of disease genes in a population. Even if a breed of dog is lucky enough to be free of serious genetic disorders, inbreeding is likely to affect our dogs in more subtle, but no less serious, ways."

The (EPS) Effective Population Size for the Boston Terrier in the UK is 36.78. UFAW adds: "EPS is a measure of how many individuals are contributing genetically to a breed population (KC-registered dogs). It is a measure of the size of the gene pool in a breed. Lower than 100 is considered critical by conservation biologists and below 50 puts a breed at grave risk."

Anyone buying a Boston puppy is advised to ask to see the relevant health certificates for the pup and its parents before committing. Prospective UK owners can also check the COI of their chosen puppy and parents using the Kennel Club's **Mate Select** programme at www.thekennelclub.org.uk/services/public/mateselect

If you are serious about getting a Boston Terrier, then study the breed standard before visiting any puppies, so you know what a well-bred example should look like. If you've already bought one, these are features your dog should display:

American Kennel Club Breed Standard (USA)

General Appearance: The Boston Terrier is a lively, highly intelligent, smooth coated, short-headed, compactly built, short-tailed, well balanced dog, brindle, seal or black in color and evenly marked with white.

The head is in proportion to the size of the dog and the expression indicates a high degree of intelligence. The body is rather short and well knit, the limbs strong and neatly turned, the tail is short and no feature is so prominent that the dog appears badly proportioned. The dog conveys an impression of determination, strength and activity, with style of a high order; carriage easy and graceful.

A proportionate combination of "Color and White Markings" is a particularly distinctive feature of a representative specimen. "Balance, Expression, Color and White Markings" should be given particular consideration in determining the relative value of General Appearance to other points.

Size, Proportion, Substance: Weight is divided by classes as follows: Under 15 pounds; 15 pounds and under 20 pounds; 20 pounds and not to exceed 25 pounds. The length of leg must balance with the length of body to give the Boston Terrier its striking square appearance. The Boston Terrier is a sturdy dog and must not appear to be either spindly or coarse. The bone and muscle must be in proportion as well as an enhancement to the dog's weight and structure.

Fault - Blocky or chunky in appearance.

Influence of Sex. In a comparison of specimens of each sex, the only evident difference is a slight refinement in the bitch's conformation.

Head: The *skull* is square, flat on top, free from wrinkles, cheeks flat, brow abrupt and the stop well defined. The ideal Boston Terrier *expression* is alert and kind, indicating a high degree of intelligence. This is a most important characteristic of the breed. The *eyes* are wide apart, large and round and dark in color. The eyes are set square in the skull and the outside corners are on a line with the cheeks as viewed from the front. Disqualify - Eyes blue in color or any trace of blue. The *ears* are small, carried erect, either natural or cropped to conform to the shape of the head and situated as near to the corners of the skull as possible.

The *muzzle* is short, square, wide and deep and in proportion to the skull. It is free from wrinkles, shorter in length than in width or depth; not exceeding in length approximately one-third of the length of the skull. The muzzle from stop to end of the nose is parallel to the top of the skull. The nose is black and wide, with a well defined line between the nostrils.

Disqualify - Dudley nose. The jaw is broad and square with short regular teeth. The bite is even or sufficiently undershot to square the muzzle. The chops are of good depth, but not pendulous, completely covering the teeth when the mouth is closed. Serious Fault - Wry mouth.

Head Faults - Eyes showing too much white or haw. Pinched or wide nostrils. Size of ears out of proportion to the size of the head. Serious Head Faults - Any showing of the tongue or teeth when the mouth is closed.

Neck, Topline and Body: The length of *neck* must display an image of balance to the total dog. It is slightly arched, carrying the head gracefully and setting neatly into the shoulders. The back is just short enough to square the body. The *topline* is level and the rump curves slightly to the set-on of the tail. The chest is deep with good width, ribs well sprung and carried well back to the loins. The body should appear short. The *tail* is set on low, short, fine and tapering, straight or screw and must not be carried above the horizontal.

(Note: The preferred tail does not exceed in length more than one-quarter the distance from set-on to hock). Disqualify - Docked tail. Body Faults - Gaily carried tail. Serious Body Faults - Roach back, sway back, slab-sided.

Forequarters: The shoulders are sloping and well laid back, which allows for the Boston Terrier's stylish movement. The elbows stand neither in nor out. The forelegs are set moderately wide apart and on a line with the upper tip of the shoulder blades. The forelegs are straight in bone with short, strong pasterns. The dewclaws may be removed. The feet are small, round and compact, turned neither in nor out, with well arched toes and short nails. Faults - Legs lacking in substance; splay feet.

Hindquarters: The thighs are strong and well muscled, bent at the stifles and set true. The hocks are short to the feet, turning neither in nor out, with a well defined hock joint. The feet are small and compact with short nails. Fault - Straight in stifle.

Gait: The gait of the Boston Terrier is that of a sure-footed, straight gaited dog, forelegs and hind legs moving straight ahead in line with perfect rhythm, each step indicating grace and power. Gait Faults - There will be no rolling, paddling, or weaving, when gaited. Hackney gait. Serious Gait Faults - Any crossing movement, either front or rear.

Coat: The coat is short, smooth, bright and fine in texture.

Color and Markings: Brindle, seal, or black with white markings. Brindle is preferred only if all other qualities are equal. (Note: Seal Defined. Seal appears black except it has a red cast when viewed in the sun or bright light). Disqualify - Solid black, solid brindle or solid seal without required white markings. Any color not described in the standard.

Required Markings: White muzzle band, white blaze between the eyes, white forechest.

Desired Markings: White muzzle band, even white blaze between the eyes and over the head, white collar, white forechest, white on part or whole of forelegs and hind legs below the hocks.

(Note: A representative specimen should not be penalized for not possessing "Desired Markings.") A dog with a preponderance of white on the head or body must possess sufficient merit otherwise to counteract its deficiencies.

Temperament: The Boston Terrier is a friendly and lively dog. The breed has an excellent disposition and a high degree of intelligence, which makes the Boston Terrier an incomparable companion.

Summary: The clean-cut short backed body of the Boston Terrier coupled with the unique characteristics of his square head and jaw, and his striking markings have resulted in a most dapper and charming American original: The Boston Terrier.

Scale of Points (for judging)

General Appearance 10

Expression 10

Head (Muzzle, Jaw, Bite, Skull & Stop) 15

Eyes 5

Ears 5

Neck, Topline, Body & Tail 15

Forequarters 10

Hindquarters 10

Feet 5

Color, Coat & Markings 5

Gait 10

Total 100

Disqualifications: *Eyes blue in color or any trace of blue. Dudley nose. Docked tail. Solid black, solid brindle, or solid seal without required white markings. Any color not described in the standard.*

Approved February 11, 2011. Effective March 30, 2011.

Kennel Club Breed Standard (UK)

Last updated October 2009.

The Kennel Club says: "A Breed Standard is the guideline which describes the ideal characteristics, temperament and appearance including the correct colour of a breed and ensures that the breed is fit for function. Absolute soundness is essential. Breeders and judges should at all times be careful to avoid obvious conditions or exaggerations which would be detrimental in any way to the health, welfare or soundness of this breed.

"From time to time certain conditions or exaggerations may be considered to have the potential to affect dogs in some breeds adversely, and judges and breeders are requested to refer to the Breed Watch section of the Kennel Club website at www.thekennelclub.org.uk/services/public/breed/watch for details of any such current issues. If a feature or quality is desirable it should only be present in the right measure. However if a dog possesses a feature, characteristic or colour described as undesirable or highly undesirable it is strongly recommended that it should not be rewarded in the show ring."

General Appearance

Smooth-coated, relatively short-headed, compactly built, short-tailed, well balanced dog of medium size, brindle in colour, evenly marked with white. Body rather short and well knit; limbs strong and neatly turned; tail short and no feature so prominent that the dog appears badly proportioned. Dog must convey an impression of determination, strength and activity, with style of a high order; carriage easy and graceful.

Characteristics - Lively and intelligent.

Temperament - Determined and strong willed.

Head and Skull - Skull square in appearance, flat on top, free from wrinkles; cheeks flat; brow abrupt, stop well defined.

Muzzle relatively short, square, wide and deep with no tendency to taper and in proportion to skull; free from wrinkles; shorter in length than in width and depth, approximately one-third of length of skull; width and depth carried out well to end; muzzle from stop to end of nose on a line parallel to top of skull; nose black, wide with well defined line between nostrils.

Jaws broad and square. Flews of good depth, not pendulous, completely covering teeth when mouth closed. Head in proportion to size of dog.

Eyes - Wide apart, round and not too large, dark in colour; expression alert, kind and intelligent. Eyes set square in skull, outside corners on a line with cheeks when viewed from front.

Ears - Carried erect; small, thin, situated as near corner of skull as possible.

Mouth - Teeth short and regular, bite even, or sufficiently undershot to square muzzle.

Neck - Of fair length, slightly arched, carrying head gracefully; neatly set into shoulders.

Forequarters - Shoulders sloping, legs set moderately wide apart on line with point of shoulders; straight in bone and well muscled; pasterns short and strong. Elbows turning neither in nor out.

Body - Deep with good width of chest; back short; ribs deep and well sprung, carried well back to loins; loins short and muscular; rump curving slightly to set-on of tail; flank very slightly cut up; body appears short but not chunky.

Hindquarters - Legs set true, good turn of stifle, hocks well let down; turning neither in nor out; thighs strong and well muscled.

Feet - Round, small, compact, turning neither in nor out; toes well arched.

Tail - Set on low; short, fine, tapering, straight or curled; devoid of fringes or coarse hair, never carried above horizontal.

Gait/Movement - Easy and graceful. Sure-footed straight-gaited, forelegs and hindlegs moving straight ahead with perfect rhythm. Each step indicating grace and power.

Coat - Short, smooth, lustrous and fine in texture.

Colour - Brindle with white markings; brindle must show throughout body distinctly; black with white markings but brindles with white markings preferred. Ideal markings: white muzzle, even white blaze over head, collar, breast, part or whole of forelegs, and hindlegs below hocks.

Size - Weight not exceeding 11.5kg (25lb) divided by classes as follows: Lightweight: under 6.8kg (15lb); Middleweight: 6.8kg (15lb) and under 9.1kg (20lb); Heavyweight: 9.1kg (20lb) and under 11.4kg (25lb).

Faults

Any departure from the foregoing points should be considered a fault and the seriousness with which the fault should be regarded should be in exact proportion to its degree and its effect upon the health and welfare of the dog and on the dog's ability to perform its traditional work.

Note: Male animals should have two apparently normal testicles fully descended into the scrotum.

Author's Notes: A "Dudley nose" is one that lacks pigment in both the puppy and adult dog and displays pink patches or spots.

"Haw" is the thin nictitating membrane at the inner corner of the lower eyelid that provides protection for the eye. It is also known as the third eyelid.

The definition of brindle is "A brownish or tawny colour of animal fur, with streaks of other colour."

NOTE: Red is NOT brindle or seal and is not an accepted colour.

4. Choosing a Boston Terrier Puppy

So you've decided that the Boston, with his gentlemanly looks and cheeky personality, is the dog for you. The next step is to pick the individual puppy; a step that should not be taken lightly as you'll have to live with the decision for more than a decade if all goes well.

Simply put, the best way to select a puppy is with your head - and not with your heart. With their appealing big eyes, silky soft fur and clownish antics, there are few more appealing things on this Earth than a litter of dapper little Boston puppies. If you go to view a litter, the pups are sure to tug at your heart strings and it will be extremely difficult – if not downright impossible - to walk away without choosing one.

So, it's essential to **do your research before you visit any litters** to make sure you know the breed, you know what features you are looking for in a Boston pup and you learn the warning signs of puppy mills and other breeders-for-profit. Armed with the knowledge in this chapter you can then select a good breeder with health-tested parents (of the puppy, not the breeder!) and who knows Bostons inside out. (Of the puppies pictured below, two or three of them are unlikely to conform to the Boston Terrier breed standard. Do you know why?)

After all, apart from getting married or having a baby, getting a puppy is one of the most important, demanding, expensive and life-enriching decisions you will ever make. Just like babies, puppies will love you unconditionally - but there is a price to pay. In return for their loyalty and devotion, you have to fulfil your part of the bargain.

In the beginning you have to be prepared to devote precious hours every day to your new pup. You have to feed him several times a day and housetrain him virtually every hour, you have to give him your attention and start to gently introduce the rules of the house as well as take care of his general health and welfare. You also have to be prepared to part with hard cash for regular healthcare and pet insurance.

If you are not prepared, or unable, to devote the time and money to a new arrival – or if you intend leaving the dog completely alone for eight or nine hours a day – then now is not the right time to consider getting a puppy.

Boston Terriers are sociable creatures that like to be with their owners. They thrive on companionship and do not do well when left alone for long periods. Lonely Bostons may end up becoming destructive (chewing on things they shouldn't) or suffering from separation anxiety and a few even experience panic attacks. If you are out at work all day, then these are not the dogs for you; to leave a Boston alone all day is just not fair on this lovable gentleman who is happiest with you.

Pick a healthy pup and he or she will probably live to 10, 12 or even into the teens, so it is definitely a long-term commitment. Before taking the plunge, ask yourself some questions:

Have I Got Enough Time?

In the first days after leaving his - or her - mother and littermates, your puppy may feel very lonely and probably even a little afraid. You and your family have to spend time with your new arrival to make him feel safe and sound. Ideally, you will be around all of the time in the beginning to help him settle and to start bonding with him. If you work, book a week - ideally two - off. (This is standard practice in the UK, but may be harder in the US, where workers tend to have shorter holidays. Wherever you live, it's still important to spend at least a few days at home with your pup in the beginning).

As well as housetraining (potty training), after the first few days and once he's feeling more settled, start to introduce short sessions of a couple of minutes of behaviour training to teach your new pup the rules of the house. Boston puppies can be boisterous and mischievous, and early training to stop your cute little arrival biting and jumping up is the way to make a good start.

Even before his vaccinations have finished, start the socialisation process by taking him out of the home to see buses, trains, noisy traffic, kids, etc. - but make sure you CARRY HIM if he's not clear after his vaccinations. Puppies can be very sensitive to all sorts of things – sights, sounds, smells, new surfaces, etc. - and it's important to start familiarisation with new things as soon as possible. The more he is introduced to at this early stage, the better. A good breeder will already have started this socialisation.

Once he has had the all-clear after his vaccinations, get into the habit of taking him out of the house and garden or yard for a short walk every day – more as he gets older. New surroundings stimulate his interest and help to stop him from becoming bored and developing unwanted character traits. He also needs to get used to different noises. Spend some time gently brushing your Boston, and check his ears are clean, to get him used to being handled right from the beginning, and enrol in a puppy class. One experienced breeder said: "I highly recommend at least one puppy/beginning training class. It helps continue to build self-confidence, reinforces the human-puppy bonding experience, and lays the foundation for a well-behaved dog."

It is also a good idea to have your pup checked out by a vet within a few days of taking him home, but don't let him come into contact with other dogs or the floor in the vet's clinic as he will still not be fully protected against disease. You'll also need to factor in time to visit the vet's clinic for regular healthcare visits and annual vaccinations.

How Long Can I Leave Him?

This is a question we get asked all of the time and one that causes a lot of debate among owners and prospective owners. All dogs are pack animals; their natural state is to be with others. So being alone is not normal for them, although many get used to it. The Boston has been bred to be a companion and family pet, not a guard dog or a hunting dog; he or she wants to be around you.

Another issue is the toilet; Bostons have much smaller bladders than humans. Forget the emotional side of it, how would you like to be left for eight hours without being able to visit the bathroom? So how many hours can you leave a dog alone? Well, a useful guide comes from the canine rescue organisations. In the UK, they will not allow anybody to adopt if they are intending to leave the dog alone for more than four or five hours a day.

Dogs left at home alone all day become bored and, in the case of Bostons and other breeds that are highly dependent on human company, they may well become depressed. Of course, it depends on the character and temperament of your dog, but a lonely Boston may display signs of unhappiness by being destructive, digging, chewing, barking or urinating.

A puppy or fully-grown dog must NEVER be left shut in a crate all day. It is OK to leave a puppy or adult dog in a crate if he or she is happy there, but all our breeders said the same, the door should never be closed for more than a few hours during the day. A crate is a place where a puppy or adult should feel safe, not a prison. Ask yourself why you want a dog – is it for selfish reasons or can you really offer a good home to a young puppy - and then adult dog - for a decade or longer? Would it be more sensible to wait until you are at home more?

Is My Home Suitable?

Bostons can happily live in apartments, but all have exercise requirements and need regular access to the outdoors. Part of this time should ideally be spent off the lead (leash) once he has the all-clear after vaccinations.

Regular trips outdoors also help to speed up the housetraining process in the early days and weeks. If you do live in an apartment and you don't want your pup to eliminate indoors, it is important to take your pup outside to perform his duty many times a day to start with. If you can continue to do this three or four times daily, then there is no need to indoor housetrain him. At a minimum, puppies should go out immediately after waking up, about 20-30 minutes after eating each meal, and right before bed.

And if you live in a house with a garden or yard, don't leave your puppy unattended; dognapping is becoming increasingly common, particularly with the high price of pups. Make sure there are no poisonous plants or chemicals out there that he could ingest, or sharp objects and other plants that could damage his protruding eyes. Common plants toxic to dogs include crocus, daffodil, azalea, wisteria, cyclamen, sweat pea, lily of the valley, tulips, hyacinth and lily. Most bulb plants are toxic.

Boston puppies are little chewing machines and puppy-proofing your home should involve moving anything sharp, breakable or chewable - including your shoes - out of reach of sharp little teeth. Make sure he can't chew electrical cords – lift them off the floor if necessary, and block off any off-limits areas of the house, such as upstairs or your bedroom, with a child gate or barrier, especially as he will probably be following you around the house in the first few days. There's more specific advice from breeders on preparing your home later in this chapter.

Other Pets

However friendly your Boston puppy is, if you already have other pets in your household, they may not be too happy at the new arrival. The good news is that Bostons rarely have a strong prey drive and generally get on well with cats and other animals. However, it might not be a good idea to leave your hamster or pet rabbit running loose with your lively pup who may regard them as a great new form of entertainment!

In the beginning, spend time to introduce them to each other gradually and supervise the sessions. Boston puppies are naturally curious and playful and they will sniff and investigate other pets. You may have to separate them to start off with, or put a boisterous puppy into a pen or crate initially to allow the cat to investigate without being mauled.

This will also prevent your pup from being injured. If the two animals are free and the cat lashes out, he or she could scratch your pup's eyes. Just type 'Boston Terrier and cat' into YouTube to see examples of how the two interact – and it's generally positive, although you MUST be careful not to let games get too rough as a cat can quite easily scratch and inadvertently damage a Boston's eyes.

A timid cat might need protection from a bold, playful Boston - or vice versa. A bold cat and a timid young Boston will probably settle down together quickest! If things seem to be going well with no aggression after one or two supervised sessions, then let them loose together. Take the process slowly, if your cat is stressed and frightened he may decide to leave. Our feline friends are notorious for abandoning home because the food and facilities are better down the road. Until you know that they can get on, don't leave them alone together.

Bostons usually get on well with other dogs. If you already have other dogs, supervised sessions from an early age will help them to get along and for the other dogs to accept your friendly new Boston. If you are thinking about getting more than one pup, you might consider waiting until your first Boston is an adolescent or adult before getting a second, so your older dog is calmer and can help train the younger one. Coping with, training and housetraining one puppy is hard enough, without having to do it with two. On the other hand, some owners prefer to get the messy part over and done with in one go and get two together – but this will require a lot of your time for the first few weeks and months.

As with all dogs, how well they get on also depends on the temperament of the individuals. If you have another dog, it is important to initially introduce the two on neutral territory (rather than in areas one pet regards as his own) as you don't want one dog to feel he has to protect his territory. If you think there may be issues, walking the dogs parallel to each other before heading home for the first time is one way of getting them used to each other.

Family and Children

If you have children they will, of course, be delighted about your new arrival; one of the wonderful things about Bostons is how naturally good they are with youngsters.

But what about the other members of your family – your husband/wife, or parents, do they all want the puppy as well? A puppy will grow into a dog that will become a part of your family for many years to come and it's important to make sure that everybody in the household is on board with the decision to get a dog.

(Photo courtesy of Susan Maxwell, of Maximum Companion Boston Terriers, California).

But remember that Boston puppies are small and delicate, as are babies, so you should never leave babies or very small children and dogs alone together – no matter how well they get along. Small kids lack co-ordination and a young pup may inadvertently get poked in the eye or trodden on if you don't keep an eye on things. Often puppies regard children as playmates (just like a small child regards a puppy as a playmate) and so the young dog might chase, jump and nip with sharp teeth. This is not aggression; this is normal play for puppies.

Train yours to be gentle with your children and your children to be gentle with your dog. See **Chapter 9 Exercise and Training** on how to deal with puppy biting. Discourage the kids from constantly picking up your gorgeous new puppy. They should learn respect for the dog, which is a living creature with his or her own needs - not a toy.

Make sure your puppy gets enough time to sleep – **which is most of the time in the beginning** - so don't let the kids constantly pester him. Sleep is very important to puppies, just as it is for babies. Also, allow your Boston to eat at his or her own pace uninterrupted; letting youngsters play with the dog while eating is a no-no as it may encourage gulping of food or food aggression. Another reason some dogs end up in rescue centres is that owners are unable to cope with the demands of small children AND a dog. On the other hand, it is also a fantastic opportunity for you to educate your little darlings (both human and canine) on how to get along with each other and set the pattern for wonderful life-long friendships.

Single People

Many single adults own dogs, but if you live alone, getting a puppy will require a lot of dedication on your part. There will be nobody to share the responsibility, so taking on a dog requires a huge commitment and a lot of your time if the dog is to have a decent life. If you are out of the house all day as well, it is not really fair to get a puppy, or even an adult dog. Left alone all day, they will feel isolated, bored and sad. However, if you work from home or are at home all day and you can spend considerable time with your dog, then great; a Boston will become your best friend.

One American breeder added: "If the owner can come home at lunch time to let the puppy out to potty and exercise, if they have a neighbour or family member who will take the puppy to a doggy day care, or will hire a dog walker to come by during day, I am very happy to place a puppy in that kind of home."

Older People

If you are older or have elderly relatives living with you, Bostons are great company. Provided their needs are met, they are affectionate, require only moderate exercise compared with larger breeds and love to be with people. If you are older, make sure you have the energy and patience to deal with a young pup. In fact, dogs can be great for older people. My father is in his mid-80s, but takes his dog out walking for an hour to 90 minutes every day - a morning and an afternoon walk - even in the rain or snow. It's good for him and it's good for the dog, helping to keep both of them fit and socialised! They get fresh air, exercise and the chance to communicate with other dogs and their humans.

Bostons are also great company indoors – you're never alone when you've got a dog. Many older people get a dog after losing a loved one (a husband, wife or previous much-loved dog). A pet gives them something to care for and love, as well as a constant companion. However, owning a dog is not cheap, so it's important to be able to afford annual pet insurance, veterinary fees, a quality pet food, etc. The RSPCA in the UK has estimated that owning a dog costs an average of around £1,300 ($1,700) a year.

Male or Female?

You have to decide whether you want a male or a female puppy. In terms of gender, much depends on the temperament of the individual dog - the differences WITHIN the sexes is greater than the differences BETWEEN the sexes. Health and temperament should be your major considerations –

unless you are buying a dog specifically for show or breeding. Males are, however, generally slightly larger than females.

When discussing gender, Pamela Preston, of ChriMaso Boston Terriers, Shingle Springs, California, says: "Generally, there is a difference, yes; but not always. I always tell people: "If boys could have puppies, I would probably ONLY have boys!" Boys, typically, are more willing to please you, more affectionate, and a bit needier than the girls. Girls tend to be a little more independent. I generally describe the difference like this: If you're sitting on the couch, a boy will want to be ON you, but a girl will be fine sitting on the other end of the couch, as long as she sees you're there. Again, this is not always the case, but very often true."

Jo Dalton, of Mumuland Boston Terriers, Lincolnshire, England, agrees: "The best way I can describe it is that males are 'in love' with you and females just 'love' you!"

Susan Maxwell of Maximum Companion Boston Terriers, California, adds: "Males seem to be more outgoing and less bossy, but we are talking about altered (neutered) animals here. Dogs that are unaltered can be a challenge for the average pet owner as hormones come into play and females in season can be difficult, as well as the males who seek them! Fights often can break out amongst unaltered pets as some try to establish dominance."

Gwion Williams, Wilarjan Boston Terriers, North Wales, UK: "Speaking from experience, I have always found males more affectionate and quicker to housetrain. I have also found a male to be more protective of his owner and territory. Not in an aggressive manner, more of an alert to let strangers know that he is the guard dog of the house."

Emily Little, of Essex, England: "Females tend to be more eager to please, higher energy levels and attentive to the owner. Males are more laid back and docile."

Another breeder added: "The female is the pack leader and the alpha; she is your best watchdog and protector. She will watch over her puppies as well as any other puppies around, and look out for the older dogs and her humans. She does not belong to you, you belong to her! Your male may be bigger, but your female is the boss."

·····

Colour

This is a controversial topic within the world of Boston Terriers. There are several aspects to it: genetics, health, temperament, conforming to breed standard and people cashing in on unusual colours purely for profit; to name but a few.

The official colours for Boston are, according to the Kennel Club: "Brindle with white markings; brindle must show throughout body distinctly; black with white markings but brindles with white markings preferred," and according to the AKC: "Brindle, seal, or black with white markings." (Seal looks black until the dog is in bright light and then the coat appears to have a red sheen).

So why is it that anyone looking for a puppy will come across adverts for red, cream, fawn, liver or chocolate, champagne, blue, grey, lilac, tricolour or splash (any colour on a white background, pictured) Bostons? Some of these colours are also known as 'dilute' or 'diluted' as they are a paler version of the traditional rich, dark coat of the breed. And why is it that so many established breeders are vehemently opposed to these so called 'rare' colours?

Canine genetics is a complicated topic that is still not fully understood. If we did, breeders would be able to produce perfect champion Boston Terriers with wonderful temperaments every litter. Here's our simplified version of the controversial colour issue:

In the 19th century The Boston Terrier came about – as all breeds do – when dog fanciers crossed a number of different breeds to create a unique look. The dogs that went into the Boston's make-up included the Bulldog, Bull Terrier and smaller French Bulldog. These different breeds all came in different colours, although the genes that produced the trademark black or dark look of the Boston were the dominant ones.

However, every now and again a recessive colour gene would pop up and a lighter coloured pup would be born. Back in the mists of time these other colours were allowed. But in 1900, the breed standard in the USA changed to ban these colours and permit only black and white dogs – seal and brindle were later added; but no other colours.

These recessive genes continue to pop up from time to time today, but the pups that display the lighter colours do not conform to the breed standard – in any country. They also often have lighter noses - pink or with pink patches; this is known as a Dudley nose. Some have one or two blue eyes.

All of these factors **disqualify** these dogs from entering conformation shows run by the breed clubs. Despite that, the Kennel Club and AKC still register these puppies if the sire and dam are Kennel Club registered – which is why you can buy a puppy in a Disqualified colour with KC or AKC papers.

If a good Boston breeder inadvertently produces one or more of these coloured puppies, he or she may sell them as pets, but will insist in the Puppy Contract that they be neutered and cannot be used for breeding. This is to protect the integrity of the breed. By the way, if you come across a 'merle' (mottled) Boston Terrier – pictured - it is not a purebred Boston at all; it has been crossed with another breed, as merle does not occur naturally in Bostons.

Are coloured dogs bad dogs? Not necessarily. But the sad truth is that unscrupulous breeders have cropped up in droves to make money by breeding unacceptable colours with no regard for the health and temperament of the puppy, the Boston Terrier breed standard or protecting the future of the breed. In other words, they are churning out puppies **purely based on colour** to make money and so you risk buying an unhealthy puppy or one with unwanted temperament traits.

And if, 25 years down the line, Bostons came in all colours with different coloured skin, eyes and noses, they wouldn't look much like Bostons, would they? These rogue colours are threatening the very future of this comparatively young breed. This, the lack of health testing among many breeders of 'rare' colours and the poor quality of their puppies are reasons why established breeders are so strongly opposed to them.

Our advice is to stick to the colours laid down by the Kennel Clubs. But if you feel you absolutely have to have one of these colours, then ensure that the pup and its parents have been **fully health tested.** Some of these genes may also carry health problems. For example, scientists don't know why, but there is evidence that Bostons with a lot of white - i.e. more than 30% of the coat - are more likely to carry the gene for deafness.

Kennel Club Assured breeder Lindsey Scanlon, Fleurdelanne Boston Terriers, Mirfield, Yorkshire, England, switched to breeding Bostons a couple of years ago, having bred French Bulldogs for several years. She founded and still runs the registered charity French Bulldog Saviours, and has helped to save more than 500 dogs so far. Lindsey has seen first-hand the effect that 'rare' colours have had on French Bulldogs and strongly campaigns against their breeding.

She said: "The whole thing is disgraceful and so sad. I think the Kennel Club is partly to blame, as it continues to register puppies in Disqualified colours. They get a fee of £15 for every puppy registered, plus another fee for a pedigree certificate, so they are making money out of them as well. It is wrong.

"With the French Bulldogs, the sheer number of blues is astronomical – I think there are almost as many blues as dogs in recognised colours. And the black and tan Frenchies are so vicious and nasty; the blues are turning exactly the same and I think it will happen with Bostons. People are breeding these dogs purely for the money; they see pound note signs in front of their eyes and they don't care about health or temperament."

Here are more comments from breeders: "A lot of back yard breeders/puppy farmers are breeding the so-called 'rare coloured' Boston Terrier, but there is no such thing. True Boston colours are brindle, seal, or black with white markings. My advice is to keep away and find a reputable breeder who will offer a lifetime of support."

"There is a huge problem with non-standard colours in the UK and these dogs often have temperament and health issues as they are bred for colour. Breeders tend to breed them and sell them for vast amounts of money as they are sold as 'RARE.'"

"Breeders advertise blue, red and champagne Boston Terriers and generally ask for more money - in excess of £2,000. These dogs are not 'rare' and are simply bred for their colour, ignoring any fault/genetics/ temperament or health issue the dog may have."

"There is most definitely a problem! They are not "illegal" per se, but they are definitely against the Boston Terrier Standard. They often pass themselves off as reputable breeders by doing one or two health tests on some of their dogs, but ultimately it is a scam as they generally charge more for these disqualified ('rare') colors than most of us charge for show potential puppies with excellent pedigrees that come from generations of health-tested ancestors."

"It is a monumental problem, causing a flood of poor quality dogs to flood the market."

One last point on colour: a phrase you may hear is 'Haggerty spot' (pictured), which is a dark dot or spot on the white blaze on top of the head. Its origins can be traced all the way back to the early 1900s to a bloodline owned by the Haggertys. According to the BTCA, international judge and highly respected Boston breeder Vincent Perry called it 'the kiss of God.'

More than One Dog

Owning two dogs can be twice as nice - or double the trouble, and double the vet's bills. There are a number of factors to consider. Here is some advice from a UK dog rescue organisation:

"Think about why you are considering another dog. If, for example, you have a dog that suffers from separation anxiety, then rather than solving the problem, your second dog may learn from your first and you then have two dogs with the problem instead of one. The same applies if you have an unruly adolescent; cure the problem first and only introduce a second dog when your first is balanced."

"A second dog will mean double vet's fees, groomer's fees, insurance and food. You may also need a larger car, and holidays will be more problematic. Sit down with a calculator and work out the expected expense – you may be surprised. Two dogs will need training, both separately and together. If the dogs do not receive enough individual attention, they may form a strong bond with each other at the expense of their bond with you.

"If you are tempted to buy two puppies from the same litter - DON'T! Your chances of creating a good bond with the puppies are very low and behaviour problems with siblings are very common.

"Your dog may be sociable with other dogs but will not necessarily accept another dog into the household. You may find it useful to borrow a friend's dog that is familiar with your own and have a "dummy run" of life in a two-dog household. Research your considered breed well, it may be best to buy a completely different breed to add balance. If you have a very active dog, would a quieter one be best to balance his high energy or would you enjoy the challenge of keeping two high energy dogs?

"You will also need to think of any problems that may occur from keeping dogs of different sizes and ages. If you decide to purchase a puppy, you will need to think very carefully about the amount of time and energy that will be involved in caring for two dogs with very different needs. A young puppy will need to have his exercise restricted until he has finished growing and will also need individual time for training."

"Dogs of the same sex can and do live amicably in the same household, although harmony is more likely with a dog and bitch combination. If you decide to keep a dog and bitch together, then you will obviously need to address the neutering issue."

Experienced US breeder Pamela Preston adds: "When considering adding a new pup to your existing pack, gender sometimes does play a role in the matching process. If you already have a female, it might be best to get a male as they tend to be less dominant than females - believe it or not, it is usually the case!

"If you have male, usually another male or female is fine. Castrated or not, I believe males actually tend to be more tolerant of another male than females are with other females."

Pet or Show?

The difference between pet and show Bostons may be great or subtle. If you buy a Boston from a show breeder, sometimes a pet has a very minor difference from a show dog due to the competitiveness of showing.

Something as minor as eye colour or the set of his ears might exclude a Boston from the show ring. Or, it could be a huge difference that is obvious, like being too long in the body, being too small or large, or having a very long, Terrier-type muzzle.

These are often common traits found in dogs bred by backyard breeders or others who are not breeding to the standard. Regardless, there is usually a difference in price and requirements as well (typically, reputable breeders require a pet to be altered – i.e. spayed/neutered).

Unless you intend to enter conformation classes with your dog, you are looking for a pet.

Showing Bostons is a specialised art, and one that can bring great pleasure to both owner and dog once you get involved. When you are starting out, you have to know what you are looking for - and be prepared to pay extra; up to £1,000 or $1,000 more than for a pet.

(Pictured is Pamela Preston's champion Can CH/Am BIS CH Kirkwood's Cosmo Knows Who DunIt - "Butler" at two years of age after he won a Best In Show award. Photo: Tom Weigard, © www.TheWinningImage.com)

If you do have plans to enter the show world with your dapper little canine, then our advice about finding a mentor is even more valid. Do your research to find someone who successfully shows and breeds Boston Terriers. They should be able to guide you on what judges look for in the ring and steer you in the direction of a good litter; if not their own, then from somebody they know with a good reputation.

This is what experienced breeder Susan Maxwell has to say on the subject: "It is impossible to know if a puppy is going to develop into a show dog at the tender age of five or six weeks! Until a puppy is at least six to nine months old, you cannot be sure about things such as top lines and movement.

"An experienced breeder may be able to tell a great deal about a puppy from its ancestors and years of experience. Puppies may fail to grow or even become larger than expected as there is a wide variety of sizes amongst this breed. There may be many reasons a 'show potential' puppy does not make it as a 'champion candidate' or even for breeding.

"Puppies that are not held back for 'show potential' are sold as 'pet quality.' Pet quality puppies are sold on 'limited' registration, which means they can compete in AKC events such as agility etc. However, they cannot be used in any breeding programs and must be spayed/neutered. We take pride in selling a well-bred, healthy pet companion to a home where it will touch the lives of all its new family members."

Top 10 Tips For Working Boston Owners

We would certainly not recommend getting a Boston if you are out at work all day, but if you're determined to get one when you're out for several hours at a time, here are some useful points:

1. Either come home during your lunch break to let your dog out or employ a dog walker (or neighbour) to take him out for a walk in the middle of the day. If you can afford it, leave him at doggie day care where he can socialise with other dogs.

2. If not, do you know anybody you could leave your dog with during the day? Consider leaving your dog with a reliable friend, relative or elderly neighbour who would welcome the companionship of a Boston without the full responsibility of ownership.

3. Take him for a walk before you go to work – even if this means getting up at the crack of dawn – and spend time with him as soon as you get home. Exercise generates serotonin in the brain and has a calming effect. A dog that has been exercised will be less anxious and more ready for a good nap.

4. Leave him in a place of his own where he feels comfortable. If you use a crate, leave the door open, otherwise his favourite dog bed or chair. You may need to restrict access to other areas of the house to prevent him coming to harm or chewing things you don't want chewed. If possible, leave him in a room with a view of the outside world; this will be more interesting than staring at four blank walls.

5. Make sure that it does not get too hot during the day and there are no cold draughts in the place where you leave him. Bostons overheat easily.

6. Food and drink: although most Bostons love their food, it is still generally a good idea to put food down at specific meal times and remove it after 15 or 20 minutes if uneaten to prevent your dog becoming fussy or 'punishing' you for leaving him alone by refusing to eat.

Make sure he has access to water at all times. Dogs cannot cool down by sweating; they do not have many sweat glands (which is why they pant, but this is much less efficient than perspiring) and can die without sufficient water.

7. Leave toys available to play with to prevent destructive chewing (a popular occupation of bored dogs or one suffering from separation anxiety). Stuff a Kong toy - pictured - with treats to keep him occupied for a while. You can even smear the inside with peanut butter or another favourite treat to keep him occupied for longer.

8. Consider getting a companion for your Boston. This will involve even more of your time and twice the expense, and if you have not got time for one dog, you have hardly time for two. A better idea is to find someone you can leave the dog with during the day.

9. Consider leaving a radio or TV on very softly in the background. The 'white noise' can have a soothing effect on some pets. If you do this, select your channel carefully – try and avoid one with lots of bangs and crashes or heavy metal music!

10. Stick to the same routine before you leave your dog home alone. This will help him to feel secure. Before you go to work, get into a daily habit of getting yourself ready, then feeding and exercising your Boston. Dogs love routine. But don't make a huge fuss of him when you leave as this can also stress the dog; just leave the house calmly.

Similarly, when you come home, your Boston will feel starved of attention and be pleased to see you. Greet him normally, but try not to go overboard by making too much of a fuss as soon as you walk through the door. Give him a pat and a stroke then take off your coat and do a few other things before turning your attention back to him. Lavishing your Boston with too much attention the second you walk through the door may encourage needy behaviour or separation anxiety.

Puppy Stages

It is important to understand how a puppy develops into a fully grown dog. This knowledge will help you to be a good owner. **The first few months and weeks of a puppy's life will have an effect on his behaviour and character for the rest of his life.** This Puppy Schedule will help you to understand the early stages:

Birth to seven weeks	A puppy needs sleep, food and warmth. He needs his mother for security and discipline and littermates for learning and socialisation. The puppy learns to function within a pack and learns the pack order of dominance. He begins to become aware of his environment. During this period, puppies should be left with their mother.
Eight to 12 weeks	A puppy should NOT leave his mother before eight weeks. At this age the brain is fully developed and **he now needs socialising with the outside world.** He needs to change from being part of a canine pack to being part of a human pack. This period is a fear period for the puppy, avoid causing him fright and pain.
13 to 16 weeks	Training and formal obedience should begin. **This is a critical period for socialising with other humans, places and situations.** This period will pass easily if you remember that this is a puppy's change to adolescence. Be firm and fair. His flight instinct may be prominent. Avoid being too strict or too soft with him during this time and praise his good behaviour.
Four to eight months	Another fear period for a puppy is between seven to eight months of age. It passes quickly, but be cautious of fright or pain that may leave the puppy traumatised. The puppy reaches sexual maturity and dominant traits are established. Your Boston should now understand the following commands: 'sit', 'down', 'come' and 'stay.'

Plan Ahead

Most Boston puppies leave the litter for their new homes when they are eight to 10 weeks old. It is important that they have time to develop and learn the rules of the pack from their mothers and litter mates. Some puppies take a little longer to develop physically and mentally, and a puppy that leaves the litter too early often suffers with issues, for example a lack of confidence and problems interacting with other dogs, throughout life.

Breeders who allow their pups to leave home at six or seven weeks are probably more interested in a quick buck than a long-term puppy placement. The pup will also still be learning lessons from his mother and littermates during those later weeks, and good breeders will use that time to continue housetraining and socialising the puppies, so that by the time you collect your puppy, he or she already knows some basics. In the USA, it is against the law in many states for a breeder to sell a puppy before eight weeks of age. To check the age requirement for your state if you live in the USA, visit www.animallaw.info/topic/table-state-laws-concerning-minimum-age-sale-puppies

Several states also have puppy 'lemon laws' to protect the buyer from unscrupulous breeders, visit www.avma.org/Advocacy/StateAndLocal/Pages/pet-lemon-laws.aspx or your state's website.

And if you want a well-bred puppy, it certainly pays to plan ahead as many breeders with good reputations have waiting lists. This is especially true if you are looking for a dog with show potential.

Choosing the right breeder is one of the most important decisions you will make. Like humans, your puppy will be a product of his or her parents and will inherit many of their characteristics. His temperament and how healthy your puppy will be now and throughout his life will largely depend on the genes of his parents. Responsible breeders DNA test their dogs, they check the health records and temperament of the parents and only breed from suitable stock - and good breeding comes at a price.

Expect to pay around £1,200 to £2,000 in the UK and around $1,500 to $2,200 in the USA for a puppy from fully health-tested parents (in 2017, show pups cost more). This figure varies from region to region, although if a Boston puppy is being sold for much less, you have to ask why. If a pup is advertised at a few hundred dollars or pounds, then it's highly unlikely that the dam and sire are superb examples of their breed, that they and the pups have been fully health tested, and that the pups and mother are being fed premium quality food. Perhaps they are not even being kept in the house with the family where the breeder should start to socialise and housetrain them.

You probably won't get much after-sales support, either. And if there is something wrong with the puppy, you could be on your own. You might be lucky with the health of your chosen pup, but is it worth the risk? Can you afford the vets' bills if he or she has a genetic illness?

Sadly, because of the high prices, unscrupulous breeders with little knowledge of the breed have sprung up, tempted by the prospect of making easy cash. A healthy Boston will be your irreplaceable companion for the next decade or more, so why buy an unseen puppy, or one from a pet shop or general advertisement?

Would you buy an old wreck of a car or a house with structural problems just because it was cheap? The answer is probably no, because you know you would be storing up stress and expense in the future.

If a healthy Boston is important to you, save up until you can afford one. Good breeders do not sell their dogs on general ad websites or in pet shops. Some do not advertise at all, such is the demand for their puppies. Many breeders - good and bad - have their own websites; you have to learn to spot the experts from the profiteers.

We strongly recommend you visit the breeder personally at least once and follow our **Top Ten Tips for Selecting a Good Breeder** to help you make the right decision. Buying a poorly-bred puppy may save you a few hundred pounds or dollars in the short term, but could cost you thousands in extra veterinary bills in the long run - not to mention the terrible heartache of having a sickly dog.

Rescue groups know only too well the dangers of buying a poorly-bred dog; years of problems can arise, usually health-related, but there can also be temperament issues, or bad behaviour due to lack of early socialisation at the breeder's.

Boston Terrier Clubs

If you live in the USA, The Boston Terrier Club of America (BTCA) is a great place to start your search for a breeder; the website lists members here: www.bostonterrierclubofamerica.org/BTCA/btca-member-links.htm

And if you are in the UK, visit the Boston Terrier Club UK and you can find details of local club secretaries who can recommend good breeders in your area at: http://thebostonterrierclub.co.uk/buying_a_boston_terrier_new

In Canada there is The Boston Terrier Club of Canada at www.bostonterrierclubofcanada.com/index.asp?ID=16

Code of Ethics

Whichever country you live in, you should be looking for a breeder who abides by the main points of the BTCA Code of Ethics, to:

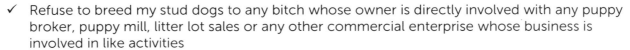

- ✓ Maintain the best possible standards of canine health, cleanliness and care

- ✓ Breed all bitches with the intention of improving the breed (with that particular breeding)

- ✓ Ensure that my dogs that are offered for stud and bitches that are accepted for stud service are in good health and free from communicable diseases and disqualifying faults

- ✓ Refuse to breed my stud dogs to any bitch whose owner is directly involved with any puppy broker, puppy mill, litter lot sales or any other commercial enterprise whose business is involved in like activities

- ✓ Keep accurate breeding records including registration papers and pedigrees

- ✓ Establish service and sales agreements that are mutually agreed upon, stated in writing and signed by all principals involved

- ✓ Furnish records to each buyer of all immunizations and worming. Also furnish buyer pedigree and American Kennel Club registration or transfer documents, unless written agreement is made at the time of sale that the papers will be withheld or they are forthcoming

- ✓ Advertise honestly and do not misrepresent or mislead a buyer of my Boston Terriers or services

- ✓ Refuse to sell any Boston Terrier to a buyer who cannot or will not provide evidence of ability to properly care for the animal

- ✓ Sell no Boston Terrier to a commercial facility, puppy broker, pet shop, puppy mill or their agent

- ✓ Hold myself responsible for the welfare of every dog I breed and/or sell

Of course, there are no cast iron guarantees that your puppy will be healthy and have a good temperament, but choosing a breeder who conforms to this code of ethics is a very good place to start. Here's some advice on what to avoid:

Where NOT to buy a Boston Puppy

No matter how nice the breeder sounds on the phone, or how many lovely photos of cute Boston puppies she or he has on their website, this is no guarantee that you are buying a quality puppy. High prices have tempted many people with limited knowledge and even fewer scruples to breeding Boston Terriers for profit.

Puppy mills are a particular problem in the USA, but they exist in most countries where dogs are kept as pets. The USA's Humane Society publishes an annual list of 100 puppy mills, here is the list for 2016: www.humanesociety.org/horrible-hundred-2016-puppy-mills-exposed.html

And here's the 2015 list: http://www.humanesociety.org/news/news/2015/05/horrible-hundred-2015-problem-puppy-mills.html]

If a US breeder is 'USDA approved (or certified)' it means he or she is a commercial breeder producing puppies for profit, so it may be wise to avoid any USDA-approved/certified breeder and choose a knowledgeable and reputable breeder whose prime motivation is a love of the breed. You should also avoid a breeder who is willing to ship a puppy without ever having met by you in person; you should be able to visit the breeder to see the puppies and the mother.

In September 2013 The UK's Kennel Club issued a warning of a puppy welfare crisis, with some truly sickening statistics. As many as one in four puppies bought in the UK may come from puppy farms - and the situation is no better in North America. The KC Press release stated: "As the popularity of online pups continues to soar:

* One in three buy online, in pet stores and via newspaper adverts - outlets often used by puppy farmers - this is an increase from one in five in the previous year

* The problem is likely to grow as the younger generation favour mail order pups, and breeders of fashionable crossbreeds flout responsible steps"

The Kennel Club said: "We are sleepwalking into a dog welfare and consumer crisis as new research shows that more and more people are buying their pups online or through pet shops, outlets often used by cruel puppy farmers, and are paying the price with their pups requiring long-term veterinary treatment or dying before six months old. The increasing popularity of online pups is a particular concern. Of those who source their puppies online, half are going on to buy 'mail order pups' directly over the internet." The KC research found that:

* Almost one in five pups bought (unseen) on websites or social media die within six months

* One third of people who bought their puppy online, over social media or in pet shops failed to experience 'overall good health'

* Some 12% of puppies bought online or on social media end up with serious health problems that require expensive on-going veterinary treatment from a young age

Caroline Kisko, Kennel Club Secretary, said: "More and more people are buying puppies from sources such as the internet, which are often used by puppy farmers. Whilst there is nothing wrong with initially finding a puppy online, it is essential to then see the breeder and ensure that they are doing all of the right things.

"This research clearly shows that too many people are failing to do this, and the consequences can be seen in the shocking number of puppies that are becoming sick or dying. We have an extremely serious consumer protection and puppy welfare crisis on our hands."

The research revealed that the problem was likely to get worse as mail order pups bought over the internet are the second most common way for the younger generation of 18 to 24-year-olds to buy a puppy (31%).

Marc Abraham, TV vet and founder of Pup Aid, said: "Sadly, if the 'buy it now' culture persists, then this horrific situation will only get worse. There is nothing wrong with sourcing a puppy online, but people need to be aware of what they should then expect from the breeder.

"For example, you should not buy a car without getting its service history and seeing it at its registered address, so you certainly shouldn't buy a puppy without the correct paperwork and health certificates and without seeing where it was bred. However, too many people are opting to buy directly from third parties such as the internet, pet shops, or from puppy dealers, where you cannot possibly know how or where the puppy was raised.

"Not only are people buying sickly puppies, but many people are being scammed into paying money for puppies that don't exist, as the research showed that 7% of those who buy online were scammed in this way." The Kennel Club has launched an online video and has a Find A Puppy app to show the do's and don'ts of buying a puppy. View the video at www.thekennelclub.org.uk/paw

What the Breeders Say

Here are some comments from Boston breeders involved in this book, starting with the UK:

"Unfortunately, as with all popular breeds, they fall victim to puppy farms/importers etc. I have even visited some 'KC Accredited Breeders' who are no better than your typical puppy farm.

"Boston Terriers are high risk whelping dogs and need to be cared for by someone who knows what they are doing and who cares; not by someone who has little or no experience. Anyone advertising a 'rare' dog or 'rare genes' - in other words charging more for a dog with a particular colour or from a different country - is in it for the money. Just because a dog is from outside the UK does not mean its genes are desirable and does not mean the dog is well bred. Bad breeders are a big problem with Bostons."

"There are not a great many imported Bostons here in the UK, but there is a big problem with puppy farmers - especially in Wales where a lot of them seem to be based. It is all about the money. You can't just put any two Bostons together, stick them in crates and feed them Pedigree Chum, but this is what some people are doing to make easy money - and then there are huge problems later."

Now some comments from breeders in the USA: "It is a monumental problem causing a flood of poor quality dogs to flood the market."

"There is most definitely a problem! We have a LOT of them in my state; it is very saddening. I've had personal experience with people buying from a puppy mill or backyard breeder only to have their puppy die of parvo in less than a week from picking it, as well as having severe behaviour problems - such as being fearful of people, being fear biters, having possessive issues regarding people, toys or food.

"These are not only unhealthy, but expensive and potentially dangerous issues. I've known of other health problems as well – bilateral deafness, severe allergies, seizures, etc. I always strongly advise potential puppy owners to do their research and make sure they are dealing with an ethical, reputable breeder."

Here is a cautionary tale from someone who got caught out by an unscrupulous breeder when she started out: "Puppy mills are a problem in the US and any place else they appear. When I first started out, I made the mistake of letting a fellow breeder and friend, who I thought at the time knew more than I did, get nice puppies for both of us.

"She had found what we both thought were beautiful puppies online from a 'well-known breeder' she had heard of. We wanted a puppy each and it was cheaper to have both puppies shipped to her, then we would meet half way (a four-hour drive). I asked my friend if both puppies looked good, and she said 'Yes, they are great' and we made plans for me to pick up my puppy and pay half of the shipping.

"As soon as I got him home I noticed he had a little soft stool, then I started watching him closely. He walked towards me in a strange way I'd never seen before; to me it looked like he walked like a duck with his hind legs. He could walk and run, but never even tried to jump like other pups his age, and I thought this was odd. By the second day something was wrong with one of his eyes, so I called one of my vets and they took him in straight away.

"As it turned out the poor baby - who came with a general health certificate - had an ulcer in one eye. When I told my vet how he walked like a duck, he looked me right in the eye and said: "That's because he is a puppy mill dog and has been living and walking on wire". It just broke my heart. Needless to say, I had all of his problems treated and taken care of. Lesson learned.

"As for that puppy, he grew up into one of the smartest, sweetest, most beautiful males you have ever seen. He still did not jump at all, but he had a wonderful forever home with us and was well loved. I do not believe all the puppies or dogs that come out of these places are that lucky. All puppy mills need to be shut down. I do know that we have enough good, clean breeders who take pride in what they are doing and who love and care for their dogs."

Caveat Emptor – Buyer Beware

Here are some signs that a puppy may have arrived via a puppy mill, a puppy broker (somebody who makes money from buying and selling puppies) or even an importer. Our strong advice is that if you suspect that this is the case, walk away - unless you want to risk a lot of trouble and heartache in the future.

You can't buy a Rolls Royce or a Lamborghini for a couple of thousand pounds or dollars - you'd immediately suspect that the 'bargain' on offer wasn't the real thing. No matter how lovely it looked, you'd be right - the same applies to Bostons. Here are some signs to look out for:

* Websites – buying a puppy from a website does not necessarily mean that the puppy will turn out

to have problems. But avoid websites where there are no pictures of the home, environment and owners. If they are only showing close-up photos of cute puppies, click the **X** button

🐾 Don't buy a website puppy with a shopping cart symbol next to his picture

🐾 Beware of any breeder offering 'rare', 'unique' or 'one of a kind' puppies. They do not conform to the Breed Standard and, in all likelihood, have not been properly health tested

🐾 Don't commit to a website puppy unless you have seen it face-to-face. If this is not possible, at the very least you must speak (on the phone) with the breeder and ask questions; don't deal with an intermediary

🐾 At the breeder's you hear: "You can't see the parent dogs because......" ALWAYS ask to see the parents and, as a minimum, see the mother and how she looks and behaves

🐾 Ignore photographs of so-called 'champion' ancestors (unless you are buying from an approved breeder), in all likelihood these are fiction

🐾 Ask to personally see all health certificates

🐾 The puppies look small for their stated age. A committed Boston breeder will not let her puppies leave before they are eight weeks or older

🐾 The person you are buying the puppy from did not breed the dog themselves

🐾 The place you meet the puppy seller is a car park or place other than the puppies' home

🐾 The seller tells you that the puppy comes from top, caring breeders from your or another country. Not true. There are reputable, caring breeders all over the world, but not one of them sells their puppies through brokers

🐾 Ask to see photos of the puppy from birth to present day. If the seller has none, there is a reason – walk away

🐾 Price – if you are offered a cheap Boston, he or she almost certainly comes from dubious stock. Careful breeding, taking good care of mother and puppies and health screening all add up to one big bill for breeders. Anyone selling their puppies at a knock-down price has cut corners

🐾 If you get a rescue Boston, make sure it is from a recognised rescue group and not a 'puppy flipper' who may be posing as a do-gooder, but is in fact getting dogs – including stolen ones - from unscrupulous sources

In fact, the whole brokering business is just another version of the puppy mill and should be avoided at all costs. Bear in mind that for every cute Boston puppy you see from a puppy mill or broker, other puppies have died. There are plenty of good breeders there, it's just a question of finding one. And the good news is that there are signs to help the savvy buyer:

Top Ten Tips for Choosing a Good Breeder

1. We cannot stress enough how important it is to choose a Boston breeder whose dogs are health tested with certificates to prove it. There are a number of inheritable illnesses within the breed and if you buy from untested stock, you risk your puppy having one or more of these. Visit the website of the Boston Terrier Club in your country or region for details of approved breeders. If your chosen breeder is not registered, read the small print on his or her website, what health tests are carried out?

2. Good breeders keep the dogs in the home as part of the family - not outside in kennel runs, garages or outbuildings. Check that the area where the puppies are kept is clean and that the puppies themselves look clean.

3. Their Bostons appear happy and healthy. Check that the pup has clean eyes, ears, nose and bum (butt) with no discharge. The pups are alert, excited to meet new people and don't shy away from visitors.

4. A good breeder will encourage you to spend time with the puppy's parents - or at least the mother - when you visit. They want your family to meet the puppy and are usually happy for you to visit more than once.

5. They are very familiar with Bostons, although some may also breed a similar breed, such as French Bulldogs. Avoid breeders who produce many types of dog; you are looking to buy from a Boston expert.

6. Most breeders will provide you with a written Puppy Contract and health guarantee. They will also show you records of the puppy's visits to the vet, vaccinations, worming medication, etc. and explain what other vaccinations your puppy will need. They will agree to take a puppy back within a certain time frame if it does not work out for you, or if there is a health problem.

7. They feed their adults and puppies high quality dog food and give you some to take home and guidance on feeding and caring for your puppy. They will also be available for advice after you take your puppy home.

8. They don't always have pups available, but keep a list of interested people for the next available litter, they might even recommend another breeder who has pups. They don't over-breed, but do limit the number of litters from their dams.

Pictured are four generations of ChriMaso Boston Terriers from AKC Breeder of Merit and mentor to new exhibitors, Pamela Preston, of Shingle Springs, California. Left to right: matriarch Ruthie, her son and first homebred champion, Taison, then Penny and daughter, Tiffany. Photo: Tom Weigard, © 2016 www.TheWinningImage.com

9. If you have selected a breeder and checked if/when she has puppies available, go online to the Boston forums before you visit and ask if anyone out there already has a dog from this breeder. If you are buying from a good breeder, the chances are someone will know her dogs or at least her reputation. If the feedback is negative, cancel your visit and start looking elsewhere. A good breeder will, if asked, provide references from other people who have bought their puppies; call at least one before you commit.

10. And finally ... good Boston breeders want to know their beloved pups are going to good homes and will ask YOU a lot of questions about your suitability as owners. DON'T buy a puppy from a website or advert where a PayPal or credit card deposit secures you a puppy without any questions.

Boston puppies should not be regarded as must-have accessories. They are not objects, they are warm-blooded, living, breathing creatures. Healthy, happy puppies and adult dogs are what everybody wants. Taking the time now to find a responsible and committed breeder is time well spent. It could save you a lot of time, money and heartache in the future and help to ensure that you and your chosen canine companion are happy together for many years to come.

The Most Important Questions to Ask a Breeder

Some of these points have been covered in the previous section, but here's a reminder and checklist of the questions you should be asking.

Have the parents and puppies been health screened? Ask to see original copies of health certificates. In the UK these will have been issued by the BVA and Kennel Club; in the USA: OFA (patellas and eyes), CAER (eyes) and BAER (deafness). In the USA, you should be able to see health test results on the OFA website: http://www.ofa.org/breedtests.html? If they have not been submitted and posted, ask to see the original certificates.

If no certificates are available, ask what guarantees the breeder is offering in terms of genetic illnesses, and how long these guarantees last – 12 weeks, a year, a lifetime? It will vary from breeder to breeder, but good ones will definitely give you some form of guarantee – it should be stated in the Puppy Contract. They will also want to be informed of any hereditary health problems with your puppy, as they may choose not to breed from the dam or sire (mother or father) again. Some breeders keep a chart documenting the full family health history of the pup – ask if one exists and if you can see it.

Is the puppy KC or AKC registered and can I pick up the registration papers with the pup? (This is no guarantee of health, it just means that the puppy's parents are both registered Boston Terriers).

Do you have a Puppy Contract?

Can you put me in touch with someone who already has one of your puppies?

Are you a member of a breed club? Not all good Boston breeders are members, but this is a good place to start. This little chap is a health-tested puppy from BTCA member Susan Maxwell, of Maximum Companion Boston Terriers, California. Susan has been breeding Bostons for 20 years.

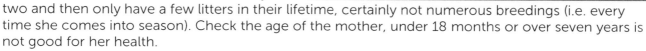

How long have you been breeding Bostons? You are looking for someone who has a track record with the breed.

How old will the puppy be when I can take him or her home? Anything less than eight weeks should set alarm bells ringing.

How many litters has the mother had? Females should not have litters until they are two and then only have a few litters in their lifetime, certainly not numerous breedings (i.e. every time she comes into season). Check the age of the mother, under 18 months or over seven years is not good for her health.

What happens to the female(s) once she/they have finished breeding? Are they kept as part of the family, rehomed in loving homes or sent to animal shelters?

Do you breed any other types of dog? Buy from a Boston specialist, preferably one who does not breed lots of other dogs - unless you know they have a particularly good reputation.

What is so special about this litter? You are looking for a breeder who has used good breeding stock and his or her knowledge to produce healthy, handsome dogs with good temperaments, not just cute dogs. All Boston puppies look cute, don't buy the first one you see – be patient and pick the right one. If you don't get a satisfactory answer, look elsewhere.

What do you feed your adults and puppies? A reputable breeder will feed a top quality dog food and advise that you do the same.

What is the average lifespan of your dogs? Pups bred from healthy stock tend to live longer.

How do you socialise and housetrain the puppy? Good breeders will raise their puppies as part of the household and start the socialisation and housetraining process before they leave.

What healthcare have the pups had so far? Ask to see records of flea treatments, wormings and vaccinations.

Why aren't you asking me any questions? A good breeder will be committed to making a good match between the new owners and their puppies. If the breeder spends more time discussing money than the welfare of the puppy and how you will care for him, you can draw your own conclusions as to what his or her priorities are – and they probably don't include improving the breed.

If you feel uneasy about the breeder or anything else, walk away - even if it means losing a deposit on a puppy.

Take your puppy to a vet to have a thorough check-up within 48 hours of purchase. If your vet is not happy with the health of the dog, no matter how painful it may be, return the pup to the breeder. Keeping an unhealthy puppy will only cause more distress and expense in the long run.

Puppy Contracts

A Puppy Contract protects both buyer and seller by providing information about both parties along with guarantees on both sides. You should also have a health guarantee for a specified time period, hopefully, a year at least. Some breeders even require a visit to **your** home. This is typically done to set the breeder's mind at ease about the environment the puppy will be living in, as well as allowing the breeder to look around (particularly the garden or yard) to see if they can identify any hazards you may not have been aware of.

A Puppy Contract will answer such questions as whether the puppy:

- Is covered by breeder's insurance and can be returned if there is a health issue within a certain period of time (some breeders offer free four-week insurance with the pup)
- Was born by Caesarean section
- Has been micro-chipped and/or vaccinated and details of worming treatments
- Has had a health check by a vet
- The puppy has been partially or wholly toilet trained
- Has been socialised and where it was kept
- And what health issues the pup and parents have been screened for
- What the puppy is currently being fed by the breeder and if any food is being supplied
- Details of the dam and sire
- Details of health screening

It's not easy for caring breeders to part with their puppies after they have lovingly bred and raised them to eight weeks of age or older, and so many supply extensive care notes for new owners, which may include details such as:

- The puppy's daily routine
- Feeding schedule and diet
- Vet and vaccination schedule
- General puppy care
- Toilet training
- Socialisation

New owners should do their research before visiting a litter as, once there, the cute Boston puppies will undoubtedly be irresistible and you will buy with your heart rather than your head. If you have any doubts at all about the breeder, seller or the puppy, WALK AWAY.

In the UK, The Royal Society for the Prevention of Cruelty to Animals (RSPCA) has a downloadable puppy contract endorsed by vets and animal welfare organisations .You can see a copy here and should be looking for something similar from the breeder or seller of the puppy:
http://puppycontract.rspca.org.uk/webContent/staticImages/Microsites/PuppyContract/Downloads/PuppyContractDownload.pdf

Some breeders will sell their puppies with 'endorsements,' or conditions that cover, usually, the neutering and showing of the dog. Ask if the breeder is placing any endorsements on the sale.

Californian breeder Susan Maxwell said: "Pet companions puppies must be cared for properly, given proper vaccinations, must be spayed/neutered, fed proper food and taken to a vet within a reasonable amount of time after purchase – usually 48 hours. A guarantee is given for life-threatening congenital issues. I have never had issues with allergies, but I also feel that dogs with allergies etc. should NOT be in a breeding program.

"Contracts for show puppies are different, depending on sex. Basically they state that you must fulfil all obligations of genetic health testing, dogs must be shown to their fullest potential and, if it is agreed that the dog is to be bred, you must follow agreed stipulations."

Fellow California breeder and Boston Terrier Club of America member, Pamela Preston, added: "My puppy contracts for both companion and show prospects are very detailed and include a realistic health guarantee, as well as requirements for both the buyer and the breeder. All companion puppies are placed on mandatory spay/neuter agreements and all show prospects are placed with guidelines for showing expectations."

Top 10 Tips for Choosing a Healthy Boston

Once you've selected your breeder and a litter is available, you then have to decide WHICH puppy to pick. Some breeders will advise and even select a puppy for you based on the personality and temperament of the puppy, along with your lifestyle and activity level. The breeder knows his or her puppies better than anyone else, and can be the best person for matching the right puppy to the right family.

Here are some signs that you should look for when selecting a puppy:

1. Your chosen puppy should have a well-fed appearance. He or she should not, however, have a distended abdomen (pot belly) as this can be a sign of worms - or other illnesses (such as Cushing's disease in adults). The ideal puppy should not be too thin either; you should not be able to see his ribs.

2. His (or her) nose should be cool, damp and clean with no discharge.

3. The pup's eyes should be bright and clear with no discharge or tear stain. Steer clear of a puppy that blinks a lot, this could be the sign of a problem.

4. His gums should be clean and pink.

5. The pup's ears should be clean with no sign of discharge, soreness or redness and no unpleasant smell.

6. Check the puppy's rear end to make sure it is clean and there are no signs of diarrhoea.

7. A puppy's coat should look clean, feel soft, not matted - and puppies should smell good! The coat should have no signs of ticks or fleas. Red or irritated skin or bald spots could be a

sign of infestation or a skin condition. Also check between the toes of the paws for signs of redness or swelling. .

8. Choose a puppy that moves freely without any sign of injury or lameness. It should be a fluid movement, not jerky or stiff, which could be a sign of joint problems.

9. When the puppy is distracted, clap or make a noise behind him - not so loud as to frighten him - to make sure he is not completely deaf. There is an issue with congenital unilateral (in one ear) or bilateral (both ears) deafness in some Boston bloodlines, particularly those with a lot of white in their coat. If the pup is deaf in one ear, he may cock his head. Unilateral deafness has no negative impact to the quality of the dog's (or your) life; however, a bilaterally deaf puppy requires special training, patience and understanding. Without proper training, they can be fear biters as well, since they cannot hear and can be easily startled.

10. Finally, ask to see veterinary records to confirm your puppy has been wormed and had his first injections. Some US breeders do their own vaccinations and wormings, but will still have records to pass on to the new owner.

If you are unlucky enough to have a health problem with your pup within the first few months, a reputable breeder will allow you to return the pup. Also, if you get the Boston puppy home and things don't work out for whatever reason, good breeders should also take the puppy back. Make sure this is the case before you commit.

....

Breeders' Advice

Our breeders have lots of advice on what to look out for when considering choosing a breeder and then the individual puppy. Emily Little, UK: "A good breeder asks personal questions about the potential owner and wants to get to know you. A good breeder will not try to 'sell' you a puppy; they want to ensure you are the best match for their breed/pups.

"Never buy a puppy: from anyone who has not had their breeding stock health tested (with documented evidence and results), if neither of the parents are present - unless the bitch had been lost at whelp, if they are advertising 'rare' colours, nor if there are signs of multiple litters.

"You should be concerned if the breeder does not display a relationship with their bitch or allow the puppy to walk/play around when shown to the potential buyer.

"The puppy should be clean, well fed and in perfect health. No wheezing or signs of neglect. They should be playful and inquisitive. The puppy should not shy away or show any signs of aggression. Eyes should not bulge and the head should be in proportion to their body. A responsible breeder will never double up on faults, (should not breed two Bostons with similar issues/faults), and ideally, both parents should be viewed to see both temperament and physical characteristics.

"A good breeder should always know more about their breed than the buyer. If appropriate research into the breed is done by the buyer, they will get a feel for the knowledge of the breeder. And a knowledgeable and responsible breeder will produce well-adjusted and healthy puppies. A responsible breeder does not just get any two dogs together and hope for the best."

Gwion Williams, UK: "Always visit and view the litter. A good breeder will not put any pressure on you to commit there and then. They will answer any questions you may have about the breed and will give you guidance on how to raise your Boston Terrier puppy from their experiences. Contact the breeder if you intend on buying a puppy sometime in the future. I have found that when people follow a litter from when they are born it gives that added bond between the person or family and dog."

Jo Dalton, UK: "Find a reputable breeder. We are a KC Assured breeder and have a list of things we must provide for and with our puppies, both before and when they leave us. Any good breeder will not mind what or how many questions you ask, because it should be important to them to learn about who you are and help and advise all they can.

"It is also worth mentioning that most good breeders do not need to advertise their puppies for sale on puppy sales websites as they have a waiting list of some sort or use the Kennel Club's puppy sales register. (Photo courtesy of Jo).

"Unfortunately due to the economic downturn, people are turning to other ways to make money and dog breeding is often seen as 'easy money.' At the present time there are lots of examples of bad breeding practices occurring in very popular breeds such as the Boston Terrier and French Bulldog, amongst others.

"People are breeding their pet KC-registered dogs together and simply either do not know or do not care about researching into what they are breeding, and we are seeing many dogs being born to these inexperienced breeders having not been fully health tested and with very high inbreeding percentages, which in turn leads to health problems.

"There are lots of puppy farmers and bad breeders out there and by no means are they limited to crossbreed or unregistered dogs. These puppies are often raised in basic and unsanitary conditions without care and attention to details with the sole purpose of making money. The puppies are often sick and unsocialised, many die within a few days of being purchased. Be aware that people lie and rarely is the sob story true.

"If something does not feel right, then chances are it isn't right and you are best to go on gut instinct and walk away. Buying a puppy because you feel sorry for it, is never a good idea for you or the puppy. The best thing you can do is to report the sellers to the RSPCA."

Pamela Preston, USA: "Puppies should be in a clean, healthy environment with friendly, outgoing, confident personalities. They should be willing to interact with you and the other animals in the environment. Puppies should be clean with no discharge coming from the eyes or nose. Be cautious of breeders who do not want you to visit their home or see the parents of the puppies. Puppies from reputable breeders are well-socialized, self-confident, energetic, and are health tested (at a minimum, BAER for hearing, and if possible, CAER for eye diseases). Their eyes should be clear and their coat clean and shiny."

Susan Maxwell, USA: "Puppy buyers should always be comfortable with whom they are buying from and should not be hesitant to ask questions, as it is their right. You are relying on the honesty of your breeder to help you find a puppy that will fit the right lifestyle of your family.

"When you visit a breeder, take note if all dogs kept seem happy...Are conditions clean? Is there adequate space? Is your breeder able to answer all your questions? Are the dogs part of the breeder's family or just kennelled in excess to make profit? This seems to be a big problem as 'puppy mill' dogs are often unsocialised and have numerous health problems and often have no health guarantee or, more important, a guarantee for your broken heart when your puppy does not fit in or is unhealthy, etc. Responsible breeders can produce health testing results on your puppy's parents as well as some testing on your puppy."

Lynda Montgomery, USA: "If I phoned to see a puppy and the seller told me they would meet me somewhere to let me see the puppy, I would move on, because there is a reason they do not want you to see how the puppies are being cared for. Or if you ask to see the parents and they tell you they do not have them; that's a red flag. The first thing you should ask is whether the puppy is JHC (Juvenile Hereditary Cataracts) clean and get a copy of the paperwork.

"If you see an ad on the internet that sounds too good to be true, for example a puppy for $500 - no matter what kind of story or how sad it is - never send these people money. They just want your money and they post pictures of the most beautiful puppies and tell the saddest stories. I know of people who have been scammed; it's awful! These people take all your information and want the money by Western Union, e-check or even Walmart to Walmart now, but there is no puppy.

"A nice healthy puppy has clear eyes, a healthy coat with good fur which is not thin. A bloated tummy can be a sign of worms. Always look at their gums, they should be pink, not pale and white. The puppy should have lots of energy and be playful, it runs toward people to be patted and played; it should not be afraid. A healthy puppy smells good (there is nothing else in the world that smells like a puppy) - but a sickly puppy can have a sour smell."

....

Picking the Right Temperament

You've picked a Boston, presumably, because you love this breed's handsome looks and outgoing, get-along-with-everybody personality. Presumably you're planning to spend a lot of time with your new puppy, as Bostons love being with humans. While different dogs may share many characteristics, each puppy also has his own individual temperament, just like humans.

The affectionate nature and positive attitude of the Boston suits most people. Also, Bostons are very adaptable to different lifestyles, as long as you start as you mean to carry on.

Visit the breeder to see how your chosen pup interacts and get an idea of his character in comparison to his littermates. Some puppies will run up to greet you, pull at your shoelaces and playfully bite your fingers. Others will be more content to stay in the basket sleeping. Watch their behaviour and energy levels.

Are you an active person who enjoys lots of daily exercise or would a less hyper puppy be more suitable? Choose the puppy that will best fit in with your family and lifestyle.

A more submissive dog will by nature be more passive, less energetic and also possibly easier to train. A dominant dog will usually be more energetic and lively. He or she may also be more stubborn and need a firmer hand when training or socialising with other dogs. If you already have a dominant dog at home, you have to be careful about introducing a new dog into the household; two dominant dogs will probably not live together comfortably.

There is no good or bad, it's a question of which type of character will best suit you and your lifestyle. Here are a couple of quick tests to try and gauge your puppy's temperament; they should be carried out by the breeder in familiar surroundings so the puppy is relaxed. It should be pointed out that there is some controversy over temperament testing as a dog's personality is formed by a combination of factors, which include inherited temperament, socialisation, training and environment (or how you treat your dog):

- The breeder puts the pup on his or her back on her lap and gently rests her hand on the pup's chest, or
- She puts her hands under the pup's tummy and gently lifts the pup off the floor for a few seconds, keeping the pup horizontal. A puppy that struggles to get free is less patient than one that makes little effort to get away. A placid, patient dog is likely to fare better in a home with young children than an impatient one.

Here are some other useful signs to look out for –

- Watch how he interacts with other puppies in the litter. Does he try and dominate them, does he walk away from them or is he happy to play with his littermates? This may give you an idea of how easy it will be to socialise him with other dogs
- After contact, does the pup want to follow you or walk away from you? Not following may mean he has a more independent nature
- If you throw something for the puppy is he happy to retrieve it for you or does he ignore it? This may measure their willingness to work with humans
- If you drop a bunch of keys behind the Boston puppy, does he act normally or does he flinch and jump away? The latter may be an indication of a timid or nervous disposition. Not reacting could also be a sign of deafness

The breeder may help you decide which temperament would fit in with you and your family and the rest is up to you. Whatever hereditary temperament your Boston has, it is true to say that dogs that have constant positive interactions with people and other animals during the first four months of life will generally be happier and more stable.

In contrast, a Boston puppy plucked from its family too early (i.e. before eight weeks of age) and/or isolated at home alone for long periods will be less happy, less socialised, needier and may well display behaviour problems later on.

Puppies are like children. Being properly raised contributes to their confidence, sociability, stability and intellectual development. The bottom line is that a pup raised in a warm, loving environment with people is likely to be more tolerant and accepting, and less likely to develop behaviour issues.

For those of you who prefer a scientific approach to choosing the right puppy, we are including the full Volhard Puppy Aptitude Test (PAT), developed by the highly respected Wendy and Jack Volhard who have built an international reputation over the last 30 years for their valuable contribution to dog training, health and nutrition. Their philosophy is: "We believe that one of life's great joys is living in harmony with your dog."

They have written several books and the Volhard PAT is regarded as an excellent method for evaluating the nature of young puppies. Jack and Wendy have also written the Dog Training for Dummies book. Visit www.volhard.com for details of their upcoming dog training camps, as well as their training and nutrition groups.

The Volhard Puppy Aptitude Test

Here are the ground rules for performing the test: the testing is done in a location unfamiliar to the puppies. This does not mean they have to be taken away from home. A 10-foot square area is perfectly adequate, such as a room in the house where the puppies have not been.

- ✓ The puppies are tested one at a time. There are no other dogs or people, except the scorer and the tester, in the testing area

- ✓ The puppies do not know the tester

- ✓ The scorer is a disinterested third party and not the person interested in selling you a puppy

- ✓ The scorer is unobtrusive and positions himself so he can observe the puppies' responses without having to move

The puppies are tested before they are fed. The puppies are tested when they are at their liveliest. Do not try to test a puppy that is not feeling well.

Puppies should not be tested the day of or the day after being vaccinated. Only the first response counts! Tip: During the test, watch the puppy's tail. (NOTE: Not all Bostons have one!) It will make a difference in the scoring whether the tail is up or down. The tests are simple to perform and anyone with some common sense can do them. You can, however, elicit the help of someone who has tested puppies before and knows what they are doing.

Social attraction - the owner or caretaker of the puppies places it in the test area about four feet from the tester and then leaves the test area. The tester kneels down and coaxes the puppy to come to him or her by encouragingly and gently clapping hands and calling. The tester must coax the puppy in the opposite direction from where it entered the test area. Hint: Lean backward, sitting on your heels instead of leaning forward toward the puppy. Keep your hands close to your body encouraging the puppy to come to you instead of trying to reach for the puppy.

Following - the tester stands up and slowly walks away encouraging the puppy to follow. Hint: Make sure the puppy sees you walk away and get the puppy to focus on you by lightly clapping your hands and using verbal encouragement to get the puppy to follow you. Do not lean over the puppy.

Restraint - the tester crouches down and gently rolls the puppy on its back for 30 seconds. Hint: Hold the puppy down without applying too much pressure. The object is not to keep it on its back but to test its response to being placed in that position.

Social Dominance - let the puppy stand up or sit and gently stroke it from the head to the back while you crouch beside it. See if it will lick your face, an indication of a forgiving nature. Continue stroking until you see a behaviour you can score. Hint: When you crouch next to the puppy avoid leaning or hovering over it. Have the puppy at your side, both of you facing in the same direction.

During testing maintain a positive, upbeat and friendly attitude toward the puppies. Try to get each puppy to interact with you to bring out the best in him or her. Make the test a pleasant experience for the puppy.

Elevation Dominance - the tester cradles the puppy with both hands, supporting the puppy under its chest and gently lifts it two feet off the ground and holds it there for 30 seconds.

Retrieving - the tester crouches beside the puppy and attracts its attention with a crumpled up piece of paper. When the puppy shows some interest, the tester throws the paper no more than four feet in front of the puppy encouraging it to retrieve the paper.

Touch Sensitivity - the tester locates the webbing of one of the puppy's front paws and presses it lightly between his index finger and thumb. The tester gradually increases pressure while counting to ten and stops when the puppy pulls away or shows signs of discomfort.

Sound Sensitivity - the puppy is placed in the centre of the testing area and an assistant stationed at the perimeter makes a sharp noise, such as banging a metal spoon on the bottom of a metal pan.

Sight Sensitivity - the puppy is placed in the centre of the testing area. The tester ties a string around a bath towel and jerks it across the floor, two feet away from the puppy.

Stability - an umbrella is opened about five feet from the puppy and gently placed on the ground. During the testing, make a note of the heart rate of the pup, this is an indication of how it deals with stress, as well as its energy level. Puppies come with high, medium or low energy levels. You have to decide for yourself, which suits your life style. Dogs with high energy levels need a great deal of exercise, and will get into mischief if this energy is not channelled into the right direction.

Finally, look at the overall structure of the puppy. You see what you get at 49 days' age (seven weeks). If the pup has strong and straight front and back legs, with all four feet pointing in the same direction, it will grow up that way, provided you give it the proper diet and environment. If you notice something out of the ordinary at this age, it will stay with puppy for the rest of its life. He will not grow out of it.

Scoring the Results

Following are the responses you will see and the score assigned to each particular response. You will see some variations and will have to make a judgment on what score to give them –

TEST	RESPONSE	SCORE
SOCIAL ATTRACTION	Came readily, tail up, jumped, bit at hands	1
	Came readily, tail up, pawed, licked at hands	2
	Came readily, tail up	3
	Came readily, tail down	4
	Came hesitantly, tail down	5
	Didn't come at all	6
FOLLOWING	Followed readily, tail up, got underfoot, bit at feet	1
	Followed readily, tail up, got underfoot	2
	Followed readily, tail up	3

	Followed readily, tail down	4
	Followed hesitantly, tail down	5
	Did not follow or went away	6
RESTRAINT	Struggled fiercely, flailed, bit	1
	Struggled fiercely, flailed	2
	Settled, struggled, settled with some eye contact	3
	Struggled, then settled	4
	No struggle	5
	No struggle, strained to avoid eye contact	6
SOCIAL DOMINANCE	Jumped, pawed, bit, growled	1
	Jumped, pawed	2
	Cuddled up to tester and tried to lick face	3
	Squirmed, licked at hands	4
	Rolled over, licked at hands	5
	Went away and stayed away	6
ELEVATION DOMINANCE	Struggled fiercely, tried to bite	1
	Struggled fiercely	2
	Struggled, settled, struggled, settled	3
	No struggle, relaxed	4
	No struggle, body stiff	5
	No struggle, froze	6
RETRIEVING	Chased object, picked it up and ran away	1
	Chased object, stood over it and did not return	2
	Chased object, picked it up and returned with it to tester	3
	Chased object and returned without it to tester	4
	Started to chase object, lost interest	5
	Does not chase object	6
TOUCH SENSITIVITY	8-10 count before response	1
	6-8 count before response	2
	5-6 count before response	3
	3-5 count before response	4
	2-3 count before response	5

	1-2 count before response	6
SOUND SENSITIVITY	Listened, located sound and ran toward it barking	1
	Listened, located sound and walked slowly toward it	2
	Listened, located sound and showed curiosity	3
	Listened and located sound	4
	Cringed, backed off and hid behind tester 5	5
	Ignored sound and showed no curiosity	6
SIGHT SENSITIVITY	Looked, attacked and bit object	1
	Looked and put feet on object and put mouth on it	2
	Looked with curiosity and attempted to investigate, tail up	3
	Looked with curiosity, tail down	4
	Ran away or hid behind tester	5
	Hid behind tester	6
STABILITY	Looked and ran to the umbrella, mouthing or biting it	1
	Looked and walked to the umbrella, smelling it cautiously	2
	Looked and went to investigate	3
	Sat and looked, but did not move toward the umbrella	4
	Showed little or no interest	5
	Ran away from the umbrella	6

The scores are interpreted as follows:

Mostly 1s - Strong desire to be pack leader and is not shy about bucking for a promotion. Has a predisposition to be aggressive to people and other dogs and will bite. Should only be placed into a very experienced home where the dog will be trained and worked on a regular basis.

Tip: Stay away from the puppy with a lot of 1s or 2s. It has lots of leadership aspirations and may be difficult to manage. This puppy needs an experienced home. Not good with children.

Mostly 2s - Also has leadership aspirations. May be hard to manage and has the capacity to bite. Has lots of self-confidence. Should not be placed into an inexperienced home. Too unruly to be good with children and elderly people, or other animals. Needs strict schedule, loads of exercise and lots of training. Has the potential to be a great show dog with someone who understands dog behaviour.

Mostly 3s - Can be a high-energy dog and may need lots of exercise. Good with people and other animals. Can be a bit of a handful to live with. Needs training, does very well at it and learns quickly. Great dog for second-time owner.

Mostly 4s - The kind of dog that makes the perfect pet. Best choice for the first time owner. Rarely will buck for a promotion in the family. Easy to train, and rather quiet. Good with elderly people, children, although may need protection from the children. Choose this pup, take it to obedience classes, and you'll be the star, without having to do too much work!

Tip: The puppy with mostly 3s and 4s can be quite a handful, but should be good with children and does well with training. Energy needs to be dispersed with plenty of exercise.

Mostly 5s - Fearful, shy and needs special handling. Will run away at the slightest stress in its life. Strange people, strange places, different floor or surfaces may upset it. Often afraid of loud noises and terrified of thunderstorms. When you greet it upon your return, may submissively urinate. Needs a very special home where the environment doesn't change too much and where there are no children. Best for a quiet, elderly couple. If cornered and cannot get away, has a tendency to bite.

Mostly 6s – So independent that he doesn't need you or other people. Doesn't care if he is trained or not - he is his own person. Unlikely to bond to you, since he doesn't need you. A great guard dog for gas stations! Do not take this puppy and think you can change him into a lovable bundle - you can't, so leave well enough alone.

Tip: Avoid the puppy with several 6s. It is so independent it doesn't need you or anyone. He is his own person and unlikely to bond to you.

The Scores

Few puppies will test with all 2s or all 3s, there'll be a mixture of scores. For that first time, wonderfully easy to train, potential star, look for a puppy that scores with mostly 4s and 3s. Don't worry about the score on Touch Sensitivity - you can compensate for that with the right training equipment.

It's hard not to become emotional when picking a puppy - they are all so cute, soft and cuddly. Remind yourself that this dog is going to be with you for eight to 16 years. Don't hesitate to step back a little to contemplate your decision. Sleep on it and review it in the light of day.

Avoid the puppy with a score of 1 on the Restraint and Elevation tests. This puppy will be too much for the first-time owner. It's a lot more fun to have a good dog, one that is easy to train, one you can live with and one you can be proud of, than one that is a constant struggle.

Getting a Dog from a Shelter - Don't overlook an animal shelter as a source for a good dog. Not all dogs wind up in a shelter because they are bad. After that cute puppy stage, when the dog grows up, it may become too much for its owner. Or, there has been a change in the owner's circumstances forcing him or her into having to give up the dog.

Most of the time these dogs are housetrained and already have some training. If the dog has been properly socialized to people, it will be able to adapt to a new environment. Bonding may take a little longer, but once accomplished, results in a devoted companion.

5. Bringing Your Puppy Home

Before you bring your precious little bundle of joy home, it's a smart idea to prepare your home before he or she arrives while you still have the chance. All puppies are demanding and, once they land, they will swallow up most of your time. Here's a list of things you ought to think about getting beforehand:

Puppy Checklist

✓ A dog bed or basket

✓ Bedding – old towels or a blanket that can easily be washed (avoid strong detergents)

✓ If possible, a towel or piece of cloth which has been rubbed on the puppy's mother to put in the bed

✓ A collar or harness and lead (leash)

✓ An identification tag for the collar or harness

✓ Food and water bowls, preferably stainless steel

✓ Puppy food – find out what the breeder is feeding and stick with it initially

✓ Puppy treats (preferably healthy ones, not rawhide)

✓ Lots of newspapers for housetraining

✓ Poo(p) bags

✓ Toys and chews suitable for puppies

✓ A puppy coat or sweater for cold days, or if you have cool seasons (Bostons are sensitive to cold as well as heat)

✓ A crate

✓ Old towels for cleaning your puppy and covering the crate

✓ AND PLENTY OF TIME!

Later on you'll also need a grooming brush, dog shampoo, flea and worming products (which you can buy from your vet) and maybe a travel crate.

This is a list of items provided by Kennel Club Assured Breeder Jo Dalton, of Mumuland Boston Terriers, Boston, Lincolnshire, UK, which is sent home with each puppy:

✓ A personalised blanket that smells of home

✓ A soft toy (that your puppy has grown up with)

✓ A soft fleece ring tug toy

✓ A Beco bone chew toy

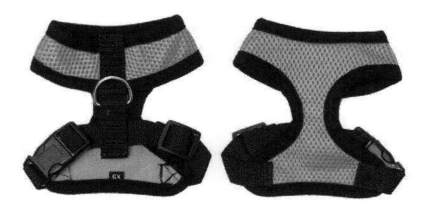

- ✓ A Beco tug rope
- ✓ A large textured ball
- ✓ A Beco Pocket (toilet bags)
- ✓ Puppy harness
- ✓ Puppy lead
- ✓ Puppy collar
- ✓ Engraved collar ID tag
- ✓ Puppy toilet training pads
- ✓ A Beco puppy bowl
- ✓ A jumper or T-shirt for the puppy, depending on the time of year
- ✓ An 800g Bag of Royal Canin Mini Junior

Puppy Proofing Your Home

Before your puppy arrives, you may have to make a few adjustments to make your home safe and suitable. Young puppies are small bundles of instinct and energy (when they are awake), with little common sense and even less self-control! All young Bostons are curious, they love to play and have a great sense of fun. They often have bursts of energy before they run out of steam and spend much of the rest of the day sleeping.

They are like babies and it's up to you to look after them and set the boundaries – both physically and in terms of behaviour – but one step at a time. Create an area where the puppy is allowed to go and then keep the rest of the house off-limits until housetraining (potty training) is complete.

You can buy a barrier specifically made for dogs or use a baby gate, which is often cheaper and,

although it has been designed for infants, works perfectly well with baby Bostons. You might even find a second-hand one on eBay.

Choose one with narrow vertical gaps or mesh and check that the puppy can't get his head stuck between the bars, or put a covering or mesh over the bottom of the gate. You can also make your own barrier, but bear in mind that cardboard and other soft materials are likely to get chewed.

Using a gate or barrier is also an effective and relatively inexpensive method of preventing a puppy from going upstairs and leaving an unwanted gift on your bedroom carpets.

A puppy's bones are soft and recent studies have shown that if very young pups are allowed to climb or descend stairs regularly, they can develop joint problems later in life.

This is worth bearing in mind, especially as some Bostons can be prone to joint problems, such as luxating patella or hip dysplasia.

You can use the baby gate to keep the puppy enclosed in a single room or area — preferably one with a floor that is easy to wipe clean and not too far away from a door to the garden or yard for housetraining.

Many owners prefer creating a safe penned area, rather than putting their dog in a crate, particularly in the UK. And several breeders we contacted use a pen to contain a pup or pups while giving them plenty of room to stretch their legs.

Tip Don't underestimate your puppy! Young Bostons are agile and can jump and climb, so choose a barrier higher than you think necessary. A 24"-high wire pen works well for puppies less than four months old; however, older than that, they get daring and will attempt to climb out, so a 36" (three feet) high wire pen is recommended (or a 24" pen with a top).

One option is to buy a manufactured playpen, and here Jo Dalton explains the pros and cons: "If you decide to opt for a playpen, ensure you monitor if and when your pup can get out of it as it grows; Bostons are known for their intelligence and will often work out a way of escaping if they want to!

"A playpen can be used in much the same way as a crate and has an advantage of being very versatile in separating eating, sleeping and - in the early days - toileting. They are ideal for the busy Mum or Dad who has other things on their mind and can't possibly watch the puppy, children and try and tidy the house or prepare dinner. Again, it is peace of mind for the owner, knowing the pup is safe and not chewing anything it shouldn't be.

"Playpens come in two types generally - the mesh panel type and the fabric type - both have advantages and disadvantages; the fabric pen can be chewed, but is easy to put up and take down, and the metal mesh panel can be expanded and will probably last longer, but it can be difficult to put up, move or take down. We have used both over the years and it will very much depend upon your personal preference."

With initial effort on your part (consistency is the key) and a willing pupil, housetraining should not take long. One of the biggest factors influencing the success and speed of housetraining is your commitment - another reason for taking time off work, if at all possible, when your puppy arrives. You may also want to remove your expensive Oriental rugs to other rooms until your little darling is fully housetrained and has stopped chewing everything.

The puppy's designated area or room should be not too hot, cold or damp and it must be free from draughts. Puppies - especially Bostons and other flat-faced breeds - are sensitive to temperature fluctuations and don't do well in very hot or very cold conditions. If you live in a hot climate, your new pup may need air conditioning in the summertime.

If you have young children, the time they spend with the puppy should be limited to a few short sessions a day. Plenty of sleep is **essential** for the normal development of a young dog. You wouldn't wake a baby every hour or so to play and the same goes for puppies. Wait a day or two - preferably longer - before inviting friends around to see your gorgeous little puppy. However excited you are, your new arrival needs a few days to get over the stress of leaving mother and siblings and to start bonding with you.

Just as you need a home, your puppy needs a den. This den is a haven where your puppy feels safe, particularly for the first few weeks after the traumatic experience of leaving his or her mother and littermates. Very young puppies sleep for over 18 hours a day. By the age of eight to 12 weeks, they are still sleeping 12 to 16 hours a day; this is normal. You have a couple of options with the den; you can get a dog bed or basket, or you can use a crate. Crates have long been popular in North America and are becoming increasingly used in the UK, particularly as it can be quicker to housetrain a puppy using a crate.

It may surprise some American readers to learn that the normal practice in the UK has often been - and still is - to initially contain the puppy in the kitchen or utility room, and later to let the dog roam around the house. Some owners do not allow their dogs upstairs, but many do. The idea of keeping a dog in a cage like a rabbit or hamster is abhorrent to many animal-loving Brits.

However, a crate can be a useful aid if used properly. Using one as a prison to contain a dog for hours on end certainly is cruel, but the crate has its place as a sanctuary for your dog. It is their own space and they know no harm will come to them in there. See **Chapter 6. Crate Training and Housetraining** for getting your Boston Terrier used to - and even to enjoy - being in a crate.

Most puppies' natural instinct is not to soil the area where they sleep. Put plenty of newspapers down in the area next to the den and your pup should choose to go to the toilet here, if you are not quick enough to get outside. Of course, they may also decide to trash their designated area by chewing their blankets and shredding the newspaper - patience is the key in this situation!

If you have a garden or yard that you intend letting your puppy roam in, make sure that every little gap has been plugged. You'd be amazed at the tiny holes puppies can escape through. Don't leave your puppy unattended in the beginning, as they can come to harm. Also, dogs are increasingly being targeted by thieves, who are even stealing from gardens. Make sure there are no poisonous plants that your pup might chew and check there are no low plants with sharp leaves or thorns which could cause eye or other injuries.

In order for puppies to grow into well-adjusted dogs, they have to feel comfortable and relaxed in their new surroundings and need a great deal of sleep.

They are leaving the warmth and protection of their mother and littermates and so, for the first few days at least, your puppy may feel very sad. It is important to make the transition from the birth home to your home as easy as possible. Your pup's life is in your hands. How you react and interact with him in the first few days and weeks will shape your relationship and his character for the years ahead.

Chewing and Chew Toys

Like babies, most puppies are mini chewing machines, and so you should remove anything breakable and/or chewable within the puppy's reach - including wooden furniture. Obviously, you cannot remove your kitchen cupboards, doors, sofas and fixtures and fittings, so don't leave your new arrival unattended for any length of time where he can chew something that is hard to replace. Don't give old socks, shoes or slippers or your pup will regard your footwear as fair game. Avoid rawhide chews as they can get stuck in the dog's throat.

Breeder Jo Dalton has some advice on the best items for chewing: "Bostons are usually exceptional chewers, so chew toys are a must for your puppy. We love the natural reindeer antler chew toys (pictured overleaf), which are a much safer alternative to real bones or plastic chew bones and have the added advantage of being packed full of calcium and, as chewing is a great way of keeping teeth clean, it is a healthy and safe option.

"A natural hemp or cotton tug rope (pictured) is also a favourite chew toy, as the cotton rope acts like dental floss and helps with teeth cleaning. It is very versatile and can be used for fetch games as well as chewing." (However, once it unravels and becomes stringy, throw it away as the strings can be swallowed and then become blockages, which could require surgery to remove). "We also recommend a natural rubber chew toy that you can fill with treats or peanut butter.

"Soft toys don't tend to last very long, so we tend to avoid them once your pup gets older. However, we have found the stuffingless soft toys last slightly longer, but are still quickly chewed to pieces. We also don't recommend vinyl dog toys, as bits can quickly and easily be chewed off and swallowed, which can also cause intestinal blockages.

"Balls can also be very dangerous, which is why we supply new owners with a large textured ball in the puppy pack. It's the only type of ball we recommend - tough enough to withstand the harsh play of an adult Boston and cannot be punctured or chewed and - although they can pick it up due to its semi-squidgy composition - it cannot easily be compressed and is too large to become lodged in your dog's mouth and cause a choking hazard.

"Tennis balls - even the Kong ones - are a huge risk to dogs as they compress almost flat and can be inhaled into the throat and then expand completely, blocking the airway. Therefore choose your toys and balls carefully."

The First Few Days

Before you collect your puppy, let the breeder know what time you will arrive and ask him or her not to feed the pup for three or four hours beforehand - unless you have a very long journey, in which case the puppy will need to eat something. He will be less likely to be car sick and should be hungry when he lands in his new home. (The same applies to an adult dog moving to a new home).

When you arrive, ask the breeder for an old towel, blanket or toy that has been with the pup's mother – you can leave one on an earlier visit to collect with the pup. Or take one with you and rub the mother with it to collect her scent and put this with the puppy for the first few days. It may help him to settle in. In the US some Boston Terriers may be shipped to your home. You can still ask for a toy or towel.

Make sure you get copies of any health certificates relating to the parents (in the UI, these should listed online with the Orthopedic Foundation for Animals at www.ofa.org) A good breeder will have a Contract of Sale or Puppy Contract that outlines everyone's rights and responsibilities - **see Chapter 4. Choosing A Boston Terrier Puppy**. It should also state that you can return the puppy if there are health issues within a certain time frame - although if you have picked your breeder carefully, it should hopefully not come to this. The breeder will give you details of worming and any vaccinations. Most good breeders supply an information sheet and puppy pack for new owners.

Find out exactly what the breeder is feeding and how much. You cannot suddenly switch a dog's diet; their digestive systems cannot cope with a sudden change. In the beginning, stick to whatever the puppy is used to. Again, good breeders will send some food home with the puppy.

The Journey Home

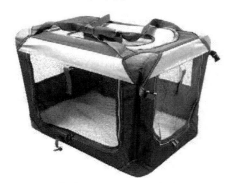

Bringing a new puppy home in a car can be a traumatic experience. Your puppy will be devastated at leaving his or her mother, brothers and sisters and a familiar environment. Everything will be strange and frightening and he may whimper and whine - or even howl or bark - on the way. If you can, take somebody with you to take care of him on that first journey. Under no circumstances have the puppy on your lap while driving. It is simply too dangerous - a Boston Terrier puppy is cute, lively and distracting - not to mention fast, so could easily jump out of the passenger's lap.

The best and safest way to transport the pup is in a crate - either a purpose-made travel crate (pictured) or a wire crate that he will use at home. Put a comfortable blanket in the bottom - preferably rubbed with the scent of the mother. Ask your travel companion to sit next to the crate and talk softly to the puppy, particularly if he is a frightened little bundle of nerves. He or she may cry or whimper. If you don't have a crate, your passenger may wish to hold the puppy. If so, have an old towel between the person and the pup as he may quite possibly urinate (the puppy, not the passenger!)

If you have a journey of more than a couple of hours, make sure that you take water and offer the puppy a drink en route. He may need to eliminate or have diarrhoea (hopefully, only due to nerves), but don't let him outside on to the ground in a strange place as he is not yet fully vaccinated. If you have a long journey, cover the bottom of the crate with a waterproof material and put newspapers in half of it, so the pup can eliminate without staining the car seats.

Arriving Home

As soon as you arrive home, let your puppy into the garden or yard and when he 'performs,' praise him for his efforts. These first few days are critical in getting your puppy to feel safe and confident in his new surroundings. Spend time with your new arrival, talk to him often in a reassuring manner. Introduce him to his den and toys, slowly allow him to explore and show him around the house - once you have puppy-proofed it.

Boston puppies are extremely curious - and amusing; you might be surprised at his reactions to everyday objects. Remember that puppies explore by sniffing and using their mouths, so don't scold for chewing. Instead, put objects you don't want chewed out of reach and replace them with toys he can chew.

If you have other animals, introduce them slowly and in supervised sessions - preferably once the pup has got used to his new surroundings, not as soon as you walk through the door. Gentleness and patience are the keys to these first few days, so don't over-face him. Have a special, gentle puppy voice and use his name often in a pleasant, encouraging manner.

Never use his name to scold or he will associate it with bad things. The sound of his name should **always** make him want to pay attention to you as something good is going to happen - praise, food, playtime, and so on.

Resist the urge to pick the puppy up all the time - no matter how cute he is! Let him explore on his own legs, encouraging a little independence. One of the most important things at this stage is to ensure that your puppy has enough sleep - which is quite a bit of the time - no matter how much you want to play with him or watch his antics when awake.

If you haven't decided what to call your new puppy yet, 'Shadow' might be a good suggestion, as he or she will follow you everywhere! Many puppies from different breeds do this, but Boston Terriers like to stick close to their owners - both as puppies and adults.

Our website receives many emails from worried new owners. Here are some of the most common concerns:

- 🐾 My puppy won't stop crying or whining
- 🐾 My puppy is shivering
- 🐾 My puppy won't eat
- 🐾 My puppy is very timid
- 🐾 My puppy follows me everywhere; she won't let me out of her sight
- 🐾 My puppy sleeps all the time, is this normal?

These behaviours are quite common at the beginning. They are just a young pup's reaction to leaving his mother and littermates and entering into a strange new world. It is normal for puppies to sleep most of the time, just like babies. It is also normal for some puppies to whine during the first couple of days.

Make your new pup as comfortable as possible, ensuring he has a warm (but not too hot), quiet den away from drafts, where he is not pestered by children or other pets. Handle him gently, while giving him plenty of time to sleep. During the first few nights your puppy may whine; try your best to ignore the pitiful cries.

Some puppies will be nervous and timid for the first few days. They will think of you as their new mother and follow you around the house. This is also quite natural, but after a few days start to leave your pup for a few minutes at a time, gradually building up the time. Boston Terriers, like other breeds selectively bred for companionship, can be prone to separation anxiety - particularly if they are used to being with you virtually 24/7. See **Chapter 8. Behaviour** for more information.

If your routine means you are normally out of the house for a few hours during the day, get your puppy on a Friday or Saturday so he has at least a couple of days to adjust to his new surroundings. A far better idea is to book time off work to help your puppy settle in, if you can and, if you don't work, leave your diary free for the first couple of weeks. Helping a new pup to settle in is virtually a full-time job.

This is a frightening time for your puppy. Is your puppy shivering with cold or is it nerves? Avoid placing your puppy under stress by making too many demands on him. Don't allow the kids to pester the pup and, until they have learned how to handle a dog, don't allow them to pick him up unsupervised, as they could inadvertently damage his tiny and delicate little body.

If your pup won't eat, spend time gently coaxing him. If he leaves his food, take it away and try it later. Don't leave it down all of the time or he may get used to turning his nose up at it and become a picky eater. The next time you put something down for him, he is more likely to be hungry. If your puppy is crying, it is probably for one of the following reasons:

- He is lonely
- He is hungry
- He wants attention from you
- He needs to go to the toilet

If it is none of these, then physically check him over to make sure he hasn't picked up an injury. Try not to fuss over him. If he whimpers, just reassure him with a quiet word. If he cries loudly and tries to get out of his allotted area, he probably needs to go to the toilet. Even if it is the middle of the night, get up (yes, sorry, this is best) and take him outside. Praise him if he goes to the toilet.

The strongest bonding period for a puppy is between eight and 12 weeks of age. The most important factors in bonding with your puppy are TIME spent with him and PATIENCE, even when he or she makes a mess in the house or chews something he shouldn't. Remember, your Boston pup is just a baby (dog) and it takes time to learn not to do these things. Spend time with your pup and you will have a loyal friend for life. Boston Terriers are very focused on their humans and that emotional attachment may grow to become one of the most important aspects of your life – and certainly his.

....

Where Should Puppy Sleep?

Where do you want your new puppy to sleep? You cannot simply allow him or her to wander freely around the house - at least not in the beginning. Ideally he will be in a contained area, such as a pen or a crate, at night. While it is not acceptable to shut a dog in a cage all day, you can keep your puppy in a crate at night until he or she is housetrained. Even then, some adult dogs still prefer to sleep in a crate.

You also have to consider whether you want the pup to sleep in your bedroom or elsewhere. If it's the bedroom, try to prevent him from jumping on and off beds and/or couches or racing up and down stairs until he has stopped growing, as this can cause joint damage.

If he is to sleep outside your bedroom, put him in a comfortable bed of his own, or a crate - and then block your ears for the first couple of nights. The whining and whimpering won't last long and he will get used to sleeping on his own, without his littermates or you. Most breeders - especially those in the US -recommend that you let your puppy sleep near you for the first couple of nights.

California breeder Pamela Preston said: "We want our puppies to know they are part of the new family, instead of being excluded from it. Sleeping nearby shows the puppy is part of your 'pack', so often helps with bonding, as well as providing comfort to the puppy in the first days or weeks in your home. Putting the puppy by himself in a crate in another room, may leave the puppy feeling as if he has been excluded from the new 'pack'. It is also helpful to you to have the puppy nearby so you can hear if he needs to be let out in the middle of the night (which is not uncommon for young puppies who cannot "hold it" all night long). If you don't let a puppy out to potty during the night and he cannot 'hold it', you are forcing him to eliminate in his crate and, once a puppy starting pottying in their crate, it is very difficult to train them not to do that."

We don't recommend letting your new pup sleep on the bed. He will not be housetrained and also a puppy needs to learn his place in the household and have his own den. It's up to you whether you decide to let him on the bed when he's older. Another point to bear in mind is that if your dog is regularly exercised, his paws and coat may pick up mud, grass, insects and other things you may not want on your bed.

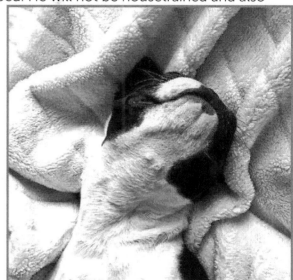

Some pups may be more confident and settle in right away - particularly if the breeder has spent time on socialisation and getting them used to being on their own for short periods.

While it is not good to leave a dog alone all day, it is also not healthy to spend 24 hours a day together. He becomes too reliant on you and this increases the chances of separation anxiety when you do have to leave him. A Boston Terrier puppy used to being on his own every night is less likely to develop attachment issues, so consider this when deciding where he should sleep.

Once your pup has settled in, you may decide you don't want him to have a permanent home in your bedroom -and remember that Bostons snuffle, snore, fart and (if not in a crate) pad around the bedroom in the middle of the night and come up to the bed to check you are still there! Some owners prefer to leave the pup in a safe draught-free place downstairs or in a different room. If you do this, you might find a set of earplugs very useful for helping (you) to survive the first few nights!

If the dog does sleep in your bedroom, make sure you spend some time apart during the day, so he is not with you 24/7, which could him to develop separation anxiety when you do have to leave him alone.

If you decide you definitely do want your pup to sleep in the bedroom from Day One, put him in a crate or similar with a soft blanket covering part of the crate initially. Some breeders recommend putting the crate very close to your bed for the first couple of nights, so that the puppy does not feel entirely alone.

....

Breeders' Tips

We asked a number of breeders what essential advice they would give to new owners of Boston Terrier puppies. They had lots of warnings and advice for puppy proofing the yard or garden, as well as some tips.

Pamela Preston, of ChriMaso Boston Terriers, California: "There's always the concern of having toxic plants in the home or yard - see this link for a detailed list, including symptoms: www.aspca.org/pet-care/animal-poison-control/dogs-plant-list especially since Bostons are curious and often like to chew on plants. One thing I always check for when I do home visits is small openings in a fence or under the house where a small dog might get out or get stuck.

"There are several good reference books that are helpful for new puppy owners to read. I usually direct my puppy people to Ian Dunbar's site at www.dogstardaily.com/training/you-get-your-puppy to download and read "Before You Get Your Puppy" before they bring their puppy home."

Susan Maxwell, of Maximum Companion Boston Terriers, California: "When bringing home a new puppy it is important that you are familiar with all vegetation in your yard and make sure that there is nothing poisonous; simple ornamental flowers like Lily of the Nile can be very dangerous - you can also go online to find a list of poisonous plants to pets." (Photo courtesy of Susan).

"Puppy proof your home making sure all cords, wires, etc. are not accessible and never leave a puppy unattended - treat them like a small baby loose in your house! Remember everything in range will get picked up and chewed and 'tasted' or eaten. Table and chair legs can be fun to chew on for a pup, as can kitchen cabinets, so be very watchful!

"If you give your puppy enough exercise and stimuli he or she should be very content and stay out of trouble. Introduce small children carefully for both puppy and child. Little puppies have sharp teeth and should not be allowed to 'teethe' on human skin - show your dislike right away for this and don't be afraid to reprimand. If a pup were to teethe hard on its momma and inflict pain its momma would growl and pin it on its back right away, letting it know it over stepped boundaries. I have taken them sharply by the scruff of their necks and scolded them for doing this...the timing of the grab with the sternness of the sound of reprimand 'NO' usually works well.

"Sharp puppy nails can also be a nuisance, so keep those hooks cut. I like to use a Dremel (pet grooming tool) and use it as early as possible. We cut nails as early as a week and introduce the Dremel at about four weeks."

Another US breeder said: "I go over many things with each new puppy parent. Also, I always advise them to take up the food and water at a certain time in the evening and to take their puppy out to potty before putting it to bed in a crate. Then to take it out one last time before they go to bed (if that is later) and to make sure that in the morning, as soon as they get up and take care of themselves, to take their puppy out to potty, because it has been a long time and it is ready to start the day. Then give them their food and water. If a puppy cries because it is lonely give it a stuffed toy to snuggle up to. It's so tempting to put the puppy in bed with you - but that is not a good idea at this stage of training.

"Introduce any older animals in the household to the new puppy, but never try to force them to be friends right away; that will come with time. Sometimes older pets need time to get used to the new puppy - and make sure that older pets get the same amount of attention that they are used to, otherwise they will really dislike the new puppy! I also tell new owners not to play rough with the puppy, because that is what will cause them to play bite. It may be cute now, but it will not be funny as they get older, so it's better not to start."

One UK breeder added: "Whatever you decide to do with your pup, stay consistent. If the puppy is to sleep in a crate, start from Day One; if the puppy is to sleep in the lounge, start from Day One. Bostons prefer a warm cosy bed to a cold floor, so they require bedding. If the pup starts crying if they are sleeping in another room to the owner, you can put the radio on low, use a ticking clock wrapped in a blanket, or a warm hot water bottle to imitate another animal. As Bostons do not have the Terrier instinct, they are not big diggers or escape artists."

(NOTE: some breeders disagree with this, saying that their Bostons DO have some Terrier instinct and some can be diggers and escape artists!)

"They will, however, chew and they may pull carpet if it's frayed. Just make sure anything that is down low is not a precious heirloom! Some dogs may chew mail, but this is easily avoided if it does become an issue. As long as there is a clear distinction between toys/chews which are 'Theirs' and other things which are 'Yours' there should not be an issue. But don't use 'human' things as toys, and giving them something to do when you leave them alone when they are old enough is always a good idea to reduce the chances of them destroying things."

Another said: "Boston Terrier puppies can be extremely clumsy and can bump into things in new environments. My advice would be make sure there is nothing that could cause them harm, especially their eyes. Puppy-proof your house, and always make sure your garden is secure for the puppy with no escape routes!"

Jo Dalton added: "Preparing and bringing your new puppy home is an exciting, but sometimes worrying time, you have so much to think about and so many choices to make. It's important to know how to make the right choices and how best to prepare for your new addition. Thorny plants are a problem and Bostons are prolific chewers - usually wood, wires and leather are the favoured items."

(Photo courtesy of Jo).

"That phone charger wire or laptop wire may look like an excellent plaything to your puppy, or the gap under the kitchen units or sofa provides an excellent place to go to toilet without anyone seeing, or simply just to run and play hide and seek under it. My advice is to check around your home to make sure there is nothing your pup can reach that is going to harm your pup in any way if he chews it."

Vaccinations and Worming

It is **always** a good idea to have your Boston Terrier checked out by a vet within a few days of picking him up. Some Puppy Contracts even stipulate that the dog should be examined by a vet within a certain time frame - often 48 hours. This is to everyone's benefit and, all being well, you are safe in the knowledge that - at least at the time of purchase - your puppy is healthy.

Keep your pup away from other dogs in the waiting room as he will not be fully protected against canine diseases until the vaccination schedule is complete. All puppies need these injections; very occasionally a pup has a reaction, but this is very rare and the advantages of immunisation far outweigh the disadvantages.

Vaccinations

An unimmunised puppy is at risk every time he meets other dogs as he has no protection against potentially fatal diseases - another point is that it is unlikely a pet insurer will cover an unvaccinated dog. It should be stressed that vaccinations are generally quite safe and side effects are uncommon. If your Boston Terrier is unlucky enough to be one of the very few that suffers an adverse reaction, here are the signs to look out for; a pup may exhibit one or more of these:

MILD REACTION - Sleepiness, irritability and not wanting to be touched. Sore or a small lump at the place where he was injected. Nasal discharge or sneezing. Puffy face and ears.

SEVERE REACTION - Anaphylactic shock. A sudden and quick reaction, usually before leaving the vet's clinic, that causes breathing difficulties. Vomiting, diarrhoea, staggering and seizures.

A severe reaction is rare. There is a far greater risk of your Boston Terrier either being ill and/or spreading disease if he does not have the injections.

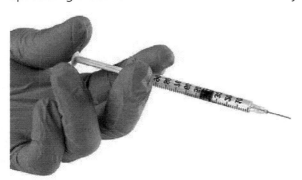

The usual schedule is for the pup to have his first vaccination at six to eight weeks of age. This will protect him from a number of diseases in one shot. In the UK these are Distemper, Canine Parvovirus (Parvo), Infectious Canine Hepatitis (Adenovirus) and Kennel Cough (Bordetella). In the US, the combination vaccine is known as DHPP (DHPP (Distemper, Hepatitis, Parvo, and Para influenza). Note that Kennel Cough and Para influenza are not the same and have different vaccines.

Puppies in the US also need vaccinating separately against Rabies, but no earlier than 16 weeks of age. There are optional vaccinations for Coronavirus and - depending on where you live and if your dog is regularly around woods or forests - Lyme Disease.

The puppy requires a second vaccination at 10 to 12 and the third and last is done at 14 to 16 weeks (USA). In the UK, the first vaccination is usually at six weeks of age (or eight) and the second one four weeks later.

Diseases such as Parvo and Kennel Cough are highly contagious and you should not let your new arrival mix with other dogs - unless they are your own and have already been vaccinated - until a week after his last vaccination; otherwise, he will not be fully immunised. Parvovirus can also be transmitted by fox faeces.

You shouldn't take your new puppy to places where unvaccinated dogs might have been, like the local park. This does not mean that your puppy should be isolated - far from it. This is an important time for socialisation. It is OK for the puppy to mix with another dog that you 100% know has been vaccinated and is up to date with its annual boosters. Perhaps invite a friend's dog around to play in your yard/garden to begin the socialisation process.

Once your puppy is fully immunised, you have a window of a few weeks when it's the best time to introduce him to many new experiences - dogs, people, traffic, noises, other animals, etc. This critical period before the age of four and a half or five months is when he is at his most receptive. Socialisation should not stop at that age, but continue for the rest of your dog's life; but it is particularly important to socialise young puppies.

Currently, in the UK, your dog will need a booster injection every year of his life, while boosters are required only every three years in the US. The vet should give you a record card or send you a reminder, but it's also a good idea to keep a note of the date in your diary. However, annual vaccines are becoming a thing of the past, particularly in the US. Tests have shown that the

Parvovirus vaccination gives most animals at least seven years of immunity, while the Distemper jab provides immunity for at least five to seven years and it is now believed that vaccinating every year can stress a dog's immune system. In the US, many vets now recommend that you take your dog for a 'titer' test once he has had his initial puppy vaccinations and one-year booster.

Titers

These are now being used by some breeders and owners in the US. The thinking behind them is to avoid a dog having to have annual vaccinations. It's fair to say that the verdict is still out in the UK. One English vet commented that a titer is only good for the day on which it is carried out, and that antibody levels may naturally drop off shortly afterwards, possibly leaving the animal at risk. He added that the dog would still need vaccinating against Leptospirosis.

NOTE: the Leptospirosis vaccine is one that Bostons CAN have an adverse reaction to; hence, most owners and breeders do not give it anymore - unless the dog frequents areas such as beaches or forests, where there is a lot of wildlife.

To 'titer or 'titering' is to take a blood sample from a dog (or cat) to determine whether he or she has enough antibodies to guarantee immunity against a particular disease, usually Parvovirus, Distemper and Adenovirus (Canine Hepatitis). If so, then an annual injection is not needed. Titering is not recommended for Leptospirosis, Bordetella or Lyme Disease, as these vaccines provide only short-term protection, and many states still require proof of a Rabies vaccination.

The vet can test the blood at his or her clinic without sending off the sample, thereby keeping costs down for the owner. A titer for Parvovirus and Distemper currently costs around $100 or less. Titer levels are given as ratios and show how many times blood can be diluted before no antibodies are detected. So, if blood can be diluted 1,000 times and still show antibodies, the ratio would be 1:1000, which is a 'strong titer,' while a titer of 1:2 would be 'weak.' A strong (high) titer means that your dog has enough antibodies to fight off that specific disease and is immune from infection. A weak titer means that you and your vet should discuss revaccination - even then your dog might have some reserve forces known as 'memory cells' that will provide antibodies when needed.

Worming

All puppies need worming (or deworming). A good breeder will give the puppies their first dose of worming medication at around two weeks old, then probably again at five and eight weeks before they leave the litter - or even more often. Get the details and inform your vet exactly what treatment, if any, your pup has already had.

The main worms affecting puppies are roundworm and tapeworm. In many areas of the US, the dreaded heartworm can also pose a risk. Roundworm can be transmitted from a puppy to humans - most often children - and can in severe cases cause blindness, or even miscarriage in women, so it's important to keep up to date with worming.

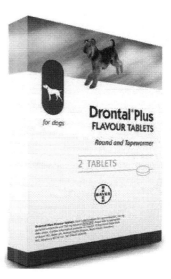

Worms in puppies are quite common; they are often picked up through their mother's milk. If you have children, get them into the habit of washing their hands after they have been in contact with the puppy - lack of hygiene is the reason why children are most susceptible. Most vets recommend worming a puppy once a month until he is six months old, and then around every two or three months.

In the US, dogs are given a monthly heartworm pill. It should be given every month when there is no heavy frost (as frost kills mosquitos that carry the disease); giving it all year round gives the best protection. The

heartworm pill is by prescription only and deworms the dog monthly for heart worm, round, hook, and whip worm.

US breeder Susan Maxwell explains her worming schedule before the pup is delivered to his or her new owner: "Puppies are wormed at two, three, four, five and six weeks with Nemex-2, and then Panacur at seven weeks for five days. We have found that using Toltrazuril is an effective way to treat coccidia/giardia (a parasitic intestinal infection); given 1 cc per 5lb for four days it 'breaks the cycle.'"

If your Boston Terrier is often out and about running through woods and fields, it is important to stick to a regular worming schedule, as he is more likely to pick up worms than one that spends more time indoors.

Fleas can pass on tapeworms to dogs, but a puppy would not normally be treated unless it is known for certain he has fleas - and then only with caution. You need to know the weight of your Boston and then speak to your vet about the safest treatment to rid your puppy of the parasites.

It is not usually worth buying a cheap worming or flea treatment from a supermarket, as they are usually far less effective than more expensive vet-recommended preparations, such as Drontal.

Many people living in the US have contacted our website claiming the parasite treatment **Trifexis** has caused severe side effects, and even death, to their dogs. Although this evidence is only anecdotal, you might want consider avoiding Trifexis to be on the safe side - even if your vet recommends it.

....

Follow the advice in this chapter and **9. Exercise and Training** and it will help your Boston to adjust to life in your household and to become the dog you dreamed of owning - and a much-loved member of the family.

6. Crate Training and Housetraining

If you are unfamiliar with them, crates may seem like a cruel punishment for a lovable and loving Boston Terrier puppy. They are, however, becoming increasingly popular to help with housetraining (potty training), to keep a dog safe at night or when you are not there. Breeders, trainers, behaviourists and people who show dogs all use them and, as you will read, often breeders believe they are a valuable aid in helping to housebreak your dog.

Getting Your Dog Used to a Crate

If you decide to use a crate, then remember that it is not a prison to restrain the dog. It should only be used in a humane manner and time should be spent to make the puppy or adult dog feel like the crate is his own safe little haven. When used correctly and time is spent getting the puppy used to the crate, it can be a godsend.

If you are leaving a dog in a crate while you are away from the home, you should always leave water inside. However, if you are putting a puppy in a crate at night, or leaving him in the crate just for an hour or two during the day, you do not need to leave water inside; this will help to speed up housetraining. One breeder said: "If puppies drink because they are bored and then have to use the restroom, they may pee inside the crate, and once that habit starts, it is very difficult to train away."

Crates may not be suitable for every Boston Terrier, which are companion creatures. They are not like hamsters or pet mice that can adapt to life permanently in a cage; they thrive on being physically close to their humans.

Being caged all day is a miserable existence, and a crate should never be used as a means of confinement because you are out of the house all day. If you do decide to use one - perhaps to put your dog in for short periods while you leave the house, or at night - the best place for it is in the corner of a room away from cold draughts or too much heat. And remember, Bostons like to be near their family – and that is you and/or any other dogs.

It is only natural for any dog to whine in the beginning. He is not crying because he is in a cage. He would cry if he had the freedom of the room and he was alone - he is crying because he is separated from you. However, with patience and the right training he will get used to it and some often come to regard the crate as a favourite place. Many breeders advise leaving the crate close to you in your bedroom for the first couple of nights. And after that it is still a good idea to leave the crate where the dog can see or hear you. Some owners make the crate their dog's only bed, so he feels comfortable and safe there.

Bostons can easily overheat. When you buy a crate, get a wire one (like the one pictured) that allows air to pass through, not a plastic one that may get very hot. If you cover the crate, don't cover it 100% or you will restrict the flow of air. The crate should be large enough to allow your dog to stretch out flat on his side without being cramped, he should be able to turn round easily and to sit up without hitting his head on the top. Here is Midwest Pet Products sizing guide for crates, based on the anticipated adult weight of your dog:
www.midwestpetproducts.com/midwestdogcrates/dog-crate-sizes.

UK breeder Jo Dalton, of Mumuland Boston Terriers, Boston, Lincolnshire, also has some advice: "The crate simply becomes the pup's bed and its own space; somewhere it knows it can go and not be disturbed - this is particularly important if you have young children. I must stress that the crate must never be used as punishment, and it's important that your dog doesn't end up in its crate the whole time. Usually we suggest that when you are home, your puppy is out with the cage door left open, so it can go in and out as necessary - unless you need to leave it to go upstairs or feel you can't give your full attention, in which case the young pup simply goes in the crate until you return.

"We recommend using a standard medium metal cage which measures around 75cm (29.5 inches) wide by 54cm (21 inches) deep, as this is big enough to divide at a young age and fit a toilet training tray at the one end. It is also big enough for a fully grown adult Boston to sleep comfortably in.

"If you are in the UK, we recommend using either the Barkshire medium crate or the Savic Residence crate, as both of these are wide enough for a small toilet training tray. You can also get a special floor grate which allows any accidents to simply drain away - useful once the toilet tray gets removed. It is very important not to have a big cage as your puppy won't feel secure and will often refuse to settle in it." (Pictured is Mumuland's black, brindle and white Stan).

Crates aren't for every owner or every Boston Terrier, but used correctly, they can:

- Create a canine den
- Be a useful housetraining tool
- Limit access to the rest of the house while your dog learns the household rules
- Be a safe way to transport your dog in a car

If you use a crate right from Day One, cover half of it with a blanket initially to help your puppy regard it as a den. He also needs bedding and it's a good idea to put a chew in as well. A large crate may allow your dog to eliminate at one end and sleep at the other, but this may slow down his housetraining. So, if you are buying a crate that will last for a fully grown Boston Terrier, get adjustable crate dividers – or make them yourself (or put a box inside) - to block part of it off while he is small so that he feels safe and secure, which he won't do in a very large crate. Once you've got your crate, you'll need to learn how to use it properly so that it becomes a safe, comfortable den for your dog and not a prison.

Here's a tried-and-tested method of getting your dog firstly to accept a crate, and then to actually want to spend time in there. Initially a pup might not be too happy about going inside, but he will be a lot easier to crate train than an adult dog that has got used to having the run of your house. These are the first steps:

1. Drop a few tasty puppy treats around and then inside the crate.
2. Put your puppy's favourite bedding or toy in there.
3. Keep the door open.
4. Feed your puppy's meals inside the crate, keeping the door open. (Some prefer to close the door at this time; one breeder said: "This is typically when I close the crate door. It helps him stay focused so the puppy eats instead of becoming distracted. It's also for a short period of time, so the puppy gets used to the closed door at a 'safe' and unthreatening time).

Place a chew or treat INSIDE the crate and close the door while your puppy is OUTSIDE the crate.

He will be desperate to get in there! Open the door, let him in and praise him for going in. Fasten a long-lasting chew inside the crate and leave the door open. Let your puppy go inside to spend some time eating the chew. IMPORTANT: If your Boston wears a collar, remove it before leaving him unattended in a crate. A collar can get caught in the wire mesh. After a while, close the crate door and feed him some treats through the mesh while he is in there.

At first just do it for a few seconds at a time, then gradually increase the time. If you do it too fast, he will become distressed. Slowly build up the amount of time in the crate. For the first few days, stay in the room, then gradually leave for a short time, first one minute, then three, then 10, 30, etc.

Next Steps

5. Put your dog in his crate at regular intervals during the day - maximum two hours.

6. Don't crate only when you are leaving the house. Place the dog in the crate while you are home as well. Use it as a 'safe' zone.

7. By using the crate both when you are home and while you are gone, your dog becomes comfortable there and not worried that you won't come back, or that you are leaving him alone. This helps to prevent separation anxiety later in life.

8. Give him a chew and remove his collar, tags and anything else that could become caught in an opening or between the bars.

9. Make it very clear to any children that the crate is NOT a playhouse for them, but a 'special room' for the dog.

10. Although the crate is your dog's haven and safe place, it must not be off-limits to humans. You should be able to reach inside at any time. The next point is important:

11. Do not let your dog immediately out of the crate if he barks or whines, or he will think that this is the key to opening the door. Wait until the barking or whining has stopped for at least ten seconds before letting him out.

A puppy should not be left in a crate for long periods, except at night, and even then he has to get used to it first. Whether or not you decide to use a crate, the important thing to remember is that those first few days and weeks are a critical time for your puppy. Try and make him feel as safe and comfortable as you can. Bond with him, while at the same time gently and gradually introducing him to new experiences and other animals and humans.

Bostons are surprisingly agile – they can climb and jump higher than you might expect. Megatron (pictured), featured in national newspapers after climbing out of his pen. He suffers from separation anxiety and his owners could not understand how he was getting out - until they secretly filmed him. You can watch Megatron's escape act here: www.dailymail.co.uk/news/article-2832950/Boston-terrier-climbs-wall-dog-cage-desperate-bid-freedom.html

A crate is a also good way of transporting your Boston Terrier in the car. Put the crate on the shady side of the interior and make sure it can't move around; put the seatbelt around it if necessary. If it's very sunny and the top of the crate is wire mesh, cover part of it so your dog has some shade and put the windows up and the air conditioning on. Never leave your Boston Terrier unattended in a vehicle; he can quickly overheat (or be targeted by thieves).

Allowing your dog to roam freely inside the car is not a safe option, particularly if you - like me – are a bit of a 'lead foot' on the brake and accelerator! Don't let him put his head out of the window either, he can slip and hurt himself or the wind pressure can cause an ear infection or bits of dust, insects, etc. to fly into your dog's eyes.

Special travel crates are useful for the car, or for taking your dog to the vet or a show. Try and pick one with holes or mesh in the side to allow free movement of air, rather than a solid plastic one.

Breeders' Advice on Crates

Traditionally crates have been more popular in America than in the UK and the rest of Europe, but opinion is slowly changing and more owners are starting to use crates on both sides of the Atlantic. This is perhaps because people's perception of a crate is shifting from regarding it as confinement to thinking of it as a safe haven, as well as a useful tool to help with housetraining and transportation, when used correctly.

Without exception, the breeders in this book believe that a crate should not be used for punishment or to imprison a dog all day while you are away from the house. This is cruel for any dog, but particularly a Boston, who loves to be with his humans. The key to successful crate training is to convince the dog that the crate is a good place; his special place. Many puppies will not initially like being in a crate, and patience - along with the right techniques - are required. Don't leave your Boston Terrier in there if he or she panics. Here's what some breeders say, starting in the US:

"I start crate training all my puppies starting at about six to seven weeks of age. I start by putting a small crate in their puppy pen and let them start sleeping in it with the door open. I graduate them to sleeping in the crate with the door closed around eight to nine weeks of age and set my alarm to wake up around 2am to take them out to potty and then put them back to bed."

(Photo courtesy of Pamela Preston, of ChriMaso Boston Terriers, California).

"Puppies can 'hold it' for about one hour for every month of age. So, a four-month-old puppy can typically hold it for about four to five hours. I also give them a tiny treat each time they go in their crate to help them be happy about being there. I will also give them a safe chew toy if they are going to be in there for more than an hour or so. This is to keep them busy, so they are not bored and become resentful of being in the crate."

"Mom is separated by five weeks and allowed to play and interact, but at five weeks, pups are sleeping on their own in a crated area with a bed, toys, food and litter box. All our pups are used to a crate before they leave and have a schedule of 5.30 or 6am wake, taken outside to potty, they play a little, eat at 7am, potty and play, nap, wake and potty, lunch, potty and play, nap and then longer play, dinner, potty and last play and potty before bed!

"I have the fortunate job that I can take pups with me as I own a pet grooming spa. As pups grow, they can be left crated for longer periods. Doggie doors work great, just remember that puppies -

like young children - get into trouble and teethe and chew. I always suggest a puppy X-pen (a portable wire pen for dogs and pups) set up in front of a doggie door, so puppies do not have free roam of the house unsupervised."

(Photo of an outdoor pen courtesy of Susan Maxwell, of Maximum Companion Boston Terriers, California).

"Each one of my dogs has their own crate. In the room where my female is with her puppies, and once the puppies are too big for the puppy bed, I replace it with an extra large crate for them and their Mom with the door locked open so they can come and go. I do this for a few reasons. I want all the puppies to see the crate as a good thing and their safe place, the way that their Mom does. When they get a little older, I start them on solid foods and potty pads and the Moms are wonderful at helping, so that when our puppies go to there forever homes, they are already half potty trained and eating solid food on their own.

"I can't tell you how many new puppy parents email or call to tell me that their new puppies don't cry or act scared at night when put to bed in their crates, and I know it's because they are not afraid of the crate. I always tell my new parents to use a crate for potty training, but to make sure the puppy is taken out as soon as they get up in the morning.

"The crate should be a good thing, not a bad thing. Our crates are left open for our dogs, and when they want private time or a nap, they go in there. I think a crate is a good training tool, but should never to be used as a punishment; they are good for puppies to sleep in at night, but not meant to be lived in. Puppies do not belong in a cage - I go over all of this in great detail with all my new puppy parents."

Here are some comments from the UK:

"I strongly condone the use of a crate, it should be your dog's safe haven, should your dog feel it needs its own space. Never trick a dog into a crate. Introduce the crate as a positive place where the dog can find peace and security. Place their bed, blanket, toys in the crate and the pup will soon recognise that it is their special place. Bostons or any dog should not be left alone for extended periods of time and I wouldn't recommend a dog being left alone in a crate for more than a few hours."

"I crate the puppies from a young age, also for short periods of time as part of their training regime. Exhibitors need to keep dogs in crates on benches at dog shows, so it's good that they are used to them from a young age."

One new owner added: "I do not crate due to the fact I work from home and never leave her alone for long. I do think my Boston is better with company, and she would not like being left alone as she is very affectionate."

Top 12 Housetraining Tips

How easy are Boston Terriers to housetrain (potty train)?

Well, it's fair to say, it varies! Some of it depends on what sort of start the puppy has had – puppies from good breeders should be partly housetrained by the time you collect them. But the dog is only as good as his or her owners. In other words, the speed and success often depends largely on one factor: YOU.

The more vigilant you are during the early days, the quicker your dog will be housetrained. It's as simple as that. Taking the advice in this chapter and being consistent with your routines and repetitions is the quickest way to toilet train your preoccupied little baby. You have three big factors in your favour:

1. Boston Terriers are intelligent.

2. They are food-motivated.

3. They are eager to please their owners and love being praised.

A further piece of good news is that a puppy's instinct is not to soil his own den. From around three weeks, a pup will leave his sleeping area to go to the toilet. As the breeder will have already started the toileting process, all you have to do is ensure that you carry on the good work.

If you're having to start from scratch when you bring your new pup home, your new arrival thinks that the whole house or apartment is his den and doesn't realise it is not the place to eliminate. Therefore you need to gently and persistently teach him that it is unacceptable to make a mess inside the home. Boston Terriers, like all dogs, are creatures of routine - not only do they like the same things happening at the same times every day, but establishing a regular routine with your dog also helps to speed up toilet training.

Dogs are also very tactile creatures, so they will pick a toilet area that feels good under their paws. Many dogs like to go on grass - but this will do nothing to improve your lawn, so you should think carefully about what area to encourage your Boston to use. You may want to consider a small patch of gravel crushed into tiny pieces in your garden, or a dog litter tray if you live in an apartment. Some breeders advise against using puppy pads for any length of time as puppies like the softness of the pads, which can encourage them to eliminate on other soft areas - such as your carpets or bed. Follow these tips to speed up housetraining:

1. **Constant supervision** is essential for the first week or two if you are to housetrain your puppy quickly. This is why it is important to take time off work when you bring him home. Make sure you are there to take him outside regularly. If nobody is there, he will learn to urinate or poo(p) inside the house.

2. Take your pup outside at the following times:

- ❀ As soon as he wakes – every time
- ❀ Shortly after each feed
- ❀ After a drink
- ❀ When he gets excited
- ❀ After exercise or play
- ❀ Last thing at night
- ❀ Initially every hour during the day - whether or not he looks like he wants to go

You may think that the above list is an exaggeration, but it isn't. Housetraining a pup is almost a full-time job for the first few days. If you are serious about training your puppy quickly, then clear your diary for a few days and keep your eyes firmly glued on your pup...learn to spot that expression or circling motion just before he makes a puddle - or worse – on your floor.

3. Take your pup to **the same place** every time, you may need to use a leash in the beginning - or tempt him there with a treat. Some say it is better to only pick him up and dump him there in an emergency, as it is ultimately a quicker process if he learns to take himself to the chosen toilet spot. Dogs naturally develop a preference for going in the same place or on the same surface - often grass or dirt. Take him to the same patch every time so he learns this is his bathroom - preferably an area in a corner of your yard or garden.

4. **No pressure – be patient.** You must allow your distracted little darling time to wander around and have a good sniff before performing his duties – but do not leave him, stay around a short distance away. Sadly, puppies are not known for their powers of concentration; it may take a while for them to select the perfect bathroom!

5. **Housetraining is reward-based.** Praise him or give him a treat immediately after he has performed his duties in the chosen spot. Boston Terriers love affection and love treats – so reward-based training is the most successful method for this often sensitive little dog.

6. **Share the responsibility.** It doesn't have to be the same person who takes the dog outside all the time. In fact it's easier if there are a couple of you, as housetraining is a very time-consuming business. Just make sure you stick to the same principles, command and patch of ground.

7. **Stick to the same routine.** Dogs understand and like routine. Sticking to the same one for mealtimes, short exercise sessions, play time, sleeping and toilet breaks will help to not only toilet and obedience train him quicker, but help him settle into his new home.

8. **Use the same word** or command when telling your puppy to go to the toilet – or while he is in the act. He will gradually associate this phrase or word with toileting and you will even be able to get him to eliminate on command after some weeks or months.

9. **Use your voice if you catch him in the act indoors.** A short sharp negative sound is best - NO! ACK! EH! - it doesn't matter, as long as it is loud enough to make him stop. Then start running enthusiastically towards your door, calling him into the garden and the chosen place and patiently wait until he has finished what he started indoors. It is no good scolding your dog if you find a puddle or unwanted gift in the house but don't see him do it; he won't know why you are cross with him. Only use the negative sound if you actually catch him in the act.

10. **No punishment.** Accidents will happen at the beginning, do not punish your Boston Terrier for them. He is a baby with a tiny bladder and bowels, and housetraining takes time - it is perfectly natural to have accidents early on. Remain calm and clean up the mess with a good strong-smelling cleaner to remove the odour, so he won't be tempted to use that spot again.

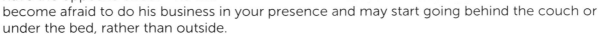

Dogs have a very strong sense of smell; use a special spray from your vet or a hot solution of washing powder to completely eliminate the odour. Smacking or rubbing his nose in it can have the opposite effect - he will become afraid to do his business in your presence and may start going behind the couch or under the bed, rather than outside.

11. **Look for the signs.** These may be whining, sniffing the floor in a determined manner, circling and looking for a place to go, or walking uncomfortably - particularly at the rear end! Take him outside straight away. Try not to pick him up. He has to learn to walk to the door himself when he needs to go outside.

12. **If you use puppy pads, only do so for a short time** (unless you live in an apartment and are indoor toilet training) or your puppy will get used to them. You can also separate a larger crate into two areas and put a pad in one area to help housetrain your pup. He will eliminate on the pad and keep his bed clean.

If you decide to keep your puppy in a crate overnight and you want him to learn not to soil the crate right from the very beginning, you need to have the crate in the bedroom so you can hear him whine when he needs to go. Initially this might be once or twice a night. By the age of five or six months a Boston Terrier pup should be able to last all night without needing the toilet – provided you let him out last thing at night and first thing in the morning (and go to bed late and get up early!)

If using a crate, remember that the door should not be closed until your Boston Terrier is happy with being inside (unless you close it for short periods initially while he is distracted, e.g. at mealtimes). He needs to believe that this is a safe place and not a trap or prison. If you don't like the idea of a crate, you can section off an area inside a room or use a puppy pen to confine the pup, with a bed and pads or newspapers in a different area that the puppy can use as a toilet area.

Apartment Living

Most Boston Terrier owners live in houses, but some do live in apartments. If you live on the 11th floor of an apartment block, housetraining can be a little trickier as you don't have easy access to the outdoors. One suggestion is to indoor housetrain your puppy. Dogs that spend much of their time indoors can be housetrained fairly easily - especially if you start early. Stick to the same principles already outlined - the only difference is that you will be placing your pup on training pads or newspaper instead of taking him outside.

Start by blocking off a section of the apartment for your new puppy. You can use a baby gate or puppy pen or make your own barrier. You will be able to keep a better eye on him than if he has free run of the whole place. It will also be easier to monitor his 'accidents.'

Select a corner away from his eating and sleeping area that will become his permanent bathroom area – carpets are to be avoided if at all possible. At first, cover a larger area than is actually needed - about three to four square feet - with newspaper (or training pads). You can reduce the area as training progresses. Take your puppy there as indicated in our Housetraining Tips. Praise him enthusiastically when he eliminates on the allotted area. If you catch him doing his business out of the toilet area, pick him up and take him back there. Correct with a firm voice - never a hand. With positive reinforcement and a strict schedule, he will soon be walking to the area on his own.

Owners attempting indoor housetraining should be aware that it often takes longer than outdoor training; some pups may resist. Also, once a dog learns to go indoors, it can be difficult to train him to eliminate outdoors. Any laziness on your part by not monitoring your puppy carefully enough - especially in the beginning – will make indoor toilet training a lot longer and more difficult process. The first week or two is crucial to your puppy learning what is expected of him.

Breeders on Housetraining

Emily Little, Essex, UK: The speed of housetraining is dependent on the dog and the owner. Bostons tend to be very easy to train and eager to please, which means they have to ability to learn quickly and the desire to do so. The breeder needs to ensure time is invested in their litter and that they are brought up in a way that makes them well-adjusted. That way when they do go to their forever homes, they are less likely to lose the skills that they have already learned from their dam. The owner needs to be consistent and patient."

Gwion Williams, of Wilarjan Boston Terriers, North Wales: "Bostons housetrain pretty quickly - especially if the breeder has already started the process. By about four months accidents are minimal. When our puppies are under six weeks of age they are encouraged to use paper, and they learn to use it pretty quickly. Between the age of six to seven weeks the puppies are then taken outside when they wake up or after meals, so that they soon learn to go outside to eliminate."

New owner Michelle Courtney-Kaye, of West Yorkshire, England: "I find my five-month-old hard to house train, slower than any other breed I've had, but I find it very hard to be cross with her - so maybe I'm the problem here."

Jo Dalton: "My pups start housetraining as soon as they can walk and have a UGO dog tray in their puppy pen. They automatically use it from around three weeks of age, so they are at least tray/paper trained when they leave us. We also start them on going outside from five weeks of age, which I have found makes housetraining a lot easier for the new owner. Kennel Club Assured Breeder Jo has a lot of advice for new owners: "It is important to remember puppies have very little

bladder control, therefore we recommend splitting the pup's crate in half to start with, with its bed at one end and newspaper or puppy pad at the other, so the pup can relieve itself if it wakes up without the need for waking you up, as you don't want to get in the habit of waking up every couple of hours to let your dog out during the night."

(Photo of Mumuland puppies courtesy of Jo).

"Puppies generally need to relieve themselves after eating and sleeping and around every 20-30 minutes while playing, so that's why we recommend having a puppy pad/dog toilet tray near where your pup is playing so it doesn't get in the habit of relieving itself just anywhere. Toilet training should start the minute you get home: simply take your dog out to the garden and allow it to relieve itself keep using the command you have chosen to use for toileting, such as 'Go Toilet' or 'Be Quick.' When your pup does relieve itself, give plenty of praise and repeat the command in your praise, e.g. 'Good Go Toilet, Teddy.'

"It is also very important to stay with your pup until it relieves itself, so the praise and reward (a small piece of cheese or wafer-thin chicken works wonders) can be given immediately, as this is how they learn. A pup that is simply put outside to go to toilet and does so without praise or reward will not know it is doing right and will continue to relieve itself when and where it wants to. Surprisingly this a common mistake many people make.

"Puppies will circle and run around with their nose to the ground when they need to go and you can guide your pup to a training pad or get it outside. You are both learning, so mistakes and accidents will happen! If you catch your pup in the act you, can correct it by saying 'No' firmly and moving it to where it should have relived itself, but it is no use punishing for an old accident, as the pup will not know or remember what it is being punished for.

"Try not to pick your pup up to go outside, as research has shown that puppies who actually physically walk to the door to go outside learn quicker and have far less accidents in the house. Research has also shown that this is why small breed dogs are thought to be traditionally harder to housetrain than some large breed dogs, i.e. a large breed puppy is harder to pick up and carry outside than a small breed dog."

If you are finding housetraining hard going, Jo has some reasons why things might not be progressing as quickly as you had hoped:

Feeding: You are feeding the puppy too much - The puppy food you are giving is unsuitable - You are not feeding at regular times - You are feeding at the wrong times (which could mean your puppy needs to go to the toilet during the night) - You are giving foods that are too salty, causing your puppy to drink more

Training Methods: Punishing your puppy for accidents indoors may make it scared of going to the toilet in front of you – even outside - Expecting your puppy to tell you when it needs to go to the toilet is unrealistic. It is far better to go outside at regular intervals - Leaving the back door or outside access open for your puppy to come and go as it pleases can cause confusion –particularly when that access is closed - You are leaving your puppy too long on its own, so it is forced to go indoors

Pamela Preston, of ChriMaso Boston Terriers, California, says: "I start litter box training my puppies around five weeks of age, then I do the initial crate training (and waking up at 2am), so that there is a good foundation before the puppy leaves my house. If done correctly, housetraining takes anywhere from a few weeks to a few months. The biggest thing is CONSISTENCY. Feed them on a set schedule and take them out to potty within about 15 to 20 minutes after eating - and **make sure** they potty before bringing them in. When they are young pups, I also pick up the water dish around 6pm or 7pm so they don't have a lot of fluid in their bladder when they go to bed. Again, take them outside frequently, to a designated area where you want them to potty, stay with them (yes, even in the rain...) until you see them potty, and then reward them with either a small treat or great praise."

Susan Maxwell, of Maximum Companion Boston Terriers, California, added: "Our puppies are trained to a litterbox before they leave for their new homes; litterbox training starts at about three or four weeks when they start walking and they start emerging from their birth bed to venture outside their box. We use a pelleted bedding that is either paper or wood base and place a litter box nearby. Some people use blankets when moms have pups, I do not as I have found it very easy for a pup to get smothered under a blanket. I use a pelleted bedding made from paper and have found not only does it make for a cleaner environment, but it also helps greatly with the structures of little Boston bodies. My dogs are fairly thick boned and stocky, and puppies produced are little 'tanks.' I find that the pellets create a very uneven surface which conforms to their bodies, so I don't get flat chests or 'swimmer' pups from not being able to get proper footing!"

One British breeder added: "If you are getting a puppy, invest in a good dressing gown and an umbrella!"

Tip As you have read, a trigger can be very effective to encourage your dog to perform his duties. Some people use a clicker or a bell - we used a word; well, two actually. Within a week or so I trained our puppy to urinate on the command of "Wee wee!" Think very carefully before choosing the word or phrase, as I often feel an idiot wandering around our garden last thing at night shouting "Max, WEE WEE!!" in an encouraging manner. (Although I'm not sure that the American expression "GO POTTY!!" sounds much better!

"How can you tell the dogs need to go out?"

7. Feeding A Boston Terrier

To keep your dog's biological machine in good working order, he or she needs the right fuel, just like a finely-tuned sports car. Feeding the correct diet is an essential part of keeping your Boston fit and healthy. However, the topic of feeding the right diet is something of a minefield. Owners are bombarded with endless choices as well as countless adverts from dog food companies, all claiming that theirs is best.

There is not one food that will give every single dog the brightest eyes, the shiniest coat, the most energy, the best digestion, the least gas, the longest life and stop him from scratching or having skin problems. Dogs are individuals, just like people, which means that you could feed a premium food to a group of dogs and find that most of them thrive on it, some do not so well, while a few might get an upset stomach or even an allergic reaction. The question is: "Which food is best for **my** Boston Terrier?"

If you have been given a recommended food from a breeder, rescue centre or previous owner, stick to this as long as your dog is doing well on it. A good breeder will know which food their dogs thrive on. If you do decide - for whatever reason - to change diet, then this must be done gradually. There are several things to be aware of when it comes to feeding:

1. Most Boston Terriers are very food motivated. Add to this their eagerness to please and you have a powerful training tool. You can use feeding time to reinforce a simple command on a daily basis.

2. However, their voracious appetites mean that most have no self-control when it comes to food, so it is up to you to control your dog's intake and keep his weight in check.

3. Some dogs have food sensitivities or allergies - more on this topic later.

4. Excess gas is a common issue with Boston Terriers and other brachycephalic (flat-faced) breeds. Their short noses mean that they often swallow a lot of air with their food, and the other main reason for flatulence is the wrong diet.

5. Many Boston Terriers do not do well on diets with a high wheat or corn content.

6. There is anecdotal evidence from breeders on both sides of the Atlantic that some Boston Terriers do well on a home-made or raw diet - if you have the time and money to stick to it.

7. Often, you get what you pay for with dog food, so a more expensive food is usually – but not always - more likely to provide better nutrition in terms of minerals, nutrients and high quality meats. Cheap foods often contain a lot of grain; read the list of ingredients to find out. Dried foods (called 'kibble' in the US) tend to be less expensive than other foods.

They have improved a lot over the last few years and some of the best ones are now a good choice for a healthy, complete diet. Dried foods also contain the least fat and most preservatives. Foods such as Life's Abundance dry formulas do not contain any preservatives.

8. Sometimes elderly dogs may just get bored with their diet and go off their food. This does not necessarily mean that they are ill, simply that they have lost interest and a new food should be gradually introduced.

Our dog Max, who has inhalant allergies, is on a quality dried food called James Wellbeloved. It contains natural ingredients and the manufacturers claim it is "hypoallergenic," i.e. good for dogs with allergies. Max seems to do well on it, but not all dogs thrive on dried food. We tried several other foods first; it is a question of each owner finding the best food for their dog. If you got your dog from a good breeder, they should be able to advise you on this.

Beware foods described as 'premium' or 'natural' or both, these terms are meaningless. Many manufacturers blithely use these words, but there are no official guidelines as to what they mean. However **"Complete and balanced"** IS a legal term and has to meet standards laid down by AAFCO (Association of American Feed Control Officials) in the USA.

Always check the ingredients on any food sack, packet or tin to see what is listed first; this is the main ingredient and it should be meat or poultry, not grain. If you are in the USA, look for a dog food endorsed by AAFCO. In general, tinned foods are 60-70% water and often semi-moist foods contain a lot of artificial substances and sugar. Choosing the right food for your Boston Terrier is important; it will certainly influence his health, coat and even temperament.

There are three stages of your dog's life to consider when feeding: Puppy, Adult and Senior (also called Veteran). Some manufacturers also produce a Junior feed for adolescent dogs. Each represents a different physical stage of life and you need to choose the right food during each particular phase. Also, a pregnant female will require a special diet to cope with the extra demands on her body; this is especially important as she nears the latter stages of pregnancy.

Most owners feed their Bostons twice a day; this helps to stop a hungry dog gulping food down in a mad feeding frenzy, and reduces the risk of Bloat (see **Chapter 10. Health** for more details). Some owners of fussy eaters feed two different meals each day to provide variety. One meal could be dried kibble, while the other might be home-made, with fresh meat, poultry and vegetables, or a moist food. If you do this, speak with your vet to make sure the two separate meals provide a balanced diet and that they are not too rich in protein.

We will not recommend one brand of dog food over another, but do have some general tips to help you choose what to feed. There is also some advice for owners of dogs with food allergies and intolerance; there is anecdotal evidence that some Bostons have an intolerance to grain and that many suffer from excess gas.

Food allergies are a growing problem in the canine world generally. Sufferers may itch, lick or chew their paws and/or legs, or rub their face. They may also get frequent ear infections as well as redness and swelling on their face. Switching to a grain-free diet can help to alleviate the symptoms, as your dog's digestive system does not have to work as hard. In the wild, a dog or wolf's staple diet would be meat with some vegetable matter from the stomach and intestines of the herbivores (plant eating animals) he ate – but no grains. Dogs do not digest corn or wheat (which are often staples of cheap commercial dog food) very efficiently. Grain-free diets still provide carbohydrates through fruits and vegetables, so your dog still gets all his nutrients.

15 Top Tips for Feeding your Boston

1. If you choose a manufactured food, don't pick one where meat or poultry content is NOT the first item listed on the bag. Foods with lots of cheap cereals or sugar are not the best choice.

2. Some dogs suffer from sensitive skin, 'hot spots' or allergies. A cheap food, often bulked up with grain, will only make this worse. If this is the case, bite the bullet and choose a high quality – usually more expensive – food, or consider a raw diet. You'll probably save money in vets' bills in the long run and your dog will be happier. A food described as 'hypoallergenic' on the sack means 'less likely to cause allergies.'

3. Feed your Boston twice a day, rather than once. Smaller feeds are easier to digest, and reduce flatulence (or gas – a common problem with Bostons!). Puppies need to be fed more often; discuss exactly how often with your breeder.

4. Establish a feeding regime and stick to it. Dogs like routine. If you are feeding twice a day, feed once in the morning and then again at tea-time. Stick to the same times of day.

   Do not give the last feed too late, or your dog's body will not have chance to process or burn off the food before sleeping. He will also need a walk or letting out in the garden or yard after his second feed to allow him to empty his bowels.

   Feeding at the same times each day helps your dog establish a toilet regime.

5. Take away any uneaten food between meals. Most Bostons LOVE their food, but any dog can become fussy if food is available all day. Imagine if your dinner was left on the table for hours. Returning to the table two or three hours later would not be such a tempting prospect, but coming back for a fresh meal would be far more appetising.

   Also, when food is left all day, some dogs take the food for granted and lose their appetite. They start leaving food and you are at your wits' end trying to find something they will actually eat. Put the food bowl down twice a day and take it up after 20 minutes – even if there is some left. If he is healthy and hungry, he'll look forward to his next meal and soon stop leaving food. If your dog does not eat anything for a couple of days, it could well be a sign that he is not well.

6. Do not feed too many titbits (tidbits) and treats between meals. Extra weight will place extra strain on your dog's joints and organs, have a detrimental effect on his health and even his lifespan. It also throws his balanced diet out of the window. Try to avoid feeding your dog from the table or your plate, as this encourages attention-seeking behaviour and drooling.

7. Never give your dog cooked bones, as these can splinter and cause choking or intestinal problems. If your Boston is a gulper, avoid giving rawhide, as dogs that rush their food have a tendency to chew and swallow rawhide without first bothering to nibble it down into smaller pieces.

8. If you switch to a new food, do the transition gradually. Unlike humans, dogs' digestive systems cannot handle sudden changes. Begin by gradually mixing some of the new food in with the old and increase the proportion so that after seven to eight days, all the food is the new one. The following ratios are recommended by Doctors Foster & Smith Inc: Days 1-3 add 25% of the new food, Days 4-6 add 50%, Days 7-9 add 75%, Day 10 feed 100% of the new food. By the way, if you stick to the identical brand, you can change flavours in one go.

9. NEVER feed the following items to your dog: grapes, raisins, chocolate, onions, Macadamia nuts, any fruits with seeds or stones, tomatoes, avocadoes, rhubarb, tea, coffee or alcohol. ALL of these are poisonous to dogs.

10. Check your dog's faeces (aka stools, poo or poop!). If his diet is suitable, the food should be easily digested and produce dark brown, firm stools. If your dog produces soft or light stools, or has a lot of gas or diarrhoea, then the diet may not suit him, so consult your vet or breeder for advice.

11. Feed your dog in stainless steel or ceramic dishes. Plastic bowls don't last as long and can also trigger an allergic reaction in some sensitive dogs. Ceramic bowls are best for keeping water cold.

12. If you have more than one dog, consider feeding them separately. Boston Terriers usually get on fine with other pets, especially if introduced at an early age. But feeding dogs together can sometimes lead to dog food aggression from a dog either protecting his own food or trying to eat the food designated for another pet.

13. If you do feed leftovers, feed them INSTEAD of a balanced meal, not as well as - unless you are feeding a raw diet. High quality dog foods already provide all the nutrients, vitamins, minerals and calories that your dog needs. Feeding titbits or leftovers may be too rich for your Boston in addition to his regular diet and cause gas, scratching or other problems, such as obesity.

 You can feed your dog vegetables as a healthy low-calorie treat. Get your puppy used to eating raw carrots, pieces of apple, etc. as a treat and he will continue to enjoy them as an adult. If you wait until he's fully grown before introducing them, he may well turn his nose up.

14. Keep your dog's weight in check. Obesity can lead to the development of serious health issues, such as diabetes, high blood pressure and heart disease. Although weight varies from dog to dog, a good rule of thumb is that your Boston Terrier's tummy should be higher than or, at worst, level with his rib cage. If his belly hangs down below it, he is overweight.

15. And finally, always make sure that your dog has access to clean, fresh water. Change the water and clean the bowl regularly – it gets slimy!

Types of Dog Food

We are what we eat. The right food is a very important part of a healthy lifestyle for dogs as well as humans. Here are the main options explained:

Dry dog food - also called kibble, this is a popular and relatively inexpensive way of providing a balanced diet. It comes in a variety of flavours and with differing ingredients to suit the different stages of a dog's life. Cheap foods are often false economy, particularly if your Boston does not tolerate grain/cereal very well, as they often contain a lot of grain. You may also have to feed larger quantities to ensure he gets sufficient nutrients. Bostons have short jaws so, if you feed a dry food, the kibble should be in small pieces.

Canned food - another popular choice – and it's often very popular with dogs too. They love the taste and it generally comes in a variety of flavours. Canned food is often mixed with dry kibble, and a small amount may be added to a dog that is on a dry food diet if he has lost interest in food. It tends to be more expensive than dried food and many owners don't like the mess. These days there are hundreds of options, some are very high quality and made from natural, organic ingredients and contain herbs and other beneficial ingredients. A part-opened tin can sometimes smell when you open the fridge door. As with dry food, read the label closely. Generally, you get what you pay for and the origins of cheap canned dog food are often somewhat dubious. Some Bostons can suffer from diarrhoea or soft stools and/or gas with too much tinned or soft food.

Semi-Moist - These are commercial dog foods shaped like pork chops, salamis, bacon, burgers or other meaty foods and they are the least nutritional of all dog foods. They are full of sugars, artificial flavourings and colourings to help make them visually appealing. Bostons don't care two hoots what their food looks like, they only care how it smells and tastes; the shapes are designed to appeal to humans. While you may give your dog one as an occasional treat, they are not a diet in themselves and do NOT provide the nutrition your dog needs. Steer clear of them for regular feeding.

Freeze-Dried - This is made by frozen food manufacturers for owners who like the convenience – this type of food keeps for six months to a year - or for those going on a trip with their dog. It says 'freeze-dried' on the packet and is highly palatable, but the freeze-drying process bumps up the cost.

Home-Cooked - Some owners want the ability to be in complete control of their dog's diet, know exactly what their dog is eating and to be absolutely sure that his nutritional needs are being met. Feeding your dog a home-cooked diet is time consuming and expensive, and the difficult thing – as with the raw diet - is sticking to it once you have started out with the best of intentions. But many owners think the extra effort is worth the peace of mind. If you decide to go ahead, you should spend the time to become proficient and learn about canine nutrition to ensure your dog gets all his vital nutrients.

What the Breeders Feed

We asked a number of Boston Terrier breeders what they feed their dogs. We are not recommending one brand over another, but the breeders' answers give an insight to what issues are important when considering food and why a particular brand has been chosen.

Gwion Williams, UK: "I feed my dogs Eden Holistic Pet Food - www.edenpetfoods.com. The reason I feed my dogs Eden is because it is rated 5/5, and is one of the best foods on the market. It has been said that this food is the next best thing to raw food, which is great as there's no preparing or defrosting involved.

"My dogs absolutely love the country cuisine flavour which contains coconut oil; this is great for their coats and gives that added shine to it. The extra benefit is that it's grain free, so even better quality. I've tried a lot of different dog food and I've been using Eden for over three years now. All our dogs are in great condition and not one fussy eater."

Pamela Preston, USA: "I feed Fromm Classic. It's a very good, holistic diet and my dogs do well on it; however, I change from time to time and generally go with a grain-free, high-quality, holistic food without artificial colors and preservatives. I add a little raw (either freeze dried, frozen, or meat from my butcher) to give them some additional flavour, but I don't do that when I travel."

Emily Little, UK: "I feed my dogs raw food mix containing chicken, offal, seaweed, peas, carrot, honey, charcoal and other trace elements. Dry food contains small mites which some dogs are allergic to, resulting in ear infections, bad stomachs etc. Also the high protein is vital to the Boston as they are active and have a high muscle percentage. The fat content gives them a good coat.

"Raw digests differently so they absorb more of the nutrients from the food, resulting in smaller hard stools which have very little odour. Also, as they are a brachycephalic breed, they can suffer from gas. When they eat standard kibble they take in a lot of air, which they then pass."

Susan Maxwell, USA: "We feed a prey raw diet and love it! Maybe that's why we never have allergy issues? Teeth seem to stay cleaner, energy levels are great, there is MINIMAL shedding, very little poop and always firm, less parasite problems, and immunity levels seem to be much greater as far as disease resistance.

"Puppies are born full of energy; they eat sooner and are weaned sooner...we let all pups wean themselves. We offer food as soon as they seem interested in momma's. They eat the same as adults (with added calcium/phosphorus) and as soon as they start eating, bowls are 'lifted' so they reach and stretch, as this helps build very strong pasterns and necks."

(Photo of the beautiful GCHCH Eviedoobee The Rock, aged seven, owned by Dona Powers and Evelyn Brand, courtesy of Susan).

Jo Dalton, UK: "I feed Royal Canin mini range - My dogs look good on it, I have trialled so many different foods - and raw - and my dogs have had issues with poor coat quality and not being able to keep weight on. I have been to so many seminars about dogs' nutritional needs and I feel Royal

Canin provides everything for every stage of a dog's life, Also, it address any allergy issues and the company has a dedicated helpline to help and advise owners if they have a problem.

"I am always complimented on how my dogs look and I put this down to feeding Royal Canin. I love their puppy milk and starter moose and biscuits - I find weaning extremely easy and I especially love their HT42d diet for pregnant bitches fed from Day One of season to Day 42 of pregnancy. I have found it has reduced absorptions in my bitches and I have had bigger litters and my bitches eat it when they often go off their food.

"Also, the moose has been quite literally a life-saver to a bitch who has just whelped as I have never known a bitch refuse to eat it. I am a breed mentor and also advise other breeders of whelping, pregnancy and raising pups of flat-faced breeds through my other business of Canine Scan and Chip. It has saved many bitches' lives."

Lynda Montgomery: "I feed IAMS Premium Protection dry dog food, because it is a good, healthy food. I called the company and checked for myself to see what it did and didn't have in it. It has two antioxidants, protein for lean muscle mass, vitamin E, Beta-Carotene, IAMS Daily Dental care for 55% less tartar build-up on teeth, probiotics, Omega 3 fatty acids for healthy skin and coat, and no by-products or fillers. My dogs eat it well; they all like it and look great. It costs a little more, but they are a part of my family and they are worth it. They are my responsibility and if I could not afford to take good care of them, I would not have them."

....

The Raw Diet

There is a quiet revolution going on in the world of dog food. After years of feeding dry or tinned dog food, increasing numbers of dog owners - and some breeders of Boston Terriers - are now feeding a raw diet to their beloved pets. However, the subject is not without controversy and, as you will read, opinions are definitely divided as far as Bostons are concerned! There is, however, anecdotal evidence that some dogs thrive on it, although scientific proof is lagging behind. Claims made by fans of the raw diet include:

- ❧ Reduced symptoms of - or less likelihood of - allergies, and less scratching
- ❧ Better skin and coats
- ❧ Easier weight management
- ❧ Improved digestion
- ❧ Less doggie odour and flatulence
- ❧ Fresher breath and improved dental health
- ❧ Helps fussy eaters
- ❧ Drier and less smelly stools, more like pellets
- ❧ Reduced risk of bloat
- ❧ Overall improvement in general health and less disease
- ❧ Higher energy levels
- ❧ Most dogs love a raw diet

If your dog is not doing well on a commercially-prepared dog food, you might consider a raw diet. It emulates the way dogs ate before the existence of commercial dog foods, which may contain artificial preservatives and excessive protein and fillers – causing a reaction in some Boston Terriers. Dry, canned and other styles of processed food were mainly created as a means of convenience, but unfortunately this convenience sometimes can affect a dog's health. Some nutritionists believe that dogs fed raw whole foods tend to be healthier than those on other diets. They say there are inherent beneficial enzymes, vitamins, minerals and other qualities in meats, fruits, vegetables and grains in their natural forms that are denatured or destroyed when cooked. Many also believe dogs are less likely to have allergic reactions to the ingredients on this diet.

Frozen food can be a valuable aid to the raw diet. The food is highly palatable, made from high quality ingredients and dogs usually wolf it down. The downsides are that not all pet food stores stock it and it is expensive.

Unsurprisingly, the topic is not without controversy. Critics of a raw diet say that the risks of nutritional imbalance, intestinal problems and food-borne illnesses caused by handling and feeding raw meat outweigh any benefits. It is true that owners must pay strict attention to hygiene when preparing a raw diet and it may not be a suitable option if there are children in the household. The dog may also be more likely to ingest bacteria or parasites such as Salmonella, E. Coli and Ecchinococcus.

Yorkshire breeder Lindsey Scanlon is one owner who says that she has never looked back since switching her Boston Terriers and French Bulldogs to raw. According to Lindsey, all of them love the raw food, they are less smelly and scratchy, and their coats shine. There is also less mess at the other end – faeces are typically hard, odourless pellets, making them easier to clean up.

Another two breeders we contacted say their dogs thrive on it; including Emily Little: "I feed my dogs raw food mix containing chicken, offal, seaweed, peas, carrot, honey, charcoal and other trace elements. Dry food contains small mites which some dogs are allergic to, resulting in ear infections, bad stomachs, etc. The high protein is vital to the Boston as they are active and have a high muscle percentage. The fat content gives them a good coat.

"Raw digests differently, so they absorb more of the nutrients from the food, resulting in smaller hard stools which have very little odour. Also, as they are a brachycephalic breed, they can suffer from gas. When Bostons eat standard kibble they take in a lot of air, which they then pass."

Another UK breeder had the opposite view: "I think the raw diet is a bad idea, unless the person is a specialist in nutrition and knows what they are doing."

Several said they either wouldn't try it or had no need to. One from the US said: "I do not feed raw, so can't offer any insight into benefits. My observations have been contradictory. For example, I know of one breeder who feeds raw and her dogs are always very thin and unhealthy looking and are often sick; however, I know of another breeder who feeds raw and her dogs look amazing. Perhaps one doesn't feed a complete diet with all the needed nutritional components and the other does. I personally don't do it because my dogs do quite well on high-quality kibble and I travel a lot, so raw would not work well for me."

A UK breeder added: "I don't like a raw diet, I know of too many people whose dogs have ended up at the vet's, from either through not feeding the correct ratios (dogs have complex requirements for vitamins and protein - not a need for certain ingredients) or intestinal rupture from bones. Also, our dogs are domesticated, they are not genetically the same their ancestors - and Bostons and other brachy(cephalic) breeds are about as far removed from wild dogs as you can get."

There are two main types of raw diet, one involves feeding raw, meaty bones and the other is known as the BARF diet (*Biologically Appropriate Raw Food* or *Bones And Raw Food),* created by Dr Ian Billinghurst.

....

Raw Meaty Bones

This diet is:

- 🐾 Raw meaty bones or carcasses, if available, should form the bulk of the diet
- 🐾 Table scraps both cooked and raw, such as vegetables, can be fed
- 🐾 As with any diet, fresh water should be constantly available. **NOTE: Do NOT feed cooked bones, they can splinter**

Australian veterinarian Dr Tom Lonsdale is a leading proponent of the raw meaty bones diet. He believes the following foods are suitable:

- 🐾 Chicken and turkey carcasses, after the meat has been removed for human consumption
- 🐾 Poultry by-products, including heads, feet, necks and wings
- 🐾 Whole fish and fish heads
- 🐾 Sheep, calf, goat, and deer carcasses sawn into large pieces of meat and bone
- 🐾 Other by-products, e.g. pigs' trotters, pigs' heads, sheep heads, brisket, tail and rib bones
- 🐾 A certain amount of offal can be included in the diet, e.g. liver, lungs, trachea, hearts, tripe

He says that low-fat game animals, fish and poultry provide the best source of food for pet carnivores. If you feed meat from farm animals (cattle, sheep and pigs), avoid excessive fat and bones that are too large to be eaten.

Some of it will depend on what's available locally and how expensive it is. If you shop around you should be able to source a regular supply of suitable raw meaty bones at a reasonable price. Start with your local butcher or farm shop. When deciding what type of bones to feed your Boston Terrier, one point to bear in mind is that dogs are more likely to break their teeth when eating large knuckle bones and bones sawn lengthwise than when eating meat and bone together.

You'll also need to think about WHERE you are going to feed your dog. A dog takes some time to eat a raw bone and will push it around the floor, so the kitchen may not be the most suitable or hygienic place. Outside is one option, but what do you do when it's raining?

Establishing the right quantity to feed your Boston Terrier is a matter of trial and error. You will reach a decision based on your dog's activity levels, appetite and body condition. High activity and a big appetite show a need for increased food, and vice versa. A very approximate guide, based on raw meaty bones, for the average dog is 15%-20% of body weight per week, or 2%-3% a day. So, if your Boston weighs 15lb (just under 7kg), he or she will require 2.25lb-3lb (1-1.5kg) of carcasses or raw meaty bones weekly. Table scraps should be fed as an extra component of the diet.

These figures are only a rough guide and relate to adult pets in a domestic environment. Pregnant or lactating females and growing puppies may need much more food than adult animals of similar body weight.

Dr Lonsdale says: "Wherever possible, feed the meat and bone ration in one large piece requiring much ripping, tearing and gnawing. This makes for contented pets with clean teeth. Wild carnivores feed at irregular intervals, in a domestic setting regularity works best and accordingly I suggest that you feed adult dogs and cats once daily. If you live in a hot climate I recommend that you feed pets in the evening to avoid attracting flies.

"I suggest that on one or two days each week your dog may be fasted - just like animals in the wild. On occasions you may run out of natural food. Don't be tempted to buy artificial food, fast your dog and stock up with natural food the next day. Puppies...sick or underweight dogs should not be fasted (unless on veterinary advice)."

Table scraps and some fruit and vegetable peelings can also be fed, but should not make up more than one-third of the diet. Liquidising cooked and uncooked scraps in a food mixer can make them easier to digest.

Things to Avoid

- Excessive meat off the bone - not balanced
- Excessive vegetables - not balanced
- Small pieces of bone - can be swallowed whole and get stuck
- Cooked bones - get stuck
- Mineral and vitamin additives - create imbalance
- Processed food - leads to dental and other diseases
- Excessive starchy food - associated with bloat
- Onions, garlic and chocolate, grapes, raisins, sultanas, currants - toxic to pets
- Fruit stones (pips) and corn cobs - get stuck
- Milk - associated with diarrhoea. Animals drink it whether thirsty or not and consequently get fat

Points of Concern

- Old dogs used to processed food may experience initial difficulty when changed on to a natural diet. Discuss the change with your vet first and then, if he or she agrees, switch your dog's diet over a period of a week to 10 days
- Raw meaty bones are not suitable for dogs with dental or jaw problems
- This diet may not be suitable if your dog gulps his food, as the bones can become lodged inside him, larger bones may prevent gulping
- The diet should be varied, any nutrients fed to excess can be harmful
- Liver is an excellent foodstuff, but should not be fed more than once weekly
- Other offal, e.g. ox stomachs, should not make up more than half of the diet
- Whole fish are an excellent source of food, but avoid feeding one species of fish constantly. Some species, e.g. carp, contain an enzyme that destroys thiamine (vitamin B1)

- If you have more than one dog, do not allow them to fight over the food, feed them separately if necessary

- Be prepared to monitor your dog while he eats the bones, especially in the beginning, and do not feed bones with sharp points. Take the bone off your dog before it becomes small enough to swallow

- Make sure that children do not disturb the dog when he is feeding or try to take the bone away

- Hygiene: Make sure the raw meaty bones are kept separate from human food and clean thoroughly any surface the uncooked meat or bones have touched. This is especially important if you have children. Feeding bowls are unnecessary, your dog will drag the bones across the floor, so feed them outside if you can, or on a floor that is easy to clean

- Puppies can and do eat diets of raw meaty bones, but you should consult the breeder or a vet before embarking on this diet with a young dog

You will need a regular supply of meaty bones - either locally or online - and you should buy in bulk to ensure a consistency of supply. For this you will need a large freezer. You can then parcel up the bones into daily portions. You can also feed frozen bones; some dogs will gnaw them straight away, others will wait for them to thaw.

More information is available from the website www.rawmeatybones.com and I would strongly recommend discussing the matter with your breeder or vet first before switching to raw meaty bones.

The BARF diet

A variation of the raw meaty bones diet is the BARF created by Dr Ian Billinghurst, who owns the registered trademark 'Barf Diet'. A typical BARF diet is made up of 60%-75% of raw meaty bones (bones with about 50% meat, such as chicken neck, back and wings) and 25%-40% of fruit and vegetables, offal, meat, eggs or dairy foods. Bones must not be cooked or they can splinter inside the dog.

There is a great deal of information on the BARF diet on the internet.

One point to consider is that a raw diet is not always suitable for the jaws and teeth conditions of brachycephalic breeds - dogs with short, broad skulls - like the Boston Terrier. You could consider a gradual shift and see how your Boston Terrier copes with the raw bones. You might also consider feeding two different daily meals to your dog - one dry kibble and one raw diet or home-cooked food, for example. If you do, then research the subject, and consult your veterinarian to make sure that the two combined meals provide a balanced diet.

NOTE: Only start a raw diet if you have done your research and are sure you have the time and money to keep it going. There are numerous websites and canine forums with information on switching to a raw diet and everything it involves.

Boston Terriers and Food Allergies

Symptoms

Dog food allergies affect about one in 10 dogs. They are the third most common canine allergy for dogs after atopy (inhaled or contact allergies) and flea bite allergies. While there's no scientific evidence of links between specific breeds and food allergies, there is anecdotal evidence from owners that some bloodlines do suffer from food allergies or intolerances.

Food allergies affect males and females in equal measure as well as neutered and intact pets. They can start when your dog is five months or 12 years old - although the vast majority start when the dog is between two and six years old. It is not uncommon for dogs with food allergies to also have other types of allergies.

If your Boston Terrier is not well, how do you know if the problem lies with his food or not? Here are some common symptoms of food allergies to look out for:

- Itchy skin (this is the most common). Your Boston Terrier may lick or chew his paws or legs and rub his face with his paws or on the furniture, carpet, etc.
- Excessive scratching
- Ear infections
- Hot patches of skin
- Hair loss
- Redness and inflammation on the chin and face
- Recurring skin infections
- Increased bowel movements (maybe twice as often as usual)
- Skin infections that clear up with antibiotics but recur when the antibiotics run out

Allergies or Intolerance?

There's a difference between dog food *allergies* and dog food *intolerance*:

Typical reactions to allergies are skin problems and/or itching

Typical reactions to intolerance are diarrhoea and/or vomiting

Dog food intolerance can be compared to people who get diarrhoea or an upset stomach from eating spicy food. Both can be cured by a change to a diet specifically suited to your dog, although a food allergy may be harder to get to the root cause of. As they say in the canine world: "One dog's meat is another dog's poison".

With dogs, certain ingredients are more likely to cause allergies than others. In order of the most common triggers, they are: **Beef, dairy products, chicken, wheat, eggs, corn, and soy.** There is also evidence that some Boston Terriers are sensitive to wheat or grain.

Unfortunately, these most common offenders are also the most common ingredients in dog foods! By the way, don't think if you put your dog on a rice and lamb kibble diet that it will automatically cure the problem. It might, but then again there's a fair chance it won't. The reason lamb and rice were thought to be less likely to cause allergies is simply because they have not traditionally been included in dog food recipes - therefore fewer dogs had reactions to them.

It is also worth noting that a dog is allergic or sensitive to an **ingredient**, not to a particular brand of dog food, so it is very important to read the label on the sack or tin. If your Boston Terrier has a reaction to beef, for example, he will react to any food containing beef, regardless of how expensive it is or how well it has been prepared.

Symptoms of food allergies are well documented. Unfortunately, the problem is that these conditions may also be symptoms of other issues such as environmental or flea bite allergies, intestinal problems, mange and yeast or bacterial infections. You can have a blood test on your dog for food allergies, but many veterinarians now believe that this is not accurate enough.

The only way to completely cure a food allergy or intolerance is complete avoidance. This is not as easy as it sounds. First you have to be sure that your dog does have a food allergy, and then you have to discover which food is causing the reaction. Blood tests are not thought to be reliable and, as far as I am aware, the only true way to determine exactly what your dog is allergic to, is to start a food trial. If you don't or can't do this for the whole 12 weeks, then you could try a more amateurish approach, which is eliminating ingredients from your dog's diet one at a time by switching diets – remember to do this over a period of a week to 10 days.

A food trial is usually the option of last resort, due to the amount of time and attention that it requires. It is also called '*an exclusion diet*' and is the only truly accurate way of finding out if your dog has a food allergy and what is causing it. Before embarking on one, try switching dog food. A hypoallergenic dog food, either commercial or home-made, is a good place to start. There are a number of these on the market and they all have the word '*hypoallergenic*' in the name.

Although usually more expensive, hypoallergenic dog food ingredients do not include common allergens such as wheat protein or soya, thereby minimising the risk of an allergic reaction. Many may have less common ingredients, such as venison, duck or types of fish. Here are some things to look for in a high quality food: meat or poultry as the first ingredient, vegetables, natural herbs such as rosemary or parsley, oils such as rapeseed (canola) or salmon.

Here's what to avoid: corn, corn meal, corn gluten meal, meat or poultry by-products (as you don't know exactly what these are or how they have been handled), artificial preservatives (including BHA, BHT, Propyl Gallate, Ethoxyquin, Sodium Nitrite/Nitrate and TBHQBHA), artificial colours, sugars and sweeteners like corn syrup, sucrose and ammoniated glycyrrhizin, powdered cellulose, propylene glycol. If you can rule out all of the above, and you have tried switching diet without much success, then a food trial may be the only option left.

....

Food Trials

Before you embark on one of these, you need to know that they are a real pain-in-the-you-know-what to monitor. You have to be incredibly vigilant and determined, so only start one if you 100% know you can see it through to the end, or you are wasting your time. It is important to keep a diary during a food trial to record any changes in your dog's symptoms, behaviour or habits.

A food trial involves feeding one specific food for 12 weeks, something the dog has never eaten before, such as rabbit and rice or venison and potato. Surprisingly, dogs are typically NOT allergic to foods they have never eaten before. The food should contain no added colouring, preservatives or flavourings.

There are a number of these commercial diets on the market, as well as specialised diets that have proteins and carbohydrates broken down into such small molecular sizes that they no longer trigger an allergic reaction. These are called *'limited antigen'* or *'hydrolysed protein'* diets.

Home-made diets are another option as you can strictly control the ingredients. The difficult thing is that this must be the **only thing** the dog eats during the trial. Any treats or snacks make the whole thing a waste of time. During the trial, you shouldn't allow your dog to roam freely, as you cannot control what he is eating or drinking when he is out of sight outdoors. Only the recommended diet must be fed. Do NOT give:

- Treats
- Rawhide (you shouldn't feed these to a Boston Terrier, anyway)
- Pigs' ears
- Cows' hooves
- Flavoured medications (including heartworm treatments) or supplements
- Flavoured toothpastes
- Flavoured plastic toys

If you want to give a treat, use the recommended diet. (Tinned diets can be frozen in chunks or baked and then used as treats). If you have other dogs, either feed them all on the trial diet or feed the others in an entirely different location. If you have a cat, don't let the dog near the cat litter tray. And keep your pet out of the room when you are eating. Even small amounts of food dropped on the floor or licked off of a plate can ruin a food trial, meaning you'll have to start all over again.

....

Boston Terriers and Grain

Although beef is the food most likely to cause allergies in the general dog population, there is plenty of anecdotal evidence to suggest that the ingredient most likely to cause a problem in many Boston Terriers is grain – just visit any internet forum to see some of the problems owners are experiencing with their Bostons. 'Grain' is wheat or any other cultivated cereal crop.

Boston Terriers, as well as Bully breeds such as Bulldogs, Boxers, Bull Terriers and French Bulldogs, **are prone to a build-up of yeast in the digestive system.** Foods that are high in grains and sugar can cause an increase in unhealthy bacteria and yeast in the stomach. This crowds out the good bacteria in the stomach and can cause toxins to occur that affect the immune system.

When the immune system is not functioning properly the itchiness related to food allergies can cause secondary bacterial and yeast infections, which often show as ear infections, skin disorders, bladder infections and reddish or dark brown tear stains. Symptoms of a yeast infection also include:

- Itchiness
- A musty smell
- Skin lesions or redness on the underside of the neck, the belly or paws

Although drugs such as antihistamines and steroids will temporarily help, they do not address the cause. Switching to a grain-free diet may help your dog get rid of the yeast and toxins. Some owners also feed their Bostons a daily spoonful of natural or live yoghurt, as this contains healthy bacteria and helps to balance the bacteria in your dog's digestive system - by the way, it works for humans too! Others have switched their dogs to a raw diet.

Switching to a grain-free diet may help to get rid of yeast and bad bacteria in the digestive system. Introduce the new food over a week to 10 days and be patient, it may take two to three months for symptoms to subside — but you will definitely know if it has worked after 12 weeks. Wheat products are also known to produce flatulence in some Boston Terriers, while corn products and feed fillers may cause skin rashes or irritations. It is also worth noting that some of the symptoms of food allergies - particularly the scratching, licking, chewing and redness - can also be a sign of inhalant or contact (environmental) allergies, which are caused by a reaction to such triggers as pollen, grass or dust. Some dogs are also allergic to flea bites. See **Chapter 11. Skin and Allergies** for details.

If you suspect your dog has a food allergy, the first port of call should be to the vet to discuss the best course of action. However, many vets' practices promote specific brands of dog food, which may or may not be the best for your dog. Don't buy anything without first checking every ingredient on the label. The website www.dogfoodadvisor.com provides useful information with star ratings for grain-free and hypoallergenic dogs' foods. We have no vested interest in this website, but have found it to be a good source of independent advice.

How Much Food?

This is another question I am often asked. The answer is ... there is no easy answer! The correct amount of food for your dog depends on a number of factors:

- Breed
- Gender
- Age
- Energy levels
- Amount of daily exercise
- Health
- Environment
- Number of dogs in house
- Quality of the food

Some breeds have a higher metabolic rate than others and energy levels vary tremendously from one dog to the next. Some Bostons are very energetic, while others veer towards the couch potato in personality. Our photo shows Jo Dalton's lively Boston enjoying playing in the grass.

Generally, smaller dogs have faster metabolisms so require a higher amount of food per pound of body weight. Female dogs may be slightly more prone to putting on weight than male dogs. Some people say that dogs that have been spayed or neutered are more likely to put on weight, although this is disputed by others. Growing puppies and young dogs need more food than senior dogs with a slower lifestyle.

Every dog is different; you can have two Boston Terriers with different temperaments. The energetic dog will burn off more calories. Maintaining a healthy body weight for dogs – and humans – is all about balancing what you take in with how much you burn off. If your dog is exercised a couple of times a day and has play sessions with humans or other dogs, he will need more calories than the couch potato Boston Terrier. And certain health conditions such as an underactive thyroid, diabetes, arthritis or heart disease can lead to dogs putting on weight, so their food has to be adjusted accordingly. Just like us, a dog kept in a very cold environment will need more calories to keep warm than a dog in a warm climate, as they burn extra calories to keep themselves warm. Here's an interesting fact: a dog kept on his own is more likely to be overweight than a dog kept with other dogs, as he receives all of the food-based attention.

Manufacturers of cheaper foods usually recommend feeding more to your dog, as much of the food is made up of cereals, which are not doing much except bulking up the weight of the food – and possibly triggering allergies in your Boston Terrier. The daily recommended amount listed on the dog food sacks or tins is generally too high – after all, the more your dog eats, they more they sell! Because there are so many factors involved, there is no simple answer. However, below we have listed a broad guideline of the average number of **calories** a Boston Terrier with medium energy and activity levels needs.

We feed our dog a dried hypoallergenic dog food made by James Wellbeloved in England. Max has seasonal allergies that make him scratch, but he seems to do pretty well on this food. Here we list James Wellbeloved's recommended feeding amounts for dogs, listed in kilograms and grams. (28.3 grams=1 ounce. 1kg=2.2lb). The number on the left is the dog's **adult weight** in kilograms. The numbers on the right are the amount of daily food that an average dog with average energy levels requires, measured in grams (divide this by 28.3 to get the amount in ounces). For example, a three-month-old Boston puppy that will grow into a 5kg (11lb) adult would require around 110 grams of food per day (3.9 ounces).

NOTE: These are only very general guidelines; your dog may need more or less than this. Use the chart as a guideline only and if your dog loses or gains weight, adjust meals accordingly.

....

Canine Feeding Chart

PUPPY

Size type	Expected adult body weight in kg (lb)	Daily serving in grams (ounces)					
		2 mths	3 mths	4 mths	5 mths	6 mths	> 6 mths
Toy	2kg (4.4lb)	50g (1.75oz)	60g (2.1oz)	60g (2.1oz)	60g (2.1oz)	55g (1.9oz)	Change to Adult or Small Breed Adult

Size type	Weight						
Small	5kg (11lb)	95g (3.5oz)	110g (3.9oz)	115g (4oz)	115g (4oz)	110g (3.9oz)	
Small	10kg (22lb)	155g (5.5oz)	185g (6.5oz)	195g (6.9 oz)	190g (6.7oz)	185g (6.5oz)	
Medium	17kg (37.5lb)	215g (7.6oz)	265g (9.3oz)	285g (10.1oz)	285g (10.1oz)	280g (9.9oz)	Change to Junior

JUNIOR

Size type	Expected adult body weight in kg (lb)	Daily serving in grams (ounces)						
		6 mths	7 mths	8 mths	10 mths	12 mths	14 mths	16 mths
Small	10kg (22lb)	195g (6.9 oz)	185g (6.5oz)	175g (6.2oz)	160g (5.6oz)	Change to Adult		
Medium	17kg (37.5lb)	290g (10.2)	285g (10.1oz)	270g (9.5oz)	245g (8.6oz)			

ADULT

Size type	Bodyweight in kg (lb)	Daily serving in grams (ounces)		
		High activity	Normal activity	Low activity
Small	5-10kg (11-22lb)	115-190g (4-6.7oz)	100-170g (3.5-6oz)	85-145g (3-5.1oz)
Medium	10-15 (22-33lb)	190-255g (6.7-9oz)	170-225g (6-7.9oz)	145-195g (5.1-6.9oz)

SENIOR

Size type	Bodyweight in kg (lb)	Daily serving in grams (ounces)	
		Active	Normal
Small	5-10kg (11-22lb)	105-175g (3.7-6.2oz)	90-150g (3.2-5.3oz)
Medium	10-15kg (22-33lb)	175-235g (6.2-8.3oz)	150-205g (3.2-7.2oz)

Overweight Dogs

It is far easier to regulate your Boston Terrier's weight and keep it at a healthy level than to try and slim down a voraciously hungry Boston Terrier when he becomes overweight. Boston Terriers are, however, prone to putting on weight and, sadly, overweight and obese dogs are susceptible to a range of illnesses. According to James Howie, Veterinary Advisor to Lintbells, some of the main ones are:

Joint disease – excessive body weight may increase joint stress, which is a risk factor in joint degeneration (arthrosis), as is cruciate disease (knee ligament rupture). Joint disease tends to lead to a reduction in exercise that then increases the likelihood of weight gain which reduces exercise further. A vicious cycle is created. Overfeeding Boston Terriers while they are growing can lead to various problems, including the worsening of hip dysplasia. Weight management may be the only measure required to control clinical signs in some cases.

Heart and lung problems – fatty deposits within the chest cavity and excessive circulating fat play important roles in the development of cardio-respiratory and cardiovascular disease.

Diabetes – resistance to insulin has been shown to occur in overweight dogs, leading to a greater risk of diabetes mellitus.

Tumours – obesity increases the risk of mammary tumours in female dogs.

Liver disease – fat degeneration may result in liver insufficiency.

Reduced Lifespan - one of the most serious proven findings in obesity studies is that obesity in both humans and dogs reduces lifespan.

Exercise intolerance – this is also a common finding with overweight dogs, which can compound an obesity problem as fewer calories are burned off and are therefore stored, leading to further weight gain.

Obesity also puts greater strain on the delicate respiratory system of Boston Terriers, making breathing even more difficult for them. Most Boston Terriers are very attached to their humans. However, beware of going too far in regarding your dog as a member of the family. It has been shown that dogs regarded as 'family members' (i.e. anthropomorphosis) by the owner are at greater risk of becoming overweight. This is because attention given to the dog often results in food being given as well.

The important thing to remember is that many of the problems associated with being overweight are reversible. Increasing exercise increases the calories burned, which in turn reduces weight. If you do put your dog on a diet, the reduced amount of food will also mean reduced nutrients, so he may need a supplement during this time.

Feeding Puppies

Feeding your Boston Terrier puppy the right diet is important to help his young body and bones grow strong and healthy. Puppyhood is a time of rapid growth and development, and puppies require different levels of nutrients to adult dogs.

For the first six weeks, puppies need milk about five to seven times a day, which they take from their mother. Generally they make some sound if they want to feed. The frequency is reduced when the pup reaches six to eight weeks old. Boston Terrier puppies should stay with their mothers and littermates until **at least** eight weeks old. During this time, the mother is still teaching her offspring some important rules about life. For the first few days after that, it's a good idea to continue feeding the same puppy food and at the same times as the breeder. Dogs do not adapt to changes in their diet or feeding habits as easily as humans.

You can then slowly change his food based on information from the breeder and your vet. This should be done very gradually by mixing in a little more of the new food each day over a period of seven to 10 days. If at any time your puppy starts being sick, has loose stools or is constipated, slow the rate at which you are switching him over. If he continues vomiting, seek veterinary advice as he may have a problem with the food you have chosen. Puppies that are vomiting or that have diarrhoea quickly dehydrate.

Because of their special nutritional needs, you should only give your puppy a food that is approved either just for puppies or for all life stages. If a feed is recommended for adult dogs only, it won't have enough protein, and the balance of calcium and other nutrients will not be right for a pup. Puppy food is very high in calories and nutritional supplements, so you want to switch to a junior or adult food once he leaves puppyhood. Feeding puppy food too long can result in obesity and orthopaedic problems – check with your vet on the right time to switch.

Getting the amount and type of food right for your pup is important. Feeding too much will cause him to put on excess pounds, and overweight puppies are more likely to grow into overweight adults. As a very broad guideline, dogs normally mature into fully developed adults at around two years old.

DON'T:

- Feed table scraps from the table. Your Boston Terrier will get used to begging for food, it will also affect a puppy's carefully balanced diet

- Feed food or uncooked meat that has gone off. Puppies have sensitive stomachs; stick to a prepared puppy food suitable for Boston Terriers, preferably one recommended by your breeder

DO:

- Regularly check the weight of your growing puppy to make sure he is within normal limits for his age. There are charts available on numerous websites, just type "puppy weight chart" into Google – you'll need to know the exact age and current weight of your puppy

- Take your puppy to the vet if he has diarrhoea or is vomiting for two days or more

- Remove his food after it has been down for 15 to 20 minutes. Food available 24/7 encourages fussy eaters

How Often?

Puppies have small stomachs but large appetites, so feed them small amounts on a frequent basis. Establishing a regular feeding routine with your puppy is a good idea, as this will also help to toilet train him. Get him used to regular mealtimes and then let him outside to do his business straight away when he has finished. Puppies have fast metabolisms, so the results may be pretty quick!

Don't leave food out for the puppy so that he can eat it whenever he wants. You need to be there for the feeds because you want him and his body on a set schedule. Smaller meals are easier for him to digest and energy levels don't peak and fall so much with frequent feeds. There is some variation between recommendations, but as a general rule of thumb:

- Up to the age of three or four months, feed your puppy three or four times a day

- Then three times a day until he is six months old

- Then twice a day for the rest of his life

Boston Terriers are known for their healthy appetites and will eat most things put in front of them, it's up to you to control their intake and manage their diet. Stick to the correct amount; you're doing your pup no favours by overfeeding him.

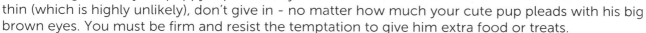

Unless your puppy is particularly thin (which is unlikely if he has been well bred), don't give in - no matter how much your cute pup pleads with his big, soulful eyes. You must be firm and resist the temptation to give him extra food or treats.

A very broad rule of thumb is to feed puppy food for a year, but some owners start earlier on adult food, while others delay switching until their Boston Terrier is 18 months or even two years old. If you are not sure, consult your breeder or your vet.

It's up to you to control your dog's intake and manage his or her diet. Stick to the correct amount; you're doing your pup no favours by overfeeding. Unless your puppy is particularly thin (which is highly unlikely), don't give in - no matter how much your cute pup pleads with his big brown eyes. You must be firm and resist the temptation to give him extra food or treats.

 Bostons are very loving companions. If your dog is not responding well to a particular family member, a useful tactic is to get that person to feed the dog every day. The way to a dog's heart is often through his or her stomach!

Feeding Seniors

Once your adolescent dog has switched to an adult diet he will be on this for several years. As a dog moves towards old age, his body has different requirements to those of a young dog. This is the time to consider switching to a senior diet.

Dogs are living to a much older age than they did 30 years ago. There are many factors contributing to this, including better vaccines and veterinary care, but one of the most important factors is better nutrition. Generally a dog is considered to be 'older' or senior if he is in the last third of his normal life expectancy.

Some owners of large breeds, such as Great Danes with a lifespan of nine years, switch their dogs from an adult to a senior diet when they are only six or seven years old. A Boston Terrier's lifespan is from 10 years upwards and when you switch depends on your individual dog, his or her energy levels and general health.

Look for signs of your dog slowing down or having joint problems. That may be the time to talk to your vet about moving to a senior diet. You can describe any changes at your dog's annual vaccination appointment, rather than having the expense of a separate consultation. As a dog grows older, his metabolism slows down, his joints may stiffen, his energy levels decrease and he needs less exercise, just like with humans. You may notice in middle or old age that your dog starts to put weight on. The adult diet he is on may be too rich and have too many calories, so it may be the time to consider switching.

Even though he is older, keep his weight in check, as obesity in old age only puts more strain on his body - especially joints and organs - and makes any health problems even worse. Because of lower activity levels, many older dogs will gain weight and getting an older dog to slim down can be very difficult.

It is much better not to let your Boston get too chunky than to put him on a diet.

But if he is overweight, put in the effort to shed the extra pounds. This is one of the single most important things you can do to increase your Boston Terrier's quality AND length of life.

Other changes in canines are again similar to those in older humans and might include stiff joints or arthritis, moving more slowly and sleeping more. His hearing and vision may not be so sharp and organs don't all work as efficiently as they used to; his teeth may have become worn down.

When this starts to happen, it is time to feed your old friend a senior diet, which will take these changes into account. Specially formulated senior diets are lower in protein and calories but help to create a feeling of fullness.

Older dogs are more prone to develop constipation, so senior diets are often higher in fibre - at around 3% to 5%. Wheat bran can also be added to regular dog food to increase the amount of fibre - but do not try this if your Boston has a low tolerance or intolerance to grain. If your dog has poor kidney function, then a low phosphorus diet will help to lower the workload for the kidneys.

Ageing dogs have special dietary needs, some of which can be provided in the form of supplements, such as glucosamine and chondroitin, which help joints. If your dog is not eating a complete balanced diet, then a vitamin/mineral supplement is recommended to prevent any deficiencies. Some owners also feed extra antioxidants to an older dog – ask your vet's advice on your next visit. Antioxidants are also found naturally in fruit and vegetables.

While some older Bostons suffer from obesity, others have the opposite problem – they lose weight and are disinterested in food. If your old dog is getting thinner and not eating well, firstly get him checked out by the vet to rule out any possible diseases. If he gets the all-clear, your next challenge is to tempt him to eat. He may be having trouble with his teeth, so if he's on a dry food, try smaller kibble or moistening it with water or gravy.

Our dog loved his twice daily feeds until he recently got to the age of 10 when he suddenly lost interest in his food, which is a hypoallergenic kibble. We tried switching flavours within the same brand, but that didn't work. After a short while we mixed his daily feeds with a little gravy and a spoonful of tinned dog food – Bingo! He's wolfing it down again and lively as ever.

Some dogs can tolerate a small amount of milk or eggs added to their food, and home-made diets of boiled rice, potatoes, vegetables and chicken or meat with the right vitamin and mineral supplements can also work well.

See **Chapter 14. Caring for Older Dogs** for more information on looking after a senior.

Reading Dog Food Labels

A NASA scientist would have a hard job understanding some manufacturers' labels, so it's no easy task for us lowly dog owners. Here are some things to look out for on the manufacturers' labels:

- The ingredients are listed by weight and the top one should always be the main content, such as chicken or lamb. Don't pick one where grain is the first ingredient; it is a poor quality feed and some Boston Terriers can develop grain intolerances or allergies, and often it is specifically wheat they have a reaction to

- High on the list should be meat or poultry by-products, these are clean parts of slaughtered animals, not including meat. They include organs, blood and bone, but not hair, horns, teeth or hooves

Ingredients: Chicken, Chicken By-Product Meal, Corn Meal, Ground Whole Grain Sorghum, Brewers Rice, Ground Whole Grain Barley, Dried Beet Pulp, Chicken Fat (preserved with mixed Tocopherols, a source of Vitamin E), Chicken Flavor, Dried Egg Product, Fish Oil (preserved with mixed Tocopherols, a source of Vitamin E), Potassium Chloride, Salt, Flax Meal, Sodium Hexametaphosphate, Fructooligosaccharides, Choline Chloride, Minerals (Ferrous Sulfate, Zinc Oxide, Manganese Sulfate, Copper Sulfate, Manganous Oxide, Potassium Iodide, Cobalt Carbonate), DL-Methionine, Vitamins (Ascorbic Acid, Vitamin A Acetate, Calcium Pantothenate, Biotin, Thiamine Mononitrate (source of vitamin B1), Vitamin B12 Supplement, Niacin, Riboflavin Supplement (source of vitamin B2), Inositol, Pyridoxine Hydrochloride (source of vitamin B6), Vitamin D3 Supplement, Folic Acid), Calcium Carbonate, Vitamin E Supplement, Brewers Dried Yeast, Beta-Carotene, Rosemary Extract.

- Guaranteed Analysis – This guarantees that your dog's food contains the labelled percentages of crude protein, fat, fibre and moisture. Keep in mind that wet and dry dog foods use different standards. (It does not list the digestibility of protein and fat and this can vary widely depending on their sources). While the Guaranteed Analysis is a start in understanding the food quality, be wary about relying on it too much. One pet food manufacturer made a mock product with a guaranteed analysis of 10% protein, 6.5% fat, 2.4% fibre, and 68% moisture (similar to what's on many canned pet food labels) – the ingredients were old leather boots, used motor oil, crushed coal and water!

- Chicken meal (dehydrated chicken) has more protein than fresh chicken, which is 80% water. The same goes for beef, fish and lamb. So, if any of these meals are number one on the ingredient list, the food should contain enough protein

- A certain amount of flavourings can make a food more appetising for your dog. Choose a food with a specific flavouring, like '*beef flavouring*' rather than a general '*meat flavouring*', where the origins are not so clear

- Find a food that fits your dog's age, breed and size. Talk to your vet or visit an online Boston Terrier forum and ask other owners what they are feeding their dogs

- If your Boston has a food allergy or intolerance to wheat, check whether the food is gluten free. All wheat contains gluten

Crude Protein (min)	32.25%
Lysine (min)	0.43%
Methionine (min)	0.49%
Crude Fat (min)	10.67%
Crude Fiber (max)	7.3%
Calcium (min)	0.50%
Calcium (max)	1.00%
Phosphorus (min)	0.44%
Salt (min)	0.01%
Salt (max)	0.51%

❧ Natural is best. Food labelled *'natural'* means that the ingredients have not been chemically altered, according to the FDA in the USA. However, there are no such guidelines governing foods labelled *'holistic'* – so check the ingredients and how it has been prepared

❧ In the USA, dog food that meets minimum nutrition requirements has a label that confirms this. It states: *"[food name] is formulated to meet the nutritional levels established by the AAFCO Dog Food Nutrient Profiles for [life stage(s)]"*

Even better, look for a food that meets the minimum nutritional requirements *'as fed'* to real pets in an AAFCO-defined feeding trial, then you know the food really delivers the nutrients that it is *'formulated'* to AAFCO feeding trials on real dogs are the gold standard. Brands that do costly feeding trials (including Nestlé and Hill's) indicate so on the package.

NOTE: Dog food labelled *'supplemental'* isn't complete and balanced. Unless you have a specific, vet-approved need for it, it's not something you want to feed your dog for an extended period of time. Check with your vet if in doubt.

If it all still looks a bit baffling, you might find the following website, mentioned earlier, very useful: www.dogfoodadvisor.com run by Mike Sagman. He has a medical background and analyses and rates hundreds of brands of dog food based on the listed ingredients and meat content. You might be surprised at some of his findings.

To recap: no one food is right for every dog; you must decide on the best for yours. If you have a puppy, initially stick to the same food that the breeder has been feeding the litter, and only change diet later and gradually. Once you have decided on a food, monitor your puppy or adult. The best test of a food is how well your dog is doing on it.

If your Boston Terrier is happy and healthy, interested in life, has enough energy, is not too fat and not too thin, doesn't scratch a lot and has healthy-looking stools, then...

Congratulations, you've got it right!

8. Canine Behaviour

Just as with humans, a Boston Terrier's personality is made up of a combination of temperament and character.

Temperament is the nature - or inherited traits - a dog is born with, a predisposition to act or react in a certain way. Not only will a responsible breeder produce puppies from physically healthy dams and sires, but she will also look at the temperament of her dogs and breed from those with good traits.

Character is what develops through the dog's life and is formed by a combination of temperament and environment. How you treat your Boston will have a huge effect on his or her personality and behaviour. Starting off on the right foot with good routines for your puppy is very important; so treat your dog well, spend time with him, socialise, exercise and play with him.

All dogs need different environments, scents and experiences to keep them stimulated and well-balanced. Praise good behaviour, use positive methods and keep training short and fun. At the same time, be consistent so your dog learns the guidelines quickly. All of these measures will help your Boston grow into a happy, well-adjusted and well-behaved adult dog that is a delight to be with.

If you adopt a dog from a rescue centre, you may need a little extra patience. These eager-to-please people-loving dogs may often arrive with some baggage. They have been abandoned by their previous owners for a variety of reasons - or perhaps forced to produce puppies in a puppy mill - and may still carry the scars of that trauma. They may feel nervous and insecure or they may not know how to properly interact with a loving owner. Your time and patience is needed to teach these poor animals to trust again and to become happy in their new forever homes.

Understanding Canine Emotions

As pet lovers, we are all too keen to ascribe human traits to our dogs; this is called *anthropomorphism* - 'the attribution of human characteristics to anything other than a human being.' Most of us dog lovers are guilty of that, as we come to regard our pets as members of the family - and Boston Terriers certainly regard themselves as members of our family...in fact some are convinced that they are the centre of it and we belong to them!

An example of anthropomorphism might be that the owner of a male dog might not want to have him neutered because he will 'miss sex,' as a human might if he or she were no longer able to have sex. This is simply not true. A male dog's impulse to mate is entirely governed by his hormones, which kick in when a female is in season, not his emotions. If he gets the scent of a bitch on heat, his hormones (which are just chemicals) tell him he has to mate with her. He does not stop to consider how attractive she is or whether she is 'the one' to produce his puppies. No, his reaction is entirely physical, he just wants to dive in there and get on with it!

It's the same with females. When they are on heat, a chemical impulse is triggered in their brain making them want to mate - with any male, they aren't at all fussy. So don't expect your little princess to be all coy when she is on heat, she is not waiting for Prince Charming to come along - the tramp down the road or any other scruffy pooch will do! It is entirely physical, not emotional. Food is another issue. A dog will not stop to count the calories of that lovely treat (you have to do that). No, he or she is driven by food and just thinks about getting the treat.

Boston Terriers are very affectionate, lively and eager to please, and if yours doesn't make you laugh from time to time, you must have had a humour by-pass. They also want to spend most of their time with their owners. All of these characteristics add up to one thing: an extremely endearing and loving family member that it's all too easy to reward - or spoil. Treating a Boston Terrier like a child - or a puppy like a baby - is a habit to be avoided.

It's fine to treat your dog like a member of the family - as long as you keep in mind that he is canine and not human. Understand his mind, patiently train him to learn his place in the household and that there are some rules he needs to follow and you will be rewarded with a companion that is second to none and fits in beautifully with your family and lifestyle.

Dr Stanley Coren is a psychologist well known for his work on canine psychology and behaviour. He and other researchers believe that in many ways a dog's emotional development is equivalent to that of a young child. Dr Coren says: "Researchers have now come to believe that the mind of a dog is roughly equivalent to that of a human who is two to two-and-a-half years old. This conclusion holds for most mental abilities as well as emotions. Thus, we can look to the human research to see what we might expect of our dogs.

"Just like a two-year-old child, our dogs clearly have emotions, but many fewer kinds of emotions than found in adult humans. At birth, a human infant only has an emotion that we might call excitement. This indicates how excited he is, ranging from very calm up to a state of frenzy. Within the first weeks of life, the excitement state comes to take on a varying positive or a negative flavor, so we can now detect the general emotions of contentment and distress. In the next couple of months, disgust, fear, and anger become detectable in the infant. Joy often does not appear until the infant is nearly six months of age and it is followed by the emergence of shyness or suspicion. True affection, the sort that it makes sense to use the label 'love' for, does not fully emerge until nine or ten months of age."

So, Boston Terriers can truly love us - but we knew that already! According to Dr Coren, dogs can't feel shame, so if you are housetraining your puppy, don't expect him to be ashamed if he makes a mess in the house, he can't; he simply isn't capable of feeling shame. But he will not like it when you ignore him when he's behaving badly, and he will love it when you praise him profusely for eliminating outdoors. He is simply responding to your reaction with his simplified range of emotions.

Dr Coren also believes that dogs cannot experience guilt, contempt or pride. I'm no expert but I'm not sure I 100% agree. Take your Boston to a local dog training class or agility event and just watch him perform - surely your dog's delight is something akin to pride? Some Bostons have a 'presence' in the show ring; they carry themselves with pride. They can certainly experience joy. Boston Terriers love your attention, and when they are showing off and lapping up your attention, their reaction can only be described as a mixture of pure joy and pride.

And like many companion breeds, the Boston Terrier can be a sensitive little soul. You can hurt his feelings by speaking to him too harshly or loudly, so don't be surprised if he 'punishes' you by sulking (or even peeing in the house when you aren't looking!) The sensitivity is also part of the Boston's charm, and after a while Bostons get into tune with the rhythms of the household and settle into their place there.

One emotion that all dogs can experience is jealousy - with Boston Terriers this may be displayed by food guarding or if you give your precious attention to animals other than themselves. An interesting article was published in the PLOS (Public Library of Science) Journal in summer 2014, following an experiment into whether dogs get jealous. Building on research that shows that six-month old infants display jealousy, scientists studied 36 dogs in their homes and video recorded their actions when their owners displayed affection to a realistic-looking stuffed canine (pictured).

Over three-quarters of the dogs were likely to push or touch the owner when they interacted with the decoy. The envious mutts were more than three times as likely to do this for interactions with the stuffed dog, compared to when the owners gave their attention to other objects, including a book. Around a third tried to get between the owner and the plush toy, while a quarter of the put-upon pooches snapped at the dummy dog!

"Our study suggests not only that dogs do engage in what appear to be jealous behaviors, but also that they were seeking to break up the connection between the owner and a seeming rival," said Professor Christine Harris from University of California in San Diego. The researchers believe that the dogs understood that the stuffed dog was real. The authors cite the fact that 86% of the dogs sniffed the toy's rear end during and after the experiment!

"We can't really speak of the dogs' subjective experiences, of course, but it looks as though they were motivated to protect an important social relationship. Many people have assumed that jealousy is a social construction of human beings - or that it's an emotion specifically tied to sexual and romantic relationships," said Professor Harris: "Our results challenge these ideas, showing that animals besides ourselves display strong distress whenever a rival usurps a loved one's affection."

Typical Boston Terrier Traits

1. Boston Terriers are bred as companion dogs. They are social and sociable dogs and should have a naturally sweet and happy temperament. The definition of 'social' is 'needing companionship and therefore best suited to living in communities (or families).'

2. When properly socialised, they make wonderful companions and family dogs and are known for being good with children and the elderly. Some breeders say that their Bostons are drawn to children and even have an affinity with them.

3. They are sensitive critters and can pick up on emotions, moods, etc. Two people involved in this book have children with special needs and both have said how one of their Boston Terriers has a special affinity with the child. This sensitivity also means that Bostons do not respond well to harsh words or treatment.

4. Boston Terriers do not like being left alone for long periods. If you are away from the home a lot, consider another breed not so dependent on humans for happiness - or wait until you have more time to devote to a dog.

5. Despite being descended from fighting dogs, Bostons have been bred as companions and they are not aggressive dogs, generally getting on well with other dogs - provided they have been properly socialised and introduced.

(Photo courtesy of Jo Dalton, Mumuland Boston Terriers, Lincolnshire, England)

6. They have been described as 'Velcro dogs;' they want to be with you 24/7 and may even follow you from room to room. Spend some time apart from them in the beginning to avoid separation anxiety, which is stressful for both dog and owner.

7. One thing that surprises some new owners is the amount of exercise some Bostons need. These are generally energetic little dogs that love to be involved in everything. They are more physically active than some other Bully breeds, such as the Bulldog or French Bulldog, but still do not require an excessive amount of exercise.

8. They are intelligent and eager to please. More Boston owners are training their dogs to take part in canine competitions, where physical and mental agility is required. The breed's affectionate nature also makes them suitable as therapy dogs. They need mental as well as physical stimulation, and enjoy both indoor and outdoor games.

9. The same goes for housetraining (potty training); a Boston can pick it up quickly, as long as you are extremely vigilant in the beginning.

10. An under-exercised, under-stimulated Boston Terrier will display poor behaviour, as any dog would.

11. Some can be a bit stubborn and/or wilful. This is not uncommon with Bully breeds. If this is the case, the owner needs to be firm and consistent with training - but this does not mean shouting at your Boston; this will have the opposite effect to what you are trying to achieve.

Cause and Effect

Treated well, socialised and trained, Boston Terriers make excellent family dogs. They are attractive, affectionate and sociable, love being around people, form close bonds and enjoy entertaining their humans - which is why once you've had one, no other breed seems quite the same. But sometimes Boston Terriers, just like other breeds and crossbreeds, can develop behaviour problems.

There are numerous reasons for this. Every dog is an individual with his or her own temperament and environment, both of which influence their interaction with you and the world. Poor behaviour may result from a number of factors, including:

- Poor breeding
- Lack of socialisation
- Boredom, due to lack of exercise or mental challenges
- Being left alone too long
- A change in living conditions
- Anxiety or insecurity
- Fear
- Being too spoiled
- Being badly treated

A Boston's bad behaviour may show itself in a number of different ways, such as:

- Constantly demanding attention
- Chewing or destructive behaviour
- Being possessive with food, toys or humans
- Jumping up
- Excessive barking
- Nipping or biting
- Soiling or urinating inside the house
- Growling
- Aggression towards other dogs or people

This chapter looks at some familiar behaviour problems. Although every dog is different, some common causes of unwanted behaviour are covered, along with tips to help improve the situation.

The best way to avoid poor behaviour is to put in the time early on to socialise and train your dog, and nip any potential problems in the bud. If you are taking in a rescue dog, you may need extra time and patience to help your new arrival unlearn some bad habits he has picked up along the way.

Ten Ways to Avoid Bad Behaviour

Different dogs have different reasons for exhibiting bad behaviour; there is no simple cure for everything. Your best chance of ensuring your dog does not become badly behaved is to start out on the right foot by following these simple guidelines:

1. **Buy from a good breeder** - They use their expertise to match suitable breeding couples, taking into account health, temperament and conformation.

2. **Start training early** - You can't start too soon. Like babies, Boston Terrier puppies have incredibly enquiring minds that can quickly absorb a lot of new information. You can start teaching your puppy to learn his own name as well as some simple commands as soon as you bring him home.

3. **Basic training should start with good manners** - E.g. housetraining, chew prevention, puppy biting and not jumping up, followed by simple obedience commands such as 'Sit', 'Come', 'Stay,' 'No,' and 'Down' or 'Off' and familiarisation with a collar and lead (leash) or harness. Adopt a gentle approach and keep training sessions short. Bostons can pick up on your mood and do not respond well to harsh words or treatment. Start with five or 10 minutes a couple of times a day and build up. Often, the way a dog responds to his or her environment is a result of owner training and management - or lack of it. Puppy classes or adult canine obedience classes are a great way to start, but make sure you do your homework afterwards. Spend a few minutes each day reinforcing what you have both learned in class - owners need training as well as dogs!

4. **Start socialisation right away** - We now realise the vital role that early socialisation plays in developing a well-rounded adult dog. It is essential to expose your dog to other people, places, animals and experiences as soon as possible. Give him a few days to settle in and then start - even if this means carrying him places until his vaccination schedule is complete. Lack of socialisation is one of the major causes of unwanted behaviour traits, and exposing your puppy to as many different things as possible goes a long way to help him to become a more stable, happy and trustworthy companion.

   IMPORTANT: Socialisation does not end at puppyhood. Bostons are social creatures that thrive on seeing, smelling and even licking. While the foundation for good behaviour is laid down during the first few months, good owners reinforce social skills and training throughout a dog's life. Many Bostons love to be the centre of attention and it's important that they learn when young that they are not the centre of the universe! Socialisation helps them to learn their place in that universe and to become comfortable with it.

5. **Reward your dog for good behaviour** - All training should be based on positive reinforcement; so praise and reward your dog when he does something good. Generally Boston Terriers are very food-motivated and keen to please their owners, and this speeds up the training process. The main aim of training is to build a good understanding between you and your dog.

6. **Ignore bad behaviour**, no matter how hard this may be. If, for example, your dog is chewing his way through your shoes, couch or toilet rolls, remove the object, give the dog an object or toy that he is allowed chew and then ignore him. This way, the dog knows what is and is not appropriate to chew. For some dogs, even negative attention is some attention. Or if he is constantly demanding your attention, ignore him.

Remove yourself from the room so he learns you give attention when **you** want to give it, not when he demands it. The more time you spend praising and rewarding good behaviour while ignoring bad behaviour, the more likely he is to respond to you. If your pup is a chewer - and most young Bostons are - make sure he has plenty of durable toys to keep him occupied; they can chew their way through flimsy toys in no time (and even swallow parts).

7. **Take the time to learn what sort of temperament your dog has.** Is she by nature a nervous or confident girl? What was she like as a puppy, did she rush forward or hang back? Did she fight to get upright when on her back or was she happy to lie there? Is she a couch potato or a ball of fire? Your puppy's temperament will affect her behaviour and how she responds to the world around her. A timid Boston Terrier will certainly not respond well to a loud approach on your part, whereas an energetic, strong-willed one will require more patience and exercise.

8. **Exercise and stimulation.** A lack of either is another major reason for dogs behaving badly. Regular daily exercise, indoor or outdoor games and toys are all ways of stopping your dog from becoming bored or frustrated.

9. **Learn to leave your dog.** Just as leaving your dog alone for too long can lead to problems, so can being with him 100% of the time. The dog becomes over-reliant on you and then gets stressed when you leave him. This is called *separation anxiety* and something that some Bostons can be susceptible to, like many breeds that thrive on human contact. When your dog is a puppy, or when he arrives at your house as an adult, start by leaving him for a few minutes every day and gradually build it up so that after a few weeks or months you can leave him for up to four hours.

10. **Love your dog - but don't spoil him,** however difficult that might be. You don't do him any favours by giving him too many treats, constantly responding to his demands for attention or allowing him to behave as he wants inside the house.

Separation Anxiety

It's not just Boston Terriers that experience separation anxiety - people do too. About 7% of adults and 4% of children suffer from this disorder. Typical symptoms for humans are:

- ❧ Distress at being separated from a loved one
- ❧ Fear of being left alone

Our canine companions aren't much different to us. When a dog leaves the litter, his owners become his new family or pack. **Separation anxiety is on the increase and recognised by behaviourists as the most common form of canine stress.**

PLEASE DON'T LEAVE ME!

Millions of dogs suffer from it - as much as 10% to 15% of the canine population. Both male and female Bostons can be susceptible because they are companion dogs and thrive on being with people. It is an exaggerated fear response caused by separation from their owner.

It can be equally distressing for the owner - I know because our dog, Max, suffers from this. He howls whenever we leave home without him. Fortunately his problem is only a mild one. If we return after only a short while, he's usually quiet. Although if we silently sneak back home and look, he's never asleep. Instead he's waiting by the patio door looking and listening for our return.

It can be embarrassing. Whenever I go to the Post Office, I tie him up outside and even though he can see me through the glass door, he still barks his head off - so loud that the people inside can't make themselves heard. Luckily the lady behind the counter is a dog lover and, despite the large **'GUIDE DOGS ONLY'** sign outside, she lets Max in. He promptly dashes through the door and sits down beside me, quiet as a mouse!

Tell-Tale Signs

Does your Boston Terrier do any of the following?

- Follow you from room to room whenever you're home?

- Get anxious or stressed when you're getting ready to leave the house?

- Howl, whine or bark when you go out, or when somebody leaves the room or car - even though other people are still with him?

- Tear up paper or chew cushions, couches or other things?

- Dig, chew, or scratch at doors and windows trying to join you?

- Foul or urinate inside the house, even though he is housetrained? (This **only** occurs when left alone)

- Exhibit restlessness - such as licking his coat excessively, pacing or circling?

- Greet you ecstatically every time you come home - even if you've only been out to empty the trash?

- Wait by the window or door until you return?

- Dislike spending time alone in the garden or yard?

If so, he or she may suffer from separation anxiety. Fortunately, in many cases this can be cured, or at least reduced. Dogs are pack animals and being alone is not a natural state for them. Puppies should be patiently taught to get used to isolation slowly and in a structured way if they are to be comfortable with it. A puppy will emotionally latch on to his new owner, who has taken the place of his mother and siblings.

He will want to follow you everywhere initially and, although you want to shower him with love and attention, it's important to leave your new puppy alone for short periods in the beginning to avoid him becoming totally dependent on you. In our case, I was working from home when we got Max. With hindsight, we should have regularly left him alone for short periods more often in the first few months.

Adopted dogs may be particularly susceptible to separation anxiety. They may have been abandoned once already and fear it happening again. And separation anxiety is not uncommon in elderly dogs. Pets age and, like humans, their senses - such as hearing and sight - deteriorate. They become more dependent on their owners and can then get more anxious when they are separated from them - or even out of view.

It may be very flattering and cute that your dog wants to be with you all the time, but insecurity and separation anxiety are forms of panic, which is distressing for your dog. If he shows any signs, help him to become more self-reliant and confident; he will be a happier dog. So what can you do if your dog is showing signs of canine separation anxiety? Every dog is different, but here are tried and tested techniques that have proved effective for some dogs.

Ten Tips to Reduce Separation Anxiety

1. Practise leaving your dog for short periods, starting with a minute or two and gradually lengthening the time you are out of sight.

2. Tire your Boston Terrier before you leave him alone. Take him for a walk or play a game before leaving.

3. Keep arrivals and departures low key and don't make a big fuss. For example, when I come home, Max is hysterically happy and runs round whimpering with a toy in his mouth. I make him sit and stay and then let him out into the garden without patting or acknowledging him. I pat him several minutes later. (He is improving).

4. Leave your dog a 'security blanket,' such as an old piece of clothing you have recently worn that still has your scent on it, or leave a radio (or TV) on - not too loud - in the room with the dog. Avoid a heavy rock station! If it will be dark when you return, leave a lamp on a timer.

5. Associate your departure with something good. As you leave, give your dog a rubber toy, like a Kong, filled with a tasty treat. This may take his mind off of your departure. (We've tried this with Max, but he sometimes refuses to touch the treat until we return home - and then wolfs it down).

6. If your dog is used to a crate, then crate him when you go out. Many dogs feel safe there, and being in a crate can also help to reduce destructiveness. Always take the collar off first. Pretend to leave the house, but listen for a few minutes. Never leave a dog in a crate all day.

   Warning: if your dog starts to show major signs of distress, remove him from the crate immediately as he may injure himself. You can also leave your dog in a pen, which gives him more freedom.

7. Structure and routine can help to reduce anxiety. Carry out regular activities, such as feeding and exercising, at the same time every day.

8. Dogs read body language very well; many Boston Terriers are intuitive. They may start to fret when they think you are going to leave them. One technique is to mimic your departure routine when you have no intention of leaving. So put your coat on, grab your car keys, go

out of the door and return a few seconds later. Do this randomly and regularly and it may help to reduce your dog's stress levels when you do it for real.

9. Some dogs show anxiety in new places, get him used to different environments and people.

10. Getting another dog to keep the first one company can help, but first ask yourself whether you have the time and money for two or more dogs. Can you afford double the bills?

 Breeder Pamela Preston added: "I have also found that taking a single drop of lavender essential oil, rubbing it in the palms of my hands, and then stroking the dog's neck and chest (where he cannot lick) will calm and ease anxiousness as well."

Sit-Stay-Down

Another technique for helping to reduce separation anxiety is to practise the common 'sit-stay' or 'down-stay' exercises using positive reinforcement. The goal is to be able to move briefly out of your dog's sight while he is in the 'stay' position. Through this your dog learns that he can remain calmly and happily in one place while you go about your normal daily life.

You have to progress slowly with this. Get your dog to sit and stay and then walk away from him for five seconds, then 10, 15 and so on, gradually increase the distance you move away from your dog. Reward your dog with a treat every time he stays calm.

Then move out of sight or out of the room for a few seconds, return and give him the treat if he is calm, gradually lengthen the time you are out of sight. If you're watching TV with your Boston Terrier snuggled up at your side and you get up for a snack, say 'Stay' and leave the room. When

you come back, give him a treat or praise him quietly. It is a good idea to practise these techniques after exercise or when your dog is a little sleepy (but not exhausted), as he is likely to be more relaxed.

Canine Separation Anxiety is not the result of disobedience or lack of training. It's a psychological condition; your dog feels anxious and insecure. Never punish your Boston Terrier for showing signs of separation anxiety - even if he has chewed your best shoes. This will only make him worse.

NEVER leave your dog unattended in a crate for long periods or if he is frantic to get out, it can cause physical or mental harm. If you're thinking of leaving an animal all day in a crate while you are out of the house, get a rabbit or a hamster - not a dog.

Excessive Barking

Boston Terriers, especially headstrong youngsters and adolescents, will behave in ways you might not want them to, until they learn that this type of unwanted behaviour doesn't earn any rewards. Bostons are not normally excessive barkers, but any dog can bark a lot, until he learns not to.

Some puppies start off by being noisy from the outset, while others hardly bark at all until they reach adolescence or adulthood. Our website gets emails from dog owners worried that their young dogs are not barking enough. However, we get many more from owners whose dogs are barking too much!

Some Bostons bark if someone comes to the door - and then welcome them like old friends - while others remain quiet. However, they do not make good guard dogs, as they want to be friends with everyone. There can be a number of reasons why your dog barks too much. He may be lonely, bored or demanding your attention. He may be possessive and over-protective and so barks (or howls) his head off when others are near you. Excessive, habitual barking is a problem that should be corrected early on before it gets out of hand and drives you and your neighbours nuts.

The problem often develops during adolescence or early adulthood as your dog becomes more confident. If your barking dog is an adolescent, he is probably still teething, so get him a good selection of hardy chew toys, such as a Nylabone, or stuff a Kong Toy with a treat or peanut butter to keep him occupied and gnawing. But give him these when he is quiet, not when he is barking, so he doesn't think they are rewards for barking.

Your behaviour can inadvertently encourage excessive barking. If your dog barks non-stop for several minutes and then you give him a treat to quieten him, he associates his barking with getting a nice treat. A better way to deal with it is to say in a firm voice: 'Shush' after he has made a few barks. When he stops, praise him and he will get the idea that what you want him to do is stop. The trick is to nip the bad behaviour in the bud before it becomes ingrained.

If he's barking to get your attention, ignore him. If that doesn't work, leave the room and don't allow him to follow you, so you deprive him of your attention. Do this as well if his barking and attention-seeking turns to nipping. Tell him to 'Stop' in a firm voice - not shouting - remove your hand or leg and, if necessary, leave the room.

As humans, we can use our voice in many different ways: to express happiness or anger, to scold, to shout a warning, and so on. Dogs are the same; different barks and noises give out different messages. **Listen** to your dog and try and get an understanding of 'Boston Terrier language'! Learn to recognise the difference between an alert bark, an excited bark, a demanding bark, a nervous, high pitched bark, an aggressive bark or a plain 'I'm barking 'coz I can bark' bark!

If your Boston is barking at other dogs, arm yourselves with lots of treats and spend time calming your dog down. When he starts to bark wildly at another dog - usually this happens when your dog is on a lead - distract him by letting him sniff a treat in your hand. Make your dog sit down and give a treat. Talk in a gentle manner and keep showing and giving your dog a treat for remaining calm and not barking. . (Keep in mind that the treats should be VERY small as too many treats throughout the day can make your dog fat, which is very unhealthy – another option is to reduce the amount of each meal to compensate for the extra treats during training). There are several videos on YouTube that show how to deal with this problem in the manner described here.

Pamela Preston added: "Use commands or words consistently, such that each command uses one word and one word only. So, for example, if you want a dog to get off the furniture or to get off you, I use the word 'Off' - rather than down - because 'Down' means lie down. If you use multiple words for a single command or action, it is confusing to the dog and takes longer to train him."

Speak and Shush!

Boston Terriers are not good guard dogs, they couldn't care less if somebody breaks in and walks off with the family silver - they are more likely to approach the burglar for a pat or a treat.

But if you do have a problem with excessive barking when somebody visits your home, the 'Speak and Shush' technique is one way of getting a dog to quieten down. If your Boston Terrier doesn't bark and you want him to, a slight variation of this method can also be used effectively to get him to bark as a way of alerting you that someone is at the door.

When your dog barks at an arrival at your house, gently praise him after the first few barks. If he persists, gently tell him that enough is enough. Like humans, some dogs can get carried away with the sound of their own voice, so try and discourage too much barking from the outset. The Speak and Shush technique teaches your dog or puppy to bark and be quiet on command.

Get a friend to stand outside your front door and say 'Speak' - or 'Woof' or 'Alert.' This is the cue for your accomplice to knock or ring the bell - don't worry if you both feel like idiots; it will be worth the embarrassment!

When your Boston barks, praise him profusely. You can even bark yourself in encouragement...After a few good barks, say 'Shush' and then dangle a tasty treat in front of his nose. He will stop barking as soon as he sniffs the treat, because it is physically impossible for a dog to sniff and woof at the same time.

Praise him again as he sniffs quietly and then give him the treat. Repeat this routine a few times a day and your dog will quickly learn to bark whenever the doorbell rings and you ask him to speak. Eventually your dog will bark after your request but BEFORE the doorbell rings, meaning he has learned to bark on command. Even better, he will learn to anticipate the likelihood of getting a treat following your 'Shush' request and will also be quiet on command.

With Speak and Shush training, progressively increase the length of required shush time before offering a treat - at first just a couple of seconds, then three, five, 10, 20, and so on. By alternating instructions to speak and shush, the dog is praised and rewarded for barking on request and also for stopping barking on request.

To get your Boston Terrier to bark on command, you need to have some treats at the ready, waiting for that rare bark. Wait until he barks - for whatever reason - then say 'Speak' or whatever word you want to use, praise him and give him a treat. At this stage, he won't know why he is receiving the treat. Keep praising him every time he barks and give him a treat.

After you've done this for several days, hold a treat in your hand in front of his face and say 'Speak.' Your Boston Terrier will probably still not know what to do, but will eventually get so frustrated at not getting the treat that he will bark. At which point, praise him and give him the treat. We trained our dog to do this quite quickly and now he barks his head off when anybody comes to the door or whenever we give him the command: 'Speak' (he's not quite so good on the Shush!).

Always use your encouraging 'teacher voice' when training; speak softly when instructing your dog, and reinforce the Shush with whisper-praise. The more softly you speak, the more your dog will be likely to pay attention. Boston Terriers respond very well to training when it is kept fun and short.

Aggression

Some breeds are more prone to aggression than others. Fortunately, this is a problem rarely seen in Boston Terriers. However, given a certain set of circumstances, any dog can growl, bark or even bite. As well as snarling, lunging, barking or biting, other physical signs of aggression include raised hackles (hair on the dog's back), top lip curled back to bare teeth, ears set high and tail raised.

All puppies bite; they explore the world with their noses and mouths. But it is important to train your cute little pup not to bite people, as he may cause injury if he continues as an adult. **And remember, any dog can bite** when under stress - even an affectionate Boston Terrier. Here are some different types of aggressive behaviour:

- Growling at you or other people

- Being possessive with toys

- Growling if you pet or show attention to another animal or human

- Growling or biting if you or another animal goes near his food

- Snarling, growling or lunging at other dogs while on the lead

- Marking territory by urinating inside the house

- Growling and chasing other small animals or cars or joggers and/or strangers

- Standing in your way, blocking your path

 As an owner, you should learn to recognise the difference between a warning growl from your dog and an aggressive growl. A warning growl is perfectly normal and acceptable - such as when another dog or child is playing too rough - whereas aggressiveness is not.

Boston Terriers love your attention, but they can also become possessive of you, their food or toys, which in itself can lead to bullying behaviour. Aggression may be caused by a lack of socialisation, an adolescent dog trying to see how far he can push the boundaries, nervousness, being spoiled by the owner, jealousy or even fear. This fear often comes from a bad experience the dog has suffered or from lack of proper socialisation. Another form of fear-aggression is when a dog becomes over-protective/possessive of his owner, which can lead to barking or lunging at other dogs or humans.

An owner's treatment of a dog can be a further reason. If the owner has been too harsh with the dog, such as shouting, using physical violence or reprimanding the dog too often, this in turn causes poor behaviour. Aggression breeds aggression. Dogs can also become hostile if they are consistently left alone, cooped up, under-fed or under-exercised. A bad experience with another dog or dogs can be a further cause. If your dog has been the victim of an attack by another dog or dogs, you may find that he starts to snarl at other dogs, particularly while on the lead. This is fuelled by fear and he needs to slowly regain his confidence and learn that not all dogs want to attack him, so don't overface him with too many dogs at once.

In fact, many dogs are more combative on the lead. This is because once on it, they cannot run away and escape - **fight or flight** - they know they can't run away, so they make themselves as frightening as possible. They therefore bark or growl to warn off the other dog or person.

Socialising your dog when young is vital. If your Boston Terrier **suddenly** shows a change of behaviour and becomes aggressive, have him checked out by a vet to rule out any underlying medical reason for the crankiness, such as toothache or earache. Raging hormones can be another reason for aggressive actions. Consider having your dog spayed or neutered if he or she has not already been done. A levelling-off of hormones can lead to a more laid-back dog. Another reason for dogs to display aggression is because they have been spoiled by their owners and have come to believe that the world revolves around them. Not spoiling your Boston and teaching him or her what is acceptable behaviour in the first place is the best preventative measure. Early training, especially during puppyhood and before he or she develops unwanted habits, can save a lot of trouble in the future.

Professional dog trainers employ a variety of techniques with a dog that has become aggressive. Firstly they will look at the causes and then they almost always use reward-based methods to try and cure aggressive or fearful dogs. **Counter conditioning** is a positive training technique used by many to help change a dog's aggressive behaviour towards other dogs. A typical example would be a dog that snarls, barks and lunges at other dogs while on the lead. It is the presence of other dogs that is triggering the dog to act in a fearful or anxious manner. Every time the dog sees another dog, he or she is given a tasty treat to counter the aggression - this is done when the dog looks at you and not when the dog is trying to lunge at the other dog. With enough steady repetition, the dog starts to associate the presence of other dogs with a tasty treat. Properly and patiently done, the final result is a dog that calmly looks to the owner for the treat whenever he or she sees another dog while on the lead.

 If you encounter a potentially aggressive situation, divert your dog's attention by turning his head away from the other dog and towards you, so that he cannot make eye contact with the other dog.

Aggression Towards People

Desensitisation is the most common method of treating aggression. It starts by breaking down the triggers for the behaviour one small step at a time. The aim is to get the dog to associate pleasant things with the trigger, e.g. people or a specific person whom he previously feared or regarded as a threat. This is done through using positive reinforcement, such as praise or treats. Successful desensitisation takes time, patience and knowledge. If your dog is starting to growl at people, there are a couple of techniques you can try to break him off this bad habit before it develops into full-blown biting.

One method is to arrange for some friends to come round, one at a time. When they arrive at your house, get them to scatter kibble on the floor in front of them so that your dog associates the arrival of people with tasty treats. As they move into the house, and your dog eats the kibble, praise your dog for being a good boy or girl. Manage your dog's environment. Don't over-face him.

Most Boston Terriers love children, but if yours is at all anxious around them, separate them or carefully supervise their time together in the beginning. Children typically react enthusiastically to dogs and some dogs may regard this as frightening or an invasion of their space.

Some dogs, particularly spoiled companion dogs, may show aggression towards the partner of the owner. Several people have contacted our website on this topic and it usually involves a partner or husband. Often the dog is jealous of the attention the owner is giving to the other person, or it could be that the dog feels threatened by him. This is not uncommon with small dogs. If this does arise, the key is for the partner to gradually gain the dog's trust of the dog. He or she should show that they are not a threat by speaking gently and giving treats for good behaviour. Avoid eye contact, as the dog may see this as a challenge. If the subject of the aggression lives in the house, then let this person give the dog his daily feeds. The way to a Boston's heart is often through his stomach!

A crate is also a useful tool for removing an aggressive dog from the situation for short periods of time, allowing him out gradually and praising good behaviour. As with any form of aggression, the key is to take steps to deal with it **immediately.**

Coprophagia (Eating Faeces)

It is hard for us to understand why a dog would want to eat his or any other animal's faeces (stools, poop or poo, call it what you will), but it happens. There is plenty of evidence from owners that some dogs love the stuff! Nobody fully understands why dogs do this, it may simply be an unpleasant behaviour trait or there could be an underlying reason. It is also thought that the inhumane and useless housetraining technique of 'sticking the dog's nose in it' when he has eliminated inside the house can also encourage coprophagia.

If your dog eats faeces from the cat litter tray - a problem several owners have also contacted us about - the first thing to do is to place the litter tray somewhere where your dog can't get to it - but the cat can. Perhaps on a shelf or put a guard around it, small enough for the cat to get through but not your Boston. Our dog sometimes eats cow or horse manure when out in the countryside. He usually stops when we tell him to and he hasn't suffered any after effects - so far. But again, this is a very unpleasant habit as the offending material sticks to the fur around his mouth and has to be cleaned off.

Think of it as a product recall!

Sometimes he rolls in the stuff and then has to be washed down. You may find that your Boston will roll in fox poop to cover the fox's scent. It's a good idea to avoid areas you know are frequented by foxes if you can, as their faeces can transmit several diseases, including Canine Parvovirus or lungworm - although neither of these should pose a serious health risk if your dog is up to date with vaccinations/titers and worming medication.

Vets have found that canine diets with low levels of fibre and high levels of starch increase the likelihood of coprophagia. If your dog is eating poop, first check his diet is nutritionally complete - is the first ingredient on the packet or tin corn (bad) or meat (good)? Does he look underweight?

Check you are feeding the right amount. If there is no underlying medical reason, you'll have to try and modify your dog's behaviour. Remove cat litter trays, clean up after your dog and don't allow him to eat his own faeces. If it's not there, he can't eat it. Don't reprimand for this behaviour.

A better technique is to distract your dog while he is in the act and then remove the offending material. Coprophagia is sometimes seen in pups aged between six months to a year and often disappears after this age.

According to one breeder: "When there is more than one dog, the poo-eating dog generally only eats the other dogs' poo and not their own. Poo-eaters are typically female; very few males. Some things that breeders have said that ways to stop your dog from eating faeces are:

1. Add crushed pineapple (or pineapple cottage cheese) to the dog's meals. Not much is needed, just a teaspoon or so, but you must give it to all the dogs you have, not just the offender.

2. Add meat tenderiser (just a shake or two) to the food.

3. There are also commercial supplements you can add to the meals available (such as 'Forbid')."

In extreme cases, when a dog exhibits persistent bad behaviour that the owner is unable to correct, a canine professional may be the answer. However, this is not inexpensive. Far better to spend time training and socialising your dog as soon as you get him or her.

Important: This chapter provides a general overview of canine behaviour. If your Boston Terrier exhibits persistent behavioural problems - particularly if he or she is aggressive towards people or other dogs - consider seeking help from a reputable canine behaviourist who uses positive reinforcement techniques, such as those listed the Association of Professional Dog Trainers at https://apdt.com or www.apdt.co.uk

9. Exercise and Training

One thing all dogs have in common – including every Boston Terrier ever born - is that they need daily exercise. Here is what daily exercise does for your dog - and you:

- ❧ It strengthens respiratory and circulatory systems
- ❧ Helps get oxygen to tissue cells
- ❧ Wards off obesity
- ❧ Keeps muscles toned and joints flexible
- ❧ Aids digestion
- ❧ Releases endorphins that trigger positive feelings
- ❧ Helps to keep dogs mentally stimulated and socialised

Whether you live in a small house, an apartment or on a farm, start regular exercise patterns early so that your dog gets used to his daily routine and gets chance to blow off steam and excess energy. Daily exercise helps to keep your dog content, healthy and free from disease.

How Much Exercise?

The Boston Terrier is regarded as a breed with 'medium' exercise requirements, but the amount of exercise that each individual dog needs varies tremendously. It depends on a number of issues, including natural energy levels, temperament, your living conditions, whether your dog is kept with other dogs and, importantly, what he gets used to. Boston Terriers tend to be flexible and, unless you have a particularly high spirited or high energy dog, yours should settle down to a regular routine.

However, be aware that Bostons are often bubbly, lively dogs. They are not often couch potatoes and, as a breed, generally have higher energy levels than other Bully breeds such as French Bulldogs, Bulldogs and most Pugs. They are also more muscular and sleeker in body and coat that those breeds.

All dogs need exercise. Don't make the mistake of thinking your Boston's easy going nature means

he doesn't need exercising; he does. For some that will mean a walk of maybe 20 or 30 minutes a couple of times a day. Some Bostons enjoy walking much further, while others are happy to run around the garden or yard or spend more time indoors burning off steam by playing games with you – and each other, if you have more than one dog. There is no one-rule-fits-all solution.

Often, a Boston will tell you that they do or do not want to go outdoors. When you take your dog for a walk, try and factor in some time off the lead (leash) playing games, which Bostons love more than walking on a lead. Some may have a stubborn streak and even lay down or stop dead when they have had enough of walking on the lead!

Make sure it is safe to let your dog run free, away from traffic and other hazards. And do not let him off the lead until he has learned the recall. There is also growing concern in both North America and the UK about attacks from loose dogs in public parks and dog parks. If you are at all worried about this, avoid public areas and find woodlands, fields, a beach or open countryside where your dog can exercise safely.

By the way, when we talk about 'exercise' it also means exercising your Boston's mind; i.e. mental stimulation. Play sessions and challenging games – or even canine competitions – are a great way of achieving this. Most Bostons absolutely love playing games with their humans.

NOTE: It should also be pointed out that there is a cultural difference between the USA and UK. Whereas most UK Boston owners expect to take their dogs out for a walk once or twice a day, many US owners have larger houses and 'yards' or plots of land and so it is more common for the dog(s) to play in the 'yard' and not be taken out for a daily walk – something which many UK owners would frown on!

The difference can be summed up in the way the two Kennel Clubs describe the Boston's exercise needs. The (UK) Kennel Club states "Up to an hour a day". While the AKC states: "Compact, easily trained, people-oriented, and always up for a walk, Boston Terriers are a perfect pet for urban life. Of course, whether their home is the city, suburbs, or country doesn't matter much to Bostons, as long as they can be the star of their family.

"If simply let out into the yard most Bostons will stand near the door waiting for their owners to join them, especially if they do not have canine companions with whom to play. The type of exercise provided for your Boston may depend on your own activity level and housing arrangements. Bostons love to run and play but should be contained in a fenced area or on a leash at all times." (Most UK Boston owners would disagree with keeping a dog on a lead at all times!)

The AKC continues: "If your Boston enjoys lots of activity and your home has a fenced yard, playing fetch, tossing flying discs and playing with a large ball are activities that provide plenty of exercise and allow him to use his energy. Some Bostons prefer less activity, but still need regular exercise. Daily walks are a good activity for these dogs. Bostons usually enjoy visits to the dog park where they can interact with other dogs and people and run off-leash. ..Many Bostons enjoy the activity and mental stimulation provided by agility or obedience classes."

...

Establish a Routine

Establish an exercise regime early in the dog's life. Dogs like routine. If possible, get him used to walks or play sessions at the same time every day, at a time that fits in with your daily routine. For example, let him out into the garden or yard first thing in the morning, then take him out after his morning feed, then perhaps again in the afternoon or when you come home from work, and a short toilet trip to the yard or garden again last thing at night.

Daily exercise could mean a walk, a jog, playtime, playing fetch or swimming. It is a common myth that no Bostons can swim. While some may be shy or frightened of water, others love it. If you do introduce your dog to water, do it gradually; don't throw him in the deep end of the swimming pool or off a jetty; that will frighten the life out of him and may even end in tragedy. **Never** force a dog into water if he doesn't want to go.

If your dog likes water, swimming is a great way to exercise; so much so that many veterinary clinics are now incorporating small water tanks, not only for remedial therapy, but also for canine recreation.

Remember that swimming is a lot more strenuous for a dog than walking or even running. Don't constantly throw that stick or ball into the water - your Boston Terrier will fetch it back until he drops - he wants to please you and it's great fun. He should exercise within his limits. Some owners whose dogs swim regularly buy a canine lifejacket for their Boston (pictured). And even if your dog doesn't want to swim, he may well enjoy dashing in and out of a paddling pool at home.

Whatever routine you decide on, ideally your dog should be getting walked at least once or more a day and you should stick to it. If you begin by going out three times a day and then suddenly stop, he will become restless and attention-seeking because he has been used to having more exercise. Conversely, don't expect a dog used to very little exercise to suddenly go on four-hour hikes; he will struggle.

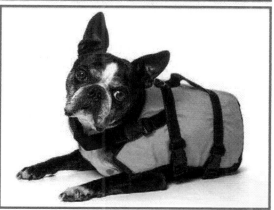

To those owners who say their dog is happy and getting enough exercise playing in the yard or garden, just show him his lead and see how he reacts. Is he excited at the prospect of leaving the house and going for a walk — or does he hide behind the sofa? For most dogs, nothing can compensate for interesting new scents, people, animals and places and, of course, playing games. Bostons are very playful with a great sense of fun.

Getting a Boston Terrier requires a big commitment from owners — you are looking at daily exercise for 10 or more years. Don't think that as your dog gets older, he won't need exercising. Older dogs need exercise to keep their body, joints and systems functioning properly. They need a less strenuous regime, but still enough to keep them physically and mentally active. Regular exercise can add months or even years to a dog's life.

Boston Terriers are very intelligent and, when it comes to training, they can learn quickly. But the downside is that this intelligence needs to be fed. Without sufficient mental challenges, your dog can become bored, unresponsive, destructive, attention-seeking and/or needy. You should factor in play sessions with your Boston — even old ones.

If your dog's behaviour deteriorates or he suddenly starts chewing things he's not supposed to, or barking a lot, the first question you should ask yourself is: "Is he getting enough exercise and mental stimulation?" Boredom (such as that caused by being alone and staring at four walls a lot) leads to bad behaviour and it's why some Bostons end up in rescue centres through no fault of their own. On the other hand, a Boston Terrier at the heart of the family getting plenty of daily exercise and play time is a happy dog and a companion second to none.

Exercising Puppies

There are strict guidelines to stick to with puppies, as it is important not to over-exercise young pups. Their bones and joints are still soft and developing and cannot tolerate a great deal of stress - so playing fetch for hours on end with your adolescent or baby Boston Terrier is not a good option. You'll end up with an injured dog and a pile of vet's bills.

Puppies, like babies, have different temperaments and some will be livelier and need more exercise than others. The golden rule is to start slowly and build it up. The worst danger is a combination of over-exercise and overweight when the puppy is growing. Do not take him out of the yard or garden until he has completed his vaccinations and it is safe to do so – unless you carry him around to start the socialisation process. Then start with short walks on the lead every day.

A good guideline is:

Five minutes of on-lead exercise per month of age

until the puppy is fully grown. That means a total of 15 minutes when he is three months (13 weeks old), 20 minutes when four months (17 weeks) old, and so on.

Slowly increase the time as he gets used to being exercised on the lead and this will gradually build up his muscles and stamina. Too much walking on pavements early on places stress on young joints. It's OK, however, for your young pup to have free run of your garden or yard (once you have plugged any gaps in the fence), provided it has a soft surface such as grass, not concrete. He will take things at his own pace and stop to sniff or rest. Once he is fully grown, your dog can go out for much longer walks on the lead. And when your little pup has grown into an adorable adult with a skeleton capable of carrying him through a long and healthy life, it will have been worth it.

A long, healthy life is best started slowly

Boston puppies have enquiring minds; get yours used to being outside the home environment and experiencing new situations as soon as he is clear after vaccinations. Start to teach him the recall so that you are soon confident enough to let him roam off the lead. Don't leave a puppy imprisoned in a crate for hours on end during the day. Boston Terriers are extremely sociable; they love being physically close to their humans.

Some days, you and your Boston may not feel like going out for a walk, but it is far better to stick to your routine and for the pair of you to winkle yourselves out of your nice, comfortable home and into the 'Great Outdoors.' A brisk walk is a great way of keeping both you and your dog fit and interested in life!

If you are considering getting two puppies, you might consider waiting until the first pup is older so he can teach the new arrival some good habits. Some people say that if you keep two puppies from the same litter, their first loyalty may be to each other, rather than to you as their owner. (Others say this is simply untrue!)

To recap: your Boston Terrier will get used to an exercise routine. If you over-stimulate and constantly exercise him as a puppy, he will think this is the norm. This is fine with your playful little pup, but may not be such an attractive prospect when your adult dog constantly needs and demands your attention and exercise a year or two later, or your work patterns change and you have not so much time to devote to him. The key is to start a routine that you can stick to.

Exercise Tips

🐾 Boston Terriers are intelligent and playful with a sense of fun. They need to use their brains. Make time to play indoor and outdoor games, such as Fetch or Hide-The-Toy, regularly with your dog - even elderly Bostons like to play

🐾 Don't strenuously exercise your dog straight after or within an hour of a meal as this can cause bloat, particularly if your dog gulps his food. Canine bloat causes gases to build up quickly in the stomach, blowing it up like a balloon, which cuts off normal blood circulation to and from the heart. The dog can go into shock and then cardiac arrest within hours. If you suspect this is happening, get to a vet immediately

🐾 If you want your dog to fetch a ball, don't fetch it back yourself or he will never learn to retrieve! Train him when he's young by giving him praise or a treat when he brings the ball or toy back to your feet

🐾 Do not throw a ball or toy repeatedly; your Boston will fetch it back again and again. Stop the activity after a while - no matter how much he begs you to throw it again. He may become over-tired, damage his joints, pull a muscle, strain his heart or otherwise injure himself. Keep an eye out for heavy panting and other signs of over-exertion or overheating

🐾 If you are playing Fetch, train your dog to release the ball for a treat. (The treat shouldn't be necessary once he has learned to drop the ball at your command). Some Bostons can get possessive - and even obsessive - with their toys or balls; do not get into a tug of war if he refuses to let go

🐾 Swimming is an exhausting exercise for a dog. Repeatedly retrieving an object from water may cause him to overstretch himself and get into difficulties

🐾 Some dogs, particularly adolescent ones, may try to push the boundaries when out walking on the lead. If your Boston Terrier stares at you and tries to pull you in another direction, ignore him. Do not return his stare, just continue along the way you want to go, not him!

🐾 Vary your exercise route – it will be more interesting for both of you

🐾 If exercising off-lead at night, buy a battery-operated flashing/illuminated collar for your dog

🐾 Exercise older dogs slowly and gently once they start to slow down - especially in cold weather when it is harder to get their bodies moving. Have a cool-down period at the end of the exercise to reduce stiffness and soreness - it helps to remove lactic acids

🐾 Invest in a set of doggie boots (pictured) if your dog spends a lot of time in snow. It can actually be quite painful when his legs and face become covered in snow and ice. Bathe your dog's legs in lukewarm water - **never** hot - at home afterwards to wash off snowballs and salt

❖ Make sure your dog has constant access to fresh water. Dogs can't sweat and Bostons can soon overheat. They need to drink water to cool down

Admittedly, when it is pouring down with rain, freezing cold (or scorching hot), the last thing you want to do is to venture outdoors with your dog. But the lows are more than compensated for by the highs. Exercise helps you to bond with your dog, keeps you both fit; you see different places and meet new companions - both canine and human. In short, it enhances both your lives.

....

Socialisation

Your adult dog's character will depend largely on two things. The first is his temperament, which he is born with, and presumably one of the reasons you have chosen a Boston Terrier. (The importance of picking a good breeder who selects breeding stock based on temperament, physical characteristics and health cannot be over-emphasised). The second factor is environment – or how you bring him up and treat him. In other words, it's a combination of **nature and nurture**. These two factors will form his character. And one absolutely essential aspect of nurture is **socialisation**.

Scientists have come to realise the importance that socialisation plays in a dog's life. We also now know that there is a fairly small window that is the optimum time for socialisation - and this is up to

the age of around four months (16 weeks) of age. Most young animals, including dogs, are naturally able to get used to their everyday environment - until they reach a certain age. When they reach this age, they become much more suspicious of things they haven't yet experienced. This is why it often takes longer to train an older dog. The age-specific natural development allows a puppy to get comfortable with the normal sights, sounds, people and animals that will be a part of his life. It ensures that he doesn't spend his life jumping in fright or growling at every blowing leaf or bird in song.

The suspicion that dogs develop in later puppyhood - after the critical window - also ensures that they do react with a healthy dose of caution to new things that could really be dangerous - Mother Nature is clever!

Socialisation means learning to be part of society, or integration. When we talk about socialising

puppies, it means helping them learn to be comfortable within a human society that includes many different types of people, environments, buildings, sights, noises, smells, other dogs and animals. Your Boston Terrier may already have a wonderful temperament, but he still needs socialising to avoid him thinking that the world is tiny and it revolves around him, which leads to unwanted adult behaviour traits.

The ultimate goal of socialisation is to have a happy, well-adjusted dog that you can take anywhere. Socialisation will give your dog confidence and teach him not to be afraid of new experiences. Ever seen a therapy or service dog in action and noticed how incredibly well-adjusted to life they are? This is no coincidence. These dogs have been extensively socialised and are ready and able to deal in a calm manner with whatever situation they encounter. They are relaxed and comfortable in their own skin - just like you want your own dog to be.

Start socialising your puppy as soon as you bring him home - waiting until he has had all his vaccinations is leaving it a bit late. Start by getting him familiar with the house and garden or yard, and, if it is safe, carry him out of the home environment - but do not put him on the floor or allow him to sniff other dogs until he's got the all-clear after his shots.

Regular socialisation should continue until your dog is around 18 months of age. After that, don't just forget about it. Socialisation isn't just for puppies; it should continue throughout your dog's life. As with any skill, if it is not practised, your dog will become less proficient at interacting with other people, animals, and environments.

Developing the Well-Rounded Adult Dog

Well-socialised puppies usually develop into safer, more relaxed and enjoyable adult dogs. This is because they're more comfortable in a wider variety of situations than poorly socialised canines. Dogs that have not been properly integrated are much more likely to display fear or aggression or develop obsessions or repetitive habits.

Boston Terriers that are relaxed about loud noises, other dogs, honking horns, cats, cyclists, veterinary examinations and crowds are easier to live with than dogs that find these situations challenging or frightening. Well socialised dogs also live more relaxed, peaceful and happy lives than dogs that are constantly stressed by their environment. Socialisation isn't an 'all or nothing' project. You can socialise a puppy a bit, a lot, or a whole lot. The wider the range of experiences you expose him to, the better his chances are of becoming a more relaxed adult.

Don't over-face your little puppy. Socialisation should never be forced, but approached systematically and in a manner that builds confidence and curious interaction. If your pup finds a new experience frightening, take a step back, introduce him to the scary situation much more gradually, and make a big effort to do something he loves during the situation or right afterwards.

For example, if your puppy seems to be frightened by noise and vehicles at a busy junction, a good method would be to go to a quiet road, sit with dog away from - but within sight of - the traffic. Every time he looks towards the traffic say 'YES!' and reward him with a treat. Keep each session short and if he is still stressed, you need to move further away. When your dog takes the food in a calm manner, he is becoming more relaxed and getting used to traffic sounds, so you can edge a bit nearer - but still just for short periods until he becomes totally relaxed.

Meeting Other Dogs

When you take your gorgeous and vulnerable little pup out to meet another dog(s) for the first few times, both of you are bound to be a little nervous. To start with, introduce your puppy to just one other dog — one that you know to be friendly, rather than taking him straight to the park where there are lots of dogs of all sizes racing around, which might frighten the life out of your timid little

darling. Always make the initial introductions on neutral ground, so as not to trigger territorial behaviour. You want your Boston Terrier to approach other dogs with confidence, not fear.

From the first meeting, help both dogs experience good things when they're in each other's presence. Let them sniff each other briefly, which is normal canine greeting behaviour. As they do, talk to them in a happy, friendly tone of voice. Don't allow them to sniff each other for too long as this may escalate to an aggressive response.

After a short time, get the attention of both dogs and give each a treat in return for obeying a simple command, such as 'Sit' or 'Stay.' Continue with the 'happy talk,' food rewards and simple commands.

Here are some signs of fear to look out for when your dog interacts with other canines:

- Running away
- Freezing on the spot
- Tail lifted in the air
- Ears high on the head
- Frantic/nervous behaviour, such as excessive sniffing, drinking or playing with a toy frenetically
- A lowered body stance or crouching
- Lying on his back with his paws in the air – this is a submissive gesture
- Lowering of the head, or turning the head away
- Lips pulled back baring teeth and/or growling
- Hair raised on his back (hackles)

Some of these responses are normal. A pup may well crouch on the ground or roll on to his back to show other dogs he is not a threat. Try not to be over-protective; your pup has to learn how to interact with other dogs. But if the situation looks like escalating into something more aggressive, calmly distract the dogs or remove your puppy – don't shout or shriek. The dogs will pick up on your fear and this in itself could trigger an unpleasant situation.

Another sign to look out for is eyeballing. In the canine world, staring a dog in the eyes is a challenge and may trigger an aggressive response. This is more relevant to adult dogs, as a young pup will soon be put in his place by bigger or older dogs; it is how they learn. The rule of thumb is to keep a close eye on your pup's reaction to whatever you expose him to so that you can tone things down if he seems at all frightened.

Always follow up a socialisation experience with praise, petting, a fun game or a special treat. One positive sign from a dog is the play bow (pictured), when he goes down on to his front elbows but keeps his backside up in the air. This is a sign that he is feeling friendly towards the other dog and wants to play.

Although Boston Terriers are not naturally aggressive dogs, aggression is often grounded in fear, and a dog that mixes easily is less likely to be aggressive. Similarly, without frequent and new experiences, some dogs can become timid and nervous when introduced to new experiences – particularly if they are at home all day and not getting out and about to mingle with other people and animals.

Take your new dog everywhere you can. You want him to feel relaxed and calm in any situation, even noisy and crowded ones. Take treats with you and praise him when he reacts calmly to new situations. Once he has settled into your home, introduce him to your friends and teach him not to jump up. If you have young children, it is not only the dog that needs socialising! Youngsters also need training on how to act around dogs, so both parties learn to respect the other.

One excellent method of getting your new puppy to meet other dogs in a safe environment is to join a puppy or kindergarten class. Ask around locally if any classes are being run. Some vets and dog trainers run puppy classes for very junior pups that have had all their vaccinations. These help pups get used to other dogs of similar age.

Breeders on Exercise and Socialisation

This is what breeders have to say on exercise and socialisation:

Jo Dalton, of Mumuland Boston Terriers, Lincolnshire, England: "An important part of a dog's life is exercise. In fact, exercise times and feeding times are often the most exciting parts of a dog's day, and your puppy will grow to keenly anticipate them - often getting very excited as soon as the harness and lead come out.

"Puppies need much less exercise than fully-grown dogs. If you over-exercise a growing puppy, you can quickly overtire it and, more importantly, damage its developing joints, which may cause early arthritis or which can be one of the contributing factors to 'slipping patella' issues.

"At three to four months of age - and after vaccinations - is the time when you can now start adventuring out with your puppy properly. Don't be alarmed if your puppy refuses to walk on its harness and lead - everything can seem very overwhelming to a pup that has only been in the garden or carried everywhere. Gradually your pup will work out that walks are fun and become accustomed to the noise and new smells. Treats and praise work wonders. If you have a friend who has an older dog that you could walk with a few times, this will encourage your pup to forget about its fears and concentrate on enjoying spending time with the other dog. It will naturally want to follow and be involved in what the other dog is doing.

"Walks still need to be kept short at this age, so around 10 to 15 minutes maximum. Start off at 10 minutes and as you near four months of age, you can start doing 15-minute walks. Ideally around two walks a day is all that is needed, so one first thing in the morning and one in the afternoon is ideal. You can then increase your duration of walks with your pup's age.

"It is important that puppies and dogs go out for exercise every day in a safe and secure area, or they may become frustrated. Time spent in the garden (however large) is no substitute for exploring new environments, and socialising with other dogs. It should go without saying that before letting your puppy off the lead in a public park, make sure it is trained to recall, so that you are confident your puppy will return to you when called.

"Bostons are naturally sociable, but it is still very important to introduce things at a young age, so I always tell new owners get them out and about and get them to experience as much as possible in the time before they are fully vaccinated and, of course, afterwards. I also use a socialisation noise CD from three weeks of age and take my pups for trips in the car and do as much socialisation as possible before they leave us - they meet older dogs, puppies of a similar age, children and people old and young."

Bill and Anne Connor, of Ringablok Boston Terriers, Carmarthen, Wales, have been breeding Bulldogs for 42 years and Bostons for 11: "Our Boston Terriers like a good walk and running around the garden, we also visit the beach. We give them as much socialisation as possible; the earlier the better, and we start as early as five weeks old. We find Boston Terriers to be very affectionate towards their owners and if trained from a young age to be left for a short time, they do not develop anxiety separation issues. Boston Terriers are very intelligent, but they can be naughty as pups!" The Connors recommend a fence height of at least four feet around the garden or yard to contain Bostons.

Gwion Williams, of Wilarjan Boston Terriers, Bangor, North Wales: "We walk our dogs for 30 minutes per day split into two 15-minute walks when they are under eight months. The reason for this is because their bones are still maturing and you don't want to over exercise at a young age. All our dogs have access to the garden to play and they absolutely love it. Adult Boston Terriers love long walks when the weather is not too hot for them - especially forests and beaches.

"Good socialisation starts very early. Handling puppies from a young age, daily household noises, children playing with the puppies, showing the puppies new things...the list is endless for socialising puppies by a good breeder. The best way to socialise a puppy is to introduce new things every day."

Susan Maxwell, of Maximum Companion Boston Terriers, California, has been breeding Bostons for 20 years: "I feel that the Boston Terrier can handle the 'exercise load' better than Pugs and Frenchies who tend to have a bigger weight load. Frenchies and Pugs are built heavier in the chest and shorter in the leg, which makes exercise for them a shorter duration. I see more Bostons in agility and very few Pugs and Frenchies, if any.

"Socialization begins from Day One as we handle all pups, getting them used to our hands, etc. We pick them all up daily and when their eyes and ears open, they get used to us and all sounds. By four to five weeks they are ready to walk on non-slippery surfaces and they are exposed to grandkids etc.! By the time they are six weeks, they are running on tile and almost ready to go outside on the patio and sand area we have made for puppies. The sand is excellent for working their pasterns (areas above the dog's feet). They get their first neonatal shot at five weeks. We go to a lot of dog shows and are exposed to a lot of dogs, so we use 'NeoPar' puppy shots."

Pamela Preston, of ChriMaso Boston Terriers, California: "I live on acreage, so my dogs have plenty of room to run and play every day - and they do. We go for a walk and play fetch and that's about it.

They do love to chase the wildlife - deer, rabbits, birds, skunks, gophers, etc. - off our property and that keeps them pretty fit and trim.

"Bostons are generally social anyway, so I would say start socializing them as soon as you feel it is safe. I have family members and friends come visit my puppies and take my puppies to visit them. I also take them for car rides so they can get used to the motion and not get car sick. I'll take them to the post office and to Starbucks as well."

Obedience Training

Training a young dog is like bringing up a child. Put in the effort early on to teach them the guidelines and you will be rewarded with a well-adjusted, sociable, individual who will be a joy to live with. Boston Terriers are intelligent, incredibly eager to please and love being with their humans. All of this adds up to one of the easiest breeds of all to train - but only if you are prepared to put in the time too.

Boston Terriers make such natural companions for humans - after all, that is what they are bred for – that it becomes all too easy to treat them like a human and spoil them. Let yours behave exactly however he wants and you may well finish up with a wilful, attention-seeking adult. The secret of successfully training Boston Terriers can be summed up in a few words:

Praise, Rewards, Patience and Consistency

Praise and treats are the two prime motivators; training should ALWAYS be reward-based, never punishment-based. Boston Terriers are sensitive; many owners would even say they have empathy (the ability to understand the feelings of others) and they do not respond well to heavy-handed training methods. They are also intelligent, making it easy for them to pick up comands - provided you make it clear exactly what you want them to do; don't give conflicting signals.

Psychologist and renowned canine expert Dr Stanley Coren has written a book called *'The Intelligence of Dogs'* in which he ranks 140 breeds. The rankings are from one to 79 – as some breeds share the same scoring. He used 'understanding of new commands' and 'obey first command' as his standards of intelligence, surveying dog trainers to compile the list. He says there are three types of dog intelligence:

- ❧ Adaptive Intelligence (learning and problem-solving ability). This is specific to the individual animal and is measured by canine IQ tests

- ❧ Instinctive Intelligence. This is specific to the individual animal and is measured by canine IQ tests
- ❧ Working/Obedience Intelligence. This is breed-dependent

The brainboxes of the canine world are the 10 breeds ranked in the 'Brightest Dogs' section of his list. All dogs in this class:

- ❧ Understand New Commands with Fewer than Five Repetitions
- ❧ Obey a First Command 95% of the Time or Better

It will come as no surprise to anyone who has ever been into the countryside and seen sheep being worked by a farmer and his right-hand man (his dog) to learn that the Border Collie is the most intelligent of all dogs. The second smartest dog is the Poodle, followed by the German Shepherd Dog and Golden Retriever.

Fans of Boston Terriers may be disappointed to learn that, along with the Akita, their beloved breed is languishing at Number 54 in the table (98th out of 140) at the very bottom of the group described as 'Average Working/Obedience Intelligence, Understanding of New Commands: 25 to 40 repetitions. Obey First Command: 50% of the time or better.' The full list can be seen here: http://petrix.com/dogint/intelligence.html

By the author's own admission, the drawback of this rating scale is that it is heavily weighted towards obedience-related behavioural traits, which are often found in working dogs, rather than understanding or creativity (found in hunting dogs). As a result, some dogs, such as the Bully breeds – like Boston Terriers, Bulldogs, Mastiffs, Bull Terriers, Pugs, French Bulldogs, etc. - are ranked quite low on the list, due to their independent or stubborn nature.

However, as far as Boston Terriers are concerned, it's true to say that you are starting out with a puppy that has the intelligence to pick up new commands quickly and he really wants to please you. You just have to convince him that HE WANTS TO OBEY your commands as good things will happen when he does! Three golden rules when training a Boston are:

1. Training must be reward based, not punishment based.
2. Keep sessions short or your dog will get bored.
3. Keep sessions fun, give your Boston a challenge and a chance to shine.

You might also consider enlisting the help of a professional trainer - although that option may not be within the budget of many new owners. If it is, then choose a trainer registered with the Association of Professional Dog Trainers (APDT); you can find a list for all countries here: https://apdt.com or www.apdt.co.uk Make sure the one you choose uses positive reward-based training methods, as the old alpha-dominance theories have been discredited.

When you train your dog, it should never be a battle of wills between you and him; it should be a positive learning experience for you both. Bawling at the top of your voice or smacking should play no part in training.

If you have a high spirited, high energy Boston, you have to use your brain to think of ways that will make training challenging for your dog and to persuade him that what you want him to do is actually what **he** wants to do. He will come to realise that it's in his own interest to do what you ask of him, i.e. he receives verbal praise, pats, treats, or play time, etc.

Establishing the natural order of things is not something forced on a dog through shouting or violence; it is brought about by mutual consent and good training. Like most dogs, Boston Terriers are happiest and behave best when they know and are comfortable with their place in the household. They may push the boundaries, especially as youngsters, but stick to your rules and everything will run much smoother. All of this is done with positive techniques.

Sometimes your dog's concentration will lapse, particularly with a pup or adolescent dog. Keep training short and fun. If you have adopted an older dog, you can still train him, but it will take a little longer to get rid of bad habits and instil good manners. Patience and persistence are the keys here.

Common Training Questions

1. **At what age can I start training my puppy?** As soon as he arrives home. Begin with a few minutes a day.

2. **How important is socialisation for Boston Terriers?** Extremely, this can't be emphasised enough. Your puppy's breeder should have already begun this process with the litter and then it's up to you to keep it going when the pup arrives home. Up to 16 weeks' old puppies can absorb a great deal of information, but they are also vulnerable to bad experiences. Pups that are not properly exposed to different people and other animals can find them very frightening when they do finally encounter them when older. They may react by cowering, barking, growling, or biting. Food possession can also become an issue with some dogs. But if they have positive experiences with people and animals before they turn 16 weeks of age, they are less likely to be afraid or try to establish dominance later. Don't just leave your dog at home in the early days, take him out and about with you, get him used to new people, places and noises. Puppies that miss out on being socialised can develop behavioural issues as adults.

3. **What challenges does training involve?** Chewing is an issue with most Boston puppies; mouthing and nipping are natural behaviours for young dogs, it's one of the ways in which they explore the world. So train your puppy only to chew the things you give him – don't give him your footwear, an old piece of carpet or anything that resembles anything you

don't want him to chew. Buy purpose-made long-lasting chew toys. Jumping up can also be an issue with lively youngsters. They love everybody and are so enthusiastic about life, so it's often a natural reaction when they see somebody.

11 Tips for Training Your Boston Terrier

1. **Start training and socialising early.** Like babies, puppies learn quickly and it's this learned behaviour that stays with them through adult life. Old dogs can be taught new tricks, but it's a lot harder to unlearn bad habits. It's best to start training with a clean slate. Puppy training should start with a few minutes a day from Day One when you bring him home.

2. **Your voice is a very important training tool.** Your dog has to learn to understand your language and you have to understand him. Commands should be issued in a calm, authoritative voice - not shouted. Praise should be given in a happy, encouraging voice, accompanied by stroking or patting. If your dog has done something wrong, use a stern voice, not a harsh shriek. This applies even if your dog is unresponsive at the beginning.

3. **Avoid giving your dog commands you know you can't enforce.** Every time you give a command that you don't enforce, he learns that commands are optional. And one command equals one response. Give your dog only one command - twice maximum - then gently enforce it. Repeating commands or nagging will make your Boston Terrier tune out. They also teach him that the first few commands are a bluff. Telling your dog to 'SIT, SIT, SIT, SIT!!!' is neither efficient nor effective. Give your dog a single 'SIT' command, gently place him in the sitting position and then praise him.

4. **Train your dog gently and humanely.** Boston Terriers do not respond well to being shouted at or hit. Keep training sessions short and upbeat so the whole experience is enjoyable for you and him. If obedience training is a bit of a bore, pep things up a bit by 'play training'. Use constructive, non-adversarial games such as Go Find, Hide and Seek or Fetch.

5. **Begin your training around the house and garden or yard.** How well your dog responds to you at home affects his behaviour away from the home as well. If he doesn't respond well at home, he certainly won't respond any better when he's out and about where there are 101 distractions, such as food scraps, other dogs, people, cats, interesting scents, etc.

6. **Mealtimes are a great time to start training your dog.** Teach him to sit and stay at dinnertime and breakfast, rather than simply putting the dish down and allowing him to dash over immediately. He might not know what you mean in the beginning, so gently place him into the sitting position while you say 'Sit.' Then place a hand on his chest during the 'Stay' command - gradually letting go - and then give him the command to eat his dinner, followed by encouraging praise - he'll soon get the idea.

7. **Use your dog's name often and in a positive manner.** When you bring your pup or new dog home, start using his name often so he gets used to the sound of it. He won't know what it means in the beginning, but it won't take him long to realise you're talking to him. DON'T use his name when reprimanding, warning or punishing. He should trust that when he hears his name, good things happen. His name should always be a word he responds to with enthusiasm, never hesitancy or fear. Use the words 'No' or 'Bad Boy/Girl' in a stern - not shouted - voice instead. Some parents prefer not to use the word 'No' with their dog, as they use it often around the human youngsters and it is likely to confuse the young canine! You

can make a sound like 'ACK!' instead. Say it sharply and the dog should stop whatever it is he is doing wrong.

8. **Have a 'No' sound.** When a puppy is corrected by his mother – for example if he bites her with his sharp baby teeth – she growls at him to warn him not to do it again. When your puppy makes a mistake, make a short sharp sound like 'Ack!' to tell the puppy not to do that again. This works surprisingly well with a sensitive Boston.

9. **Timing is critical to successful training.** When your puppy does something right, praise him immediately. If you wait more than a few seconds he will have no idea what he has done right. Similarly, when he does something wrong, correct him straight away. For example, if he eliminates in the house, don't shout and certainly don't rub his nose in it; this will only make things worse. If you catch him in the act, use your 'No' or 'Ack' sound and immediately carry him out of the house. Then use the toilet command (whichever word you have chosen) and praise your pup or give him a treat when he performs. If your pup is constantly eliminating indoors, you are not keeping a close enough eye on him.

10. **Don't give your dog lots of attention (even negative attention) when he misbehaves.** Boston Terriers love their owners' attention. If he gets lots of attention when he jumps up on you, his bad behaviour is being reinforced. If he jumps up, push him away, use the command 'No' or 'Down' and then ignore him. Give your dog attention when YOU want to – not when he wants it. If he starts jumping up, nudging you constantly or barking to demand your attention, ignore him. Don't give in to his demands. Wait a while and pat him when you want **after** he has stopped demanding your attention.

11. **Start as you mean to go on.** In other words, in terms of rules and training, treat your cute little Boston pup as though he were fully grown; introduce the rules you want him to live by as an adult. If you don't want your dog to take over your couch or bed or jump up at people when he is an adult, don't allow him to do it when he is small. You can't have one set of rules for a pup and one set for a fully grown dog; he won't understand. Also, make sure that everybody in the household sticks to the same set of rules. Your dog will never learn if one person lets him jump on the couch and another person doesn't.

Remember this simple phrase: TREATS, NOT THREATS.

··

Teaching Basic Commands

Sit

Teaching the Sit command to your Boston is relatively easy. Teaching a young pup to sit still is a bit more difficult! In the beginning you may want to put your protégé on a lead to hold his attention.

1. Stand facing each other and hold a treat between your thumb and fingers just an inch or so above his head. Don't let your fingers and the treat get any further away or you might have trouble getting him to move his body into a sitting position. In fact, if your dog jumps up when you try to guide him into the Sit, you're probably holding your hand too far away from his nose. If your dog backs up, you can practise with a wall behind him. NOTE: It's rather pointless paying for a high quality, possibly hypoallergenic dog food and then filling him with trashy treats. Buy premium treats with natural ingredients that won't cause allergies, or use natural meat, fish or poultry titbits.

2. As he reaches up to sniff it, move the treat upwards and back over the dog towards his tail at the same time as saying 'Sit'. Most dogs will track the treat with their eyes and follow it with their noses, causing their snouts to point straight up.

3. As his head moves up toward the treat, his rear end should automatically go down towards the floor. TaDa! (drum roll!).

4. As soon as he sits, say 'Yes!' give him the treat and tell your dog(s) he's a good boy or girl. Stroke and praise him for as long as he stays in the sitting position. If he jumps up on his back legs and paws you while you are moving the treat, be patient and start all over again. Another method is to put one hand on his chest and with your other hand, gently push down on his rear end until he is sitting, while saying 'Sit'. Give him a treat and praise, even though you have made him do it; he will eventually associate the position with the word 'sit'.

5. Once your dog catches on, leave the treat in your pocket (or have it in your other hand). Repeat the sequence, but this time your dog will just follow your empty hand. Say 'Sit' and bring your empty hand in front of your dog's nose, holding your fingers as if you had a treat. Move your hand exactly as you did when you held the treat.

6. When your dog sits, say 'Yes!' and then give him a treat from your other hand or your pocket.

7. Gradually lessen the amount of movement with your hand. First, say 'Sit' then hold your hand eight to 10 inches above your dog's face and wait a moment. Most likely, he will sit. If he doesn't, help him by moving your hand back over his head, like you did before, but make a smaller movement this time. Then try again. Your goal is to eventually just say 'Sit' without having to move or extend your hand at all.

Once your dog reliably sits on cue, you can ask him to sit whenever you meet and talk to people (admittedly, it may not work, but it might calm him down a bit). The key is anticipation. Give your Boston the cue before he gets too excited to hear you and before he starts jumping up on the person just arrived. Generously reward your dog the instant he sits. Say 'Yes' and give him treats every few seconds while he holds the Sit.

Whenever possible, ask the person you're greeting to help you out by walking away if your dog gets up from the sit and lunges or jumps towards him or her. With many consistent repetitions of this exercise, your dog will learn that lunging or jumping makes people go away, and polite sitting makes them stay and give him attention.

'Sit' is a useful command and can be used in a number of different situations. For example, when you are putting his lead on, while you are preparing his meal, when he returned the ball you have just thrown, when he is jumping up, demanding attention or getting over-excited.

Come

This is another basic command that you can teach right from the beginning. Teaching your dog to come to you when you call (known as the recall) is an important lesson. A dog that responds quickly and consistently can enjoy freedoms that other dogs cannot. Although you might spend more time teaching this command to your Boston than any other, the benefits make it well worth the investment. By the way, 'Come' or a similar word is better than 'Here' if you intend using the 'Heel' command, as these words sound too similar.

No matter how much effort you put into training, no dog is ever going to be 100% reliable at coming when called and especially not a strong-willed Boston or one with a high prey drive. Dogs are not machines. They're like people in that they have their good days and their bad days. Sometimes they don't hear you call, sometimes they're paying attention to something else, sometimes they misunderstand what you want, and sometimes a Boston simply decides that he would rather do something else.

Whether you're teaching a young puppy or an older dog, the first step is always to establish that coming to you is the best thing he can do. Any time your dog comes to you whether you've called him or not, acknowledge that you appreciate it. You can do this with smiles, praise, affection, play or treats. This consistent reinforcement ensures that your dog will continue to 'check in' with you frequently.

1. Say your dog's name followed by the command **'Come!'** in an enthusiastic voice. You'll usually be more successful if you walk or run away from him while you call. Dogs find it hard to resist chasing after a running person, especially their owner.

2. He should run towards you. NOTE: Dogs tend to tune us out if we talk to them all the time. Whether you're training or out for an off-lead walk, refrain from constantly chattering to your dog - no matter how much of a brilliant conversationalist you are! If you're quiet much of the time, he is more likely to pay attention when you call him. When he does, praise him and maybe give him a treat.

3. Often, especially outdoors, a dog will start off running towards you but then get distracted and head off in another direction. Pre-empt this situation by praising your dog and cheering him on when he starts to

come to you and before he has a chance to get distracted. Your praise will keep him focused so that he'll be more likely to come all the way to you. If he stops or turns away, you can give him feedback by saying 'Oh-oh!' or 'Hey!' in a different tone of voice (displeased or unpleasantly surprised). When he looks at you again, smile, call him and praise him as he approaches you.

Progress your dog's training in baby steps. If he's learned to come when called in your kitchen, you can't expect him to be able to do it straight away at the park, at the beach or in the woods when he's surrounded by distractions. When you first try this outdoors, make sure there's no one around to distract your dog. It's a good idea to consider using a long training lead - or to do the training within a safe, fenced area. Only when your dog has mastered the recall in a number of locations and in the face of various distractions can you expect him to come to you regularly.

Down

There are a number of different ways to teach this command. It is one that does not come naturally to a young pup, so it may take a little while for him to master. Don't make it a battle of wills and, although you may gently push him down, don't physically force him down against his will. This will be seen as you asserting dominance in an aggressive manner and your Boston will not like it, nor will he respond well.

1. Give the **Sit** command.

2. When your dog sits, don't give him the treat immediately, keep it in your closed hand. Slowly move your hand straight down toward the floor, between his front legs. As your dog's nose follows the treat, just like a magnet, his head will bend all the way down to the floor. When the treat is on the floor between your dog's paws, start to move it away from him, like you're drawing a line along the floor. (The entire luring motion forms an L-shape).

3. At the same time say '**Down**' in a firm manner.

4. To continue to follow the treat, your dog will probably ease himself into the Down position. The instant his elbows touch the floor, say 'Yes!' and immediately let him eat the treat. If your dog doesn't automatically stand up after eating the treat, just move a step or two away to encourage him to move out of the Down position. Then repeat the sequence above several times. Aim for two short sessions of five minutes a day.

If it doesn't work, try using a different treat. And if your dog's back end pops up when you try to lure him into a Down, quickly snatch the treat away. Then immediately ask your dog to sit and try again. It may help to let your dog nibble on the treat as you move it toward the floor. If you've tried to lure your dog into a Down but he still seems confused or reluctant, try this trick:

❧ Sit down on the floor with your legs straight out in front of you. Your dog should be at your side. Keeping your legs together and your feet on the floor, bend your knees to make a 'tent shape'

❧ Hold a treat right in front of your dog's nose. As he licks and sniffs the treat, slowly move it down to the floor and then underneath your legs. Continue to lure him until he has to crouch down to keep following the treat

❧ The instant his belly touches the floor, say Yes! and let him eat the treat. If your dog seems nervous about following the treat under your legs, make a trail of treats for him to eat along the way

Some dogs find it easier to follow a treat into the Down from a standing position.

- Hold the treat right in front of your dog's nose, and then slowly move it straight down to the floor, right between his front paws. His nose will follow the treat

- If you let him lick the treat as you continue to hold it still on the floor, your dog will probably plop into the Down position

- The moment he does, say 'Yes!' and let him eat the treat

Many dogs are reluctant to lie on a cold floor. It may be easier to teach yours to lie down on a carpet or warm surface. The next step is to introduce a hand signal. You'll still reward him with treats, though, so keep them nearby or hidden behind your back.

- Start with your dog in a Sit

- Say 'Down'

- Without a treat in your fingers, use the same hand motion you did before

- As soon as your dog's elbows touch the floor, say 'Yes!' and immediately get a treat to give him

- Clap your hands or take a few steps away to encourage him to stand up. Then repeat the sequence from the beginning several times for a week or two

 Even though you're not using a treat to lure your dog into position, you should still give him a reward when he lies down. You want your dog to learn that he doesn't have to see a treat to get one.

When your dog readily lies down as soon as you say the cue and then use your new hand signal, you're ready for the next step. You probably don't want to keep bending all the way down to the floor to make your Boston lie down. To make things more convenient, you can gradually shrink the signal so that it becomes a smaller movement. To make sure your dog continues to understand what you want him to do, you'll need to progress slowly.

Repeat the hand signal, but instead of guiding your dog into the Down by moving your hand all the way to the floor, move it almost all the way down. Stop moving your hand when it's an inch or two above the floor. Practice the Down exercise for a day or two, using this slightly smaller hand signal. Then you can make your movement an inch or two smaller, stopping your hand three or four inches above the floor.

After practising for another couple of days, you can shrink the signal again. As you continue to gradually stop your hand signal farther and farther from the floor, you'll bend over less and less. Eventually, you won't have to bend over at all. You'll be able to stand up straight, say 'Down,' and then just point to the floor.

Your next job is a bit harder - it's to practise your dog's new skill in many different situations and locations so that he can lie down whenever and wherever you ask him to. Slowly increase the level of distraction, for example, first practise in calm places, like different rooms in your house or in your garden, when there's no one else around. Then increase the distractions, practise at home when family members are moving around, on walks and then at friends' houses, too.

Stay

This is a very useful command, but it's not so easy to teach a lively and distracted young Boston pup to stay still for any length of time.

Here is a simple method to get your dog to stay; if you are training a young dog, don't ask him to stay for more than a few seconds at the beginning.

1. This requires some concentration from your dog, so pick a time when he's relaxed and well exercised or just after a game or mealtimes, especially if training a youngster. Start with your dog in the position you want him to hold, either the Sit or Down position.

2. Command your dog to sit or lie down, but instead of giving a treat as soon as he hits the floor, hold off for one second. Then say 'Yes!' in an enthusiastic voice and give him a treat. If your dog tends to bounce up again instantly, have two treats ready. Feed one right away, before he has time to move; then say 'Yes!' and feed the second treat.

3. You need a release word or phrase. It might be 'Free!' or 'Here!' or a word that you only use to release your dog from this command. Once you've given the treat, immediately give your release cue and encourage your dog to get up. Then repeat the exercise several times in one training session, gradually wait a tiny bit longer before releasing the treat. (You can delay the first treat for a moment if your dog bounces up).

4. A common mistake is to hold the treat high and then give the reward slowly. As your dog doesn't know the command yet, he sees the treat coming and gets up to meet the food. Instead, bring the treat toward your dog quickly - the best place to deliver it is right between his front paws. If you're working on a Sit-Stay, give the treat at chest height.

5. When your dog can stay for several seconds, start to add a little distance. At first, you'll walk backwards, because your Boston Terrier is more likely to get up to follow you if you turn away from him. Take one single step away, then step back towards your dog and say 'Yes!' and give the treat. Give him the signal to get up immediately, even if five seconds haven't passed. The stay gets harder for your dog depending on how long it is, how far away you are, and what else is going on around him.

6. Trainer shorthand is **'distance, duration, distraction.'** For best success in teaching a stay, work on one factor at a time. Whenever you make one factor more difficult, such as distance, ease up on the others at first, then build them back up. That's why, when you take that first step back from your dog, adding **distance**, you should cut the **duration** of the stay.

7. Now your dog has mastered the Stay with you alone, move the training on so that he learns to do the same with distractions. Have someone walk into the room, or squeak a toy or bounce a ball once. A rock-solid stay is mostly a matter of working slowly and patiently to start with. Don't go too fast, the ideal scenario is that your Boston never breaks out of the Stay position until you release him.

8. If he does get up, take a breather and then give him a short refresher, starting at a point easier than whatever you were working on when he cracked.

9. Don't use the 'Stay' command in situations where it is unpleasant for your dog. For instance, avoid telling him to stay as you close the door behind you on your way to work. Finally, don't use Stay to keep a dog in a scary situation.

If you think he's tired or had enough, leave it for the day and come back later – just finish off on a positive note by giving one very easy command you know he will obey, followed by a reward.

 Training requires lots of treats. From the beginning feed your puppy healthy treats, such as carrot pieces or apple slices, and he will continue to regard these as rewards when older. Just as with humans, it is difficult to convince an adult dog that fruit and veg are something special if they have not eaten them much as a child!

Puppy Biting

All puppies spend a great deal of time chewing, playing, and investigating objects. All of these normal activities involve them using their mouths and their needle-sharp teeth. Like babies, this is how they investigate the world. When puppies play with people, they often bite, chew and mouth on people's hands, limbs and clothing.

Play biting is normal for puppies, they do it all the time with their littermates. They bite moving targets with their sharp teeth; it's a great game. But when they arrive in your home, they have to be taught that human skin is sensitive and body parts are not suitable material for biting. Biting humans is never acceptable, not even from a small dog or puppy.

As a puppy grows and feels more confident in his surroundings, he may become bolder and his bites may hurt someone – especially if you have children or elderly people at home. Make sure every time you have a play session, you have a toy nearby and when he starts to chew your hand or feet, clench your fingers (or toes!) to make it more difficult and distract him with a toy in your other hand.

Keep the game interesting by moving the toy or rolling it around in front of him. (He may be too young to fetch it back if you throw it). He may continue to chew you, but will eventually realise that the toy is far more interesting and lively than your boring hand.

If he becomes over-excited and too aggressive with the toy, if he growls a lot, stop playing with him and **walk away**. Although it might be quite cute and funny now, you don't want your Boston doing this as an adult. Remember, if not checked, any unwanted behaviour traits will continue into adulthood, when you certainly don't want him to bite a child's hand – even accidentally.

When you walk away, don't say anything or make eye or physical contact with your puppy. Simply ignore him; this is extremely effective and often works within a few days. If your pup is more persistent and tries to bite your legs as you walk away, thinking this is another fantastic game, stand still and ignore him.

If he still persists, tell him 'No!' in a very stern voice, then praise him when he lets go. If you have to physically remove him from your trouser leg or shoe, leave him alone in the room for a while and ignore his demands for attention if he starts barking.

Many Boston Terriers are sensitive and another method that can be very effective is to make a sharp cry of 'Ouch!' when your pup bites your hand – even when it doesn't hurt. This worked very well for us. Your pup may well jump back in amazement, surprised that he has hurt you.

Divert your attention from your puppy to your hand. He will probably try to get your attention or lick you as a way of saying sorry. Praise him for stopping biting and continue with the game. If he bites you again, repeat the process. A sensitive Boston will soon stop biting you. You may also think about keeping the toys you use to play with your puppy separate from other toys. That way he will associate certain toys with having fun with you and will work harder to please you.

Boston Terriers love playing and you can use this to your advantage by teaching your dog how to play nicely with you and the toy and then by using play time as a reward for good behaviour.

 If your puppy is either in a hyperactive mood or over-tired, he is not likely to be very receptive to training. Choose your moments; he will respond better when relaxed.

Clicker Training

Clicker training is a method of training that uses a sound - a click - to tell an animal when he does something right. The clicker is a tiny plastic box held in the palm of your hand, with a metal tongue that you push quickly to make the sound.

The clicker creates an efficient language between a human trainer and a trainee. First, the owner or trainer teaches a dog that every time he hears the clicking sound, he gets a treat. Once the dog understands that clicks are always followed by treats, the click becomes a powerful reward. When this happens, the trainer can use the click to mark the instant the animal performs the right behaviour. For example, if a trainer wants to teach a dog to sit, she'll click the instant his rump hits the floor and then deliver a tasty treat. With repetition, the dog learns that sitting earns rewards.

So the 'click' takes on huge meaning. To the animal it means: "Whatever I was doing the moment my trainer clicked, *that's* what she wants me to do." The clicker in animal training is like the winning buzzer on a game show that tells a contestant he's just won the money! Through the clicker, the trainer communicates precisely with the dog, and that can speed up training.

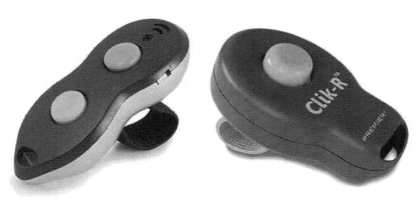

Although the clicker is ideal because it makes a unique, consistent sound, you do need a spare hand to hold it. For that reason, some trainers prefer to keep both hands free and instead use a one-syllable word like 'Yes!' or 'Good!' – rather than a clicker - to mark the desired behaviour.

In the following steps, you can substitute the word in place of the click to teach your Boston what the sound means. It's easy to introduce the clicker, spend half an hour or so teaching your dog that the sound of the click means 'Treat!' Here's how:

1. Sit and watch TV or read a book with your dog in the room. Have a container of treats within reach.

2. Place one treat in your hand and the clicker in the other. (If your dog smells the treat and tries to get it by pawing, sniffing, mouthing or barking at you, just close your hand around the treat and wait until he gives up and leaves you alone).

3. Click once and immediately open your hand to give your dog the treat. Put another treat in your closed hand and resume watching TV or reading. Ignore your dog.

4. Several minutes later, click again and offer another treat.

5. Continue to repeat the click-and-treat combination at varying intervals, sometimes after one minute, sometimes after five minutes. Make sure you vary the time so that your dog doesn't know exactly when the next click is coming. Eventually, he'll start to turn toward you and look expectantly when he hears the click - which means he understands that the sound of the clicker means a treat is coming his way.

If your dog runs away when he hears the click, you can make the sound softer by putting it in your pocket or wrapping a towel around your hand that's holding the clicker. You can also try using a different sound, like the click of a retractable pen or the word 'Yes.'

Clicker Training Basics

Once your dog seems to understand the connection between the click and the treat, you're ready to get started.

1. Click just once, right when your dog does what you want him to do. Think of it like pressing the shutter of a camera to take a picture of the behaviour.

2. Remember to follow every click with a treat. After you click, deliver the treat to your dog's mouth **as quickly as possible.**

3. It's fine to switch between practising two or three behaviours within a session, but work on one command at a time. For example, say you're teaching your Boston to sit, lie down and raise his paw. You can do 10 repetitions of sit and take a quick play break. Then do 10 repetitions of down, and take another quick break. Then do 10 repetitions of stay, and so on. Keep training sessions short and stop before you or your dog gets tired of the game.

4. End training sessions on a good note, when your dog has succeeded. If necessary, ask him to do something you know he can do well at the end of a session.

Collar and Lead Training

You have to train your Boston Terrier to get used to a collar or harness and lead, and then he has to learn to walk nicely with them. Teaching these manners can be challenging because many young Bostons are very lively and don't necessarily want to walk at the same pace as you.

All dogs will pull on a lead initially. This isn't because they want to show you who is boss, it's simply that they are excited to be outdoors and are forging ahead.

Many Boston owners and breeders prefer to use a body harness (pictured) instead of a collar. Bostons are brachycephalic breeds and a harness takes the pressure away from a dog's sensitive neck area and distributes it more evenly around the body. Harnesses with a chest ring for the lead can be effective for training. When your dog pulls, the harness turns him around.

Another option is to start your dog on a padded collar and then change to a harness once he has learned some lead etiquette – although padded collars can be quite heavy. Some Bostons don't mind collars; some will try to fight them, while others will slump to the floor like you have hung a two-ton weight around their necks! You need to be patient and calm and proceed at a pace comfortable for your puppy; don't fight your dog and don't force the collar on.

1. The secret to getting a collar is to buy one that fits your puppy now - not one he is going to grow into - so choose a small lightweight one that he will hardly notice. A big collar may be too heavy and frightening. You can buy one with clips to start with, just put it on and clip it together, rather than fiddling with buckles, which can be scary when he's wearing a collar for the first time. Stick to the principle of positive reward-based training and give him a treat once the collar is on, not after you have taken it off. Then gradually increase the length of time you leave the collar on.

IMPORTANT: If you leave your dog unattended in a crate, or leave him alone in the house, take off the collar. He is not used to it and it may get caught on something, causing panic or injury.

So put the collar on when there are other things that will occupy him, like when he is going outside to be with you, or in the home when you are interacting with him. Or put it on at mealtimes or when you are doing some basic training. Don't put the collar on too tight, you want him to forget it's there. If he scratches the collar - which he almost certainly will - get his attention by encouraging him to follow you or play with a toy so that he forgets the irritation.

2. Once your puppy is happy wearing the collar, introduce the lead. An extending or retractable one is not particularly suitable for starting off with, as they are not very strong and no good for training him to walk close. Buy a fixed-length lead. Start off in the house; don't try to go out and about straight away. Think of the lead as a safety device to stop him running off, not something to drag him around with. You want a Boston that doesn't pull, so don't start by pulling him around. You don't want to get into a tug-of-war contest.

3. Attach the lead to the collar and give him a treat while you put it on. The minute it is attached, use the treats (instead of pulling on the lead) to lure him beside you, so that he gets used to walking with the collar and lead. As well as using treats you can also make good use of toys to do exactly the same thing - especially if your dog has a favourite. Walk around the house with the lead on and lure him forwards with the toy.

It might feel a bit odd but it's a good way for your pup to develop a positive relationship with the collar and lead with the minimum of fuss. Act as though it's the most natural thing in the world for you to walk around the house or apartment with your dog on a lead – and just hope that the neighbours aren't watching! Some dogs react the moment you attach the lead and they feel some tension on it – a bit like when a horse is being broken in for the first time. Drop the lead and allow him to run around the house or yard, dragging it after him, but be careful he doesn't get tangled and hurt himself. Try to make him forget about it by playing or starting a short fun training routine with treats. Treats are a huge distraction for most Bostons. While he is concentrating on the new task, occasionally pick up the lead and call him to you. Do it gently and in an encouraging tone.

4. The most important thing is not to yank on the lead. If it is gets tight, just lure him back beside you with a treat or a toy while walking. All you're doing is getting him to move around beside you. Remember to keep your hand down (the one holding the treat or toy) so your dog doesn't get the habit of jumping up at you. If you feel he is getting stressed when walking outside on a lead, try putting treats along the route you'll be taking to turn this into a rewarding game: good times are ahead... That way he learns to focus on what's ahead of him with curiosity and not fear.

Take collar and lead training slowly, give your Boston Terrier time to process all this new information about what the lead is and does. Let him gain confidence in you, and then in the lead and himself. Some dogs can sit and decide not to move. If this happens, walk a few steps away, go down on one knee and encourage him to come to you using a treat, then walk off again.

For some pups, the collar and lead can be restricting and they will react with resistance. Some dogs are perfectly happy to walk alongside you off-lead, but behave differently when they have one on. Proceed in tiny steps if that is what your puppy is happy with, don't over face him, but stick at it if you are met with resistance. With training, your puppy will learn to walk nicely on a lead; it is just a question of when, not if.

Walking on a Lead

There are different methods, but we have found the following one to be successful for quick results. Initially, the lead should be kept fairly loose. Have a treat in your hand as you walk, it will encourage your dog to sniff the treat as he walks alongside. He will not pull ahead, as he will want to remain near the treat.

Give him the command **Walk** or **Heel** and then proceed with the treat in your hand, keep giving him a treat every few steps initially, then gradually extend the time between treats. Eventually, you should be able to walk with your hand comfortably at your side, periodically (every minute or so) reaching into your pocket to grab a treat to reward your dog.

If your dog starts pulling ahead, first give him a warning, by saying 'No' or 'Easy,' or a similar command. If he slows down, give him a treat. But if he continues to pull ahead so that your arm becomes fully extended, stop walking and ignore your dog. Wait for him to stop pulling and to look up at you. At this point reward him for good behaviour before carrying on your walk. Be sure to quickly reward him with treats and praise any time he doesn't pull and walks with you with the lead slack. If you have a lively young pup that is dashing all over the place on the lead, try starting training when he is already a little tired - after a play or exercise session - (but not exhausted).

Another method is what dog trainer Victoria Stillwell describes as the Reverse Direction Technique. When your dog pulls, say 'Let's Go!' in an encouraging manner, then turn away from him and walk off in the other direction, without jerking on the lead. When he is following you and the lead is slack, turn back and continue on your original way.

It may take a few repetitions, but your words and body language will make it clear that pulling will not get your dog anywhere, whereas walking calmly by your side - or even slightly in front of you - on a loose lead will get him where he wants to go.

There is an excellent video (in front of a beautiful house!) which shows Victoria demonstrating this technique and highlights just how easy it is with a dog that's easy to please. It only lasts three minutes and is well worth watching: https://positively.com/dog-behavior/basic-cues/loose-lead-walking.

CREDIT: With thanks to the American Society for the Prevention of Cruelty to Animals for assistance with parts of this chapter. The ASPCA has a great deal of good advice and training tips on its website at: www.aspca.org/pet-care/virtual-pet- behaviorist/dog- behaviour/training-your-dog

....

Breeders on Training

"They learn obedience pretty quickly as they thrive on impressing their owners. If you want an obedient puppy, then take your puppy to obedience/puppy socialisation classes. They will give you great advice and guidance."

"They are very intelligent dogs. Having come from a German Shepherd Dog background, I am used to a dog responding to what I have asked it to do. My Mini Dachshunds were stubborn and understood, but would only respond on their terms, but Bostons have a natural inbuilt need to please. You occasionally get the stubborn few who will push the boundaries and want to dominate you or the pack. But usually this is a phase at around eight to 10 months and with training and a caring but firm approach, it is easy to get them through it. After that you have a dog who you only have to look at in a certain way if it has displeased you."

"Some Bostons are stubborn but most are eager to learn. The breed as a whole is highly intelligent - therefore they are easy to train. When compared to the temperament of a Pug, Bostons are by far easier to train."

"Boston Terriers are very intelligent. Get their attention and help them to understand what you want them to do and they will be glad to do it. They really want to please you."

"Bostons are easy to train in general. They're very smart. Boys are often easier to train because they are such pleasers. They typically respond to treats and praise pretty equally. Girls tend to be a little more independent, so may take just a bit longer, but they are smart as well (sometimes smarter than us!)".

(Photo courtesy of Bill and Anne Connor, of Ringablok Boston Terriers, Carmarthen, Wales).

"Never correct or scold a puppy for something you didn't catch it doing! They have no idea what you are correcting them for. They may cower and you may think they know what you are upset about, but most likely they are reading your body language! This is very important. I grew up training domestic and exotic animals for movies, etc. and I saw this happen so many times. Correction happens at the time of an undesirable act."

"Bostons are very smart and quick to learn - don't let them train you! Remember you are the 'pack leader' and, believe me, they love to learn new things. I teach all the pups to chase a lure (a fuzzy animal toy on the end of a lunge whip). It is a great form of exercise and teaches them all to share and all play with one another."

British breeder Jo Dalton added: "A trained dog is a happy dog. Housetraining aside, every puppy also needs to be taught good manners and have constructive lessons in basic control and social interaction. This includes:

- 🐾 Responding to its name
- 🐾 Learning how to greet and behave politely around other people and dogs
- 🐾 To come back when called
- 🐾 To walk nicely on the lead
- 🐾 To sit down and stay on command
- 🐾 To allow itself to be groomed and examined by you and your vet

"Most owners can benefit from attending good training classes, and training in the company of other dogs is very useful, because of the realistic distractions it involves. Ideally, you should start your classes as soon as your puppy's vaccinations are complete, but classes can be invaluable for older dogs too.

"There are lots of schools of thought on dog training and it is naturally important that you find a class and training Instructors with the right approach for you and your puppy. You can find training classes by using the Kennel Club's Find a Club service – visit www.findaclub.org.uk to find a club near you running training classes. You can also ask your vet and other dog owners for recommendations. Dog training can be lots of fun and very rewarding. After all, a trained dog is a happy dog, and a happy dog makes for a happy owner too."

'Terrible Teens'

The teenage years – with dogs, anything from six to 18 months old – can be a difficult time for some owners. It may seem as though your pleasant, affectionate little Boston has turned into a pint-sized terror – chewing through things he or she knows perfectly well are off-limits, stealing things or eliminating inside the house after they have been successfully housetrained. Their reactions to previously acceptable things might also become heightened, so they may become more fearful, bolder or more aggressive in certain situations.

What many owners forget is that their cute little puppy doesn't turn into a perfectly behaved adult overnight — there is the small issue of the 'Terrible Teens' to contend with first. As with humans, the adolescent dog's hormones are raging and their bodies are often ahead of their minds. Your 18-month-old Boston may look like an adult, but inside they are still a teenager, finding his or her way in the world - and often this involves pushing the boundaries to see just what they can get away with.

Jo Dalton has this advice for new owners: "At around the age of around six to nine months your puppy may become extremely naughty and difficult - this is known as your dog's adolescent age. And if a Boston is going to need to be re-homed due to behaviour issues, it is often around this sort of age.

"It is the time when your puppy will try your patience and push the boundaries to their limits. Difficult behaviour can range from chewing things up, barking, attempting to assert themselves over other dogs or humans (in extreme cases this can result in aggression) and messing in the house or scent/territory marking, to just generally not listening and acting like they have never had a single training session in their life.

"A firm hand and routine is needed during this time in your puppy's development as it's this period that sets a precedent for your dog's behaviour in adult life. It is important that regular training continues during this time and why puppy training is so important, as it gives an owner a support network.

"The most common thing owners say to me is: 'It's like he has forgotten everything he has learned up to now, even his toilet training has gone backwards.' Even though it feels this way, your dog hasn't actually forgotten anything, it is simply pushing the boundaries to see how far it can take things before you bring it back into line. As hard as it is to do, it is very important you pull rank at this time as, if left unchecked, the behaviour will only worsen and become the normal behaviour for your dog.

"So what should you do? Very simply. **go back to basics with everything**; so back to the basic principles of toilet training and back to the basics of positive reinforcement training. Do go back to your dog training classes if you have already stopped them - I would always recommend continuing through classes from very basic puppy classes to when your pup is around one year old, that way when you do hit this difficult period of adolescence, you have the help and support you need.

"Your dog won't have forgotten what it has learnt (even though it may act like it has) and it won't take long for your dog to realise that the unruly behaviour is not going to be tolerated. If necessary, put methods in place to remove any status your dog has gained over you and other family members."

Another point to remember is that, although your adolescent dog may look almost like an adult, he or she is still teething. So make sure you still have plenty of toys and chews to satisfy the dog's urge to mouthe and chew.

It is also important to ensure that your teenage Boston has enough opportunities to let off steam — both physically with plenty of exercise, and mentally with a range of games and challenges.

10. Boston Terrier Health

Health has a major impact on the quality of life of any dog, or person. It's difficult for any individual – canine or human - to enjoy life to the full with ill health, and he or she may also have a shortened life span. When it comes to choosing and raising a dog, good health should always be a major consideration. Firstly, select a puppy from a breeder who tests her dogs and then play your part in keeping your Boston healthy throughout his or her life.

There is not a single breed without a genetic weakness. Most breeds have not just one, but several ailments that they are more likely to inherit than other breeds. For example, German Shepherds are more prone to hip problems than some other breeds, and 30% of Dalmatians have problems with their hearing.

If you get a German Shepherd or a Dalmatian, your dog may not automatically suffer from these issues, but will statistically be more likely to have them than a breed with no genetic history of the issue if the parents have not been health tested as 'Unaffected.'

Boston Terriers are one of the 'Bull' or 'Bully' breeds, which means they are also from the **brachycephalic** family of dogs. All dogs have one of three shapes of head:

- Long and narrow (dolichocephalic), like the Borzoi, Afghan Hound, Saluki and Dachshund

- Wolf–like (mesaticephalic), or equally proportioned, in which the width of the dog's skull is similar to the length of the nasal cavity, like a Beagle, Border Collie, Cocker Spaniel or Labrador Retriever

- Short and broad (brachycephalic), like the Boston Terrier, Boxer, Bulldog, Bullmastiff, Cavalier King Charles Spaniel, Dogue de Bordeaux, French Bulldog, Lhasa Apso, Pekingese, Pug and Shih Tzu.

"Brachy" means shortened and "cephalic" means head. Although the exaggerated features are not as pronounced in the Boston Terrier as, for example, the Bulldog, being brachycephalic can still cause health problems in some Bostons. Some of the most common ailments are eye problems – particularly juvenile cataracts, luxating patellas (dislocated kneecaps), breathing problems, due to stenotic nares or elongated soft palate, and various skin issues. Good breeders will be able to produce health clearances for eyes, hearing and patellas.

Over the years, successive selective breeding has led to the skull bones of brachycephalic dogs being shortened to give the face and nose a "pushed in" appearance. This skull shape gives the characteristic flattened face and short nose. While this makes the dogs appear extremely appealing - a feature that matches the Boston's big personality - it can also cause some major health issues. While the bone structure has been compressed, all the soft pink tissue inside has not. The oversized and shortened head can lead to breathing, skin, eye, mating and birthing problems and an intolerance to heat and anaesthetics − all of which are covered in this book.

Don't skimp on price. If you are buying a Boston as a pet (as opposed to a show dog), a more expensive puppy from a reputable breeder usually means that the breeder is taking better care and producing better puppies - in terms of health, temperament and socialisation - than someone selling cheap or 'rare' puppies. Ask to see both parents, or at least the mother, as well as all of their and the puppy's health certificates, and check that the puppy breathes easily.

The Media on Canine Health

Health problems with the brachycephalic dog breeds were highlighted in the BBC documentary *Pedigree Dogs Exposed* which investigated health and welfare issues caused by the breeding of some purebred dogs. It was aired on TV in the UK in 2008 and caused a stir around the world.

In it, the Kennel Club - the UK's governing body for purebred dogs that runs the prestigious dog show Crufts - was criticised for allowing breed standards, judging standards and breeding practices to compromise the health of pedigree (purebred) dogs. The BBC had previously broadcast the highly popular Crufts for 42 years, but withdrew its coverage in an effort to persuade breeders to place more emphasis on the health of their puppies, rather than on just their physical appearance. The KC lodged a complaint with the broadcasting regulator, claiming unfair treatment and editing.

However, due to strong public opinion, the KC later rolled out new health plans and reviewed standards for every breed. Three separate health reports were commissioned and they concluded that current breeding practices were detrimental to the welfare of dogs and made various recommendations to the KC and UK breeders to improve pedigree dog health.

I attend Crufts every year and it is clear that health is a priority among responsible breeders, who are now making serious efforts to improve health. At the show (held every March) the Discover Dogs section has more than 200 stands representing the breeds and, if you live in the UK, it's a great place to discover which breed is best for you, or to find out more about your chosen breed.

The change in the Boston Terrier has been less pronounced than with many other dogs, but even so, a modern Boston looks slightly different from his ancestor at the turn of last century (pictured is Champion Halloo Prince), when the breed had a longer tail, lighter body and often a smaller head.

Following *Pedigree Dogs Exposed*, the Kennel Club set up its Breed Watch programme, which it describes as: *"An 'early warning system' to identify points of concern for individual breeds. Its primary purpose is to enable anyone involved in the world of dogs, but in particular dog show judges, to find out about any breed specific conformational issues which may lead to health problems. These conditions are known as a 'point(s) of concern.'"*

All breeds are in one of three categories:

1 Breeds with no current points of concern reported

2 Breeds with Breed Watch points of concern

3 Breeds where some dogs have visible conditions or exaggerations that can cause pain or discomfort (previously known as High Profile)

The good news is that the Boston Terrier is in Category 1: "Currently no points of concern specific to this breed have been identified for special attention by judges, other than those covered routinely by the Kennel Club Breed Standard." Pay attention to the Breed Standard when selecting a puppy, and if you haven't got yours yet, there's more information on how to select a healthy pup in **Chapter 4. Choosing a Boston Terrier Puppy.**

Moves have also been made in the USA to improve the health of the breed. The AKC Canine Health Foundation was set up in the mid-1990s in response to Time Magazine's article **"A Terrible Beauty"** that covered the increasing genetic disease in purebred dogs. The Boston Terrier Club of America (BTCA) Health Committee was formed in 1999, which states:

"The Mission of the Health Committee shall be to assist Boston Terrier breeders in improving the health of the purebred Boston Terrier breeding stock by helping bring their dog's natural qualities to perfection, and in so doing advance and protect the interests of the breed.

"The Committee shall also provide education on health matters to all Boston Terrier owners and shall keep abreast of new developments in the field of canine veterinary medicine and canine genetics affecting our breed."

The BTCA Health Committee has a voluntary Health Certification programme available to members whose dogs have passed certain health requirements. "We are hopeful that certification can begin to reduce genetic problems and improve the overall health of the Boston Terrier Breed by raising breeder awareness of genetic problems." Lists of U.S. Boston Terriers that have completed the health certification program for 2003-2015 can be found at: www.bostonterrierclubofamerica.org/boston-terrier-health/btca-health-certification-program.htm

We are not recommending that you don't get a Boston Terrier; far from it! However, if the Boston is definitely the dog for you, we advise you to do your homework and choose one bred from healthy stock - for the sake of you and your dog.

The information in this chapter is not written to frighten new owners, but to help you to recognise symptoms of the main conditions affecting Boston Terriers and enable you to take prompt action, should the need arise. There are also a number of measures you can take to prevent or reduce the chances of certain physical and behavioural problems developing, including keeping your dog's weight in check, feeding the right diet, giving daily exercise and not leaving your Boston in very hot or cold places.

....

Insuring a Boston Terrier

Insurance for your new puppy or adult dog is something else to consider. The best time to get pet insurance is immediately after you bring your dog home and before any health issues develop. Don't wait until you need to seek veterinary help – bite the bullet and take out annual insurance.

If you can afford it, take out life cover. This may be more expensive, but will cover your dog throughout his or her lifetime - including for recurring or chronic ailments, such as eye, joint or breathing problems. Some breeders may give free 30-day insurance coverage in their puppy packs, which gives new owners sufficient time to sort out long term cover.

Insuring a healthy puppy or adult dog is the only sure fire way to ensure vet bills are covered before anything unforeseen happens - and you'd be a rare owner if you didn't use your policy at least once during your dog's lifetime. Bostons are not one of the most expensive dogs to insure - even so, it's not cheap. Insurance may cost up to £50 a month in the UK, depending on the level of cover ($25 to $75 in the US) - and if you make a claim, the monthly premium may well increase. On the plus side, you'll have peace of mind and you'll know how much you have to shell out every month.

In the UK, Bought By Many has teamed up with insurers More Than to launch a policy specifically for Boston Terriers which offers a 20% discount at: https://boughtbymany.com/offers/boston-terrier-insurance. Current rates for a 13-week-old Boston Terrier puppy range from around £26 a month for Basic cover to £54 for Premier coverage. (I'm not on commission, just trying to save you money!) Always shop around for the best price – and check the exclusions and excess (i.e. the amount of money you have to contribute to each claim). The bigger the excess, the cheaper the policy.

Advances in veterinary science mean that there is so much more vets can do to help an ailing dog - but at a cost. Surgical procedures often rack up bills of thousands of pounds or dollars. In the US, the cost of treating patella luxation may range from $1,500 to $3,000 per knee – or £2,000 in the UK, including pre-surgery fees - and $4,000 if both eyes need surgery for cataracts. (around £2,000 In the UK).

Also, pedigree dogs like the Boston Terrier are at increasing risk of theft by criminals, including organised gangs. With the purchase price of puppies rising, dognapping more than quadrupled in the UK between 2010 and 2015; with some 50 dogs a day being stolen. Some 49% of dogs are snatched from owners' gardens and 13% from peoples' homes. If you take out a policy, check that theft is included. Although nothing can ever replace Man's Best Friend, a good insurance policy will ensure that you are not out of pocket.

In the US, Consumers' Advocate has named the top 10 pet insurance companies, taking into account reimbursement policies, coverage and customers' reviews. Here is their league table: 1. Healthy Paws, 2. PetPlan, 3. Trupanion, 4. Embrace, 5. Pets Best, 6. PetFirst, 7. VPI Pet Insurance, 8. Pet Partners, 9. ASPCA Pet Health Insurance, 10. Pet Premium.

Three Golden Tips for New Boston Terrier Owners

There are three golden tips for anybody thinking of getting a Boston Terrier, which will in all likelihood save you a lot of money and heartache.

1: Buy a well-bred puppy.

Scientists have come to realise the important role that genetics play in determining a person's long-term health. Well, the same is true of dogs. This means ensuring you get your puppy from a reputable breeder who selects the parent dogs based on a number of factors, the main ones of which are health and temperament. A good breeder selects their breeding stock based on:

- 🐾 health history
- 🐾 bloodline
- 🐾 conformation
- 🐾 temperament

If you talk to owners with healthy, happy Bostons, the one factor that many have in common is that they did their homework, spent time researching the breed and found a reputable breeder before taking the plunge.

Although puppies are expensive, many responsible breeders make little money on the sale of their puppies. Boston Terrier breeding is a specialised art and the main concern of good breeders is to improve the breed by producing healthy puppies with good temperaments that are as close to the Breed Standard as possible.

It is far better to spend time beforehand choosing a puppy that has been properly bred than to spend a great deal of time and money later as your wonderful pet develops health problems due to poor breeding; not to mention the heartache that goes along with it.

- 🐾 Don't buy a Boston from a pet shop. No reputable breeder allows their pups to end up here. You will, in all probability, be buying a Boston with questionable heritage and breeding – and you'll be extremely lucky if this does not result in problems at some point in the dog's life
- 🐾 Never buy a puppy from a small ad on the internet unless you can personally visit or check out the owners and get full details of the pup's background, parents and health history
- 🐾 Never buy a pup or adult Boston unseen with a credit card deposit without first thoroughly checking out the breeder – you are storing up trouble and expense for yourself

 **2: Find a vet that knows and understands the Boston Terrier.**

This is a breed that may require specialised veterinary care. Like all brachycephalic breeds, Bostons can have an adverse reaction to common anaesthesia, and surgery should not be undertaken lightly. You could waste a lot of time and money by visiting a vet who is not familiar with Bostons and their healthcare requirements. If you already have a vet, check if he or she is experienced with Bull breeds, if not you'd be advised to switch to one who is.

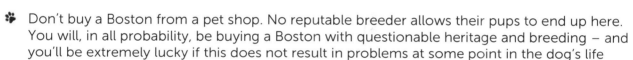 **3: Get pet insurance as soon as you get your dog.**

Don't wait until he or she has a health issue and needs to see a vet. When you are working out your finances for a puppy or adult dog, factor in the cost of good pet insurance and trips to the vet for check-ups, annual vaccinations, etc.

We all want our dogs to be healthy -so how can you tell if yours is? Well, our **Top Signs** are a good start. Here are some positive things to look for in a healthy Boston Terrier.

Top 13 Signs of a Healthy Boston

1. **Breathing** – Many Boston Terriers snuffle and snore - and even 'sing' or 'yodel' - but they should not pant or wheeze excessively, nor should their breathing be excessively noisy or laboured when excited or exercising. Regular, quiet breathing is a good sign.

2. **Coats** – These are easy-to-monitor indicators of a healthy dog. A Boston Terrier has a single coat of short, smooth hair that sheds somewhat (not excessively like many other breeds). The coat should be glossy; a dull, lifeless coat, a discoloured one or a coat that loses excessive hair can be a sign that something is amiss.

3. **Skin** – A healthy skin should be smooth without redness. Some Bostons are prone to skin complaints and/or allergies. If your dog is scratching, licking or biting himself a lot, he may have a condition that needs addressing before he makes it worse. Red or bald patches, sores, scales, scabs or growths can be a sign of a problem. Any signs of fleas, ticks or other external parasites should be treated immediately.

4. **Ears** – A small percentage of Bostons suffer from deafness, particularly those with a lot of white in their coat. According to the USA's OFA (Orthopedic Foundation for Animals) the Boston was ranked second overall for breeds tested for deafness; it was found in 1.7% of dogs. The deafness can be unilateral – in one ear, or bilateral - in both ears. Brain Auditory Evoked Response (BAER) testing is performed to determine the dog's hearing capability.

US breeder Pamela Preston says: "The way I tell if a puppy is a unilaterally deaf is to stand in the next room, but where I can see the puppy, and then call him (or clap my hands). A normal hearing dog will immediately turn around and run to me. A 'uni' (unilaterally deaf puppy) will stand there and cock his head trying to determine which direction the sound came from. When a puppy hears only in one ear, he loses the ability to determine the direction from which the sound originated, so has to wait for other clues - usually visual or felt clues."

The BTCA says: "Make sure your breeder has had your puppy BAER tested and ask to see records of the puppy's parents' BAER test results."

Ear infections are a problem with many breeds of dog and the Boston is no different. The ears should be inspected, gently cleaned and dried as part of your weekly grooming routine. Unpleasant smells, redness or inflammation are all signs of infection.

5. **Mouth** – Gums should be a healthy pink colour. Bostons shouldn't have dark gums unless they are one of the Disqualified colours. A change in colour can be an indicator of a health issue. Paleness or whiteness can be a sign of anaemia, lack of oxygen due to heart or breathing problems, or severe pain. Blue gums or tongue are a sign that your dog is not breathing properly. Red, inflamed gums can be a sign of gingivitis or other tooth disease. Again, your dog's breath should smell OK. Young dogs will have sparkling white teeth, whereas older dogs will have darker teeth, but they should not have any hard white, yellow,

green or brown bits - tartar and plaque build-up should be removed to minimise the risk of tooth decay or infection.

A tiny percentage of Bostons are born with a cleft palate, which is an opening between the mouth and the nose that happens when the tissues separating these two cavities do not grow together properly. Often these puppies are put to sleep at birth, but not always. There is a French Bulldog called Lentil that has survived and made it on to Facebook with a mission to "raise awareness for those with craniofacial differences and to teach all of us to be kind." His page has more than 146,000 Likes at www.facebook.com/MyNameIsLentil.

6. **Weight** – Boston Terriers can be sturdy dogs with relatively large bones for their height. The Kennel Clubs have three classes: lightweight at under 15lbs, middleweight at 15lbs to 20lbs, and heavyweight at 20lbs to 25lbs. However, the sturdiness does not excuse obesity, which is bad for any dog as it causes strain on joints and organs. Dogs may have weight problems due to factors such as diet, lack of exercise, allergies, diabetes, thyroid or other health issues. A Boston has a deep chest and a general rule of thumb is that your dog's stomach should be above his rib cage when standing. If his stomach is level or hangs below, he is overweight (or he may have a pot belly, which can also be a symptom of other conditions, such as Cushing's Disease).

7. **Nose** – A dog's nose is an indicator of health. It should normally be moist and cold to the touch as well as free from discharge and secretions. Any yellow, green or foul smelling discharge is not normal - in younger dogs this can be a sign of canine distemper. Many puppies are born with pink noses, but these normally turn to jet black. A Dudley nose may have pink areas and it does not affect the dog's health, but makes the dog ineligible for conformation shows under Kennel Club rules, as the Breed Standard states that a Boston Terrier's nose should be black).

8. **Eyes** – Healthy eyes are shiny and bright with no yellowish tint. The area around the eyeball (the conjunctiva) should be a healthy pink; paleness could be a sign of underlying problems. A red swelling in the corner of one or both eyes could by a sign of Cherry Eye, an ailment which some Bostons can get. There should be no thick, green or yellow discharge from the eyes. A cloudy eye could well be a sign of cataracts.

9. **Attitude** – A generally lively disposition and positive attitude are signs of good health. Symptoms of illness may include one or all of the following: not eating food, a general lack of interest in his or her surroundings, or lethargy and sleeping a lot (even more than normal). The important thing is to look out for any behaviour that is out of the ordinary for your individual dog.

10. **Energy** – Levels vary from one Boston to the next, but the breed is generally regarded as having medium energy levels, although some are more active in short bursts – especially puppies and adolescents. Your dog should have good energy levels with fluid and pain-free movements. Lethargy or lack of energy – if it is not the dog's normal character – could be a sign of an underlying problem.

11. **Stools** – Poo, poop, business, faeces – call it what you will - it's the stuff that comes out of the less appealing end of your dog on a daily basis! It should be firm and brown, not runny, with no signs of worms or parasites. Watery stools or a dog not eliminating regularly are both signs of an upset stomach or other ailments. If it continues for a more than a day or two, consult your vet. If puppies have diarrhoea they need checking out much quicker as they can soon dehydrate.

12. **Smell** – Your Boston Terrier should have a pleasant "doggie" smell. If there is a musty, "off" or generally unpleasant odour coming from his body, it could be a sign of yeast, or other, infection. There can be a number of reasons for this, such as an ear infection, skin problem and/or reaction to a certain type of food. You need to get to the root of the problem.

13. **Temperature** – The normal temperature of a dog is 101°F to 102.5°F. Excited or exercising dogs may run a slightly higher temperature. Anything above 103°F or below 100°F should be checked out. The exceptions are female dogs about to give birth; they will often have a temperature of 98°F or 99°F. If you take your dog's temperature, make sure he or she is relaxed and *always* use a purpose-made canine thermometer.

So now you know some of the signs of a healthy dog – what are the signs of an unhealthy one? There are many different symptoms that can indicate your beloved canine companion isn't feeling great. If you don't yet know your dog, his habits, temperament and behaviour patterns, then spend some time getting acquainted with them.

What are his normal character and temperament? Lively or sedate, playful or serious, outgoing or introverted, happy to be left alone or loves to be with people, a keen appetite or a fussy eater? How often does he empty his bowels? Does he ever vomit? (Dogs will often eat grass to make themselves sick, this is perfectly normal and a canine's natural way of cleansing his digestive system).

You may think your Boston Terrier can't talk, **but he can!** If you really know your dog, his character and habits, then he CAN tell you when he's not well. He does this by changing his patterns. Some symptoms are physical, some emotional and others are behavioural. It's important for you to be able to recognise these changes as soon as possible. Early treatment can be the key to keeping a simple problem from snowballing into a serious illness.

If you think your dog is unwell, it is useful to keep an accurate and detailed account of his symptoms to give to the vet. You might even want to film your dog's behaviour on your mobile phone. This will help the vet to correctly diagnose and effectively treat your dog. Most canine illnesses are detected through a combination of signs and symptoms.

....

Five Vital Signs of Illness

1. **Temperature** - New-born puppies have a temperature of 94-97°F, and they cannot regulate their body temperature like adults can, so you will need to make sure yours is kept very warm. This will reach the normal adult body temperature of 101°F to 102.5°F at about four weeks old. Like all dogs, a Boston's temperature is normally taken via the rectum. If you do this, be very careful. It's easier if you get someone to hold your dog while you do it. Digital thermometers are a good choice, but **only use one specifically made for rectal use,** as normal glass thermometers can easily break off in the rectum.

Ear Thermometer

Ear thermometers are now available, making the task much easier, although they can be expensive and don't suit all dogs' ears. (Walmart has started stocking them). Remember that exercise or excitement can cause the temperature to rise by 2°F to 3°F when your dog is actually in good health, so better to wait until he is relaxed and calm before taking his temperature. If it is above or below the norms, give your vet a call.

2. **Respiratory Rate** - Another symptom of canine illness is a change in breathing patterns. This varies a lot depending on the size and weight of the

dog. An adult dog will have a respiratory rate of 15-25 breaths per minute when resting. You can easily check this by counting your dog's breaths for a minute with a stopwatch handy. Don't do this if the dog is panting – it doesn't count.

3. **Heart Rate** - You can feel your Boston's heartbeat by placing your hand on his lower ribcage – just behind the elbow. Don't be alarmed if the heartbeat seems irregular compared to a human. It IS irregular in some dogs. Your Boston will probably love the attention, so it should be quite easy to check his heartbeat. Just lay him on his side and bend his left front leg at the elbow, bring the elbow in to his chest and place your fingers or a stethoscope on this area and count the beats.

   - Small dogs, like Bostons, have a normal rate of 90 to 140 beats per minute
   - Medium-sized dogs have a normal rate of 80 to 120 beats per minute
   - Big dogs have a normal rate of 70 to 120 beats per minute
   - A young puppy has a heartbeat of around 220 beats per minute
   - An older dog has a slower heartbeat

4. **Behaviour Changes** - Any inexplicable behaviour changes can also be symptoms of illness. If there has NOT been a change in the household atmosphere, such as another new pet, a new baby, moving home or the absence of a family member, then the following symptoms may well be a sign that all is not well with your Boston Terrier:

   - Depression
   - Anxiety
   - Tiredness
   - Trembling
   - Falling or stumbling
   - Loss of appetite
   - Walking in circles

5. **Breathing Patterns** - Boston Terriers are susceptible to breathing problems due to their anatomy. Here are some signs to look out for:

   - Belly and chest move when breathing
   - Nostrils flare open or pinch closed when breathing
   - Breathing with an open mouth
   - Breathing with the elbows sticking out from the body
   - Noisy breathing
   - Fast breathing and shallow breaths
   - Excessive panting
   - Neck and head are held low and out in front of the body

Your Boston Terrier may normally show some of these signs, but if any of them appear for the first time or worse than usual, you need to keep him under close watch for a few hours or even days. Quite often he will return to normal of his own accord. Like humans, dogs have off-days too.

If he is showing any of the above symptoms, then don't over-exercise him, and avoid stressful situations and hot or cold places. Make sure he has access to clean water. There are many other signals of ill health, but these are five of the most important. Keep a record for your vet. If your dog does need professional medical attention, most vets will want to know:

WHEN the symptoms first appeared

WHETHER they are getting better or worse, and

HOW FREQUENT the symptoms are. Are they intermittent, continuous or increasing?

We have highlighted some of the indicators of good and poor health to help you monitor your dog's wellbeing. Getting to know his character, habits and temperament will go a long way towards spotting the early signs of ill health. The next section looks in detail at some of the most common ailments affecting Boston Terriers, with much of the complicated medical terminology explained in simple terms. We also cover the symptoms and treatments of various conditions.

What the Breeders Say

We asked several breeders what the Boston Terrier's main health issues were and which health certificates new owners should ask for. This is what they said, starting in the UK:

Gwion and Lisa Williams, Wilarjan Boston Terriers, Bangor, North Wales: "We health test all of our dogs. DNA tests for Juvenile Hereditary Cataracts, Patella Score using the Putnam (1968) scoring system to detect any patella luxation, Heart test to detect any heart murmurs, BVA Eye scheme screening programme for hereditary eye disease in dogs, run in conjunction with the Kennel Club."

Jo Dalton, Mumuland Boston Terriers, Boston, Lincolnshire: "Early Onset Hereditary Cataracts (HC HSF4 test) and BVA Late Onset Hereditary Cataracts. Also, patellas seem to be a big problem, so evidence of patella scoring is a must. We were one of the first breeders to patella score our dogs - even before the breed clubs were starting to recognise a problem.

"We also see a lot of Corneal Ulcers, which often take longer to heal and become quite severe very quickly if not treated quickly." Photo, courtesy of Jo, of Kizzybas Tiny Tearaway To Mumuland, or Mabel to her friends, looking very fit and active at 13 months old.

Emily Little, Basildon, Essex: "Juvenile Hereditary Cataracts (JHC);there is an HSF4 DNA test available and certificate from the AHT (Animal Health Trust). Also luxating patellas - these are checked and 'scored' by an experienced vet. Food/substance intolerance or allergy - this can't be tested, but is apparent in the dog's coat, brown staining and bowel movements."

In the USA, Pamela Preston, ChriMaso Boston Terriers, Shingle Springs, California, says: "There are several issues that are known to be prevalent in Boston Terriers. Numerous eye diseases, including juvenile cataracts (there is now a DNA test for that), slipping patella, mitral valve disease (MVD), which is a common heart issue in older, small breeds in general, and hip dysplasia (HD).

"HD typically does not negatively affect Bostons as they are small and have little weight bearing on their hips, so even if they are affected with HD, they generally have no (or very few/minor) symptoms. Also, hemivertebrae, which can be identified via X-rays, is seen in Bostons and other short-backed breeds such as French Bulldogs. Again, often even if the dog has a few hemivertebrae, as long as they are in the thoracic region and there are not too many, chances are there will be no impact on the quality of life.

"For each of my breeding dogs, I have the following tests done: Brain Auditory Evoked Response (BAER) to test for deafness, Companion Animal Eye Registry (CAER) exam to test for eye diseases, JC DNA to test for juvenile cataracts, Patella to test for slipping/lose knees, echocardiogram to test for heart disease, spine x-rays to identify hemivertebrae and other spinal anomalies, trachea X-rays to make sure the trachea is not too tiny (tracheal stenosis) or large, and hip X-rays to determine if the dog has HD. All of the results are sent to the Orthopedic Foundation for Animals for inclusion in their databases for research purposes."

Susan Maxwell, Maximum Companion Boston Terriers, California, has been breeding Bostons for 20 years and says: "Bostons, Pugs and Frenchies (French Bulldogs) are similar in the fact that they are all brachycephalic breeds with pushed-in, shorter faces, normal lower jaws and somewhat shorter upper ones. This makes all prone to what is called brachycephalic syndrome.

"The nostrils can be very small and pinched (called stenotic nares), restricting airflow, as well as an elongated soft palate, which can be compressed like an accordion with flaps of skin in its throat and causes snorting, mild regurgitation (some extreme cases require surgery to remove flaps of skin) and various respiratory sounds.

"This group is also prone to narrow windpipes (tracheal stenosis). Always use caution with these types of dogs going for any treatments that require anaesthesia. These breeds do not handle hot or humid weather well because of their restricted breathing problems, so always be familiar with how temperature affects your dog's breathing. We use 'cool coats' (chamois) soaked in water if we are outside in warm weather. Always be in tune with the sounds your brachycephalic pet makes."

Brachycephalic Syndrome

Like other brachycephalic breeds, the Boston Terrier's skull has been successively bred to be shorter, so the face now appears "pushed-in." However, the amount of soft pink tissue inside has remained the same size. This includes the soft palate, the cartilage inside the nose and the tongue, which are all now crammed into a smaller space. There is also a lack of nasal bone which can result in the nostrils being very narrow, like small slits instead of open holes.

Brachycephalic Syndrome - also called Brachycephalic Airway Obstruction Syndrome (BAOS) - is used to describe the range of abnormalities that result from this and includes an **elongated soft palate (ESP), stenotic nares, a hypoplastic trachea** and **everted laryngeal saccules.** A dog with this syndrome may have one or a combination of these conditions, with variable effects on his breathing, ranging from mild to life threatening.

An **elongated soft palate,** (the soft part of the roof of the mouth) is too long for the short mouth and so partially blocks the entrance to the trachea (windpipe) at the back of the throat. Dogs with **stenotic nares** have nostrils that are too narrow, restricting the amount of air that can be inhaled. Sometimes the narrow opening is on the inside (the actual nasal cavity) and cannot be seen, but it still exists.

A **hypoplastic trachea** (or **tracheal stenosis**) means that the windpipe is narrower than normal. Although there is no treatment for this, it's important to keep the dog's weight in check. If this is the dog's only issue and it is not severe, the dog may be able to successfully live with the condition, but should not be used for breeding.

In severe cases of BAOS, the knock-on effect of a dog struggling to breathe can create another problem. Unfortunately the increased effort creates a suction effect in the back of the throat at the opening to the windpipe. This opening into the windpipe is called the larynx (or voice box in people) and it has a tough cartilage frame that keeps it open wide.

However, constant suction in this area over a period of months or years can cause it to fold inwards, which narrows the airway even further and really does cause serious breathing difficulty. This secondary problem is called **laryngeal collapse**. The **laryngeal saccules** are small pouches just inside the larynx. They evert (turn outwards) causing a further obstruction of the airways.

Symptoms of BAOS

- Loud snoring
- Noisy breathing – especially during excitement or exercise
- Panting
- Poor ability to exercise
- Broken sleep patterns
- Intolerance to heat
- Choking on food
- Regurgitating
- Blue gums or tongue
- Fainting

Affected dogs may also suffer from:

- Difficulty swallowing
- Tooth or gum disease
- Increased eye problems
- Infections in the facial skin folds
- Strange body posture as the dog tries to breathe more efficiently

The problem is that a large number of brachycephalic dogs may show a mild form of some of these symptoms in their daily lives. Some vets believe that our tolerance of what is acceptable in brachycephalic breeds has shifted to think that the above signs are normal, which they are not.

They are, however, all signs that the respiratory system is under stress. The good humour may hide the fact that he is in distress, so it's up to you to monitor your dog.

Vets are keen to get the message out that **these symptoms are not normal** and if your Boston is displaying some of them then he needs help. If you are thinking of getting a puppy, do not choose one exhibiting any of the above symptoms.

Treatment - Fortunately there are things that can be done to reduce the breathing problems associated with this syndrome. Various forms of surgery can be carried out to help brachycephalic dogs breathe better. Although these treatments will not produce a normal airway, they improve the flow of air, helping dogs to breathe more easily and improving their quality of life and ability to exercise. Exercise is important to avoid obesity, which makes things much worse.

One of the most important factors in deciding outcomes is how early the problem(s) are diagnosed. Tackling breathing issues early in the Boston's life helps to reduce the amount of suction at the back of the throat and to prevent or delay the development of the dreaded laryngeal (voice box) collapse, for which there are only limited options.

The vet may have a good idea that BAOS is the problem, based on symptoms, age and the fact that your dog is a breed prone to the condition. But before he or she can make a proper diagnosis, the dog may have to be examined under general anaesthetic – which is also not without risk for brachycephalic breeds. The vet may also take a biopsy (small tissue sample) and blood sample to check carbon dioxide and alkaline levels.

A small flexible camera called an **endoscope** (pictured) may be used to examine the throat, larynx and possibly the windpipe. Many vets prefer to perform corrective surgery to remodel some of the soft tissue at the same time, so that the dog is only knocked out once. Dogs that still have excessive soft tissue have a higher risk of problems with anaesthetic. Your vet will discuss all of the options, which include:

An **elongated soft palate** can be surgically shortened so it no longer protrudes into the back of the throat.

Everted laryngeal saccules can be surgically removed to increase the size of the laryngeal airway.

Stenotic nares (pinched or narrow nostrils, pictured) can be surgically opened by removing a wedge of tissue from the nares allowing better airflow through the nose.

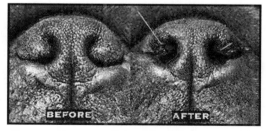

With today's laser technology some of these procedures can be performed with a minimal amount of bleeding and no need for stitches. The level of success depends on the age of the animal and when these procedures are performed. The earlier BAOS is diagnosed and treated, the better, as the condition can worsen with time and cause other abnormalities.

Note that sometimes a puppy may display signs of ESP and the vet may want to do surgery right away; however, many bloodlines take some time for the head to fully mature and the breeder may recommend you wait (as long as it is not a severe condition) until the dog is one year old to see if the condition resolves itself as the head matures.

Everted laryngeal saccules and a weakening of the windpipe can result when the dog has to breathe through a restrictive airway for a long time. If the veterinary surgeon can increase the size of the airway and decrease the inspiratory (breathing in) pressure before the airway is damaged, then the dog can breathe much easier.

The key here is to keep a lookout for the tell-tale signs and if you are at all worried that your dog is showing one or several of the symptoms, then consult a vet, and speak to your breeder about any past history in the line. The earlier BAOS is diagnosed and treated, the better the outlook for your dog.

Bostons and Anaesthetic

It is always a concern for owners if their beloved Boston needs to be anaesthetised for a surgical procedure – and it's also a factor to be considered when deciding when or whether to have your dog spayed or neutered. (Some breeders may stipulate in the Puppy Contract that the dog has to be spayed or neutered if it is not a show dog).

The problem with many brachycephalic dogs is that there is simply too much soft tissue squashed into their shortened heads. In practical terms what this means is that Bostons may have difficulty breathing, or at least have smaller airways than many other breeds.

Dogs that cope perfectly well on a daily basis can have difficulty with anaesthetic when all their muscles are relaxed and the narrow airways effectively become blocked. Keeping your dog's weight under control is important' as obesity increases the risk of breathing problems, as well as many other health issues.

Pick a vet who is familiar with brachycephalic breeds, as they can react differently to other dogs under anaesthetic.

Tip Here are some points to be familiar with before agreeing to surgery – and ask your vet beforehand to outline the extra care he or she will be taking with your Boston:

- Food and water should be restricted 12 hours before surgery as vomiting can have serious consequences -discuss this with your vet

- The vet should provide oxygen before anaesthesia to help saturate the dog's lungs with extra oxygen

- Some Bostons should not be masked, they can become anxious and experience breathing difficulties

- The dog should have an endotracheal tube (ET) in his or her windpipe (trachea) to keep the airway open at all times. The tube should be kept in place as long as possible and until the dog is fully awake

- The vet should have a special anaesthetic procedure or protocol for Bostons and other brachycephalic breeds

- This protocol should take into account anti-vomiting, anti-inflammatory, anti-anxiety measures and pain management to reduce common complications

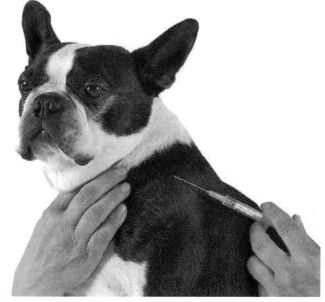

The French Bulldog Rescue Network has an Anaesthesia Protocol developed by Dr Lori Hunt, DVM and Dr Dawn Ruben, DVM, who advise AGAINST the use of the following drugs: Acepromazine, Phenobarbital (injectable anaesthetic), Xylazine (sedative) and Halothane (gas anaesthetic). See their full Anaesthesia Protocol for brachycephalic dogs at: www.frenchbulldogrescue.org/adoption-info/faq/anesthesia-policy.

A critical time is the recovery phase after the surgical procedure - and this is where YOU come in. Here are some tips to help your Boston towards a full and speedy recovery:

- Keep your dog within sight for 12 to 24 hours after surgery
- Monitor the colour of your dog's tongue – pink is good, blue is bad
- Keep your Boston well ventilated. If your dog is panting excessively, check his temperature (with a canine thermometer). If it is several degrees above the normal above 101°F, turn a fan on and face it towards him
- Keep your dog in a quiet, stress-free place, and try and keep him relaxed

....

Hemivertebrae

Hemivertebrae is the name given to a genetic abnormality of the spine that occurs when the puppy is still a foetus in the mother's womb. 'Hemi' means half and 'vertebrae' are the series of small bones that link to make up the backbone or spine. It occurs when one side of the vertebrae does not develop properly. The vertebrae can be fused or they are wedge-shaped, causing a twisting of the spine.

The condition is not uncommon in Boston Terriers and other brachycephalic breeds like the Bulldog, Pug and French Bulldog (pictured). It is a consequence of being bred for a short back. How it affects each individual Boston varies; if the deformity is restricted to the thoracic region (the section of back near the shoulders), it is not a problem. But when it affects the rest of the spine it can cause serious problems, as the deformed vertebrae create a wedging effect that twists the spine, which can cause compression (squashing) of the spinal cord.

Signs usually first appear in puppies and often progressively get worse, until they level off at about nine to 12 months, once the spine stops growing. Symptoms include weakness in the hind limbs, pain, and incontinence –of both urine and faeces. It can be a very painful condition and in extreme cases when no more treatment is available, it may well be kinder to have the dog put to sleep.

Diagnosis is relatively straightforward. A vet will take X-rays to see if the condition is present in the spine. He or she may then use more advanced technologies like myelograms, CT scans or MRIs to see if there is any compression of the spinal cord. Because this is a condition the dog is born with, it cannot be cured; although surgery may be an option in some cases, this is a VERY expensive surgery and success is rarely guaranteed). The best way to ensure that your Boston does not have it is to get the dog from a responsible breeder.

With thanks to the UK's Universities Federation for Animal Welfare (UFAW) for the following, more scientific, explanation of Hemivertebrae:

"Boston Terriers commonly have deformities of the bones of the spine. These can lead to pressure on the spinal cord resulting in progressive pain and loss of hind limb function and incontinence. Hemivertebrae are bones of the spine that are abnormally shaped. Because of their abnormal shape, these bones tend not to align correctly with their neighbouring bones in the spine. This can lead to instability and deformity of the spinal column, which in turn can lead to the spinal cord or the nerves arising from it becoming squashed and damaged.

"This causes pain – which can be severe - wobbliness (ataxia) on the hind legs and can also cause loss of hind leg function and incontinence (inability to control passing urine or faeces). It appears that the disease is a consequence of selecting for the screw (curly) tail conformation of this breed. The screw-tail shape is due to abnormal shape of tail bones but this abnormality can also affect other parts of the spine with serious consequences as outlined above.

"Pain from spinal cord compression (squashing) can be severe. Affected dogs can also lose function in their hind limbs and sometimes lose bladder and bowel control. Not all animals with hemivertebrae develop these signs; some have milder signs of ataxia or no signs at all. Dogs with severe signs may need major surgical interventions, which have their own welfare impacts, and, despite this, some may not recover and need to be euthanized on humane grounds.

"Young dogs are most commonly affected when problems associated with skeletal deformities develop as their skeleton grows. The skeletal deformity is permanent without surgery. The clinical signs associated with the condition can develop rapidly over days, or gradually over weeks and months. Severely affected individuals would, without surgery, have permanent major disability. Even where surgery is possible, some animals may have unacceptable levels of disability necessitating euthanasia. Thus this condition can severely limit both the quality and length of life.

"The exact numbers affected are not known, but it is considered a common problem in Boston Terriers and other brachycephalic (short-nosed) breeds that have screw-tails. Selection for screw tails, which are caused by deformed vertebrae, has the unintended consequence of causing deformity higher up the spine also.

"Screw tail describes a tail which, in its relaxed position, is coiled, usually to one side. The most

severely affected tails cannot be straightened at all, others can be manually straightened but relax back into the coiled position. The exact genetics of this condition have yet to be worked out; however, Boston Terriers are considered to be predisposed to hemivertebrae because of the breed characteristic of a screw-tail. The gene(s) causing the screw-tail deformity (which involves hemivertebrae in the tail) are thought also to be involved in producing hemivertebrae elsewhere in the spine.

Methods and prospects for elimination of the problem are not known, though whilst the breed standard includes a screw-tail the condition seems likely to persist. It seems likely, since the screw tail is caused by hemivertebrae in the tail, that out-breeding to dogs with straight tails, then selection for a straight tail might be a way forward to eliminate this welfare problem."

Hypothyroidism

Hypothyroidism is a common hormonal disorder in dogs generally and is due to an under-active thyroid gland. The gland (located on either side of the windpipe in the dog's throat) does not produce enough of the hormone thyroid, which controls the speed of the metabolism. Dogs with very low thyroid levels have a slow metabolic rate. It occurs mainly in dogs over the age of five.

Scientists are not exactly sure what causes it, but it is thought that 50% of the time it is the dog's own immune system that damages the thyroid gland, so in these cases it is an auto immune disease. The BTCA's own Health Survey found that 3% of Boston Terriers had the condition, and the Club says that the thyroid testing laboratories at Michigan State University report that 2.1% of Bostons tested were affected.

Generally, hypothyroidism occurs most frequently in larger, middle-aged dogs of either gender. The symptoms are often non-specific and quite gradual in onset, and they may vary depending on breed and age. Most forms of hypothyroidism are diagnosed with a blood test and the OFA provides a registry for thyroid screening in the USA.

Common Symptoms - These have been listed in order, with the most common ones being at the top of the list:

- High blood cholesterol
- Lethargy
- Hair loss
- Weight gain or obesity
- Dry coat or excessive shedding
- Hyper pigmentation or darkening of the skin, seen in 25% of cases
- Intolerance to cold, seen in 15% of dogs with the condition

The BTCA adds that with Bostons, another symptom can be 'rat (i.e. bald) tail.'

Treatment - Although hypothyroidism is a type of auto-immune disease and cannot be prevented, symptoms can usually be easily diagnosed and successfully treated. Most cases can be well-managed on thyroid hormone replacement therapy tablets.

The affected dog is placed on a daily dose of a synthetic thyroid hormone called thyroxine (levothyroxine). The dog is usually given a standard dose for his weight and then blood samples are taken periodically to monitor him and the dose is adjusted accordingly. Depending upon your dog's preferences and needs, the medication can be given in different forms, such as a solid tablet, in liquid form, or a gel that can be rubbed into his ears. Once treatment has started, he will be on it for the rest of his life.

In some less common situations, surgery may be required to remove part or all of the thyroid gland. Another treatment is radioiodine, where radioactive iodine is used to kill the overactive cells of the thyroid. While this is considered one of the most effective treatments, not all dogs are suitable for the procedure and lengthy hospitalisation is often required. Happily, once the diagnosis has been made and treatment has started, whichever treatment your dog undergoes, the majority of symptoms disappear.

Eye Problems

One of the Boston Terrier's most endearing features is also one of the biggest potential areas of concern - and that is his big, beautiful eyes. The large, protruding eyes can easily become injured, so owners need to take special care to protect them. In addition, there are a number of diseases that can affect Bostons' eyes.

Avoid buying an puppy with one of the inheritable eye diseases by choosing a reputable breeder who can show you eye certificates to prove that the parents have not passed eye disease to your chosen puppy. It may cost you more than buying from a breeder who doesn't health test, but it will be worth it in the long run. Illness and constant visits to the vet are costly and very distressing for you and the dog.

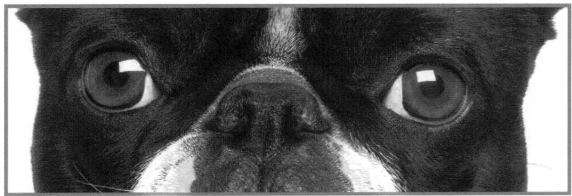

The Boston Terrier Club of America (BTCA) says: "There are over 20 different eye diseases that are known to occur in Boston Terriers ... The one we fear the most is Juvenile Cataracts, which will cause total blindness in very young dogs. With Boston Terriers it is recommended that CAER exams be given every year." (BVA screening in the UK).

"Our personal recommendation if you don't want to do it every year, is to do it before every breeding or in any year you breed your Boston Terrier. This should ensure that you don't pass a serious eye disease on to the puppies. Also make sure that all puppies are CAER-tested before they go to their new homes."

 Here are some things owners can do to help keep eyes safe:

🐾 Remove thorny plants, such as roses, from your garden - or fence them off

🐾 Don't let your dog stick his head out of the car window when travelling; the pressure is bad for his eyes and they may also get damaged by particles in the air

🐾 Don't leave your Boston in bright sunshine for long periods, as it can damage his eyes (too much heat is generally bad for Bostons, anyway) - you can buy a doggie sun visor to give shade to your dog's eyes.

🐾 Be careful when heading off into the countryside - avoid sharp plants and objects and very dusty areas; Bostons' eyes are magnets for dust and other particles

🐾 Don't play too rough with your dog - and don't let the kids rough-house, either

🐾 Use a harness, not a collar when our walking. Straining against a collar can force dangerous pressure onto shallow eyeballs

🐾 Carry eye wash when out and about with your dog

Hereditary Cataracts

Juvenile Hereditary Cataract (JHC), sometimes also referred to as Early Onset Hereditary Cataract (EHC), is a condition that is known to affect the Boston Terrier – and one which the breeders involved in this book regard as a major issue. Studies by the USA's OFA ranked the Boston Terrier second worst out of all breeds for the incidence of cataracts.

The purpose of the transparent lens is to focus the rays of light form an image on the retina. A cataract occurs when the lens becomes cloudy. Less light enters the eye, images become blurry and the dog's sight diminishes as the cataract becomes larger. Untreated, it can result in blindness. One or both eyes may be affected and the cataracts may not appear at the same time. Other affected breeds are the Staffordshire Bull Terrier and French Bulldog.

JHC may be seen as early as eight weeks old, when owners might notice small white flecks in their dog's eye(s). The condition develops and dogs with JHC are completely blind by two years of age or so. The mutated gene has been identified by scientists as the HSF4, and the DNA test, called 'Juvenile Hereditary Cataract HC-HSF4' (HSF4 in the USA) is available both in the UK and USA. The gene is recessive and dogs get one of three results:

CLEAR - dogs have no copies of the mutant gene and will neither develop the condition nor pass the gene on to their offspring.

CARRIER - dogs have one copy of the normal gene and one copy of the mutant gene. They will not develop the condition, but will pass a mutant gene on to some 50% of their offspring. These dogs, if bred, should be bred only to Clear dogs.

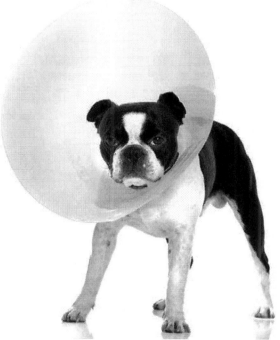

AFFECTED - dogs have two copies of the mutant gene that causes the condition and WILL develop the disease. These dogs should not be bred.

Ask to see the parents' eye certificates if you are buying a puppy. All good Boston Terrier breeders should eye test and will show you the current certificate for the mother and a copy of the father's, if he is elsewhere. The gene is 'autosomal recessive' which means that BOTH parents have to be Affected for the pup to inherit JHC. A Carrier and a Clear can be bred together to produce a litter with no Affecteds, but half of the litter will be Carriers.

Although a Carrier has no outward signs of JHC, breeding two Carriers together will result in both Carrier and Affected pups. There is also a middle-aged onset cataract, which develops when a dog is a bit older (not a juvenile, but not yet a senior). Older Bostons can also be afflicted by Late Onset Hereditary Cataracts, but the HSF4 gene mutation is not responsible for this. Scientists have yet to identify the responsible gene for these two cataracts.

Diagnosis - Hereditary cataracts are usually first diagnosed when the owner sees their dog bumping into furniture, or when his pupils have changed colour. You may also see that the middle of the pupil has a white spot or area. Try shining a torch at your dog's eyes or taking a picture with a flash and you should see a coloured reflection in his eye. If you see something grey or dull white, your pup may have a cataract. The vet will refer the pet to an ophthalmic specialist to carry out the same eye exam that is done for breeding stock.

The process is painless and simple; drops are put into the eyes and the dog is taken into a dark room after a few minutes for examination and diagnosis.

Treatment - If you think your Boston Terrier may have cataracts, it is important to get him to a vet as soon as possible. Cataracts progress at varying rates; some have a slow onset, while others can rapidly cause blindness. Occasionally, if a puppy's cataracts are small, they can be watched and may not need treatment. They won't go away, but they may not get bigger quickly. Discuss this with your vet and if you agree on this option, you have to be extremely vigilant and monitor your puppy's eyes for any signs of change.

Puppies born with congenital cataracts can sometimes improve as they mature. That's because the lens inside the puppy's eye grows along with the dog. When the area of cloudiness on the lens remains the same size, by the time the puppy becomes an adult, the affected portion of the lens is relatively small. By adulthood, some dogs born with cataracts are able to compensate and see 'around' the cloudiness.

However, the only treatment for more severe canine cataracts is surgery, unless the cataracts are caused by another underlying condition, such as diabetes. (Not all cataracts are operable). Despite what you may have heard, laser surgery does not exist for canine cataracts, neither is there any proven medical treatment other than surgery.

Surgery runs into thousands of pounds or dollars, as discussed in the **Insurance** section, but the good news is that it is almost always (85-90%) successful and restores excellent vision. The dog has to have a general anaesthetic (again, this needs discussion with your vet), and the procedure is similar to small incision cataract surgery in people, with the lens being replaced. The good news is that once the cataract has been removed, it does not recur. One point to note is that cataract surgery can occasionally trigger glaucoma, and the dog will then require lifetime daily eye drops. Before your Boston can undergo this procedure, though, he has to be passed fit and a suitable candidate for surgery.

After the operation, he will probably have to stay at the surgery overnight so that the professionals can keep an eye on him. And once back home, he will demand a lot of your care and attention. He has to wear a protective Elizabethan collar, or E collar, usually for one to three weeks while his eye is healing. The next part is important: you have to keep him quiet and calm (not always easy with Bostons!) You'll also have to give him eye drops, perhaps four times a day for the first week and then less frequently after that – maybe for up to six months. The success of cataract surgery depends very much on the owner doing all the right things. But all the effort will be worth it when your dog regains his sight.

Corneal Ulcers

The protruding eyes of the Boston Terrier make the breed prone to this problem, which is also called Ulcerative Keratitis. The transparent part of the eye known as the cornea forms a cover over the iris and pupil and admits light to the inside of the eye. When dust and larger particles get into the Boston's eye, they cause irritation - just as they do with humans – and, if left untreated, can cause infection and corneal ulcers.

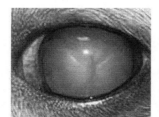 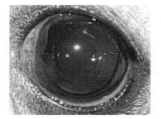

Left: eye with cataracts. Right: same eye with artificial lens

The BTCA says: "Perhaps one dog in ten will experience a corneal ulcer sometime during its life, based on the l,903 dogs surveyed in the 2000 Boston Terrier Health Survey.

"Corneal Ulcers can be difficult and expensive to treat and often result in the loss of the eye. This is a case where an "ounce of prevention is worth a pound of cure." Some of these reasons for lack of good healing are inherited problems that can be picked up in a CAER examination before a dog is bred."

The symptoms of this painful condition are:

- 🐾 Red, painful or watery eye
- 🐾 Squinting
- 🐾 Sensitivity to light
- 🐾 Rubbing the eyes with the paw
- 🐾 Eye remaining closed
- 🐾 Discharge or film over the eye

Treatment depends on the cause, and if the ulcers are deep or are growing, surgery may be necessary. The vet may also put an E collar on your dog to prevent him from scratching his eyes. Less severe cases do not require surgery. Instead, the condition will be treated with antibiotics and ointment applied to the eye. It is critical to treat the eye religiously to help ensure proper healing.

Inflammation and pain may be treated with nonsteroidal anti-inflammatory drugs (NSAIDs). In certain cases, the vet may insert contact lenses to reduce eyelid irritation, which can sometimes substitute for surgery.

Corneal Dystrophy is a different progressive disease and affects a small number of dogs. It occurs when fluid builds up, causing the cornea to turn white, and can affect dogs of any age. It is thought to be inherited, but it is not yet known how. Corneal Dystrophy usually starts in the corner of the eyes and spreads. It can be difficult to treat and may cause a Corneal Ulcer. However, although the affected areas may be highly visible, they rarely cause blindness. Treatment depends of severity and includes low fat, high fibre diet, ointments and, in extreme cases, a surgical procedure called keratectomy.

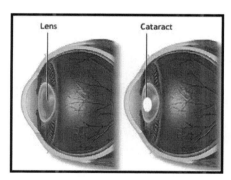

Cherry Eye

Humans have two eyelids, but dogs have a third eyelid, called a nictating membrane. This third eyelid is a thin, opaque tissue with a tear gland that rests in the inner corner of the eye. Its purpose is to provide additional protection for the eye and to spread tears over the eyeball. Usually it is retracted and therefore you can't see it, although you may notice it when your dog is relaxed and falling asleep. When the third eyelid becomes visible it may be a sign of illness or a painful eye.

Cherry Eye is a medical condition, officially known as *nictitans gland prolapse*, or prolapse of the gland of the third eyelid. Boston Terriers are one breed with a susceptibility to this, although it is not known whether the condition is inherited. Other susceptible breeds include the Bulldog, Beagle, Bloodhound, French Bulldog, Bull Terrier, Cocker Spaniel, Lhasa Apso, Saint Bernard and Shar-Pei. Studies have shown that around 6% of Bostons are affected by it.

Causes - The exact cause of Cherry Eye is not known, but it is thought to be due to a weakness of the fibrous tissue which attaches the gland to the surrounding eye. This weakness allows the gland to fall down, or prolapse. Once this has happened and the gland is exposed to the dry air and irritants, it can become infected and/or begin to swell. The gland often becomes irritated, red and swollen. There is sometimes a mucous discharge and if the dog rubs or scratches it, he can further damage the gland and even possibly create an ulcer on the surface of the eye.

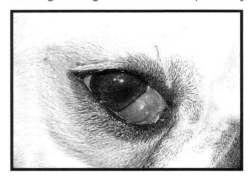

Symptoms - The main visible symptom in a red, often swollen, mass in the corner of one or both eyes, which is often first seen in young dogs up to the age of two years. It can occur in one or both eyes and may be accompanied by swelling and/or irritation. Although it may look sore, it is not a painful condition for your dog.

Treatment - At one time, it was popular to surgically remove the gland to correct this condition. While this was often effective, it could create problems later on. The gland of the third eyelid is very important for producing tears, without which dogs could suffer from 'Dry Eye', also known as Keratoconjunctivitis Sicca (KCS). These days, removing the gland is not considered a good idea.

A far better and straightforward option is to surgically reposition the gland by tacking it back into place with a single stitch that attaches the gland to the deeper structures of the eye socket. There is also another type of operation during which the wedge of tissue is removed from directly over the gland. Tiny dissolving stitches are used to close the gap so that the gland is pushed back into place. After surgery the dog may be placed on antibiotic ointment for a few days.

Mostly, surgery is performed quickly and for most dogs that's the end of the matter. However, a few dogs do have a recurrence of cherry eye. The eye should return to normal after about seven days, during which time there may be some redness or swelling. If the affected eye suddenly seems uncomfortable or painful for your dog, or you can see protruding stitches, then take him back to the vet to get checked out. Other options include anti-inflammatory eye drops to reduce the swelling and manually manipulating the gland back into place.

 Sometimes a dog will develop Cherry Eye in one eye and then the condition will also appear some time later in the other eye. If you have a young dog diagnosed with Cherry Eye, discuss waiting a few weeks or months before having any surgery to see if the second eye is affected. This will save the dog being anesthetised twice and will also save you money. Discuss this with your vet.

Glaucoma

Glaucoma is a condition that puts pressure on the eye, and if the condition becomes chronic or continues without treatment, it will eventually cause permanent damage to the optic nerve, resulting in blindness.

A normal eye contains a fluid called aqueous humour to maintain its shape, and the body is constantly adding and removing fluid from inside of the eye to maintain the pressure inside the eye at the proper level. Glaucoma occurs when the pressure inside the eyeball becomes higher than normal. Just as high blood pressure can damage the heart, excessive pressure inside the eye can damage the eye's internal structures. Unless glaucoma is treated quickly, temporary loss of vision or even total blindness can result.

The cornea and lens inside the eye are living tissues, but they have no blood vessels to supply the oxygen and nutrition they need; these are delivered through the aqueous humour. In glaucoma, the increased pressure is most frequently caused by this fluid not being able to properly drain away from the eye.

Fluid is constantly being produced and if an equal amount does not leave the globe, then the pressure starts to rise, similar to a water balloon. As more water is added the balloon stretches more and more. The balloon will eventually burst, but the eye is stronger so this does not happen. Instead the eye's internal structures are damaged irreparably.

Secondary glaucoma means that it is caused by another problem, such as a wound to the eye. Primary glaucoma is normally inherited.

Symptoms - Even though a puppy may carry the gene for this disorder, the disease itself does not usually develop until a dog is at least two or three years old; usually a little while after reaching maturity. The dog has to first reach maturity, with primary glaucoma, both eyes are rarely affected equally or at the same time, it usually starts in one eye several months or even years before it affects the second one. Glaucoma is a serious disease and it's important for an owner to be able to immediately recognise early signs. If treatment is not started within a few days - or even hours in some cases - of the pressure increasing, the dog will probably lose sight in that eye. Here are the early signs:

- ❧ Pain
- ❧ Dilated pupil or one pupil that looks bigger than the other
- ❧ Rapid blinking
- ❧ Cloudiness in the cornea at the front of the eye
- ❧ Redness in the whites of an eye (bloodshot)
- ❧ One eye looks larger or sticks out further than the other one
- ❧ Loss of appetite, which may be due to headaches
- ❧ Change in attitude, less willing to play, etc.

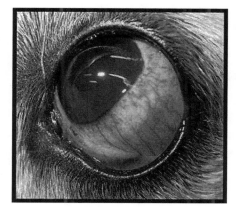

Most dogs will not display all of these signs at first, perhaps just one or two. A dog rubbing his eye with his paw, against the furniture or carpet or your leg is a common - and often unnoticed- early sign. Some dogs will also seem to flutter the eyelids or squint with one eye.

The pupil of the affected eye will usually dilate (get bigger) in the early stages of glaucoma. It may still react to all bright light, but it will do so very slowly. Remember that glaucoma is usually going to initially affect just one of the eyes. If the pupil in one eye is larger than in the other, something is definitely wrong and it could be glaucoma.

If you suspect your dog has glaucoma, get him to the vet as soon as possible, i.e. **immediately,** not the day after, this is a medical emergency. The vet will carry out a manual examination and test your dog's eye pressure using a tonometer on the surface of the eye. There is still a fair chance that the dog may lose sight in this eye, but a much better chance of saving the second eye with the knowledge and preventative measures learned from early intervention.

Treatment revolves around reducing the pressure within the affected eye, draining the aqueous humour and providing pain relief, as this can be a painful condition for your dog. There are also surgical options for the long-term control of glaucoma. As yet it cannot be cured.

Distichiasis

This is the medical term for abnormally growing eyelashes irritating a dog's eyes. With this condition small eyelashes abnormally grow on the inner surface or the very edge of the eyelid, and both upper and lower eyelids may be affected. Some breeds are affected more than others, suggesting that it is an inherited trait, including the Boston Terrier, Cocker Spaniel, Golden Retriever, Boxer and Pekingese.

The affected eye becomes red, inflamed, and may develop a discharge. The dog will typically squint or blink a lot, just like a human with a hair or other foreign matter in the eye. The dog will often rub his eye against furniture, other objects or the carpet. In severe cases, the cornea can become ulcerated and it looks a blue colour. If left, the condition usually worsens and severe ulcerations and infections develop that can lead to blindness.

The dog can make the condition worse by scratching or rubbing his eyes. The constant rubbing of the eyelash against the eye can also cause Corneal Ulcers or scarring on the eye if left untreated.

Treatment usually involves surgery or electro- or cryo-epilation, where a needle is inserted into the hair follicle and an ultra-fast electric current is emitted. This current produces heat which destroys the stem cells responsible for hair growth. This procedure may need to be repeated after several months because all of the abnormal hairs may not have developed at the time of the first treatment -although this is not common with dogs older than three years.

During surgery, the lid is split and areas where abnormal hairs grow are removed. Both treatments require anaesthesia and usually result in a full recovery. After surgery, the eyelids are swollen for four to five days and the eyelid margins turn pink. Usually they return to the normal colour within four months. Antibiotic eye drops are often used following surgery to prevent infections.

Entropion

This is a condition in which the edge of the lower eyelid rolls inward, causing the dog's fur to rub the surface of the eyeball, or cornea. In rare cases the upper lid can also be affected, and one or both eyes may be involved.

This painful condition is thought to be hereditary and is more commonly found in dog breeds with a wrinkled face, like the Bulldog, French Bulldog and Boston Terrier. Other affected breeds include the Chow Chow, Bloodhound, Pug, Bull Mastiff, Great Dane, Rottweiler, Akita, Shar Pei, Spaniel, Poodle and Labrador Retriever.

The affected dog will scratch at his painful eye with his paws and this can lead to further injury. If your Boston is to suffer from Entropion, he will usually show signs at or before his first birthday. You will notice that his eyes are red and inflamed and they will produce tears. He will probably squint.

The tears typically start off clear and can progress to a thick yellow or green mucus. If the Entropion causes Corneal Ulcers, you might also notice a milky-white colour develop. This is caused by increased fluid, which affects the clarity of the cornea. For your poor dog, the irritation is constant.

Imagine how painful and uncomfortable it would be if you had permanent hairs touching your eyes. It makes my eyes water just thinking about it.

It's important to get your dog to the vet as soon as you suspect Entropion, before he scratches his cornea and makes matters worse. The condition can cause scarring around the eyes or other issues which can jeopardise a dog's vision if left untreated. A vet will make the diagnosis after a painless and relatively simple inspection of your dog's eyes. But before he or she can diagnose Entropion, they will have to rule out other issues, such as allergies, which might also be making your dog's eyes red and itchy. That's another reason why it is a good idea to find a vet who is familiar with brachycephalic breeds and their associated health issues.

In young Bostons, some vets may delay surgery and treat the condition with medication until the dog's face is fully formed to avoid having to repeat the procedure at a later date. In mild cases, the vet may successfully prescribe eye drops, ointment or other medication. However, the most common treatment for more severe cases is a fairly straightforward surgical procedure to pin back the lower eyelid. Discuss the severity of the condition and all possible options with your vet before proceeding to surgery.

Dry Eye (Keratitis Sicca)

Also known as **Keratoconjunctivitis sicca** or **KCS**, this is a condition thought to affect 2% of young Bostons and occurs when not enough tears are produced. With insufficient tears, a dog's eyes can become irritated and the conjunctiva appears to be red.

The eyes typically develop a thick, yellowy discharge. Infections are common as tears also have anti-bacterial and cleansing properties, and inadequate lubrication allows dust, pollen and other debris to accumulate. The nerves of these glands may also become damaged.

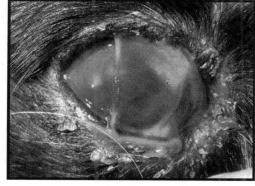

In many cases the reason for Dry Eye is not known, other times it may be caused by injuries to the tear glands, eye infections, reactions to drugs, an immune reaction or even the gland of the third eyelid being surgically removed by mistake. Left untreated, the dog will suffer painful and chronic eye infections. Repeated irritation of the cornea results in severe scarring and ulcers may develop, which can lead to blindness.

Treatment usually involves drugs; cyclosporine, ophthalmic ointment or drops being the most common. In some cases another eye preparation – Tacrolimus - is also used and may be effective when cyclosporine is not. Often artificial tear solutions are also prescribed. In very severe cases, an operation can be performed to transplant a salivary duct into the upper eyelid, causing saliva to drain into and lubricate the eye. This procedure is rarely used, but is an option.

Eye Care for Boston Terriers

Some eye conditions affecting Boston Terriers may be inherited, but there are other issues, such as dirt or pollen in the eye, which are environmental. Bostons' eyes can easily attract irritating material, which makes your dog rub or scratch them, potentially causing injury. Also, some Boston Terriers may suffer from allergies that also cause their eyes to become irritated.

Whatever the reason, it is a good idea to get into the habit of checking your dog's eyes and the surrounding skin folds (wrinkles) at least once a week. This also enables you to monitor any changes in the eyes and, if a problem such as infection or cherry eye does occur, you can get on top of it right away.

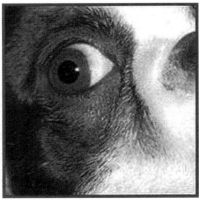

Tear staining is not uncommon with Bostons, and it is especially noticeable on white areas of skin. These brownish, wet stains are also a breeding ground for bacteria and yeast. The most common is Red Yeast, usually associated with reddish-brown facial stains and which may emit an odour.

Tear staining can be related to shallow eye sockets, health and diet as well as genetics. Most vets agree that face staining results from excessive tear production and a damp face. Also any skin folds around the face attract dirt, so keeping them clean should be a regular part of your BTMP (Boston Terrier Maintenance Programme!)

Wet a cotton ball with a sterile eye wash -or use eye wipes - to gently rub the folds around your dog's eyes, clearing them of any dried discharge. Repeat with clean cotton balls or wipes until the area is clean. There are videos on YouTube that demonstrate how to do it. Remember to dry after cleaning to deter yeast infections. There are many canine tear stain removers on the market - some are quite expensive, but if it saves you having to visit the vet's with eye infections it will be worth it in the long run.

Some owners have tried home remedies with some success, such as using an astringent to clean and dry the area. Remedies involving vinegar and other natural ingredients are also used, but regardless of what you use, be extremely careful of anything you put near your dog's eyes. If in any doubt at all about a product or remedy, check with your vet.

Also be on the lookout for ingrowing eyelashes or Dry Eye, which occurs when the eyes are not producing enough tears. A green discharge is usually present, and a hazy blue film can appear on the eyeball. Your vet can carry out a simple test to diagnose the problem, and may prescribe artificial tears that you should apply daily. (Humans can get the same problem, particularly when they get older).

Eye Testing

There are various ways of testing for hereditary eye conditions. In the USA there is the OptiGen PRA Test and the annual CAER test associated with the Orthopedic Foundation for Animals (OFA). The aim of the OFA is to promote the health and welfare of companion animals through a reduction in the incidence of genetic disease

In the UK there is the British Veterinary Association (BVA) Eye Test, an annual test, carried out due to the fact some diseases have a late onset. If you are buying a puppy, it is highly advisable to check if the parents have been tested and given the all-clear. Always ensure the breeder lets you see the original certificate (which is white in the UK) and not a photocopy.

Identification of dogs that do not carry diseased genes is the key to eradicating the problem within the breed.

Luxating Patella

Luxating patella, also called 'floating kneecap' or 'slipped stifle' can be a painful condition akin to a dislocated knee cap in humans.

It is sometimes congenital (present from birth) and typically affects small and miniature breeds. It is one of the most common ailments affecting Boston Terriers — studies show it may affect up to 10% of Bostons. In mild cases the kneecap may pop back into its socket of its own accord, while more severe cases can lead to a rupturing of the anterior cruciate ligament and surgery.

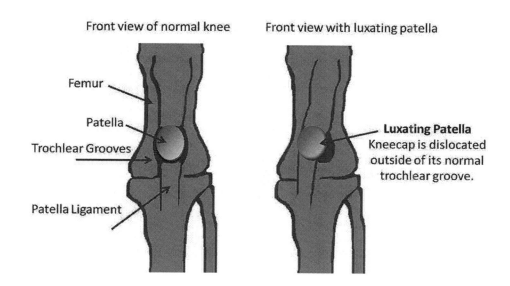

Front view of normal knee   Front view with luxating patella

Femur

Patella

Trochlear Grooves

Patella Ligament

Luxating Patella
Kneecap is dislocated outside of its normal trochlear groove.

Symptoms - A typical sign would be if your dog is running across the park when he suddenly pulls up short and yelps with pain. He might limp on three legs and then after a period of about 10 minutes, drop the affected leg and start to walk normally again. Another sign is that you might notice him stretching out a rear leg quite often or 'skipping' once in a while when walking or running.

If the condition is severe, he may hold up the affected leg up for a few days. Dogs that have a luxating patella on both hind legs may change their gait completely, dropping their hindquarters and holding the rear legs further out from the body as they walk. In the most extreme cases they might not even use their rear legs, but walk like a circus act by balancing on their front legs so their hindquarters don't touch the ground.

Genetics, injury and malformation during development can all cause this problem. Because it is difficult to determine if the luxation is genetic, it is best not to breed a dog that is affected (unless there is documented proof of injury). If you are buying a puppy, ask if there is any history in either parent and ask to see screening certificates for the parents. Typically many sufferers are middle-aged dogs with a history of intermittent lameness in the affected rear leg or legs, although the condition may appear as early as four to six months old.

A groove in the end of the femur (thigh bone) allows the knee cap to glide up and down when the knee joint is bent, while keeping it in place at the same time. If this groove is too shallow, the knee cap may luxate — or dislocate. It can only return to its natural position when the quadriceps muscle relaxes and increases in length, which is why a dog may have to hold his leg up for some time after the dislocation.

Sometimes the problem can be caused – and is certainly worsened - by obesity, the excess weight putting too much strain on the joint – another good reason to keep your Boston's weight in check.

Treatment - There are four grades of patellar luxation, ranging from Grade I, which sometimes has no symptoms at all, to Grade IV, in which the patella cannot be realigned manually. This gives the dog a bow-legged appearance. If left untreated, the groove will become even shallower and the dog will become progressively lamer, with arthritis prematurely affecting the joint. This will cause a permanently swollen knee and reduce your Boston's mobility. It is therefore important to get your dog in for a veterinary check-up ASAP if you suspect he may have a luxating patella.

Surgery is often required for Grade III and IV luxation, although this should not be undertaken lightly, due to potential breathing problems under anaesthetic. In these cases, known as a **trochlear modification**, the groove at the base of the femur is surgically deepened to better hold the knee cap in place. The good news is that dogs generally respond well, whatever the type of surgery, and are usually completely recovered within one to two months.

Hip Dysplasia

Canine Hip Dysplasia (CHD) is the most common cause of hind leg lameness in dogs. It is generally a hereditary condition that occurs mainly in large breeds, but it is not uncommon for Boston Terriers to also be affected.

With big breeds the effects are obvious, but this is not the case with small, lighter breeds like the Boston. Some Bostons may have CHD (also referred to as Hip Dysplasia or HD), yet often show no outward signs of it and live perfectly normal lives.

OFA studies carried out in the USA before December 2015 show that of the 263 Boston Terriers tested, 11.8% were found to have abnormal hips. However, the breed is still only ranked 96th out of all breeds for this problem.

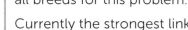

Currently the strongest link to contributing factors is genetic predisposition and rapid growth and weight gain; the latter two apply to large dogs, rather than the Boston Terrier.

The hip is a ball and socket joint. Hip dysplasia is caused when the head of the femur (thigh bone) fits loosely into a shallow and poorly-developed socket in the pelvis. The right hand side of the diagram shows a shallow hip socket and a deformed femur head, causing hip dysplasia. The healthy joint is on the left.

Most dogs with dysplasia are born with normal hips, but due to their genetic make-up – and possibly other factors such as diet – the soft tissues that surround the joint develop abnormally. The joint carrying the weight of the dog becomes loose and unstable, muscle growth lags behind normal development and is often followed by degenerative joint disease or osteoarthritis, which is the body's attempt to stabilise the loose hip joint. Early diagnosis gives your vet the best chance to tackle the problem as soon as possible, minimising the chance of arthritis developing.

Symptoms are not often seen in the Boston, but when they are, they can range from mild discomfort to extreme pain. A pup with hip dysplasia often starts to show signs between five and 13 months old.

Symptoms

- 🐾 Lameness in the hind legs, particularly after exercise
- 🐾 Difficulty or stiffness when getting up or climbing uphill
- 🐾 'Bunny hop' gait
- 🐾 Dragging the rear end when getting up
- 🐾 Waddling rear leg gait
- 🐾 Painful reaction to stretching the hind legs, resulting in a short stride
- 🐾 Side-to-side sway of the croup (area above the tail) with a tendency to tilt the hips down if you push down on the croup
- 🐾 Reluctance to jump, exercise or climb stairs
- 🐾 Sitting like a frog with legs splayed behind (although this can be normal for some dogs)

OFA states that hip evaluations are not 'official' until the dog is two years of age. Anything between one year and younger than two years is considered 'preliminary.' and anything younger than one year of age is not considered. Using a technique called palpation and hip manipulation, vets can often detect hip dysplasia before symptoms become evident and when radiographs fail to identify abnormalities. Moving the knee towards the centre causes the hip to fall out of its socket and moving the knee away from the centre causes the hip to return to the socket.

Causes and Triggers - Canine hip dysplasia is usually an inherited condition. But there are also factors that can trigger or worsen the condition, including:

1. Overfeeding, especially on a diet high in protein and calories
2. Excess calcium, also usually due to overfeeding
3. Extended periods without exercise – or too much vigorous exercise – especially when a young Boston and his bones are growing
4. Obesity
5. Excess time, particularly sleeping and lying down, on concrete or very hard surfaces

Advances in nutritional research have shown that diet plays an important role in the development of hip dysplasia. It's important for owners to realise that, no matter how cutely your Boston stares at you pleading for food with those beautiful big brown eyes, excess pounds will place a strain on your dog and eventually take their toll.

Feeding a high-calorie or high calcium diet to growing dogs can trigger a predisposition to hip dysplasia, as the rapid weight gain places increased stress on the hips. Make sure your dog is on the right diet for his age. When you take your puppy to the vet's for his injections, ask for advice on the best diet. Also speak to your breeder, a good breeder will remain at the end of a phone line to give advice throughout your Boston's life.

Exercise may be another risk factor. Dogs that have a predisposition to hip dysplasia may have an increased chance of getting it if they are over-exercised at a young age. On the other hand, dogs with large leg muscle mass are likely to cope better with hip dysplasia than dogs with small muscle mass.

The key here is moderate, low-impact exercise for fast-growing young dogs. High impact activities that apply a lot of force to the joint, such and jumping and catching Frisbees, is not recommended for young dogs.

Treatment - Most cases of CHD in Bostons require no treatment. However, as with most conditions, early detection leads to a better outcome. Your vet will take X-rays to make a diagnosis. Treatment is geared towards preventing the hip joint getting worse and decreasing pain. Various medical and surgical treatments are now available to ease the dog's discomfort and restore some mobility.

Treatment depends upon several factors, such as the dog's age, how bad the problem is and, sadly, how much money you can afford to spend on treatment. Management of a painful condition usually consists of restricting exercise, keeping body weight down and managing pain with analgesics and anti-inflammatory drugs. As with humans, cortisone injections may sometimes be used to reduce inflammation and swelling. Cortisone can be injected directly into the affected hip to provide almost immediate relief for a tender, swollen joint. In severe cases, surgery may be an option, especially with older dogs.

Hip Testing - The Pennsylvania Hip Improvement Program (Penn HIP) system was developed by the University of Pennsylvania to provide a reliable method for predicting the development of Canine Hip Dysplasia and can be used on dogs as young as 16 weeks old. The breed has a 'Distraction Index' of 0.71, where "there is a low risk of developing hip dysplasia with osteoarthritis when the distraction index is close to 0.30."

The Penn HIP method uses three separate radiograph taken under deep sedation or general anaesthesia. Thirty years ago the British Veterinary Association (BVA) and Kennel Club in the UK set up a hip screening program for dogs, which tests them using radiology and gives them a rating or 'hip score'. The KC is responsible for publishing hip dysplasia results for all pedigree dogs in the Kennel Club Breed Records.

Veterinary MRI and radiology specialist Ruth Dennis, of the UK's Animal Health Trust, states: *"For dogs intended for breeding, it is essential that the hips are assessed before mating to ensure that they are free of dysplastic changes or only minimally affected."*

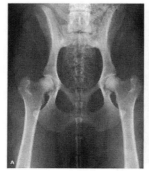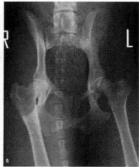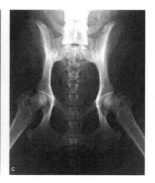

Figure A is the healthy hip, B shows lateral tilting, C shows outward rotation

Cushing's Disease

This is a complex ailment best described as a set of symptoms caused by the dog producing too much of a hormone called Cortisol. It is a condition that usually develops over a period of time, which is why it is more often seen in older dogs. It affects some Bostons.

Cortisol is released by the adrenal gland located near the kidneys. Normally it is produced during times of stress to prepare the body for strenuous activity. It alters the metabolism, allowing the body to draw energy from stored fats and sugars while retaining sodium and water. Think of an adrenaline rush.

The problem occurs when the body is constantly being exposed to Cortisol and in effect is in a persistent state of breakdown.

Symptoms - It can be very difficult to diagnose. The most common signs of Cushing's are similar to those for old age, making it hard to diagnose and then monitor. If you can, it is a good idea to keep a note of any changes you notice in your dog's habits, behaviour and appearance and take these notes with you to the vet. The most noticeable signs include:

1. Drinking excessive amounts of water
2. Urinating frequently and possible urinary incontinence
3. Ravenous appetite
4. Hair loss or recurring skin problems
5. Pot belly
6. Thin skin
7. Muscle wastage
8. Lack of energy, general lethargy
9. Excessive panting

Causes and Diagnosis - There are three types of Cushing's, but 80-85% of cases are caused by a tumour on the pituitary gland. Usually benign and often very small, this tumour puts pressure on the gland, causing an increase in the pituitary secretion. This then causes the adrenal gland to release additional Cortisol.

In some cases, the over-use of steroids (artificial hormones), such as Cortisone, Prednisone and others can lead to Cushing's Disease. There are two blood tests for Cushing's Disease. Your vet may carry out one or both of these.

You may have to leave your dog at the surgery for a few hours to have her tested, as levels of Cortisol naturally rise and fall throughout the day.

Treatment - Cushing's Disease cannot be cured, but it can be managed and controlled with medication, usually giving your dog a longer, happier life. Lysodren (Mitotane) is the drug of choice for treating the most common pituitary-dependent Cushing's Disease. This has to be given for the remainder of the dog's life. If you suspect your dog has Cushing's, you should contact your vet immediately.

Epilepsy

If you have witnessed your dog having a seizure (convulsion), you will know how frightening it can be. Seizures are not uncommon in dogs, but many dogs have only a single seizure. If your dog has had more than one seizure it may be that he or she is epileptic. Just as in people, there are medications for dogs to control seizures, allowing your dog to live a more normal life.

Epilepsy means repeated seizures due to abnormal activity in the brain and is caused by an abnormality in the brain itself. It can affect any breed of dog and in fact affects around four or five dogs in every 100, and in some breeds it can be hereditary. If seizures happen because of a problem somewhere else in the body, such as heart disease (which stops oxygen reaching the brain), this is not epilepsy. Your vet may do tests to try to find the reason for the epilepsy, but in many cases no cause can be identified.

Symptoms - Some dogs seem to know when they are about to have a seizure and may behave in a certain way. You will come to recognise these signs as meaning that a seizure is likely. Often dogs just seek out their owner's company and come to sit beside them when a seizure is about to start.

Once the seizure starts, the dog is conscious but unresponsive; he physically cannot respond to you (unlike with head tremors,) but holding him close to you or keeping him safe by wrapping in a blanket is still a good idea. Most dogs become stiff, fall onto their side and make running movements with their legs. Sometimes they will cry out and may lose control of their bowels or bladder. Most seizures last between one and three minutes - **it is worth making a note of the time the seizure starts and ends** because it often seems that a seizure goes on for a lot longer than it actually does.

After a seizure, dogs behave in different ways. With a mild seizure, also called a petit seizure, most dogs just get up and carry on with what they were doing, while others appear dazed and confused for up to 24 hours afterwards. In addition, after a severe seizure - also called a gran mal - seizure, dogs will often tremble and whimper for quite a while. Be sure your dog is in a warm, safe place to allow him time to calm down and return to normal.

Most commonly, dogs will be disorientated for only 10 to 15 minutes before returning to their old self. They often have a set pattern of behaviour that they follow - for example going for a drink of water or wanting to go outside to the toilet. If your dog has had more than one seizure, you may well start to notice a pattern of behaviour that is typically repeated.

Most seizures occur while the dog is relaxed and resting quietly. It is very rare for a seizure to occur while exercising. Often seizures occur in the evening or at night. In a few dogs, a particular event or stress may trigger an episode. It is common for a pattern to develop and, should your dog suffer from epilepsy, you will gradually recognise this as specific to your dog. The most important thing is to **stay calm**. Remember that your dog is nonresponsive during the seizure and is not in severe pain. It is likely to be more distressing for you than for him.

Make sure that he is not in a position to injure himself, for example by falling down the stairs. If you can put him in a safe place (like on a blanket on the floor rather than on an elevated bed or couch where he could fall and injure himself further), that is helpful, otherwise do not try to interfere with him. Never try to put your hand inside his mouth during a seizure or you are very likely to get bitten. Seizures can cause damage to the brain and if your dog has repeated occurrences, it is likely that further seizures will occur in the future. The damage caused is cumulative and after a lot of seizures there may be enough brain damage to cause early senility (with loss of learned behaviour and housetraining or behavioural changes).

It is not common for dogs to injure themselves during a seizure; however, if they are one of several dogs, the other dogs may attack him, so try to isolate the seizing dog from the others, if possible. Occasionally they may bite their tongue and there may appear to be a lot of blood, but is unlikely to be serious; your dog will not swallow his tongue. If a seizure goes on for a very long time (more than 10 minutes), his body temperature will rise and this can cause damage to other organs such as the liver and kidneys as well as the brain. In very extreme cases, some dogs may be left in a coma after severe seizures. If you are able to record your dog's seizure on a mobile phone or video recorder, this will be most useful to show the vet.

When Should I Contact the Vet? - Generally, if your dog has a seizure lasting more than five minutes, or is having multiple seizures, you should contact your vet. When your dog starts a seizure, make a note of the time. If he comes out of it within five minutes, allow him time to recover quietly before contacting your vet. It is far better for him to recover quietly at home rather than be bundled into the car and carted off to the vet right away.

However, if your dog does not come out of the seizure within five minutes, or has repeated seizures close together, contact your vet immediately, as he or she will want to see your dog as soon as possible. If this is his first seizure, your vet may ask you to bring him in for a check and some routine blood tests. Always call your vet's practice before setting off to be sure that there is someone there who can help your dog.

There are many things other than epilepsy which cause seizures in dogs. When your vet first examines your dog, he or she will not know whether your dog has epilepsy or another illness. It's unlikely that the vet will see your dog during a seizure, so it is **vital** that you're able to describe in some detail just what happens. You might want to make notes or record it on your mobile phone. Epilepsy usually starts when the dog is aged between one and five. So if your dog is older or younger, he may have a different problem.

The vet may need to run a range of tests to ensure that there is no other cause. These may include blood tests, possibly X-rays, and maybe even an MRI scan of your dog's brain. If no other cause can be found, then a diagnosis of epilepsy may be made. If your Boston Terrier already has epilepsy, remember these key points:

- ❧ Don't change or stop any medication without consulting your vet
- ❧ See your vet at least once a year for follow-up visits
- ❧ Be sceptical of 'magic cure' treatments

Remember, live *with* epilepsy not *for* epilepsy. With the proper medical treatment, most epileptic dogs have far more good days than bad ones. Enjoy all those good days.

Treatment - It is not usually possible to remove the cause of the seizures, so your vet will use medication to control them. How well a dog manages with epilepsy depends to some extent on the owner, who has to keep up with the medication and make sure it is administered at the right times each day. Treatment will not cure the disease, but it will manage the signs; even a well-controlled epileptic will have occasional seizures. Sadly, as yet there is no miracle cure for epilepsy, so don't be tempted with anything promising instant or permanent results from the internet.

There are many drugs used in the control of epilepsy in people, but very few of these are suitable for long-term use in a dog. Two of the most common are Phenobarbital and Potassium Bromide (check that these drugs are suitable for Boston Terriers, some dogs can have negative results with Phenobarbitol).

Many epileptic dogs require a combination of one or more types of drug to achieve the most effective control of their seizures. Treatment is decided on an individual basis and it may take some time to find the best combination and dose of drugs for your pet. You need patience when managing an epileptic pet and it is important that medication is given at the same time each day.

Once your dog has been on treatment for a while, he will become dependent on the levels of drug in his blood at all times to control seizures. If you miss a dose of treatment, blood levels can drop and this may be enough to trigger a seizure. Each epileptic dog is an individual and a treatment plan will be designed specifically for him. It will be based on the severity and frequency of the seizures and how they respond to different medications.

Keep a record of events in your dog's life, note down dates and times of seizures and record when you have given medication. Each time you visit your vet, take this diary along with you so he or she can see how your dog has been since his last check-up. If seizures are becoming more frequent, it may be necessary to change the medication. The success or otherwise of treatment may depend on YOU keeping a close eye on your Boston to see if there are any physical or behavioural changes.

It is rare for epileptic dogs to stop having seizures altogether. However, provided your dog is checked regularly by your vet to make sure that the drugs are not causing any side-effects, there is a good chance that he will live a full and happy life.

Thanks to www.canineepilepsy.co.uk for assistance with this article. If your Boston Terrier has epilepsy, we recommend reading this informative website to gain a greater understanding of the illness.

Heart Problems

Just as with humans, heart problems are relatively common among the canine population in general. Heart failure, or Congestive Heart Failure (CHF), occurs when the heart is not able to pump enough blood around the dog's body. The heart is a mechanical pump. It receives blood in one half and forces it through the lungs, then the other half pumps the blood through the entire body.

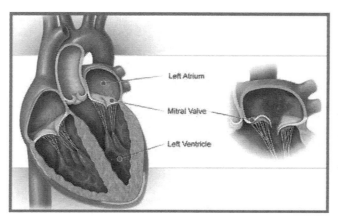

Left Atrium

Mitral Valve

Left Ventricle

Some dogs can suffer from **Pulmonic Stenosis**, which is a congenital narrowing in the region of the pulmonary valve, and many smaller breeds – including the Boston Terrier – can be prone to suffer from **Mitral Valve Disease** (MVD, also called Endocardiosis), usually seen in older dogs.

The heart muscle is a pump that moves blood through the four chambers using involuntary contractions. Blood is pumped around the body via a one-way system. The valves between the chambers form a tight seal that prevent the blood from flowing backwards into the chamber it has just come from; so the blood is always flowing forwards.

When the valves degenerate over time, they become thickened and deformed, losing their tight seal and causing some blood to seep backwards. When the valve between the left atrium and left ventricle – i.e. the mitral valve - no longer forms a tight seal, blood moves back into the left atrium. This means the heart has to work harder to pump the volume of blood the body needs for normal functions.

Symptoms

- Heart murmur
- Tiredness
- Decreased activity levels
- Restlessness, pacing around instead of settling down to sleep
- Intermittent coughing, especially during exertion or excitement. This tends to occur at night, sometimes about two hours after the dog goes to bed or when he wakes up in the morning. This coughing is an attempt to clear fluid in the lungs and is often the first clinical sign of MVD

If the condition worsens, other symptoms may appear:

- Lack of appetite
- Rapid breathing
- Abdominal swelling (due to fluid)
- Noticeable loss of weight
- Fainting (syncope)
- Paleness

Diagnosis – Unlike a heart attack in humans, heart failure in the dog is a slow insidious process that occurs over months or years. In these cases, once symptoms are noted, they will usually worsen over time until the animal is placed on treatment.

If your dog is exhibiting a range of the above symptoms, the vet may suspect heart problem, and he or she will carry out tests to make sure. These may include listening to the heart, chest X-rays, blood tests, electrocardiogram (a record of your dog's heartbeat) or an echocardiogram (ultrasound of the heart).

Treatment - If the heart problem is due to valve disease or an enlarged heart (dilated cardiomyopathy - DCM), the condition cannot be reversed. However, the vast majority of affected dogs don't require any treatment at all until they show symptoms, and then they generally do well on medication. Only in very severe cases do dogs die from the disease. The only way to prevent the disease is to remove affected dogs from the breeding pool - but it's too late for you if your Boston is already showing symptoms.

Instead, treatment focuses on managing the symptoms with various medications. These may change over time as the condition worsens. The veterinarian may also prescribe a special low salt diet for your dog, as sodium (found in salt) determines the amount of water in the blood, and the amount of exercise your dog has will have to be controlled. There is some evidence that vitamin and other supplements may be beneficial, discuss this with your vet.

The prognosis (outlook) for dogs with heart problems depends on the cause and severity, as well as their response to treatment. Once diagnosed, he can live a longer, more comfortable life with the right medication and regular check-ups.

....

Heart Murmurs

Heart murmurs are not uncommon in dogs. Our dog was diagnosed with a Grade 1-2 murmur a few years ago and, of course, your heart sinks when the vet gives you the terrible news. But once the shock is over, it's important to realise that there are several different severities of the condition and, at its mildest, it is no great cause for concern.

Literally, a heart murmur is a specific sound heard through a stethoscope. It results from the blood flowing faster than normal within the heart itself or in one of the two major arteries. Instead of the normal 'lubb dupp' noise, an additional sound can be heard that can vary from a mild 'pshhh' to a loud 'whoosh'. Murmurs are caused by a number of factors, including MVD. Other reasons include hyperthyroidism, anaemia and heartworm.

The different grades of heart murmurs are:

- ❀ **Grade I** - barely audible
- ❀ **Grade II** - soft, but easily heard with a stethoscope
- ❀ **Grade III** - intermediate loudness; most murmurs that are related to the mechanics of blood circulation are at least grade III
- ❀ **Grade IV** - loud murmur that radiates widely, often including opposite side of chest
- ❀ **Grades V and Grade VI** - very loud, audible with stethoscope barely touching the chest; the vibration is also strong enough to be felt through the animal's chest wall

In puppies, there are two major types of heart murmurs, and they will probably be detected by your vet at the first or second vaccinations. The most common type is called an innocent 'flow murmur.' This type of murmur is soft (typically Grade II or less) and is not caused by underlying heart disease. An innocent flow murmur typically disappears by four to five months of age.

However if a puppy has a loud murmur (Grade III or louder), or if the heart murmur is still easily heard with a stethoscope after four or five months of age, the likelihood of the puppy having an underlying congenital (from birth) heart problem becomes much higher. The thought of a puppy having lifelong heart disease is extremely worrying, but it is important to remember that the disease will not affect all puppies' life expectancy or quality of life.

A heart murmur can also develop suddenly in an adult dog with no prior history of the problem. This is typically due to heart disease that develops with age. In toy and small breeds, a heart murmur may develop in middle-aged to older dogs due to an age-related thickening and degeneration of one of the valves in the heart, the mitral valve. (This is the type our dog has and it was first noticed at the age of seven).

By the way, our Max was diagnosed with a Grade II heart murmur and we have taken the vet's advice and ignored it — although we are always on alert for a dry, racking cough, which is a sign of fluid in the lungs - so far, it hasn't happened. The good news is that Max is now 12 and he is, as the saying goes: "fit as a butcher's dog."

Overheating Boston Terriers

It's a fact, Boston Terriers and all brachycephalic dogs overheat more easily than other breeds. They do not cope well with high temperatures and are prone to heatstroke or hyperthermia. By the way, the Boston can also suffer from **hypo**thermia if he gets too cold.

It's also a fact that dogs can't sweat. Well, only a tiny bit through the pads of their paws. Instead of being able to cool down by sweating all over their body like humans, they have the far less efficient mechanism of panting, which circulates cooling air around their body. Couple this inefficient cooling system with the shortened head of the Boston and you have a potential recipe for disaster. Make no mistake, heat can be a killer for Boston Terriers.

Bostons have been bred to have shortened facial bone structures to give a pushed-in look. However, the soft tissue inside has stayed the same size, which means that there isn't much room for air to circulate inside the dog's mouth and throat.

Some Bostons have elongated palates and extremely narrow nostrils, which makes breathing difficult, and especially so when they are hot and need to pant. When they try to pant quickly, foam can be produced, which in turn blocks the throat and causes laboured breathing. A dog's normal body temperature is around 101-102.5ºF (a puppy's normal rectal temperature is lower). If this rises to over 106ºF, the dog is suffering from heatstroke and can die within minutes.

NOTE: As well as dying from overheating, Boston Terriers can also die or get into difficulties when they are stressed – again this is related to breathing problems. Do not let your dog get too hot or overexcited or over-exercised. If he is struggling for breath, STOP the activity immediately.

Symptoms of Overheating

- Heavy panting
- Rapid pulse rate
- High body temperature – above 104°F
- Bright red or purple tongue and possibly gums
- Tiredness and distress, perhaps becoming dizzy and staggering
- Drooling a thick, sticky saliva or foam as airways become blocked
- Possible vomiting and/or diarrhoea, sometimes with blood
- Shock
- Coma

Action

STAY CALM! Your dog will pick up on your fear if you panic, causing him more stress. Remove the dog from the hot area immediately. Lower his temperature by wetting him thoroughly with cool or tepid water (**not cold**). You can also use a towel dipped in cool water, then increase air movement around him with a fan. Part his fur with your fingers to let the cooling air get to his body. . Cooling the underbelly and the feet, in particular, can help reduce your dog's temperature. You are trying to get the body temperature down to 104 °F or below, and then you can stop the emergency measures.

CAUTION: Using very cold water can actually be counterproductive. Cooling too quickly and especially allowing the dog's body temperature to become too low can cause other life-threatening medical conditions. Similarly, some Boston Terrier owners recommend using ice on the body to cool the dog, but many veterinarians advise against this, as it closes the skin pores and could potentially make the situation worse.

Other suggestions from owners include getting your Boston used to eating ice cubes, ice pops or frozen yoghurts from an early age so that if he does start to overheat, you can feed him these and he will readily take them. Another suggestion is that if your dog has started foaming, squirt lemon juice from a plastic lemon into the back of his throat – he will hate it, but the lemon juice will help to break down the foam and clear the throat. You may also have to reach inside his throat to try and pull out the foam and clear his airways. This may sound dramatic, but if you think it would save your dog's life, you probably wouldn't hesitate.

Many owners who live in warm climates have found certain products to be helpful, these include cooling jackets, vests and blankets, and sun visors (pictured) which also protect eyes. NOTE: Ice collars are not recommended for Bostons, it is thought they may restrict the blood flow to the brain and cause other problems, such as seizures. And never force your dog to drink water when overheated, just try and coax him to drink.

The rectal temperature of an overheated dog should be checked every few minutes, if you can. Do this very carefully, preferably with somebody holding him steady. Use a special rectal thermometer and hold on to it, some dogs have been known to "suck in" the thermometer. Once the body temperature is down to 104°F, the cooling measures should be stopped and the dog should be dried thoroughly and covered so he does not continue to lose heat. Even if the dog appears to be recovering, take him to your vet as soon as possible. He should still be examined as he may be dehydrated or have other complications. Allow him access to water or an electrolyte rehydrating solution if he can drink on his own. Do not try to force-feed cold water as he may inhale it or choke.

When you have the emergency situation under control, take him to the vet immediately. He or she will lower your dog's body temperature to a safe range, if you have not already done so, and continue to monitor his temperature. They may administer fluids, and possibly oxygen and may take blood samples to test for clotting. The dog will be monitored for shock, respiratory distress, kidney failure, heart abnormalities and other complications, and treated accordingly.

Dogs with moderate heatstroke often recover without complicated health problems. However, severe heatstroke can cause organ damage that might need on-going care, such as a special diet prescribed by the vet. Dogs that suffer from heatstroke once have an increased risk of getting it again and owners must take steps to prevent it recurring.

15 Tips to Prevent a Boston Overheating

The main factor in determining whether your dog gets heatstroke is YOU. Being aware of your dog's susceptibility to heat (and stress) is the first step, taking action to prevent it is the second essential step. Bostons can overheat alarmingly quickly, here are some preventative measures:

1.   Make sure your dog has a cool place indoors.

2.   Make sure he has shade outdoors at all times.

3. Reduce exercise in warm weather. On hot days only take your dog outside for short periods; early in the morning and in the evening when temperatures are lower are the best times. For some Bostons, anything in the 70s is hot, while others may be fine outdoors for shorter periods at temperatures up to 80°F.

   Heat tolerance is partially due to where the dog is born and raised. For example, a dog born and raised in the UK may not be able to handle hot weather as well as a dog from Florida.

4. Make sure your dog has access to clean water 24/7.

5. If your dog does not want to go outside, do not force him.

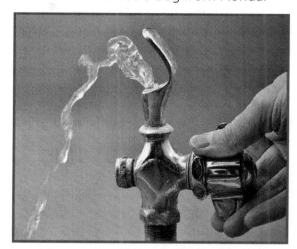

6. Have a shady toilet area in your yard or garden for your dog. On hot and sunny days, don't leave him outdoors for long periods; many Bostons enjoy sunbathing, but this doesn't stop them from overheating.

7. Monitor exercise and play time. By the time your Boston starts to feel hot, he is probably already overheating. Keep an eye on your dog, especially puppies and adolescent dogs who may want to constantly run and play for hours.

8. Take water with you on your walks in warm weather. Watch your dog carefully for indications that he is overheating, and if he shows signs, stop in a shady spot and give him some water. If symptoms don't subside, take him home and ring the vet.

9. On hot days avoid places like the beach and especially concrete or asphalt areas, where heat is reflected and there is no access to shade.

10. NEVER muzzle your Boston.

11. NEVER leave him in a parked car, even if you're in the shade or will only be gone a short time. The temperature inside a parked car can quickly reach up to 140°F.

12. Put your dog in a cool area of the house. Air conditioning is one of the best ways to keep a dog cool, but is not always reliable. You can freeze water in soda bottles, or place ice and a small amount of water in several resealable food storage bags, wrap them in a towel or tube sock and put them on the floor for your dog to lie on.

13. Do not let your dog become over-excited in warm weather and avoid strenuous games or exercise.

14. Don't go jogging with a Boston. Most dogs will try to keep up with their owners and this can put stress on the heart or cause them to overheat.

15. Do not allow your Boston to become obese. An obese dog is more likely to suffer from heatstroke.

NOTE: Bostons are also sensitive to low temperatures, so have a doggie coat or sweater for those cold days, and make sure your Boston isn't left in a draught when you are away from the house.

Canine Diabetes

This is not an issue that particularly affects Boston Terriers any more than any other breed of dog, but can affect dogs of all breeds, sizes and both genders. It does, however, affect obese dogs more than ones of a normal weight and the fact that some owners spoil their dogs with lots of treats and titbits makes their pet a candidate for obesity.

There are two types: *diabetes mellitus* and *diabetes insipidus*. Diabetes mellitus is the most common form and affects one in 400 to 500 dogs. Thanks to modern veterinary medicine, the condition is now treatable and need not shorten your dog's lifespan or interfere with his quality of life. Diabetic dogs undergoing treatment now have the same life expectancy as non-diabetic dogs of the same age and gender.

However, if left untreated, the disease can lead to cataracts - and this is especially true of Bostons as they are already susceptible - increasing weakness in the legs (neuropathy), other ailments and even death. In dogs, diabetes is typically seen anywhere between the ages of four to 14, with a peak at seven to nine years. Both males and females can develop it; unspayed females have a slightly higher risk. The typical canine diabetes sufferer is middle-aged, female and overweight, but there are also juvenile cases.

What is Diabetes?

Diabetes insipidus is caused by a lack of vasopressin, a hormone that controls the kidneys' absorption of water.

Diabetes mellitus occurs when the dog's body does not produce enough insulin and cannot successfully process sugars.

Dogs, like us, get their energy by converting the food they eat into sugars, mainly glucose. This glucose travels in the dog's bloodstream and individual cells then remove some of that glucose from the blood to use for energy. The substance that allows the cells to take glucose from the blood is a protein called *insulin.*

Insulin is created by beta cells that are located in the pancreas, which is next to the stomach. Almost all diabetic dogs have Type 1 diabetes: their pancreas does not produce any insulin. Without it, the cells have no way to use the glucose that is in the bloodstream, so the cells 'starve' while the glucose level in the blood rises. Your vet will use blood samples and urine samples to check glucose concentrations in order to diagnose diabetes. Early treatment helps to prevent further complications developing.

Symptoms - The most common ones include:

- Extreme thirst
- Excessive urination
- Weight loss
- Increased appetite
- Coat in poor condition
- Lethargy

🐾 Vision problems due to cataracts

Cataracts and Diabetes

Cataracts may develop due to high blood glucose levels causing water to build up in the eyes' lenses. This leads to swelling, rupture of the lens fibres and the development of cataracts. In many cases the cataracts can be surgically removed to bring sight back to the dog. However, some dogs may stay blind even after the cataracts are gone, and some cataracts simply cannot be removed. Blind dogs are often able to get around surprisingly well, particularly in a familiar home. Their sense of smell and hearing are much more highly developed than with us humans; we are much more heavily dependent on our sight.

Treatment starts with the right diet. Your vet will prescribe meals low in fat and sugars. He or she will also recommend medication. Many dogs can be successfully treated with diet and medication, while more severe cases may require insulin injections. In the newly-diagnosed dog, insulin therapy begins at home.

Normally, after a week of treatment, you return to the vet who will do a series of blood sugar tests over a 12-14 hour period to see when the blood glucose peaks and when it hits its lows. Adjustments are then made to the dosage and timing of the injections. Your vet will explain how to prepare and inject the insulin. You may be asked to collect urine samples using a test strip (a small piece of paper that indicates the glucose levels in urine).

If your dog is already having insulin injections, beware of a 'miracle cure' offered on some internet sites; it does not exist. There is no diet or vitamin supplement that can reduce your dog's dependence on insulin injections because vitamins and minerals cannot do what insulin does in the dog's body. If you think that your dog needs a supplement, discuss it with your vet first to make sure that it does not interfere with any other medication.

Exercise - Managing your dog's diabetes also means managing his activity level. Exercise burns up blood glucose the same way that insulin does. If your dog is on insulin, any active exercise on top of the insulin might cause him to have a severe low blood glucose episode, called *'hypoglycaemia'*.

Your usual insulin dose will take that amount of exercise into account.

 Keep your dog on a reasonably consistent exercise routine. If you plan to take your dog out for some extra demanding exercise, such as running round with other dogs, give him only half of his usual insulin dose.

🐾 You can usually buy specially formulated diabetes dog food from your veterinarian

🐾 You should feed the same type and amount of food at the same time every day

🐾 Most vets recommend twice-a-day feeding for diabetic pets. It is OK if your dog prefers to eat more often

🐾 If you have other pets in the home, they should also be placed on a twice-a-day feeding schedule, so that the diabetic dog cannot eat from their bowls. Help your dog to achieve the best possible blood glucose control by not feeding him table scraps or treats between meals

🐾 Watch for signs that your dog is starting to drink more water than usual. Call the vet if you see this happening, as it may mean that the insulin dose needs adjusting.

FINE FOODS

Menu

Peter Hesse

"I DON'T SEE TABLE SCRAPS."

Remember these simple points:

Food raises blood glucose

Insulin and exercise lower blood glucose

Keep them in balance

For more information on canine diabetes visit www.caninediabetes.org

....

Canine Cancer

This is the biggest single killer of dogs of any breed and will claim the lives of one in four dogs. It is the cause of nearly half the deaths of all dogs aged 10 years and older, according to the American Veterinary Medical Association (AMVA). Early detection is critical. Some things to look out for are:

- Swellings anywhere on the body
- Lumps in a dog's armpit or under the jaw
- Sores that don't heal
- Chronic bad breath
- Weight loss
- Poor appetite, difficulty swallowing or excessive drooling
- Changes in exercise or stamina level
- Laboured breathing
- Change in bowel or bladder habits

If your dog has been spayed or neutered, the risk of certain cancers decreases. These cancers include uterine and breast/mammary cancer in females, and testicular cancer in males (if the dog was neutered before he was six months old). Along with controlling the pet population, spaying is especially important because mammary cancer in female dogs is fatal in about 50% of all cases.

One type of cancer is relatively common in Boston Terriers and that is the Mast Cell Tumour (MCT). This is the most common skin tumour in dogs, and it can also affect other areas of the body, including the spleen, liver, gastrointestinal tract, and bone marrow.

According to Ryan Veterinary Hospital of the University of Pennsylvania: "Certain dogs are predisposed to MCT, including brachycephalic (flat-faced) breeds such as Boston Terriers, Boxers, Pugs, and Bulldogs, as well as retriever breeds, though any breed of dog can develop MCT. When they occur on the skin, MCT vary widely in appearance. They can be a raised lump or bump on or just under the skin, and may be red, ulcerated, or swollen. In addition, many owners will report a waxing and waning size of the tumor, which can occur spontaneously, or can be produced by agitation of the tumor, causing degranulation. Mast cells contain granules filled with substances that can be released into the bloodstream and potentially cause systemic problems, including stomach ulceration and bleeding, swelling and redness at and around the tumor site, and potentially life-threatening complications, such as a dangerous drop in blood pressure and a systemic inflammatory response leading to shock.

"When MCT occur on the skin, they can occur anywhere on the body. The biological behavior of these tumors can vary widely; some may be present for many months without growing much, while others can appear suddenly and grow very quickly. The most common sites of MCT spread (metastasis) are the lymph nodes, spleen and liver."

The dog's prognosis (outlook) depends on a number of factors, including: grade (severity), whether enough margins were removed with the biopsy, whether it has spread to other parts of the body, and if the MCT can be completely removed by surgery. Low grade MCTs are often successfully treated with a single surgical procedure, usually followed by daily medication. High grade tumours may require one or more procedures (or none at all) and a cocktail of drugs – 'multimodal therapy.' Success may depend on how far the cancer has already spread to other parts of the body. As with all cancers, early detection and treatment increase survival rates.

One breeder said: "One of my male dogs had an MCT on his hip. It was large (about the size of a quarter and about half an inch thick). The vet removed it with good margins and the dog has never had a recurrence - it has been more than two years now. The vet recommends one half a 25mg Benadryl tablet twice daily on an ongoing basis to help prevent recurrence, and so far there has been none."

Diagnosis - Just because your dog has a skin growth doesn't mean that it's cancerous. As with humans, tumours may be benign (harmless) or malignant (harmful). Your vet may use X-rays, blood tests, or possibly ultrasounds to help with diagnosis. He or she will carry out a biopsy, in which a tissue sample is taken from your dog and sent off for analysis. In the US, often the vet will aspirate the lump and view the cells under a microscope before taking a biopsy and sending it to the lab. Generally, the vet will remove the lump (with good 'margins') and send the sample to the lab to determine if it is benign or malignant, rather than making that claim after looking at the cells themselves.

If your dog is diagnosed with cancer, there is hope. Advances in veterinary medicine and technology offer various treatment options, including chemotherapy, radiation and surgery. Unlike with humans, a dog's hair will not fall out with chemotherapy.

Canine cancer is growing at an ever-increasing rate. One of the difficulties is that your pet cannot tell you when a cancer is developing, but if cancers can be detected early enough through a physical or behavioural change, they often respond well to treatment.

Over recent years, we have all become more aware of the risk factors for human cancer. Responding to these by changing our habits is having a significant impact on human health. For example, stopping smoking, protecting ourselves from over-exposure to strong sunlight and eating a healthy, balanced diet all help to reduce cancer rates. We know to keep a close eye on ourselves, go for regular health checks and report any lumps and bumps to our doctors as soon as they appear. Increased cancer awareness is definitely improving human health.

The same is true with your dog.

While it is impossible to completely prevent cancer from occurring, a healthy lifestyle with a balanced diet and regular exercise can help to reduce the risk. Also, be aware of any new lumps and bumps on your dog's body and any changes in his behaviour.

Treatment – Nowadays this is not dissimilar to treatment of humans with cancer and may include one or more of the following: surgery, radiation, chemotherapy and medication. The success of treatment depends on the type of cancer, how early the tumour is found and the treatment used. The sooner treatment begins, the greater the chances of success.

One of the best things you can do for your dog is to keep a close eye on him for any tell-tale signs. This shouldn't be too difficult and can be done as part of your regular handling and grooming. If you notice any new bumps, for example, monitor them over a period of days to see if there is a change in their appearance or size. If there is, then make an appointment to see your vet as soon as possible. It might only be a cyst, but better to be safe than sorry.

Research into earlier diagnosis and improved treatments is being conducted at veterinary schools and companies all over the world. Advances in biology are producing a steady flow of new tests and treatments that are now becoming available to improve survival rates and canine cancer care. If your dog is diagnosed with cancer, do not despair, there are many options and new, improved treatments are constantly being introduced.

Our Happy Ending

We know from personal experience that canine cancer can be successfully treated if it is diagnosed early enough. Our dog was diagnosed with T-cell lymphoma when he was four years old.

We had noticed a black lump on his anus that quickly grew to the size of a small grape. We took him to the vet within the first few days of seeing the lump and, after a test, he was diagnosed with the dreaded T-cell lymphoma. This is a particularly nasty and aggressive form of cancer that can spread to the lymph system and is often fatal for dogs.

As soon as the diagnosis was confirmed, our vet Graham operated and removed the lump. He also had to remove one of his anal glands, but as dogs have two this was not a serious worry. Afterwards, we were on tenterhooks, not knowing if another lump would grow or if the cancer had already spread to his lymph system. After a few months, Max had another blood test and was finally given the all-clear. I am pleased to report that Max is now happy, healthy and 12 years old. We were very lucky. I would strongly advise anyone who suspects that their dog has cancer to get him or her to your local vet as soon as possible.

DISCLAIMER: The author is not a veterinarian; this chapter has been written to provide accurate and helpful information on Boston Terrier health. It gives a broader understanding of some of the issues that can affect Boston Terriers, but should not replace professional veterinary advice. If you are at all worried about your dog's health, you are strongly advised to consult a veterinarian at the earliest opportunity.

11. Skin and Allergies

Allergies are a growing concern for owners of many breeds. Visit any busy vet's clinic these days — especially in spring and summer — and there will probably be dogs in there with some type of sensitivity. Some breeds are more prone to develop skin problems related to allergies and intolerances; unfortunately, the Boston Terrier is one of these. Visit any online Boston forum and you'll see there are plenty of itchy dogs out there.

Generally, skin conditions, allergies and intolerances are on the increase across the canine world - as well as in the human world. How many children did you hear of having asthma or a peanut allergy when you were at school? Not many, I'll bet. Yet allergies and adverse reactions are now relatively common — and it's the same with dogs. As yet the reasons are not clear; it could be to do with breeding or processed diets, but there is no clear scientific evidence to back this up.

This is a complicated topic and a whole book could be written on this subject alone. While many dogs have no problems at all, some suffer from sensitive skin, allergies, yeast infections and/or skin disorders, causing them to scratch, bite or lick themselves excessively on the paws and other areas. Symptoms may vary from mild itchiness to a severe reaction.

Sometimes sensitivities run in bloodlines. If you haven't chosen your puppy yet, ask if either of the parents has any history of allergies or hypersensitivities. If so, there is a chance that the puppy has inherited this trait -and doubly so if both parents are affected.

As with humans, the skin is the dog's largest organ. It acts as the protective barrier between your dog's internal organs and the outside world; it also regulates temperature and provides the sense of touch. Surprisingly, a dog's skin is actually thinner than ours, and it is made up of three layers:

1. **Epidermis** or outer layer, the one that bears the brunt of your dog's contact with the outside world. Humans have between 10 to15 layers in the stratum corneum (outer part of the epidermis) and canines have about five. As well as thin skin, dogs' pH is more alkaline, making their skin not only delicate, but susceptible to absorbing undesirable toxins, etc.

2. **Dermis** is the extremely tough layer mostly made up of collagen, a strong and fibrous protein. This is where blood vessels deliver nutrients and oxygen to the skin, and it also acts as your dog's thermostat by allowing his body to release or keep in heat, depending on the outside temperature and your dog's activity level.

3. **Subcutis** is a dense layer of fatty tissue that allows your dog's skin to move independently from the muscle layers below it, as well as providing insulation and support for the skin.

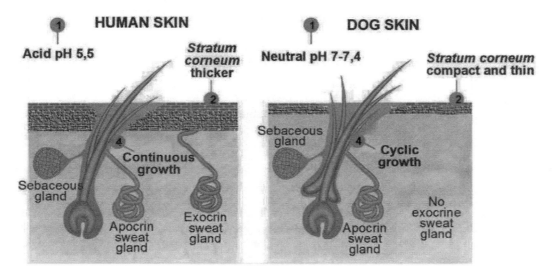

4. Just 5% of a human's body is covered by hair, while canines have 95% coverage. Our hair grows continuously, but a dog has cyclical growth – mainly in spring and autumn.

Human allergies often trigger a reaction within the respiratory system, causing us to wheeze or sneeze, whereas allergies or hypersensitivities in a dog often cause a reaction in his or her **skin.**

Skin can be affected from the **inside** by things that your dog eats or drinks.

Skin can be affected from the **outside** by fleas, parasites, inhaled or contact allergies triggered by grass, pollen, man-made chemicals, dust, mould etc. These environmental allergies are especially common in some Terriers as well as the Miniature Schnauzer, Bulldog and certain other breeds. You may hear the term '**atopic dermatitis'** from your vet, which is recurring skin issues triggered by allergies.

Skin problems may be the result of one or more of a wide range of causes - and the list of potential remedies and treatments is even longer. It's by no means possible to cover all of them in this chapter. The aim here is to give a broad outline of some of the ailments most likely to affect Bostons and how to deal with them. We have also included remedies tried with some success by ourselves (our dog has skin issues) and other owners of dogs with skin problems, as well as advice from a holistic specialist.

Like all dogs, Bostons can suffer from food allergies or intolerances as well as environmental allergies. Canine skin disorders are a complex subject. Some dogs can run through fields and woodland, dig holes and roll around in the grass with no after-effects at all. Others may spend more time indoors and have an excellent diet, but still experience severe itching.

This information is not intended to take the place of professional help. We are not animal health experts and you should always contact your vet as soon as your dog appears physically unwell or uncomfortable. This is particularly true with skin conditions.

There is anecdotal evidence from some dog owners that switching to a raw diet or raw meaty bones diet can significantly help some dogs with skin problems as well as those with food intolerances or allergies. See **Chapter 7. Feeding a Boston** for more information.

The two main problems with this type of ailment are that:

1. The exact cause is often difficult to diagnose, as the symptoms may also be common to other issues. If environmental allergies are involved, some specific allergy tests are available costing hundreds of pounds or dollars. You will have to take your vet's advice on this, as the tests are not always conclusive. If the answer is dust or pollen, it can be difficult to keep your

lively dog away from the triggers while still having a normal life - unless you and your Boston spend 100% of your time in a spotlessly clean city apartment - which is, frankly, unlikely! It is often a question of managing a skin condition, rather than curing it.

2. Once diagnosed, it is often difficult to treat and impossible to cure, so managing the issue is often the way forward.

Skin issues and allergies often develop in adolescence or early adulthood, which may be anything from a few months to two or three years old. Our dog Max was perfectly normal until he reached two when he began scratching, triggered by environmental allergies - most likely pollen. Over the years he's been on various different remedies that have all worked for a time. As his allergies are seasonal, he normally does not have any medication between October and March. But come spring and as sure as daffodils are daffodils, he starts scratching again. Luckily, they are manageable and Max lives a happy, normal life. Allergies and their treatment can cause a lot of stress for dogs and owners alike.

 The No. 1 piece of advice is DON'T DELAY. If you suspect your Boston has an allergy or skin problem, try to deal with it right away, before the all-too-familiar scenario kicks in and it develops into a chronic (recurring and long term) condition. If a vet can find the source of the problem early on, there is more chance of successfully treating it before it has chance to develop into a more serious condition with secondary issues.

(The photo shows a puppy faced with a huge bowl of dried, processed food, which can trigger dermatitis in some Bostons).

Whatever the cause, before a vet can diagnose the problem you have to be prepared to tell him or her all about your dog's diet, exercise regime, habits, medical history and local environment. He or she will then carry out a thorough physical examination, possibly followed by further (expensive) tests, before treatment can be prescribed. You'll have to decide whether these tests are worth it and whether they are likely to discover the exact root of the problem.

Breeders on Allergies

This is what some Boston Terrier breeders had to say: "Food and/or substance intolerance or allergy can be an issue. It is apparent in the dog's coat, brown staining around the face and bowel movements. Dry food is a big factor, it can affect their skin, coat and tearing (brown stains)."

Another said: "Like humans, some dogs are sensitive or intolerant to certain foods, and this can cause a variety of problems. In extreme cases, they may develop colitis (slime and blood in their stools). Always consult your vet if you notice your dog displaying any of the following symptoms: lethargy, aggressive or hyperactive behaviour, chronic skin and ear problems, light to mid-brown loose bulky stools or diarrhoea.

"Bostons can also have skin allergies to dust and traffic pollution. I have found that several of my pups who live in central London have allergies to the pollution and get very itchy. I have advised the owners to feed Royal Canin Urban range and it has helped reduce itching in all cases."

"Foods with too high a protein content can cause skin irritation."

Another British breeder added: "One breeder told me that they once lost a bitch due to a bee sting that they later discovered still inside the dog's mouth, between the cheek and gum. The dog suffered anaphylaxis and the breeder now carries an epi pen with them at all times."

Types of Allergies

'Canine dermatitis' means inflammation of a dog's skin and it can be triggered by numerous things, but the most common by far is allergies. Vets estimate that one in four dogs at their clinics is there because of some kind of allergy. Symptoms are:

- ❧ Chewing on paws
- ❧ Rubbing the face on the carpet
- ❧ Scratching the body
- ❧ Scratching or biting the anus
- ❧ Itchy ears, head shaking
- ❧ Hair loss
- ❧ Mutilated skin with sore or discoloured patches or hot spots

A Boston that is allergic to something will show it through skin problems and itching; your vet may call this 'pruritus'. It may seem logical that if a dog is allergic to something he inhales, like certain pollen grains, his nose will run; if he's allergic to something he eats, he may vomit, or if allergic to an insect bite, he may develop a swelling. But in practice this is seldom the case. The skin is an organ and with dogs it is this organ that is often affected by allergies. So instead, he will have a mild to severe itching sensation over his body and maybe a chronic ear infection.

Dogs with allergies often chew their feet until they are sore and red. You may see your Boston rubbing his face on the carpet or couch or scratching his belly and flanks. Because the ear glands produce too much wax in response to the allergy, ear infections can occur, with bacteria and yeast - which is a fungus - often thriving in the excessive wax and debris.

(Your Boston doesn't have to suffer from allergies to get ear infections. By the way, if your dog does develop a yeast infection and you decide to switch to a grain-free diet, try and avoid those that are potato-based, as these contain high levels of starch).

Holistic vet Dr Jodie Gruenstern says: "Grains and other starches have a negative impact on gut health, creating insulin resistance and inflammation. It's estimated that up to 80% of the immune system resides within the gastrointestinal system; building a healthy gut supports a more appropriate immune response. The importance of choosing fresh proteins and healthy fats over processed, starchy diets (such as kibble) can't be overemphasized."

As mentioned in **Chapter 7. Feeding a Boston Terrier,** some owners add a probiotic to their dog's meal, such as a spoonful of live natural or Greek yoghurt. Probiotics not only promote a healthy gut, they also help support the dog's immune system.

An allergic dog may cause skin lesions or 'hot spots' by constant chewing and scratching. Sometimes he will lose hair, which can be patchy, leaving a mottled appearance. The skin itself may be dry and crusty, reddened, swollen or oily, depending on the dog. It is very common to get secondary bacterial skin infections due to these self-inflicted wounds. An allergic dog's body is reacting to certain molecules called 'allergens.' These may come from:

- ❧ Trees
- ❧ Grass
- ❧ Pollens
- ❧ Foods and food additives, such as specific meats, grains or colourings
- ❧ Milk products
- ❧ Fabrics, such as wool or nylon
- ❧ Rubber and plastics
- ❧ House dust and dust mites
- ❧ Mould
- ❧ Flea bites
- ❧ Chemical products used around the house

These allergens may be inhaled as the dog breathes, ingested as the dog eats or caused by contact with the dog's body when he walks or rolls. However they arrive, they all cause the immune system to produce a protein (IgE), which causes various irritating chemicals, such as histamine, to be released. In dogs, these chemical reactions and cell types occur in sizeable amounts only within the skin, hence the scratching.

Diet and Food Allergies

Food is the third most common cause of allergies in dogs, and one that affects many Bostons. Cheap dog foods bulked up with grains and other ingredients can cause problems. Some dogs have problems with corn, wheat and other grains. If you feed your dog a dry commercial dog food, make sure that it's a high quality, preferably hypoallergenic, one and that the first ingredient listed on the sack is meat or poultry, not grain.

Without the correct food, a dog's whole body - not just his skin and coat - will continually be under stress, and this manifests itself in a number of ways. The symptoms of food allergies are similar to those of most allergies:

- ❧ Itchy skin affecting primarily the face, feet, ears, forelegs, armpits and anus
- ❧ Excessive scratching
- ❧ Chronic or recurring ear infections
- ❧ Hair loss
- ❧ Hot spots

- Increased bowel movements, maybe twice as many as normal
- Skin infections that clear up with antibiotics, but return after the antibiotics have finished

The bodily process that occurs when an animal has a reaction to a particular food agent is not very well understood. As many other problems can cause similar symptoms to food allergies (and also the fact that many sufferers also have other allergies), it is important that a vet identifies and treats any other problems before food allergies are diagnosed. Atopy, flea bite allergies, intestinal parasite hypersensitivities, sarcoptic mange and yeast or bacterial infections can all cause similar symptoms. This can be an anxious time for owners as vets try one thing after another to get to the bottom of the allergy.

The normal method for diagnosing a food allergy is elimination. Once all other causes have been ruled out or treated, then a food trial is the next step – and that's no picnic for owners either. See **Chapter 7** for much more information. As with other allergies, dogs may have short-term relief by taking fatty acids, antihistamines, and steroids, but removing the offending items from the diet is the only permanent solution.

....

Inhalant Allergies (Atopy)

Some of the most common allergies in dogs are inhalant and seasonal - at least at first, some allergies may develop and worsen. Substances that can cause an allergic reaction in dogs are similar to those causing problems for humans. A clue to diagnosing these allergies is to look at the timing of the reaction. Does it happen all year round? If so, this may be mould, dust or some other trigger that is permanently in the environment. If the reaction is seasonal, then pollens may well be the culprit.

A diagnosis can be made by allergy testing - either a blood or skin test where a small amount of antigen is injected into the dog's skin to test for a reaction. The blood test can give false positives, so the skin test is many veterinarians' preferred method.

'**Intradermal skin testing**' can be carried out by your vet or a veterinary dermatologist. The dog is given an injection with a gentle sedative and remains awake throughout the procedure. Quite a large patch of fur is then shaved off the side of his abdomen and tiny needles inject dozens of test allergens into the area. The dog is carefully monitored for signs of a reaction, such as redness or hives. The procedure can last anything from 30 to 90 minutes, depending on how many tests are performed. There is more detailed information on this commercial website:
http://aadconline.com/content/skin-testing

Whether or not you take this route, will be your decision; allergy testing is not cheap. And there's also no point doing it if you are not going to go along with the recommended method of treatment afterwards, which may be immunotherapy, or '**hyposensitisation**', and this can also be an expensive and lengthy process. It consists of a series of injections made specifically for your dog and administered over weeks or months to make him more tolerant of specific allergens. It may have to be done by a veterinary dermatologist if your vet is not familiar with the treatment. Vets in the US claim that success rates can be as high as 75% of cases.

These tests work best when carried out during the season when the allergies are at their worst. But before you get to this stage, your vet will have had to rule out other potential causes, such as fleas or mites, fungal, yeast or bacterial infections and hypothyroidism. Due to the time and cost involved in skin testing, most mild cases of allergies are treated with a combination of avoidance, fatty acids and antihistamines. (Pictured is a dog after intradermal skin testing).

Environmental or Contact Irritations

These are a direct reaction to something the dog physically comes into contact with. It could be as simple as grass, specific plants, dust or other animals. If the trigger is grass or other outdoor materials, the allergies are often seasonal. The dog may require treatment - often tablets, shampoo or localised cortisone spray - for spring and summer, but be perfectly fine with no medication for the other half of the year. This is the case with our dog.

If you suspect your Boston may have outdoor contact allergies, here is one very good tip guaranteed to reduce his scratching: get him to stand in a tray or large bowl of water on your return from a walk. Washing his feet and under his belly will get rid of some of the pollen and other allergens, which in turn will reduce his scratching and biting. This can help to reduce the allergens to a tolerable level.

Other possible triggers include dry carpet shampoos, caustic irritants, new carpets, cement dust, washing powders or fabric conditioners. If you wash your dog's bedding or if he sleeps on your bed, use a fragrance-free - if possible, hypoallergenic - laundry detergent and avoid fabric conditioner. The irritation may be restricted to one part of the dog – e.g. the underneath of the paws or belly - which has touched the offending object. Symptoms are skin irritation - either a general problem or specific hotspots - itching (pruritis) and sometimes hair loss. Readers sometimes report to us that their dog will incessantly lick one part of the body, often the paws, anus, belly or back. (Pictured are dust mites).

Flea Bite Allergies

These are a very common canine allergy and affect dogs of all breeds. To compound the problem, many dogs with flea allergies also have inhalant allergies. Flea bite allergy is typically seasonal, worse during summer and autumn - peak time for fleas - and is worse in warmer climates where fleas are prevalent.

This type of allergy is not the flea itself, but to proteins in flea saliva, which are deposited under the dog's skin when the insect feeds. Just one bite to an allergic Boston will cause intense and long-lasting itching. If affected, the dog will try to bite at the base of his tail and scratch a lot. Most of the damage is done by the dog's scratching, rather than the flea bite, and can result in his fur falling out or skin abrasions. Some Bostons will develop hot spots. These can occur anywhere, but are often on the front feet or legs and along the back and base of the tail. Flea bite allergies can only be totally prevented by keeping all fleas away from the dog. Various flea prevention treatments are available — see the section on Parasites. If you suspect your dog may be allergic to fleas, consult your vet for the proper diagnosis and medication.

Acute Moist Dermatitis (Hot Spots)

Acute moist dermatitis or 'hot spots' are not uncommon. A hot spot can appear suddenly and is a raw, inflamed and often bleeding area of skin. The area becomes moist and painful and begins spreading due to continual licking and chewing. They can become large, red, irritated lesions in a short pace of time. The cause is often a local reaction to an insect bite: fleas, ticks, biting flies and even mosquitoes have been known to cause acute moist dermatitis. Other causes include:

- Allergies - food allergies and inhalant allergies
- Mites
- Ear infections
- Poor grooming
- Burs or plant awns
- Anal gland disease
- Hip dysplasia or other types of arthritis and degenerative joint disease

Diagnosis and Treatment - The good news is that, once diagnosed and with the right treatment, hot spots can disappear as quickly as they appeared. The underlying cause should be identified and treated, if possible. Check with your vet before treating your Boston for fleas and ticks at the same time as other medical treatment (such as anti-inflammatory medications and/or antibiotics), as he or she will probably advise you to wait.

Treatments may come in the form of injections, tablets or creams — or your dog might need a combination of them. Your vet will probably clip and clean the affected area to help the effectiveness of any spray or ointment and your poor Boston might also have to wear an E-collar until the condition subsides, but usually this does not take long.

Bacterial infection (Pyoderma)

Pyoderma literally means 'pus in the skin' (yuk!) and fortunately, this condition is not contagious. Early signs of this bacterial infection are itchy red spots filled with yellow pus, similar to pimples or spots in humans. They can sometimes develop into red, ulcerated skin with dry and crusty patches.

Pyoderma is caused by several things: a broken skin surface, a skin wound due to chronic exposure to moisture, altered skin bacteria, or poor blood flow to the skin. Dogs have a higher risk of developing an infection when they have a fungal infection or an endocrine (hormone gland) disease such as hyperthyroidism, or have allergies to fleas, food or parasites. Pyoderma is often secondary to allergic dermatitis and develops in the sores on the skin that happen as a result of scratching. Puppies often develop 'puppy pyoderma' in thinly-haired areas such as the chin, groin and underarms. Fleas, ticks, yeast or fungal skin infections, thyroid disease, hormonal imbalances, heredity and some medications can increase the risk. If you notice symptoms, get your dog to the vet quickly before the condition develops from **superficial pyoderma** into **severe pyoderma**, which is extremely unpleasant and takes a lot longer to treat.

Bacterial infection, no matter how bad it may look, usually responds well to medical treatment, which is generally done on an outpatient basis. Superficial pyoderma will usually be treated with a two to six-week course of antibiotic tablets or ointment. Severe or recurring pyoderma looks awful, causes your dog distress and can take months of treatment to completely cure. Medicated shampoos and regular bathing, as instructed by your vet, are also part of the treatment. It's also important to ensure your dog has clean, dry, padded bedding.

It is also highly recommended that you discourage constant chewing, scratching and biting, as it can become a habit for a dog. When it becomes a habit, the dog continues to scratch AND BITE even after the issue has been resolved.

Parasites

Demodectic Mange in Bostons

Demodectic mange is also known as red mange, follicular mange or puppy mange. It is caused by the tiny mite Demodex canis (pictured) that can only be seen through a microscope. The mites actually live inside the hair follicles on the bodies of virtually every adult dog - and most humans - without causing any harm or irritation. In humans, the mites are found in the skin, eyelids and the creases of the nose ... try not to think about that!

According to health surveys carried out by the Boston Terrier Club of America (BTCA), approximately one in 10 Bostons has suffered localised demodectic mange, while one in 20 has had the generalised form. The spots usually occur on the face, but could form anywhere, including the paws.

The BTCA says: "One of the most difficult problems a Boston Terrier owner ever encounters is demodectic mange. This disease is caused by the presence of the mite Demodex Canis in the hair follicles of the dog, in conjunction with an impaired or deficient immune system. The disease is thought to be caused by a genetic defect in the immune system. The Boston Terrier is listed among the breeds with familial predilection to demodectic mange.

"Demodectic mange is mainly a disease of young dogs that have poorly developed immune systems. The majority of puppies are immune to the mites and will display no ill effects from them. Most dogs (90%) will have mature immune systems by the time they are 12 to 18 months of age and will 'outgrow' the problem.

"In the first hours of a puppy's life, the demodex mites begin moving to the nursing puppies from the mother. These mites will lay eggs in the hair follicles that hatch and multiply. By the time a puppy is four to six months old, he may be showing signs of hair loss around his face caused by the multiplication of the mites.

"Older dogs with demodectic mange may have a serious underlying disease problem that interferes with a well-functioning immune system. Cushing's, cancer, hypothyroid and even diabetes have been thought to be associated with a predilection for this mange

"Differentiation of localized from generalized demodectic mange is based upon the severity of the infection. In cases where there are fewer than five spots of mange on a dog it is termed 'localized;' more than five spots and the mange is termed 'generalized.' These spots usually occur on the face, but may occur anywhere including the feet."

The demodectic mite spends its entire life on the host dog. Eggs hatch and mature from larvae to nymphs to adults in 20 to 35 days and the mites are transferred directly from the mother to the puppies within the first week of life by direct physical contact. Demodectic mange is not a disease of poorly kept or dirty kennels. It is generally a disease of young dogs with inadequate or poorly developed immune systems (or older dogs suffering from a suppressed immune system).

Vets currently believe that virtually every mother carries and transfers mites to her puppies, and most are immune to the mite's effects, but a few puppies are not and they develop full-blown mange. They may have a few (less than five) isolated lesions and this is known as localised mange – often around the head. This happens in around 90% of cases, but in the other 10% of cases, it develops into generalised mange that covers the entire body or region of the body.

One US breeder said: "The general consensus among breeders is that if a puppy has localized mange and can outgrow it naturally without veterinary assistance, then it is not genetic and should not be a problem. However, conversely, if the dog has generalized mange and requires medical intervention for healing, it is usually deemed a genetic deficiency of the immune system and that dog should not be bred."

The condition is most likely to develop in puppies with parents that have suffered from mange. In other words, there is thought to be a genetic link, not necessarily with the mange itself, but rather with the suppressed immune system. Most lesions in either form develop after four months of age. Demodectic mange can also develop around the time when females have their first season, typically around nine months old, and may be due to a slight dip in the bitch's immune system.

Symptoms – In localised mange, a few circular crusty areas appear, most frequently on the head and front legs of three to six-month-old puppies. Most will self-heal as the puppies become older and develop their own immunity, but a persistent problem needs treatment.

In severe cases, bald patches are usually the first sign, usually accompanied by crusty, red skin that sometimes appears greasy or wet. Usually hair loss begins around the muzzle, eyes and other areas on the head; these areas may or may not itch.

With generalised mange, there are bald patches over the entire coat, including the head, neck, body, legs, and feet. The skin on the head, side and back is crusty, often inflamed and oozes a clear fluid. The skin itself will often be oily to touch and there is usually a secondary bacterial infection. Some puppies can become quite ill and can develop a fever, lose their appetites and become lethargic. If you suspect your puppy has generalised demodectic mange, get him to a vet straight away.

There is also a condition called pododermatitis, when the mange affects a puppy's paws. It can cause bacterial infections and be very uncomfortable, even painful. The symptoms of this mange include hair loss on the paws, swelling of the paws (especially around the nail beds) and red/hot/inflamed areas, which are often infected. Treatment is always recommended, and it can take several rounds to clear it up.

Diagnosis and Treatment – The vet will diagnose demodectic mange after he or she has taken a skin scraping. As these mites are present on every dog, they do not necessarily mean the dog has mange. Only when the mite is coupled with lesions will the vet diagnose mange. Treatment usually involves topical (on the skin) medication and sometimes tablets. Localised demodectic mange often resolves itself as the puppy grows. If the dog has just one or two lesions, these can usually be successfully treated using specific creams and spot treatments. With generalised demodectic mange, treatment can be lengthy and expensive.

Vets often prescribe Amitraz anti-parasitic dips every two weeks. This is an organophosphate available on prescription under the name Aludex (UK) or Mitaban (USA). Owners should always wear rubber gloves when treating their dog, and it should be applied in an area with adequate ventilation. It should also be noted that some dogs – especially Toy breeds - can react to this, so check very carefully with your vet as to whether it will be suitable for your Boston. This treatment is NOT suitable or advised for every dog – neither is it recommended for young Bostons with localised mange (as they usually grow out of it on their own)..

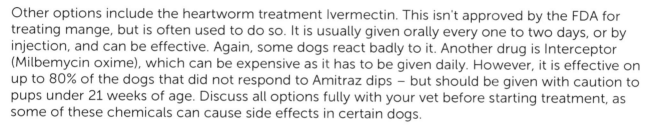

Most dogs with the severe form of the condition need from six to 14 dips every two weeks. After a while, your vet will probably take another skin scraping to check that the mites have gone. Dips continue for one month after the mites have disappeared, but dogs shouldn't be considered cured until a year after their last treatment.

Other options include the heartworm treatment Ivermectin. This isn't approved by the FDA for treating mange, but is often used to do so. It is usually given orally every one to two days, or by injection, and can be effective. Again, some dogs react badly to it. Another drug is Interceptor (Milbemycin oxime), which can be expensive as it has to be given daily. However, it is effective on up to 80% of the dogs that did not respond to Amitraz dips – but should be given with caution to pups under 21 weeks of age. Discuss all options fully with your vet before starting treatment, as some of these chemicals can cause side effects in certain dogs.

There are also a number of holistic remedies, including aloe vera, lemon and garlic, apple cider vinegar, honey, yoghurt and olive oil. We have no personal experience as to how effective they are, but there is plenty of anecdotal evidence that holistic remedies work in certain cases. Whatever option you choose, act promptly, to avoid the dreaded full-blown generalised demodectic mange developing; it is a terrible and painful ailment for a dog.

Dogs that have the generalised condition may have underlying skin infections, so antibiotics are often given for the first several weeks of treatment. Because the mite flourishes on dogs with suppressed immune systems, you should try to get to the root cause of immune system disease, especially if your Boston is older when he or she develops demodectic mange.

Sarcoptic Mange

Also known as canine scabies, this is an inflammatory disease caused by various types of the demodex mite. This microscopic parasite can cause a range of skin problems such as hair loss and severe itching, and in some cases problems with the immune system. The mites can infect other animals such as foxes and cats, with each species having a slightly different parasite. The human version is called scabies. Any dog can catch the parasite from close contact with foxes, fox dens and fox poo(p). Fox mange is less severe (for a dog) than the dog mite, but it still causes severe itching for the affected dog, who will scratch and bite himself.

The mites burrow into the dog's skin and live for up to 22 days in cool, moist environments. At normal room temperature, they live from two to six days, preferring to live on parts of the dog with less hair. These are the areas you may see him scratching, although it can spread throughout the body in severe cases.

Diagnosing canine scabies can be somewhat difficult, and it is often mistaken for inhalant allergies.

The most common way is for the vet to take a skin scraping from the dog and analyse it under a microscope.

Once diagnosed, there are a number of effective treatments, including selamectin (Revolution), an on-the-skin solution applied once a month, which also provides heartworm prevention, flea control and some tick protection. Various Frontline products are also effective – check with your vet for the correct ones.

NOTE: Some Bostons may have a reaction to Frontline and other topical solutions. Keep an eye on your dog after applying the treatment to make sure there is no negative reaction.

As with demodectic mange, washes and dips may also be necessary - in some cases the dog is completely clipped for the dip to have maximum effect.

It may take between four and six weeks for a complete course of treatment. During this time, try and limit other dogs' contact with the infected dog, as mange is highly infectious, as the mites move quickly from one animal to the next. Most cases clear up with veterinary treatment, but in extreme cases, the dog may have to be quarantined.

As well as catching it from foxes, dogs can also pick it up at kennels, veterinary clinics, the local parks, the dog groomer's or anywhere where there are lots of other dogs. Because your Boston does not have to come into direct contact with an infected dog to catch scabies, it is difficult to completely protect him.

If your dog is affected, make sure his bedding is clean and avoid washing powders and other chemicals. A healthy immune system can help prevent the recurrence of the problem, and a good diet can go some way towards prevention.

Fleas

When you see your dog scratching and biting, your first thought is probably: "He's got fleas!" and you may well be right. Fleas don't fly, but they do have very strong back legs and they will take any opportunity to jump from the ground or another animal into your Boston's lovely warm coat. You can sometimes see the fleas if you part your dog's fur.

And for every flea (pictured) that you see on your dog, there is the awful prospect of hundreds of eggs and larvae in your home. So if your dog is unlucky enough to catch fleas, you'll have to treat your environment as well as your dog in order to completely get rid of them.

The best form of cure is prevention. Vets recommend giving dogs a preventative flea treatment every four to eight weeks. This may vary depending on your climate, the season - fleas do not breed as quickly in the cold - and how much time your dog spends outdoors. Once-a-month topical insecticides - like Frontline, Advocate and Advantix - are the most commonly used flea prevention products on the market. You part the skin and apply drops of the liquid on to a small area on your dog's back, usually near the neck. Some kill fleas and ticks, and others just kill fleas - check the details. It is worth spending the money on a quality treatment, as cheaper brands may not rid your dog completely of fleas, ticks and other parasites. Sprays, dips, shampoos and collars are other options, as are tablets and injections in certain cases, such as before your dog goes into boarding kennels or has surgery. Incidentally, a flea bite is different from a flea bite allergy.

NOTE: There is considerable anecdotal evidence from dog owners of various breeds that the US flea and worm tablet Trifexis may cause severe side effects in some dogs. You may wish to read owners' comments at: www.max-the-schnauzer.com/trifexis-side-effects-in-schnauzers.html before deciding whether to use it.

Ticks

A tick is not an insect, but a member of the arachnid family, like the spider. There are over 850 types of them, divided into two types: hard shelled and soft shelled.

Ticks don't have wings - they can't fly, they crawl. They have a sensor called Haller's organ that detects smell, heat and humidity to help them locate food, which in some cases is a Boston. A tick's diet consists of one thing and one thing only – blood! They climb up onto tall grass and when they sense an animal is close, crawl on him.

Ticks can pass on a number of diseases to animals and humans, the most well-known of which is Lyme Disease, a serious condition that causes lameness and other problems. Vaccinations are available to guard against Lyme Disease. They can be expensive, but should be considered if your dog spends a lot of time outdoors in areas where this dreaded disease is a threat.

If you do find a tick on your Boston's coat and are not sure how to get it out, have it removed by a vet or other expert. Inexpertly pulling it out yourself and leaving a bit of the tick behind can be detrimental to your dog's health. Prevention treatment is similar to that for fleas. If your Boston has particularly sensitive skin, he might do better with a natural flea or tick remedy.

Heartworm

Heartworm is a serious and potentially fatal disease affecting pets in North America and many other parts of the world (but not the UK). It is caused by foot-long worms that live in the heart, lungs and associated blood vessels of affected pets, causing severe lung disease, heart failure and damage to other organs in the body.

The dog is a natural host for heartworms, allowing heartworms living inside the dog to mature into adults, mate and produce offspring. If untreated, their numbers can increase; dogs have been known to harbour several hundred worms in their bodies. Heartworm disease causes lasting damage to the heart, lungs and arteries, and can affect the dog's health and quality of life long after

the parasites are gone. For this reason, prevention is by far the best option and treatment - when needed - should be administered as early as possible.

The mosquito (pictured) plays an essential role in the heartworm life cycle. When a mosquito bites and takes a blood meal from an infected animal, it picks up baby worms that develop and mature into 'infective stage' larvae over a period of 10 to 14 days.

Then, when the infected mosquito bites another dog, cat or susceptible wild animal, the infective larvae are deposited onto the surface of the animal's skin and enter the new host through the mosquito's bite wound. Once inside a new host, it takes approximately six months for the larvae to develop into adult heartworms. Once mature, heartworms can live for five to seven years in a dog.

In the early stages of the disease, many dogs show few or no symptoms. The longer the infection persists, the more likely symptoms will develop. These include:

- A mild persistent cough
- Reluctance to exercise
- Tiredness after moderate activity
- Decreased appetite
- Weight loss

As the disease progresses, dogs may develop heart failure and a swollen belly due to excess fluid in the abdomen. Dogs with large numbers of heartworms can develop sudden blockages of blood flow within the heart leading to the life-threatening Caval Syndrome. This causes a sudden onset of laboured breathing, pale gums and dark, bloody or coffee-coloured urine. Without prompt surgical removal of the heartworm blockage, few dogs survive.

The effects that untreated heartworm can have on dogs is truly shocking, as many volunteers in rescue shelters can testify.

Although more common in south eastern states of the USA, heartworm disease has been diagnosed in all 50 states. And because infected mosquitoes can fly indoors, even dogs that spend much time inside the home are at risk. For that reason, the American Heartworm Society recommends that you get your dog tested every year and give your dog heartworm preventive treatment for the full 12 months of the year.

Thanks to the American Heartworm Society for assistance with the section

....

Ringworm

This is not actually a worm, but a fungus and is most commonly seen in puppies and young dogs. It is highly infectious and often found anywhere on the body including on the face, ears, paws or tail. The ringworm fungus is most prevalent in hot, humid climates but, surprisingly, most cases occur in autumn and winter. Ringworm infections in dogs are not that common; in one study of dogs with active skin problems, less than 3% had ringworm.

Ringworm is transmitted by spores in the soil and by contact with the infected hair of dogs and

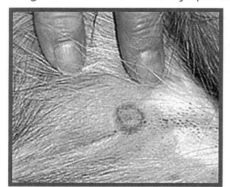

cats, which can be typically found on carpets, brushes, combs, toys and furniture. Spores from infected animals can be shed into the environment and live for over 18 months, but fortunately most healthy adult dogs have some resistance and never develop symptoms.

The fungi live in dead skin, hairs and nails - and the head and legs are the most common areas affected. Tell-tale signs are bald patches with a roughly circular shape (see photo). Ringworm is relatively easy to treat with fungicidal shampoos or antibiotics from a vet.

Humans can catch ringworm from pets, and vice versa. Children are especially susceptible, as are adults with suppressed immune systems and those undergoing chemotherapy. Hygiene is extremely important. If your dog has ringworm, wear gloves when handling him and wash your hands well afterwards. And if a member of your family catches ringworm, make sure they use separate towels from everyone else or the fungus may spread. As an adolescent, I caught ringworm from horses at stables where I worked at weekends - much to my mother's horror - and was treated like a leper by the rest of the family until it had cleared up!

....

Interdigital Cysts

More commonly seen in the Bulldog and French Bulldog, these can be very difficult to get rid of, since they are not the primary problem, but often a sign of some other condition. Actually, they are not cysts, but the result of **furunculosis**, a condition of the skin that clogs hair follicles and creates chronic infection. They can be caused by a number of factors, including allergies, excess licking, poor foot conformation, mites, yeast infections, ingrowing hairs or other foreign bodies, and obesity.

If you've ever noticed a fleshy red lump between your dog's toes that looks like an ulcerated sore or a hairless bump, then it may well be an interdigital cyst - or 'interdigital furuncle' to give the condition its correct medical term.

These nasty-looking bumps are painful for your dog and will probably cause him to limp. Vets might recommend a whole range of treatments to get to the root cause of the problem. It can be extremely expensive if your dog is having a barrage of tests or biopsies and even then you are not guaranteed to find the underlying cause.

The first thing he or she will probably do is put your dog in an E-collar to stop him licking the affected area, which will never recover properly as long as he's constantly licking it. This, again, is stressful for your dog. Here are some remedies your vet may suggest:

- Antibiotics and/or steroids and/or mite killers
- Soaking his feet in Epsom salts twice daily to unclog the hair follicles
- Testing him for allergies or thyroid problems
- Starting a food trial if food allergies are suspected
- Shampooing his feet
- Cleaning between his toes with medicated (benzoyl peroxide) wipes
- Referring him to a veterinary dermatologist
- And, in drastic cases, surgery

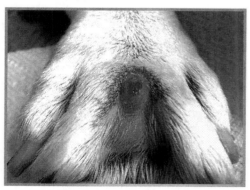

If you suspect your Boston has an interdigital cyst, take him to the vet for a correct diagnosis and then discuss the various options. A course of antibiotics may be suggested initially, along with switching to a hypoallergenic diet if a food allergy is suspected. If the condition persists, many owners get discouraged, especially when treatment may go on for many weeks.

Before you resort to any drastic action, first try soaking your Boston's affected paw in Epsom salts for five or 10 minutes twice a day.

After the soaking, clean the area with medicated wipes, which are antiseptic and control inflammation. In the US, these are sold under the brand name Stridex pads in the skin care section of any grocery, or from the pharmacy. There are other brands as well, such as Noxema and generic brands.

If you think the cause may be an environmental allergy, wash your dog's paws and under his belly when you return from a walk; this will help to remove pollen and other allergens from his body.

Surgery can be effective, but it is a drastic option and although it might solve the immediate problem, it will not deal with whatever is triggering the interdigital cysts in the first place. Not only is healing after this surgery a lengthy and difficult process, it also means your dog will never have the same foot as before - future orthopaedic issues and a predisposition to more cysts are a couple of possible scenarios.

All that said, your vet will understand that interdigital cysts aren't so simple to deal with, but they are always treatable. Get the right diagnosis as soon as possible, limit all offending factors and give medical treatment a good solid try before embarking on more drastic cures.

Ear Infections

Infection of the external ear canal (outer ear infection) is called otitis externa and is quite common in all types of dog. It is estimated that as many as one dog in five suffers from it at some point in his or her life – more with some breeds. The fact that your dog has recurring ear infections does not necessarily mean that the ears are the source of the problem – although they might be.

One reason for them is moisture in the ear canal, which, in turn, allows bacteria to flourish there. However, it's not unusual for Bostons with chronic or recurring ear infections to have food or inhalant allergies or low thyroid function (hypothyroidism). Sometimes the ears are the first sign of allergy. The underlying cause of the problem must be treated or the dog will continue to have chronic ear problems.

Tell-tale signs include your dog shaking his head, scratching or rubbing his ears a lot, or an unpleasant odour coming from the ears. If you look inside the ears, you might notice a reddish brown, blackish or yellow discharge; it may also be red and inflamed with a lot of wax. Sometimes a dog may appear depressed or irritable; ear infections are painful. In chronic cases, the inside of his ears may become crusty or thickened.

Dogs can have ear problems for many different reasons, including:

❧   Food allergies (often this is the case with ear infections in Bostons) or environmental allergies

❧   Ear mites or other parasites

- Bacteria or yeast infections
- Injury, sometimes due to excessive scratching
- Foreign bodies, e.g. plant material, lodged inside the ear(s)
- Hormonal abnormalities, e.g. hypothyroidism
- The ear anatomy and environment, e.g. excess moisture
- Hereditary or immune conditions and tumours

Treatment depends on the cause and what, if any, other conditions your dog may have. Antibiotics are used for bacterial infections and antifungals for yeast infections.

Glucocorticoids, such as dexamethasone, are often included in these medications to reduce the inflammation in the ear. Your vet may also flush out and clean the ear with special drops, something you may have to do daily at home until the infection clears.

A dog's ear canal is L-shaped, which means it can be difficult to get medication into the lower (horizontal) part of the ear. The best method is to hold the dog's ear flap with one hand and put the ointment or drops in with the other, if possible tilting the dog's head away from you so the liquid flows downwards **with gravity.**

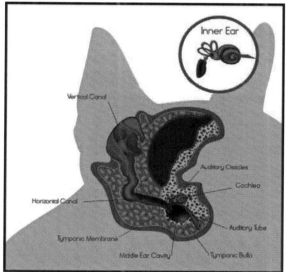

Make sure you then hold the ear flap down and massage the medication into the horizontal canal before letting go of your dog, as the first thing he will do is shake his head – and if the ointment or drops aren't massaged in, they will fly out.

Nearly all ear infections can be successfully managed if properly diagnosed and treated. But if an underlying problem remains undiscovered, the outcome will be less favourable. Deep ear infections can damage or rupture the eardrum, causing an internal ear infection and even permanent hearing loss. Closing of the ear canal (**hyperplasia** or **stenosis**) is another sign of severe infection. Most extreme cases of hyperplasia will eventually require surgery as a last resort; the most common procedure is called a 'lateral ear resection'.

Our dog had a lateral ear resection several years ago, following years of recurring ear infections and the growth of scar tissue. It was surgery or deafness, the vet said. We opted for surgery and our dog has been free of ear infections ever since. However, it is an extremely painful procedure for the dog and should only be considered as a very last resort.

To avoid or alleviate recurring ear infections, check your dog's ears and clean them regularly. If your Boston enjoys swimming, great care should be taken to ensure the inside of the ear is thoroughly dry afterwards - and after bathing at home. There is more information in **Chapter 12. Grooming.**

When cleaning your dog's ears, be very careful not to put anything too far down inside. Visit YouTube to see videos of how to correctly clean without damaging them. In a nutshell, DO NOT use cotton buds (called cotton swabs or Q-tips in the US), these are too small and can damage the ear. Some owners recommend regularly cleaning the inside of ears with cotton wool and a mixture of water and white vinegar once a week or so.

If your dog appears to be in pain, has smelly ears, or if his ear canals look inflamed, contact your vet straight away. If you can nip the first infection in the bud, there is a chance it will not return. If your dog has a ruptured or weakened eardrum, ear cleansers and medications could do more harm than good. Good hygiene and early treatment is the best way of preventing a recurrence. There is a good veterinary website here: http://animalpetdoctor.homestead.com/ears.html which describes the different causes, severity and possible treatments for ear infections.

....

Canine Acne

Acne is not uncommon and - just as with humans - generally affects teenagers, often between five and eight months of age with dogs. It occurs when oil glands become blocked causing bacterial infection and these glands are most active in teenagers. Acne is not a major health problem as most of it will clear up once the dog becomes an adult, but it can recur.

Typical signs are pimples, blackheads or whiteheads around the muzzle, chest or groin. For some young dogs, acne is a normal part of growing up and the problem will clear up on its own. Other times, it may be caused by factors such as a hormonal imbalance, an allergic reaction to something or poor hygiene – particularly if it occurs in older dogs.

You can help your dog by bathing him in a medicated canine shampoo or dabbing the affected area with a warm damp cloth or astringent. If the adolescent acne is severe with bleeding or pus, or the dog is an adult, then a visit to the vet is recommended.

....

Some Allergy Treatments

Treatments and success rates vary tremendously from dog to dog and from one allergy to another, which is why it is so important to consult a vet at the outset. Earlier diagnosis is more likely to lead to a successful treatment. Some owners whose Bostons have recurring skin issues find that a course of antibiotics or steroids works wonders for their dog's sore skin and itching. However, the scratching starts all over again shortly after the treatment stops.

Food allergies require patience, a change of diet and maybe even a food trial, and the specific trigger is notoriously difficult to isolate – unless you are lucky and hit on the culprit straight away. With inhalant and contact allergies, blood and skin tests are available, followed by hypersensitisation treatment. However, these can be expensive and often the specific trigger for many dogs remains unknown. So the reality for many owners of Bostons with allergies is that they manage the ailment with various medications and practices, rather than curing it completely.

Our Personal Experience

After corresponding with numerous other dog owners and consulting our vet, Graham, it seems that our experiences with allergies are not uncommon. This is borne out by the dozens of dog owners who have contacted our website about their pet's allergy or sensitivities. Our dog was perfectly fine until he was about two years old when he began to scratch a lot. He scratched more in spring and summer, which meant that his allergies were almost certainly inhalant or contact-based and related to pollens, grasses or other outdoor triggers.

One option was for Max to have a barrage of tests to discover exactly what he was allergic to. We decided not to do this, not because of the cost, but because our vet said it was highly likely that he was allergic to pollens. If we had confirmed an allergy to pollens, we were not going to stop taking him outside for walks, so the vet treated him on the basis of seasonal inhalant or contact allergies, probably related to pollen.

As mentioned, one method is to have a shallow bath or hose outside and to rinse the dog's paws and underbelly after a walk in the countryside. This is something our vet does with his own dogs and has found that the scratching reduces as a result. Regarding medications, initially Max was put on a tiny dose of **Piriton**, an antihistamine for hay fever sufferers (prescribed in the millions for humans and canines) and for the first few seasons this worked well.

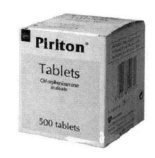

Allergies can often change and the dog can also build up a tolerance to a treatment, which is why they can be so difficult to treat. This has been the case with our dog over the past nine years. The symptoms change from season to season, although the main ones remain and they are general scratching, paw biting and ear infections. One year, he bit the skin under his tail a lot (near the anus) and this was treated effectively with a single steroid injection followed by spraying the area with cortisone once a day at home for a period. This type of spray can be very effective if the itchy area is small, but no good for spraying all over a dog's body.

A few years ago Max started nibbling his paws for the first time - a habit he persists with - although not to the extent that they become red and raw. Over the years we have tried a number of treatments, all of which have worked for a while, before he comes off the medication in autumn for six months when plants and grasses stop growing outdoors. He manages perfectly fine the rest of the year without any treatment.

If we were starting again from scratch, knowing what we know now, I would investigate a raw diet, if necessary in combination with holistic remedies. We have stuck with a high quality hypoallergenic dry food. Max's allergies are manageable, he loves his food, is full of energy and otherwise healthy, and so we are reluctant to make such a big change at this point in his life.

According to Graham, more and more dogs are appearing in his waiting room every spring with various types of allergies. Whether this is connected to how we breed our dogs remains to be seen. One season, he put Max on a short course of steroids. These worked very well for five months, but steroids are not a long-term solution, as prolonged use can cause organ damage.

Another spring, Max was prescribed a non-steroid daily tablet called **Atopica,** sold in the UK only through vets. (The active ingredient is cyclosporine, which suppresses the immune system. Some dogs can have side effects, although Max didn't, and holistic practitioners believe that it is harmful to the dog). This treatment was expensive, but initially extremely effective – so much so that we thought we had cured the problem completely. However, after a couple of seasons on cyclosporine he developed a tolerance to the drug and started scratching again.

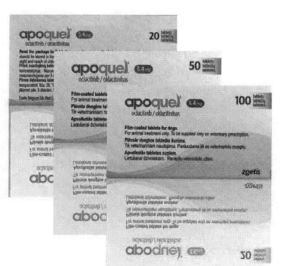

A few years ago, he went back on the antihistamine Piriton, a higher dose than when he was two years old, and this worked very well again. One advantage of this drug is that is it manufactured by the millions for dogs and is therefore very inexpensive. In the meantime, we were returning to the vet's periodically for ear drops for recurring ear infections.

In 2013, the Food and Drug Administration (FDA) approved **Apoquel** (oclacitinib) to control itching and inflammation in allergic dogs. In some quarters, it has been hailed **'a wonder drug'** for canine allergies. In fact, it proved so popular in the UK and North America that there was initially a shortage of supply, with the manufacturers not being able to produce it fast enough. The tablets cost around £1 a day - or $1.50 to

$2 – so it's not cheap, but the beauty of it is that it's a non-steroid, so dogs can take it long term without suffering the organ damage associated with long-term steroid use.

We have tried Apoquel and had excellent results; Max has been on it for about six months of the year for three years now. There was some tweaking at the beginning to get the daily dose right, but it really has proved effective for us. Max still scratches, but not so much – all dogs scratch a bit – and he has no redness or swellings at all. Normally, dogs start with a double dose for 10 days to suppress the allergic reaction and then go on to a single tablet a day mixed into one of their meals.

Many vets recommend adding fish oils (which contain Omega-3 fatty acids) to a daily feed to keep your dog's skin and coat healthy all year round – whether or not he has problems. We add a liquid supplement called Yumega Plus, which contains Omegas 3 and 6, to one of his two daily feeds all year round; this definitely seems to help his skin, and his coat positively shines.

In the past when the scratching has got particularly bad, we have bathed Max in an antiseborrhoeic shampoo (called Malaseb) twice a week for a limited time. This also helped, although it has not been necessary since he started on the Apoquel.

The main point is that most allergies are manageable. They may change throughout the life of the dog and you may have to alter the treatment. Our Max still scratches, but nowhere near as much as when he was younger. He may have allergies, but he wouldn't miss his walks for anything and, all in all, he is one very contented canine.

We've compiled some anecdotal evidence from our website from owners of dogs with various allergies. Here are some of their suggestions for alleviating the problems:

Bathing - Bathing your dog using shampoos that break down the oils that plug the hair follicles. These shampoos contain antiseborrhoeic ingredients such as benzoyl peroxide, salicylic acid, sulphur or tar. One example is Sulfoxydex shampoo, which can be followed by a cream rinse, such as Episoothe Rinse, afterwards to prevent the skin from drying out. Other natural shampoos such as oatmeal or tea tree oil are also gentle enough to use. Do not bathe your dog too often, unless instructed to do so by the vet, as it washes away natural oils in the skin.

Dabbing – Using an astringent such as witch hazel or alcohol on affected areas. We have heard of zinc oxide cream being used to some effect. In the human world, this is rubbed on to mild skin abrasions and acts as a protective coating. It can help the healing of chapped skin and nappy rash in babies. Zinc oxide works as a mild astringent and has some antiseptic properties and is safe to use on dogs, as long as you do not allow the dog to lick it off.

Daily supplements - Vitamin E, vitamin A, zinc and omega oils all help to make a dog's skin healthy. Feed a daily supplement that contains some of these, such as fish oil, which provides omega.

Here are some specific remedies from owners. We are not endorsing them; we're just passing on the information. Check with your vet before trying any new remedies.

A medicated shampoo with natural tea tree oil has been suggested by one owner. Some have reported that switching to a fish-based diet has helped lessen scratching. Ann G. said: "Try Natural Balance Sweet Potato and Fish formula. My dog Charlie has skin issues and this food has helped him tremendously! Plus he LOVES it!" Others have suggested home-cooked food is best, if you have the time to prepare the food.

This is what another reader had to say: "My eight-month-old dog also had a contact dermatitis around his neck and chest.

I was surprised how extensive it was. The vet recommended twice-a-week baths with an oatmeal shampoo. I also applied organic coconut oil daily for a few weeks. This completely cured the dermatitis. I also put a capsule of fish oil with his food once a day and continue to give him twice-weekly baths. His skin is great now."

Several owners have tried coconut oil with some success. Here is a link to an article on the benefits of coconut oils and fish oils: www.cocotherapy.com/fishoilsvsvirginoil_coconutoil.htm Check with your vet first.

....

The Holistic Approach

As canine allergies become increasingly common, more and more owners of dogs with allergies and sensitivities are looking towards natural foods and remedies to help deal with the issues. Some are finding that their dog does well for a time with injections or medication, but then the symptoms slowly start to reappear. A holistic practitioner looks at finding the root cause of the problem and treating that, rather than just treating the symptoms.

Dr Sara Skiwski is a holistic vet working in California. She writes here about canine environmental allergies: "Here in California, with our mild weather and no hard freeze in winter, environmental allergens can build up and cause nearly year-round issues for our beloved pets. Also seasonal allergies, when left unaddressed, can lead to year-round allergies. Unlike humans, whose allergy symptoms seem to affect mostly the respiratory tract, seasonal allergies in dogs often take the form of skin irritation/inflammation.

"Allergic reactions are produced by the immune system. The way the immune system functions is a result of both genetics and the environment: Nature versus Nurture. Let's look at a typical case. A puppy starts showing mild seasonal allergy symptoms, for instance a red tummy and mild itching in spring. Off to the vet!

"The treatment prescribed is symptomatic to provide relief, such as a topical spray. The next year when the weather warms up, the patient is back again - same symptoms but more severe this time. This time the dog has very itchy skin. Again, the treatment is symptomatic - antibiotics, topical spray (hopefully no steroids), until the symptoms resolve with the season change. Fast forward to another spring... in the third year, the patient is back again but this time the symptoms last longer, (not just spring but also through most of summer and into fall). By Year Five, all the symptoms are significantly worse and are occurring year round. This is what happens with seasonal environmental allergies. The more your pet is exposed to the allergens they are sensitive to, the more the immune system over-reacts and the more intense and long-lasting the allergic response becomes. What to do?

"In my practice, I like to address the potential root cause at the very first sign of an allergic response, which is normally seen between the ages of six to nine months old. I do this to circumvent the escalating response year after year. Since the allergen load your environmentally-sensitive dog is most susceptible to is much heavier outdoors, I recommend two essential steps in managing the condition. They are vigilance in foot care as well as fur care.

"What does this mean? A wipe down of feet and fur, especially the tummy, to remove any pollens or allergens is key. This can be done with a damp cloth, but my favorite method is to get a spray bottle filled with Witch Hazel and spray these areas. First, spray the feet then wipe them off with a cloth, and then spray and wipe down the tummy and sides. This is best done right after the pup has been outside playing or walking. This will help keep your pet from tracking the environmental allergens into the home and into their beds. If the feet end up still being itchy, I suggest adding foot soaks in Epsom salts."

Dr Skiwski also stresses the importance of keeping the immune system healthy by avoiding unnecessary vaccinations or drugs: "The vaccine stimulates the immune system, which is the last thing your pet with seasonal environmental allergies needs. I also will move the pet to an anti-inflammatory diet. Foods that create or worsen inflammation are high in carbohydrates. An allergic pet's diet should be very low in carbohydrates, especially grains. Research has shown that 'leaky gut,' or dysbiosis, is a root cause of immune system overreactions in both dog and cats (and some humans).

"Feed a diet that is not processed, or minimally processed; one that doesn't have grain and takes a little longer to get absorbed and assimilated through the gut. Slowing the assimilation assures that there are not large spikes of nutrients and proteins that come into the body all at once and overtax the pancreas and liver, creating inflammation.

"A lot of commercial diets are too high in grains and carbohydrates. These foods create inflammation that overtaxes the body and leads not just to skin inflammation, but also to other inflammatory conditions, such as colitis, pancreatitis, arthritis, inflammatory bowel disease and ear infections. Also, these diets are too low in protein, which is needed to make blood. This causes a decreased blood reserve in the body and in some of these animals this can lead to the skin not being properly nourished, starting a cycle of chronic skin infections which produce more itching."

After looking at diet, check that your dog is free from fleas and then these are some of her suggested supplements:

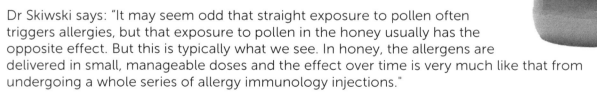

❧ **Raw (Unpasteurised) Local Honey** - an alkaline-forming food containing natural vitamins, enzymes, powerful antioxidants and other important natural nutrients that are destroyed during the heating and pasteurisation processes. Raw honey has anti-viral, anti-bacterial and anti-fungal properties. It promotes body and digestive health, is a powerful antioxidant, strengthens the immune system, eliminates allergies, and is an excellent remedy for skin wounds and all types of infections. Bees collect pollen from local plants and their honey often acts as an immune booster for dogs living in the locality.

Dr Skiwski says: "It may seem odd that straight exposure to pollen often triggers allergies, but that exposure to pollen in the honey usually has the opposite effect. But this is typically what we see. In honey, the allergens are delivered in small, manageable doses and the effect over time is very much like that from undergoing a whole series of allergy immunology injections."

❧ **Mushrooms** - make sure you choose the non-poisonous ones! Dogs don't like the taste, so you may have to mask it with another food. Medicinal mushrooms are used to treat and prevent a wide array of illnesses through their use as immune stimulants and modulators, and antioxidants. The most well-known and researched are reishi, maitake, cordyceps, blazei, split-gill, turkey tail and shiitake. The mushrooms stabilise mast cells in the body, which have the histamines attached to them. Histamine is what causes much of the inflammation, redness and irritation in allergies. By helping to control histamine production, the mushrooms can moderate the effects of inflammation and even help prevent allergies in the first place. **WARNING!** Mushrooms can interact with some over-the-counter and prescription drugs, so do your research as well as checking with your vet first.

- ❀ **Stinging Nettles** - contain biologically active compounds that reduce inflammation. Nettles have the ability to reduce the amount of histamine the body produces in response to an allergen. Nettle tea or extract can help with itching. Nettles not only help directly to decrease the itch, but also work overtime to desensitise the body to allergens, helping to reprogramme the immune system.

- ❀ **Quercetin** – is an over-the-counter supplement with anti-inflammatory properties. It is a strong antioxidant and reduces the body's production of histamines.

- ❀ **Omega-3 Fatty Acids** - these help decrease inflammation throughout the body. Adding them into the diet of all pets - particularly those struggling with seasonal environmental allergies – is very beneficial. If your dog has more itching along the top of their back and on their sides, add in a fish oil supplement. Fish oil helps to decrease the itch and heal skin lesions. The best sources of Omega 3s are krill oil, salmon oil, tuna oil, anchovy oil and other fish body oils, as well as raw organic egg yolks. If using an oil alone, it is important to give a vitamin B complex supplement.

- ❀ **Coconut Oil** - contains lauric acid, which helps decrease the production of yeast, a common opportunistic infection. Using a fish body oil combined with coconut oil before inflammation flares up can help moderate or even suppress your dog's inflammatory response.

Dr Skiwski adds: "Above are but a few of the over-the-counter remedies I like. In non-responsive cases, Chinese herbs can be used to work with the body to help to decrease the allergy threshold even more than with diet and supplements alone. Most of the animals I work with are on a program of Chinese herbs, diet change and acupuncture.

"So, the next time Fido is showing symptoms of seasonal allergies, consider rethinking your strategy to treat the root cause instead of the symptom."

With thanks to Dr Sara Skiwski, of the Western Dragon Integrated Veterinary Services, San Jose, California, for her kind permission to use her writings as the basis for this section

....

This chapter has only just touched on the complex subject of skin disorders. As you can see, the causes and treatments are many and varied. The best piece of advice we can give is that if your Boston Terrier has a skin issue, seek a professional diagnosis as soon as possible - whatever the condition - before attempting to treat it yourself and before the condition becomes entrenched.

Early diagnosis and treatment can sometimes nip the problem in the bud. Some skin conditions cannot be completely cured, but they can be successfully managed, allowing your Boston to live a happy, pain-free life. If you haven't got your puppy yet, ask the breeder if there is a history of skin issues in her bloodlines. And once you have your dog, remember that a good quality diet and attention to cleanliness and grooming go a long way in preventing and managing canine skin problems and ear infections.

....

12. Grooming

One advantage the Boston Terrier has over many other breeds is that, when it comes to grooming, this breed is low maintenance. The Boston has a single coat that does shed short hair, but not excessively. When looked after properly, a healthy Boston's coat is sleek and positively shines, adding to the breed's dapper appearance.

However, despite the easy maintenance coat, grooming doesn't just mean giving your Boston Terrier a quick tickle with a brush once a week! There are other factors to grooming that play a part in keeping your dog clean and skin-related issues at bay. Time spent grooming is also time spent bonding with your dog. It is this physical and emotional inter-reliance that brings us closer to our pets.

Routine grooming sessions allow you to examine your Boston's coat, skin, ears, teeth, eyes, paws and nails for signs of problems. Although they require fairly minimal brushing, it's important to get your puppy used to being handled and groomed from an early age; a stubborn adult Boston may not take kindly to being handled if he is not used to it.

The Boston Terrier Coat

The coat is short and smooth and sheds all year round - although more so in spring and autumn. Due to the shedding, this is not a breed suitable for people who have pet allergies. A once a week

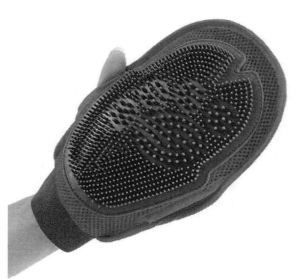

brush and check-over should be enough for your Boston - and all you need for this is a soft bristle brush and/or a rubber 'hound glove' (pictured).

Other benefits of regular brushing are that it removes dead hair and skin, stimulates blood circulation and spreads natural oils throughout the coat, helping to keep it in good condition. If brushed regularly, your dog shouldn't need many baths - unless he has a skin condition. If you do notice an unpleasant smell (in addition to your Boston's normal gassy emissions!) and he hasn't been rolling in something unmentionable, then your dog could have a yeast infection that may entail a visit to the vet.

Begin at your dog's head and brush backwards towards the tail; brush strokes should always be in the direction that the hair grows, not against the fur. It's easier to do it when your dog is standing, it's OK if he prefers to sit or lie down, just make sure you cover all areas including his legs and under his belly.

You can just brush your dog, or another method is to gently squirt the coat with a fine spray of water to prevent the hairs from breaking. Then rub with the hound glove to remove loose and dead hair, and finally use a soft bristle brush to remove all the remaining loose hair. Bristle brushes can be expensive, but they last forever.

 This tip was passed on by our groomer after we had been having difficulty getting our dog to stay still while grooming. If your Boston is resisting your efforts, take him out of his 'comfort zone' by placing him on a table - hold on to make sure he can't jump off and injure himself (or get someone to hold him). You'd be surprised what a difference this can make once he is out of his normal environment - i.e. at floor level - and at your level, where you can more easily control him.

Despite what you might read in internet ads, there are only three accepted colours for a Boston Terrier coat: brindle, seal or black - all with white markings.

Here are a few extra regular health and hygiene tasks you can do for your dog:

The Boston Face

Ears - A Boston would not be a Boston without his trademark ears. Yet this distinctive feature is not without its drawbacks. Boston Terriers, like many breeds, can be prone to ear infections - predominantly yeast infections. These can usually be detected by a nasty smell coming from the ears or when you see your dog shaking or rubbing his head a lot. In more severe cases, you may notice redness or a build-up of wax or discharge.

Ear cleaning - or at least checking the ears - should be part of your normal at-home grooming schedule, perhaps once every couple of weeks or so, to keep infection at bay. See **Chapter 11. Skin and Allergies** on how to clean your dog's ears safely. Ear canals are generally warm and moist, making them a haven for bacteria. In dogs, recurring ear infections can also be a sign of other underlying issues, such as food or environmental allergies.

If your Boston's ears have an unpleasant smell, if he scratches them a lot or they look red, consult your vet as simple routine cleaning won't clear up an infection - and ear infections are notoriously difficult to get rid of once they have arrived. Keeping your dog's ears clean is the best way to avoid problems starting in the first place.

 Never put anything sharp or narrow - like a cotton bud - inside your dog's ear.

Acne - Little red pimples on a dog's face and chin means he has got acne! A dog can get acne at any age, not just as an adolescent. Plastic bowls can also trigger the condition, which is why stainless steel ones are better. Often a daily washing followed by an application of an antibiotic cream is enough to get rid of the problem; if it persists it will mean a visit to your vet.

A Boston's skin can dry out, especially with artificial heat in the winter months. If you spot any dry patches, for example on the inner thighs or armpits, or a cracked nose, massage a little petroleum jelly or baby oil on to the dry patch.

Eyes - The eyes should be clean and clear. Cloudy eyes, particularly in an older dog, could be early signs of cataracts. Red or swollen tissue in the corner of the eye could be a symptom of cherry eye. Bostons have protruding eyes, which can attract dust or dirt. Many owners carry eye drops that they regularly use to wash away debris. You can also gently clean the eyes with warm water and cotton wool - but never put anything sharp anywhere near a Boston's eyes, your dog can suddenly jump forwards or backwards, causing injury.

Many Boston Terriers suffer from tear staining - often reddish-brown - which is most obvious on white hair and on dogs with more pronounced wrinkles. There are many reasons for tear stains;

sometimes it can be perfectly natural, other times it may be a sign of an underlying problem, e.g. an over-active tear duct, diet, or a genetic predisposition caused by the structure of the eye.

Excessive tearing results in damp facial hair, which becomes a breeding ground for bacteria and yeast, the most common of which is 'red yeast.' This often makes the tear stains a stronger red-brown colour and may emit a moderate to strong odour. Vets can prescribe medication to treat bacterial and yeast infections. If the tear staining is related to diet, it may take some time to get to the root cause of the problem, see **Chapter 7. Feeding a Boston Terrier.**

There are various manufactured products freely available to reduce tear staining, as well as a number of home remedies. One is to add a teaspoon of white cider vinegar to your dog's drinking water to alter his internal pH and control new tear stains. It may take him a while to get used to the new flavour of his water, so start with a tiny bit at a time.

Another is to use a mixture of plain white milk of magnesia and peroxide, and to mix them into a paste with corn starch. Work this into the stained area and let it dry. Then wash and condition the skin, repeat for several days, preferably every other day, until tear staining is gone. You can find other owners' experiences with this on various canine forums as the problem affects many breeds - e.g. at www.bostonterrierforums.com/forum/health-wellness/4027-tear-stains.html Always be extremely careful with peroxide or bleach near your dog's eyes and check with your vet before trying any home remedy.

While you are cleaning the eyes, you can also clean your Boston's wrinkles by wiping them with a medicated pad or baby wipe with lanolin or aloe to keep the crevices free of debris and bacteria - or you can use a drop of medicated dog shampoo from your vet in a cup of warm water. Facial wrinkles are part of what makes the breed so unique and appealing, but air cannot circulate in the hidden pockets under the wrinkles (and under some short screw tails) and they can become a breeding ground for yeast or bacteria. The skin can become red and infected, and sometimes yellow pus can be seen if not kept clean. After you have wiped the wrinkles or skin around the eyes, it's important to dry the skin to deter bacteria.

....

Nail Trimming

Not all Bostons get enough exercise outdoors on hard surfaces to wear their nails down, so they have to be clipped or filed regularly. Nails should be kept short for the paws to remain healthy. Long nails interfere with the dog's gait, making walking awkward or painful and they can also break easily,

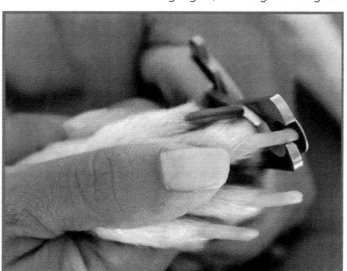

usually at the base of the nail where blood vessels and nerves are located.

Get your dog used to having his paws inspected from puppyhood. It is also a good opportunity to check for other problems such as cracked pads or interdigital cysts. These are swellings between the toes, often due to a bacterial infection that the Bully breeds tend to suffer from more than other breeds.

Be prepared: many Boston Terriers dislike having their nails trimmed, so it requires patience and persistence on your part.

To trim your dog's nails, use a specially designed clipper. Most have safety guards to prevent you cutting the nails too short. Do it before they get too long; if you can hear the nails clicking on the floor, they're too long. You want to trim only the ends, before 'the quick,' which is a blood vessel inside the nail. You can see where the quick ends on a white nail, but not on a dark nail.

Clip only the hook-like part of the nail that turns down. Start trimming gently, a nail or two at a time, and your dog will learn that you're not going to hurt him. If you accidentally cut the quick, stop the bleeding with some styptic powder.

Another option is to file your dog's nails with a nail grinder tool. Some dogs may have tough nails that are hard to trim and this may be less stressful for your dog, with less chance of pain or bleeding. The grinder is like an electric nail file and only removes a small amount of nail at a time. Some owners prefer to use one as it is harder to cut the quick, and many dogs prefer them to a clipper. However, you have to introduce your Boston gradually to the grinder - they often don't like the noise or vibration at first. If you find it impossible to clip your dog's nails, or you are at all worried about doing it, take him to a vet or a groomer - and ask him or her to squeeze your dog's anal sacs while he's there!

And while we're discussing the less appealing end of your Boston Terrier, let's dive straight in and talk about anal sacs. Sometimes called scent glands, these are a pair of glands located inside your dog's anus that give off a scent when he has a bowel movement. You won't want to hear this, but problems with impacted anal glands are not uncommon in dogs.

If your dog drags himself along on his rear end - 'scooting' - or tries to lick or scratch his anus, he could well have impacted anal glands that need squeezing, also called expressing - either by you if you know how to do it, your vet or a groomer. (He might also have worms). When a dog passes firm stools the glands normally empty themselves, but soft poo(p) or diarrhoea can mean that not enough pressure is exerted on to the glands to empty them, causing discomfort to the dog. If they become infected, this results in swelling and pain. In extreme cases one or both anal glands can be removed, but this must be weighed up against the risk of anaesthetising a Boston.

Bathing Your Boston Terrier

If you regularly groom your Boston Terrier and clean any skin folds, you shouldn't need to bathe your dog very often - unless he's been rolling is something horrible.

If a dog's coat and skin get too dirty it can cause irritation, leading to scratching and excessive shedding. It's all a question of getting the balance right, and this will to some extent depend on how much outdoor exercise your Boston gets, what sort of areas he's running in and what his natural skin condition is like. A Boston Terrier regularly exercising outside may need the odd bath every now and again (once every few weeks or months).

Although Bostons generally do not need regular bathing, one exception is if your dog has a skin problem and the vet has recommended baths to alleviate symptoms and scratching. (Another exception is if you are showing your dog, which will entail regular bathing).

Never use human shampoos on your Boston as these will only irritate his skin. A dog's skin has a different pH to that of a human. Instead use a shampoo specially medicated for dogs - such as Malaseb or similar. It is expensive, but lasts a long time. There is also a wide range of shampoos for dogs containing natural organic ingredients. If you bathe a healthy dog too often you can wash off the natural protective oils, causing the skin to dry out.

And if you do bathe your dog, make sure that you thoroughly dry him, especially in any wrinkles.

....

Teeth Cleaning

Veterinary studies show that by the age of three, 80% of dogs show signs of gum disease. Symptoms include yellow and brown build-up of tartar along the gum line, red inflamed gums and persistent bad breath.

You can give your dog a daily dental treat such as Dentastix or Nylabone to help keep his mouth and teeth clean, but you should also brush your Boston's teeth every now and again. Take things slowly in the beginning and give your dog lots of praise. Bostons love attention and many will start looking forward to teeth brushing sessions - especially if they like the flavour of the toothpaste!

Use a pet toothpaste, as the human variety can upset a canine's stomach. The real benefit comes from the actual action of the brush on the teeth, and various brushes, sponges and pads are available - the choice depends on factors such as the health of your dog's gums, the size of his mouth and how good you are at teeth cleaning.

Get your dog used to the toothpaste by letting him lick some off your finger when he is young. If he doesn't like the flavour, try a different one. Continue this until he looks forward to licking the paste - it might be instant or take days.

Put a small amount on your finger and gently rub it on one of the big canine teeth at the front of his mouth. Then get him used to the toothbrush or dental sponge - praise him when he licks it - for several days. The next step is to actually start brushing.

Lift his upper lip gently and place the brush at a 45º angle to the gum line. Gently move the brush backwards and forwards. Start just with his front teeth and then gradually do a few more. You don't need to brush the inside of his teeth as his tongue keeps them relatively free of plaque. With a bit of encouragement and patience, it can become a fun task for you both!

....

As you can see, grooming isn't just about brushing your Boston Terrier once a week. Hopefully your dog will thrive without too much maintenance, but some Bostons do require that little extra bit of care; it's all part of the bargain when you decide on this breed.

13. The Birds and the Bees

Judging by the number of questions our website receives from owners who ask about the canine reproductive cycle and breeding their dogs, there is a lot of confusion about the doggie facts of life out there.

Some owners want to know whether they should breed their dog, while others ask at what age they should have their dog spayed (females) or neutered (males).

Owners of females often ask when she will come on heat, how long this will last and how often it will occur. Sometimes they want to know how you can tell if a female is pregnant or how long a pregnancy lasts. So here, in a nutshell, is a short chapter on the facts of life as far as Boston Terriers are concerned.

Females and Heat

Just like all other mammal and human females, a female Boston Terrier has a menstrual cycle - or to be more accurate, an oestrus cycle. This is the period of time when she is ready (and willing!) for mating and is more commonly called *heat* or being *on heat*, *in heat* or *in season*.

A female Boston Terrier has her first cycle from about six to nine months old. However, there are some bloodlines with longer spans between heat cycles and the female may not have her first heat until she is anywhere from 10 months to one year old.

She will generally come on heat every six to eight months, though it may be longer between cycles, and the timescale becomes more erratic with old age. It can also be irregular with young dogs when cycles first begin.

On average, the heat cycle will last from 12 to 21 days, but can be anything from a few days up to three or four weeks. Within this period there will be several days that will be the optimum time for her to get pregnant. This middle phase of the cycle is called the *oestrus*.

The third phase, called *diestrus*, begins immediately following oestrus. During this time, her body will produce hormones whether or not she is pregnant. Her body thinks and acts like she is pregnant. All the hormones are present; only the puppies are missing. This can sometimes lead to what is known as a 'false pregnancy'.

Breeders normally wait until a female has been in heat at least twice before breeding from her, or until she is two years of age and fully health tested. Females should not be used for breeding too early, and certainly not before the age of one year. Pregnancy draws on their calcium reserves that they need for their own growing bones. And if a female breeds too early, she may break down structurally and have more health issues in later life. Good Boston Terrier breeders also limit the number of litters from each female, as breeding takes a lot out of them.

To protect females from overbreeding, the UK's Kennel Club introduced Breeding Restrictions in 2012. Now it will not register a litter from any bitch:

1. That has already had four litters.

2. If she is less than one year old at the time of mating.

3. If she is eight years or older when she whelps (gives birth).

4. If the litter is the result of any mating between father and daughter, mother and son or brother and sister.

5. If she has already had two C-Sections.

While a female dog is on heat, she produces hormones that attract male dogs. Because dogs have a sense of smell hundreds of times stronger than ours, your girl on heat is a magnet for all the males in the neighbourhood. It is believed that males can "smell" a female on heat up to two miles away! They may congregate around your house or follow you around the park, waiting for their chance to prove their manhood – or mutthood in their case.

Don't expect your precious Boston Terrier princess to be fussy. Her hormones are raging when she is on heat and during her most fertile days, she is ready, able and ... VERY willing! As she approaches the optimum time for mating, you may notice her short tail bending slightly to one side. She will also start to urinate more frequently. This is her signal to all those virile male dogs out there that she is ready for mating.

The first visual sign you may notice is when she tries to lick her swollen rear end – or vulva to be precise. She will then bleed; this is sometimes called spotting. It will be a light red or brown at the beginning of the heat cycle; some bitches bleed a lot after the first week. Some females can bleed quite heavily, this is normal. But if you have any concerns, contact your vet to be on the safe side. She may also start to 'mate' with your leg or other dogs. These are all normal signs of heat.

Breeding Boston Terriers requires much specialised knowledge on the part of the owner but, as stated, this does not stop a female on heat from being extremely interested in attention from any old mutt! To avoid an unwanted pregnancy - which could lead to complications and in extreme cases the death of the mother and puppies - you must keep a close eye on your female and not allow her to freely wander where she may come into contact with other dogs when she is on heat.

Unlike women, female dogs do not go through the menopause and can have puppies even when they are quite old. However, a litter for an elderly female Boston can also result in complications.

Ad from an animal shelter

If you don't want your gal to get pregnant, you should have her spayed (unless you intend showing her under Kennel Club or AKC rules). In Europe and North America, humane societies, animal shelters and rescue groups urge dog owners to have their pets spayed or neutered to prevent unwanted litters that contribute to too many animals in the rescue system or, even worse, having to be destroyed.

Normally all dogs from rescue centres and shelters will have been spayed or neutered. Most recognised breeders encourage the practice – and many even specify it in their Puppy Contract as a condition of sale.

Spaying and Neutering

Spaying

Spaying is the term used to describe the removal of the ovaries and uterus (womb) of a female dog so that she cannot become pregnant. Although this is a routine operation, it is major abdominal surgery and she has to be anaesthetised.

A popular myth is that a female dog should have her first heat cycle before she is spayed, but this is not the case. Even puppies can be spayed. You should consult your vet for the optimum time.

If spayed before her first heat cycle, one of the advantages is that your dog will have an almost zero risk of mammary cancer (the equivalent of breast cancer in women). Even after the first heat, spaying reduces the risk of this cancer by 92%. Some vets claim that the risk of mammary cancer in unspayed female dogs can be as high as one in four.

Some females may put weight on easier after spaying and will require slightly less food afterwards. As with any major procedure, there are pros and cons.

Spaying is a much more serious operation for a female than neutering is for a male. This is because it involves an **internal** abdominal operation, whereas the neutering procedure is carried out on the male's testicles, which are **outside** his abdomen.

For:

- Spaying prevents infections, cancer and other diseases of the uterus and ovaries
- Your dog will have a greatly reduced risk of mammary cancer
- It reduces hormonal changes that can interfere with the treatment of diseases like diabetes or epilepsy
- Spaying can reduce behaviour problems, such as roaming, aggression towards other dogs, anxiety or fear
- It eliminates the risk of the potentially fatal disease pyometra (a secondary infection that occurs as a result of hormonal changes in the female's reproductive tract), which affects unspayed middle-aged females
- You don't have to guard your female against unwanted attention from males as she will no longer have heat cycles
- You no longer have to cope with any potential mess caused by bleeding inside the house during heat cycles
- A spayed dog does not contribute to the pet overpopulation problem

Against:

- There is some scientific evidence that spaying and neutering before 12 months of age can lead to physical or behavioural issues in some dogs. You can read more here: www.dogsnaturallymagazine.com/three-reasons-to-reconsider-spayneuter and at www.akcchf.org/news-events/news/health-implications-in-early.html

- Complications can occur, including an abnormal reaction to the anaesthetic, bleeding, stitches breaking and infections; **these are not common**

- Occasionally there can be long-term effects connected to hormonal changes. These may include weight gain, urinary incontinence or less stamina and these problems can occur years after a female has been spayed

- Complications can occur, including an abnormal reaction to the anaesthetic, bleeding, stitches

- Older females may suffer some urinary incontinence, but it only affects a few spayed females - discuss it with your vet

- Cost. This can range from £100 to £300 in the UK (approximately $150-$500 at a vet's practice in the USA, or around $50 at a low cost clinic, for those that qualify)

- Boston Terriers can be sensitive to anaesthesia – select a vet who is familiar with Bostons, or at least brachycephalic (flat-faced) breeds

If you talk to a vet or a volunteer at a rescue shelter, they will say that the advantages of spaying far outweigh any disadvantages. If you have a female puppy, when you take her in for her puppy vaccinations, ask your vet whether, and at what age, spaying would be a good idea for your Boston.

Neutering

Neutering male dogs involves castration; the removal of the testicles. This can be a difficult decision for some owners, as it causes a drop in the pet's testosterone levels, which some humans – men in particular! - feel affects the quality of their dog's life.

Fortunately, dogs do not think like people and male dogs do not miss their testicles or the loss of sex. Our own experience is that our dog Max is much happier having been neutered. We decided to have him neutered after he went missing three times on walks – he ran off on the scent of a female

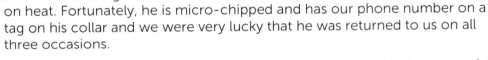

on heat. Fortunately, he is micro-chipped and has our phone number on a tag on his collar and we were very lucky that he was returned to us on all three occasions.

Unless you specifically want to breed or show your dog, or he has a special job, neutering is recommended by animal rescue organisations and vets. Even then, Guide Dogs for the Blind, Hearing Dogs for Deaf People and Dogs for the Disabled are routinely neutered and this does not impair their ability to perform their duties.

There are countless unwanted puppies, many of which are destroyed. There is also the problem of a lack of knowledge from the owners of some breeding dogs, resulting in the production of poor puppies with congenital health or temperament problems.

Neutering is usually performed around puberty, about six months old. It can, however, be done at any age over eight weeks, provided both testicles have descended. The operation is a relatively straightforward procedure. Dogs neutered before puberty tend to grow a little larger than dogs done later. This is because testosterone is involved in the process that stops growth, so the bones grow for longer without testosterone.

The neutering operation for a male is much less of a major operation than spaying for a female. Complications are less common and less severe than with spaying a female. Although he will feel tender afterwards, your dog should return to his normal self within a couple of days.

When he comes out of surgery, his scrotum (the sacs that held the testicles) will be swollen and it may look like nothing has been done. But it is normal for these to slowly shrink in the days following surgery. Here are the main pros and cons:

For:

- Behaviour problems such as aggression and wandering off are reduced
- Unwanted sexual behaviour, such as mounting people or objects, is usually reduced or eliminated
- Testicular problems such as infections, cancer and torsion (painful rotation of the testicle) are eradicated
- Prostate disease, common in older male dogs, is less likely to occur
- A submissive entire (un-neutered) male dog may be targeted by other dogs. After he has been neutered, he will no longer produce testosterone and so will not be regarded as much of a threat by the other males, so he is less likely to be bullied
- A neutered dog is not fathering unwanted puppies

Against:

- As with any surgery, there can be bleeding afterwards, you should keep an eye on him for any blood loss after the operation. Infections can also occur, generally caused by the dog licking the wound, so try and prevent him doing this. If he persists, use an Elizabethan collar (or E-collar, a large plastic collar from the vet). In the **vast majority** of cases, these problems do not occur
- Some dogs' coats may be affected, but supplementing their diet with fish oil can compensate for this
- Cost - this starts at around £80 in the UK (in the USA this might cost upwards from $100 at a private veterinary clinic or from $50 at a low cost or Humane Society clinic)
- Boston Terriers can be sensitive to anaesthesia – select a vet who is familiar with the breed

Myths

Here are some common myths about neutering and spaying:

Neutering or spaying will spoil the dog's character - There is no evidence that any of the positive characteristics of your dog will be altered. He or she will be just as loving, playful and loyal. Neutering may reduce aggression or roaming, especially in male dogs, because they are no longer competing to mate with a female.

A female needs to have at least one litter - There is no proven physical or mental benefit to a female having a litter. Pregnancy and whelping can be stressful and can have complications. In a false pregnancy, a female is simply responding to the hormones in her body.

Mating is natural and necessary - Dogs are not humans, they do not think emotionally about sex or having and

raising a family. Because Boston Terriers like the company of humans so much, we tend to ascribe human emotions to them. Unlike humans, their desire to mate or breed is entirely physical, triggered by the chemicals called hormones within their body. Without these hormones – i.e. after neutering or spaying – the desire disappears or is greatly reduced.

Male dogs will behave better if they can mate - This is simply not true; sex does not make a dog behave better. In fact, it can have the opposite effect. Having mated once, a male may show an increased interest in females. He may also consider his status elevated, which may make him harder to control or call back.

Pregnancy

A canine pregnancy will normally last for 58 to 65 days, regardless of the size or breed of the dog. Sometimes pregnancy is referred to as the *'gestation period.'*

It's a good idea to take a female for a pre-natal check-up after mating. The vet should answer any questions, such as the type of food, supplements, care and physical changes in your female.

There is a blood test available that measures levels of *relaxin*. This is a hormone produced by the ovary and the developing placenta, and pregnancy can be detected by monitoring relaxin levels as early as three weeks after mating. The levels are high throughout pregnancy and then decline rapidly after the female has given birth.

A vet can usually see the puppies using Ultrasound from around the same time. X-rays also give the breeder an idea of the number of puppies; these can help to give the vet more information, which is particularly useful if the bitch has had previous whelping problems. It is best to wait until around Day 58 or so before getting an X-ray, as that is about when the skeletons have calcified, to get an accurate puppy count.

Here are some of the signs of pregnancy:

* After mating, many females become more affectionate. (However, some will become uncharacteristically irritable and maybe even a little aggressive)

* The female may produce a slight clear discharge from her vagina about one month after mating

* Three or four weeks after mating, a few females experience morning sickness – if this is the case, feed little and often. She may seem more tired than usual

* She may seem slightly depressed and/or show a drop in appetite. These signs can also mean there are other problems, so you should consult your vet

* Her teats (nipples) will become more prominent, pink and erect 25 to 30 days into the pregnancy. Later on, you may notice a fluid coming from them

* After about 35 days, or seven weeks, her body weight will noticeably increase

* Her abdomen will become noticeably larger from around day 40, although first-time mums and females carrying few puppies may not show as much

- Many pregnant females' appetite will increase in the second half of pregnancy

- Her nesting instincts will kick in as the delivery date approaches. She may seem restless or scratch her bed or the floor

- During the last week of pregnancy, females often start to look for a safe place for whelping. Some seem to become confused, wanting to be with their owners and at the same time wanting to prepare their nest. Even if the female is having a C-section, she should still be allowed to nest in a whelping box with layers of newspaper, which she will scratch and dig as the time approaches

If your female becomes pregnant − either by design or accident - your first step should be to consult a vet.

Litter Size

According to the breeders we contacted, this varies considerably from one Boston to another, but they often have small litters. A normal range might be from two to four or to five, with any more being considered a large litter. One UK breeder's dam had a litter of 12 pups.

False Pregnancies

As many as 50% or more of intact (unspayed) females may display signs of a false pregnancy. In the wild it was common for female dogs to have false pregnancies and to lactate (produce milk). This female would then nourish puppies if their own mother died.

False pregnancies occur 60 to 80 days after the female was in heat - about the time she would have given birth − and are generally nothing to worry about for an owner. The exact cause is unknown, however, hormonal imbalances are thought to play an important role. Some dogs have shown symptoms within three to four days of spaying, these include:

- Making a nest

- Producing milk (lactating)

- Mothering or adopting toys and other objects

- Appetite fluctuations

- Barking or whining a lot

- Restlessness, depression or anxiety

- Swollen abdomen

- She might even appear to go into labour

Try not to touch your dog's nipples, as touch will stimulate further milk production. If she is licking herself repeatedly, she may need an E-collar to minimise stimulation. To help reduce and eliminate milk production, you can apply cool compresses to the nipples

Under no circumstances should you restrict your Boston Terrier's water supply to try and prevent her from producing milk. This is dangerous as she can become dehydrated.

Some unspayed bitches may have a false pregnancy with each heat cycle. Spaying during a false pregnancy may actually prolong the condition, so better to wait until it is over and then have her spayed to prevent it happening again. False pregnancy is not a disease, but an exaggerated response to normal hormonal changes. Owners should be reassured that even if left untreated, the condition almost always resolves itself.

However, if your Boston Terrier appears physically ill or the behavioural changes are severe enough to worry you, visit your vet, who may prescribe tranquilisers to relieve anxiety, or diuretics to reduce milk production and relieve fluid retention. In rare cases, hormone treatment may be necessary.

Generally, dogs experiencing false pregnancies do not have serious long-term problems, as the behaviour disappears when the hormones return to their normal levels in two to three weeks.

One exception is **Pyometra**, a disease mainly affecting unspayed middle-aged females, caused by a hormonal abnormality. Pyometra follows a heat cycle in which fertilisation did not occur and the dog typically starts showing symptoms within two to four months.

Commonly referred to as 'pyo', there are 'open' and 'closed' forms of the disease. Open pyo is usually easy to identify with a smelly discharge, so prompt treatment is easy. Closed pyo is often harder to identify and you may not even notice anything until your girl becomes feverish and lethargic. When this happens, it is very serious and time is of the essence. Typically, vets will recommend immediately spaying in an effort to save the bitch's life.

Signs of pyometra are excessive drinking and urination, with the female trying to lick a white discharge from her vagina. She may also have a slight temperature. If the condition becomes severe, her back legs will become weak, possibly to the point where she can no longer get up without help.

Pyometra is serious if bacteria take a hold, and in extreme cases it can be fatal. It is also relatively common and needs to be dealt with promptly by a vet, who will give the dog intravenous fluids and antibiotics for several days. In most cases this is followed by spaying.

Should I Breed From My Boston?

The short and simple answer is: Unless you know exactly what you are doing or have expert help, **NO, leave it to the experts.**

You need specialist knowledge to successfully breed healthy Boston Terriers with good temperaments that conform to the Breed Standard, but the rising cost of puppies and increasing number of dog owners is tempting more people to consider breeding their dogs.

Prices vary, but may be up to £2,000 for a KC-registered pet puppy in the UK - even more for one with show potential – and around $1,500 to $2,200 or more in the USA for a puppy from a breeder with a proven track record who health tests her stock. But anyone who thinks it is easy money should bear in mind that breeding Bostons is a complex, expensive and time-consuming business when all the fees, DNA and health tests, care, nutrition and medical expenses have been taken into account.

You can't just put any two dogs together and expect perfect, healthy puppies every time; ethical and successful breeding is much more scientific and time consuming than that. The Bully breeds are the hardest and most challenging of dogs to breed. Inexperience can result in tragic consequences, with the loss of the mother or pups - or both. Many approved breeders will insist in the Puppy Contract that you have your pup spayed or neutered in order to prevent you breeding him or her to protect the integrity of the breed.

Breeding Bostons is risky if you don't know what you are doing. **Many cannot give birth naturally.** In some cases it can even be dangerous to allow them to do so. Instead, many bitches have C-sections (Caesarean sections). In the UK, all C-sections have to be registered with the Kennel Club.

A major study carried out jointly by the BSAVA (British Small Animal Veterinary Association) and the UK's Kennel Club looked at 13,141 bitches from 151 breeds and the incidence of C-Sections over a 10-year period. The resulting report, published in 2010, singled out three breeds as having Caesarean rates of over 80% – the French Bulldog at 81.3%, the Bulldog at 86.1%, and the Boston Terrier at a remarkable 92.3%. It is thought that the rates were as high in the USA. The full report is here: http://bit.ly/2cV6MF3.

Although anecdotal evidence from breeders suggests that the overall percentage is now lower, the number of Boston Terriers having C-Sections is still very high.

C-sections are carried out when the mother is unable to birth the pups naturally – and timing is critical. Too early and the pups may be underdeveloped or the mother can bleed to death; too late and the pups can die.

The main reason for them is that Bostons are front-loaded. For small dogs they have a relatively large head and wide shoulders. However, their bodies taper off towards the rear and the hips and pelvis are relatively narrow. It is through here that the pups have to pass when being born. Often, the pup's head and/or shoulders are too large, or there is a fear that natural whelping (birth) may cause injury to the mother. In either case a C-section is performed.

And since 2012, the UK's Kennel Club will no longer resister puppies from a female that has had more than two C-Sections, "except for scientifically proven welfare reasons and in such cases normally provided that the application is made prior to mating."

An experienced American show breeder said: "The percentage of Bostons having C sections varies by line and breeder. Dogs from pet breeders don't have the lovely heads and bodies that show breeders' dogs typically do, so they are often free-whelpers.

"Most show breeders don't want to risk losing puppies, so will automatically go with a C-section. Although I schedule a C-section each time, I generally let my bitches go into labor and see if they can easily free-whelp. If so, I let them, but if there's a struggle at all, I will have the C- section done. I won't jeopardize my bitch or my puppies.

"From a percentage perspective, I am guessing 80% of show litters are C-sectioned and 90% of pet litters are free-whelped. That's purely a guess though, based on my knowledge of other show breeders and reading about pet breeders."

One USA breeder with 25 years' experience said: "I spent years trying to have free whelpers. If both the sire and dam are from free whelpers, it can make a big difference. Doing a C-section because it is convenient is not good for the breed. I always give the bitch a try at natural delivery on her first litter, and if she can't manage it, then it's a C section after that."

The breeder added that the narrow pelvis of the female presents a problem within the breed, and Bostons are also one of the breeds with a higher than usual incidence of open fontanels. This occurs when the bones do not fuse correctly at the top of the puppy's head, leaving the pup vulnerable to injury or hydrocephalus – 'water on the brain.'

This lovely photo of new pups was taken by Kennel Club Assured Breeder Jo Dalton, of Mumuland Boston Terriers, Boston, Lincolnshire. It may just look like a straightforward photo of cute puppies, but in describing the photo, Jo outlines some of the complexities facing anyone who wants to successfully breed healthy Bostons:

"The pups were just 36 hours old when this photo was taken. They were a litter of four, two dogs and two bitches, born to Beanz (Dreamarezzo Patty Of Mumuland) via emergency C-Section due to primary inertia."

(Primary inertia is not uncommon in Bostons and occurs when the dam is unable to birth her pups naturally as her womb muscles do not make the necessary contractions to force the pups out).

Jo continues: "Beanz was three years old when she had this litter; she is the daughter of a Polish import bitch (Baby Suburbanus). I put her to my stud dog Bolek (Aureadicta Large Glory For Mumuland), who is sired by our Jeffery.

"Bolek and Beanz are both fully health tested BVA HC - Unaffected, JHC (Juvenile Hereditary Cataracts) Clear, Patella 0/0 and heart tested normal. As is Jeffery, who at the age of six has also just been re-examined under the BVA scheme for late onset HC and is still unaffected; re-scored patellas at a score of 0/0, and he has no heart problems.

"All the pups were born JHC Hereditary Clear, and all passed their eight-week health check with no heart murmurs, etc. I kept a bitch from this litter - Bindy (Mumuland's Venus De Mumu) - who is patella scored 0/0, heart tested Normal and BVA HC Unaffected. She had her first litter of eight pups in February this year and I have kept a bitch again, Mumuland's Six Horse Judy, who is also Hereditary Clear of JHC. She has just been patella scored 0/0, but will be re-scored again at around 18 months of age. She heart tested Normal and is due to be BVA HC tested in the early part of next year."

Gwion and Lisa Williams, of Wilarjan Boston Terriers, Bangor North Wales, previously bred other dogs but are relative newcomers to Bostons. Gwion said: "Since I was about 13 I started having an interest in dogs and started researching different breeds to find which breed I would like to exhibit and breed in the future."

"Something really stood out about the look of the Boston Terrier, but I wanted to wait until the timing was right before buying one. I wanted to find the best dogs possible to be the foundation to our breeding line. In the past we have owned and bred the Parson Russell Terrier and Smooth Coat

Chihuahua. Our passion now is the Boston Terrier; no one can fully appreciate the breed until they actually own one."

Pictured is their six-month-old Norwilbeck Ted Baker For Wilarjan (Ted).

He adds: "You need a lot of money, time and dedication to breed. Think carefully before making the decision and do plenty of research. I have found 'The Book of the Bitch' to be very detailed about dog breeding. When you buy a breeding bitch from a good breeder, they will be more than happy to give you guidance. They will make you aware of the financial implications involved and the process from mating to raising the litter. Good breeders will also help you find a compatible male to breed with your bitch which is very, very valuable."

A BTCA member and US breeder of 20 years' standing shared some tips to successful breeding: "Most Bostons are delivered by C-section. I have had many free whelp, but when I breed, I do it with C-section in mind...this breed has a very large head.

"I also use a tool called 'Draminski Ovulation Detector.' I have used vets for progesterone testing for years, and have found this tool most useful and cost efficient; the company makes progesterone probes for livestock and now has one for dogs. It's simple and helps one to catch even the most difficult bitches' ovulation cycle. I also treat ALL breeding dogs with Baytril (antibiotic) seven days prior to breeding to make sure there are no possible infections. Following these two breeding practices has made all breedings successful for me."

In short, breeding good Boston Terriers is a complex issue. Responsible breeding is backed up by genetic information and screening as well as a thorough knowledge of the desired traits of the Boston. It is definitely not for the amateur hobbyist. Breeding is not just about the look of the dogs; health and temperament are important factors too. Many people do not realise that the single most important factor governing health and certain temperament traits is genetics.

Having said that, good Boston Terrier breeders are made, not born. Like any expert, they do their research and learn their trade over several years. Spend time researching the breed and its genetics and make sure you are going into it for the right reasons and not just for the money - ask yourself how you intend to improve the breed.

Tip If you are determined to breed from your dog, you must first learn a lot, and a great way of doing this is to **find a mentor**; somebody who is already successfully breeding Boston Terriers. By 'successful' we mean somebody producing healthy puppies with good temperaments, not someone who is making lots of money churning out poor quality puppies.

Visit dog shows and make contact with established breeders or look at the Kennel Club or AKC website for details of breeders near you. Contact the Boston Terrier Club UK at: http://thebostonterrierclub.co.uk or the American Boston Terrier Club of America at: www.bostonterrierclubofamerica.org and find a suitable person who is willing to help you get started - somebody already very familiar with the breed. The AKC also has a BTCA-approved mentor list: http://images.akc.org/pdf/judges/mentors/boston_terrier.pdf?_ga=1.39392103.579087550.145482 5357

And make sure you have a vet who is also familiar with Bostons and able to perform a C-section at whatever time of day or night it may be required.

Committed Boston Terrier breeders aren't in it for the cash. They use their skills and knowledge to produce healthy pups with good temperaments that conform to the Breed Standards and ultimately improve the breed. Our strong advice is: when it comes to Boston Terriers, leave it to the experts. However, if you are still thinking of breeding, these questions might help you to make up your mind if it's right for you and your dog:

Ask Yourself This...

1. Did I get my Boston Terrier from a good, ethical breeder? Dogs sold in pet stores and on general sales websites are seldom good specimens and can be unhealthy.

2. Are my dog and his or her close relatives free from health issues? Eye issues, breathing and heart problems, and Patella Luxation are just some of the illnesses Boston pups can inherit. Are you 100% sure your breeding dog is free from them all? An unhealthy female is also more likely to have trouble with pregnancy and whelping.

3. Does my dog have a good temperament? Does he or she socialise well with people and other animals? Dogs with poor temperaments should not be bred, regardless of how good they look.

4. Do I understand COI and its implications? COI stands for Coefficient of Inbreeding. It measures the common ancestors of a dam and sire and indicates the probability of how genetically similar they are. Breeding from too closely-related dogs can result in health issues for the offspring.

5. Does my dog conform to the Breed Standard as laid down by the Kennel Club or AKC? Do not breed from a Boston Terrier that is not an excellent specimen, hoping that somehow the puppies will turn out better. They won't. Talk with experienced breeders and ask them for an honest assessment of your dog.

6. Do I conform to the Boston Terrier clubs' strict Code of Ethics?

7. Is my female at least in her second heat cycle? Many breeders prefer to wait a little longer, until their female is at least two years old and fully physically mature, when they are able to carry a litter to term and are robust and mature enough to whelp and care for a litter. Also,

some health tests cannot be carried out until a dog is 18 months to two years old. Even then, not all females are suitable. Some are simply poor mothers that don't care for their puppies; others don't produce enough milk - which means you have to do it.

8. Have my dog and the dog I intend breeding mine with both been tested for Brucellosis (which can result in infertility, abortion or stillbirths)? Breeding dogs should also be clear of Canine Herpes Virus, which is the leading cause of death in new-born puppies.

9. Am I financially able to provide good veterinary care for the mother and puppies, particularly if complications occur? If you are not prepared to make a significant financial commitment to a litter, then don't breed your dog. A single litter could easily cost you £2,000 - or $3,000 in the USA – and what if you only get one or two puppies? Here is one US breeder's estimate of costs per litter: C-section $1,500, Stud fee $1,000, Dewclaw removal and vaccines $100 per puppy, Food, supplements, toys and other supplies $100 per puppy, Puppy health testing (per puppy) - BAER $65 and CAER $50, Dam health testing - CAER $50, Patella $65, JC DNA $65, Echocardiogram $215, and Spine/Hip/Trachea X-rays $350.

10. Have I got the indoor space? Mother and pups will need their own space in your home – **not outside** - which will become messy as new-born pups do not come into this world housetrained (potty trained). It should also be warm and draught-free.

11. Can I cope with lots of puppies at once? Although Bostons often have small litters, there is a big variation between females and some may have large litters of up to nine or even 10 pups.

12. Can I devote the time to breeding? Caring for mother and young pups is a 24/7 job in the beginning and involves many sleepless nights. During the day, you cannot simply go off to work or leave the house and mother and young pups unattended. It is not uncommon for a Boston dam to be unable or unwilling to provide milk for her puppies, particularly when a C-section is involved as it may take up to 72 hours for the anaesthesia to completely dissipate. In which case, you have to tube feed the puppies every three to four hours throughout the day and night. Breeding is a huge tie.

13. Am I confident enough in my breeding programme to offer a health warranty on my puppies?

14. Will I be able to find good homes for all the puppies and be prepared to take them back if necessary? Good breeders do not let their precious puppies go to any old home. They often have a waiting list for their puppies before the litter is born. However, the people on the list still have to satisfy the breeder that they will provide a loving home for the lifetime of the puppy.

You may have the most wonderful Boston Terrier in the world, but only enter the world of canine breeding if you have the right knowledge and motivation. Don't do it just for the money or the cute factor – or to show the kids 'The Miracle of Birth!' Breeding poor examples only brings heartache to owners in the long run when health or other issues develop.

14. Caring for Older Dogs

Boston Terriers are generally bubbly, energetic little dogs that live life to the full. Lifespan varies from one individual to another and is affected by factors such as bloodlines, general health, environment, lifestyle and diet. A typical lifespan may be anything from 10 or more years, with some dogs having longer or shorter lives. Occasionally a Boston is reported as having lived to the mid to late teens, but this is the exception, rather than the rule.

Many remain fit and active well into their twilight years, but eventually all dogs – even lively Bostons - slow down. At some point your old dog will start to feel the effects of ageing. Physically, joints may become stiffer and organs, such as the heart or liver, may not function as effectively. On the mental side - just as with humans - your dog's memory, ability to learn and awareness will all start to dim.

Your faithful companion might become a bit grumpier, stubborn or a little less tolerant of lively dogs and young children. You may also notice that he doesn't see or hear as well as he used to. On the other hand, your old friend might not be hard of hearing at all.

He might have developed that affliction common to many older dogs of 'selective hearing.' Our 12-year-old Max has bionic hearing when it comes to the word 'Dinnertime' whispered from 30 feet, yet now seems strangely unable to hear the commands 'Come' or 'Down' when we are right in front of him!

Your Boston will tell you in his or her own way when he is slowing down. And you can help ease your dog into old age gracefully by keeping an eye out for these signals and taking action to help as much as possible. This might involve a visit to the vet for supplements and/or medications, modifying your dog's environment, changing the food and slowly reducing the amount of daily exercise. Much depends on the individual dog. Just as with humans, a dog of ideal weight that has been active and stimulated throughout his or her life is likely to age slower than an overweight couch potato.

Keeping Bostons at that optimum weight is challenging - and important – as they age. Their metabolisms slow down, making it easier to put on the pounds unless their daily calories are reduced. At the same time, extra weight places additional, unwanted stress on joints and organs, making them work harder than they should.

We normally talk about dogs being old when they reach the last third of their lives. This varies from one dog to the next and bloodline to bloodline. Some Bostons may start to show signs of ageing as young as seven years old, while others will still be fit in mind and body at nine or 10.

Physical and Mental Signs of Ageing

If your Boston is in or approaching the last third of his life, here are some signs that his body is feeling its age:

- 🐾 He doesn't want to go outside in bad weather (even less than usual!)

- 🐾 He has generally slowed down and no longer seems as keen to go out on his walks. He tires more easily on a walk

- 🐾 He gets up from lying down and goes up and down stairs more slowly. He can no longer jump on to the couch or bed or into the car. These are all signs that his joints are stiffening, often due to arthritis

- 🐾 He urinates more frequently

- 🐾 He has the occasional 'accident' (incontinence) inside the house

- 🐾 He is getting grey hairs, particularly around the face and muzzle

- 🐾 He has put on a bit of weight

- 🐾 He drinks more water

- 🐾 He gets constipated

- 🐾 The foot pads thicken and nails may become more brittle

- 🐾 He has one or more lumps or fatty deposits on his body. Our dog Max developed two on his head recently and we took him straight to the vet, who performed an operation to remove them. They were benign - harmless - but you should always get them checked out ASAP in case they are an early form of cancer

- 🐾 He can't regulate his body temperature as he used to and so feels the cold and heat more

- 🐾 He doesn't hear as well as he used to

- 🐾 His eyesight may deteriorate – if his eyes appear cloudy he may be developing cataracts; see your vet as soon as you notice the signs

- 🐾 He has bad breath (halitosis), which could be a sign of dental or gum disease. Some dogs are prone to poor dental health. Brush his teeth regularly and/or give him a daily dental stick, such as Dentastix or similar. If the bad breath persists, get him checked out by a vet

- 🐾 If he's inactive he may develop callouses on the elbows, especially if he lies down on hard surfaces – although this is more common with larger breeds

Your dog may display one, several or many of these symptoms as he ages. And it's not just his body that deteriorates, his mind does too. It's all part of the normal ageing process. Here are some symptoms. Your dog may display some, all or none of these signs of mental deterioration:

- His sleep patterns change - an older dog may be more restless at night and sleepy during the day - and he sleeps deeper

- He barks more

- He stares at objects or wanders aimlessly around the house

- He forgets or ignores commands or habits he once knew well, such as housetraining and recall

- He displays increased anxiety (e.g. with loud noises) or aggression

- Often Bostons may become more clingy and dependent on you, which may result in separation anxiety, while a few 'switch off' and become less interested in human contact

Understanding the changes happening to your dog and acting on them compassionately and effectively will help ease your dog's passage through his senior years.

Your dog has given you so much pleasure during his lifetime, now he needs you to give that bit of extra care for a happy, healthy old age. You can also help your Boston to stay mentally active by playing gentle games and getting new toys to stimulate interest.

Helping Seniors

The first thing you can do is monitor your dog and be on the lookout for any changes in actions or behaviour. Then there are lots of things you can do for him.

Food and Supplements - As dogs age they need fewer calories, so many owners switch to a food specially formulated for older dogs. These are labelled 'Senior,' 'Ageing' or 'Mature.' Check the

labelling; some are specifically for small dogs aged over eight, others may be for 10-year-olds. If you are not sure if a senior diet is necessary for your dog, talk to your vet the next time you are there for vaccinations or a check-up. Remember, if you do change the brand, switch the food gradually over a week to 10 days. Unlike with humans, a dog's digestive system cannot cope with sudden changes of diet.

Consider feeding your Boston a supplement, such as Omega-3 fatty acids for the brain and coat, or one to help joints. There are also medications and homeopathic remedies to help relieve anxiety. Again, check with your vet before introducing anything new.

Exercise - Take the lead from your dog; if he doesn't want to walk as far, then don't. But if your dog doesn't want to go out at all, you will have to coax him out. ALL senior dogs need some physical exercise to keep their joints moving and to exercise their heart and lungs.

Environment - Make sure your dog has a nice soft place to rest his old bones, which may mean adding an extra blanket to his bed. This should be in a place that is not too hot or cold, as he may not be able to regulate his body temperature as well as when he was younger. If his eyesight is failing, move obstacles out of his way, reducing the chance of injuries. Jumping on and off furniture or in or out of the car is high impact for old joints and bones.

He may need a helping hand on to and off the couch or your bed (if he's allowed up there) and maybe a ramp or step to get in and out of the car. Make sure he has plenty of time to sleep and is not pestered and/or bullied by younger dogs, other animals or young children.

Weight - No matter how old your Boston is, he still needs a waist! Maintaining a healthy weight with a balanced diet and regular, gentler exercise are two of the most important things you can do for your dog.

Consult a Professional - If your dog is showing any of the following signs, get him checked out by your vet:

- Increased urination or drinking - this can be a sign of something amiss, such as reduced liver or kidney function, Cushing's Disease or Diabetes

- Incontinence, which could be a sign of a mental or physical problem

- Constipation or not urinating regularly could be a sign of something not functioning properly with the digestive system or organs

- Cloudy eyes, which could be cataracts

- Lumps or bumps on the body - which are most often benign, but can occasionally be malignant (dangerous)

- Decreased appetite – loss of appetite is often a sign of an underlying problem

- Excessive sleeping or a lack of interest in you and his or her surroundings

- Diarrhoea or vomiting

- A darkening and dryness of skin that never seems to get any better - this can be a sign of hypothyroidism

- Any other out-of-the-ordinary behaviour for your dog. A change in patterns or behaviour is often your dog's way of telling you that all is not well

The Last Lap

Huge advances in veterinary science have meant that there are countless procedures and medications that can prolong the life of your dog, and this is a good thing. But there comes a time when you have to let go. If your dog is showing all the signs of ageing, has an ongoing medical condition from which he or she cannot recover, or is showing signs of pain, mental anxiety or distress and there is no hope of improvement, then the dreaded time has come to say goodbye.

You owe it to him or her. There is no point keeping an old dog alive if all they have to look forward to is pain and death. I'm even getting upset as I write this, as I think of parting from our 12-year-old dog in the not-too-distant future, as well as the wonderful dogs we have had in the past. But we have their lives in our hands and we can give them the gift of passing away peacefully and humanely at the end when the time is right.

Losing our beloved companion, our best friend, a member of the family, is truly heart-breaking for many owners.

But one of the things we realise at the back of our minds when we get that lively little puppy is the pain that comes with it, knowing that we will live longer than him or her and that we will probably have to make this most painful of decisions at some point. It's the worst thing about being a dog owner.

If your Boston has had a long and happy life, then you could not have done any more. You were a great owner and your dog was lucky to have you. Remember all the good times you have had together.

And try not to rush out and buy another dog; wait a while to grieve for your Boston. Assess your current life and lifestyle and, if your situation is right, only then consider getting another dog and all that that entails in terms of time, commitment and expense. Bostons are sensitive, often intuitive, creatures. One coming into a happy, stable household will get off to a much better start in life than a dog entering a home full of grief.

Whatever you decide to do, put your dog first.

15. Boston Terrier Rescue

Are you thinking of adopting a Boston Terrier from a rescue organisation? What could be kinder and more rewarding than giving a poor, abandoned dog a happy and loving home for the rest of his life?

Not much really; adoption saves lives. The problem of homeless dogs is truly depressing. It's a big issue in Britain, but even worse in the US, where the sheer numbers in kill shelters is hard to comprehend. Randy Grim states in "Don't Dump The Dog" that 1,000 dogs are being put to sleep every hour in the States.

According to Jo-Anne Cousins, former Executive Director at IDOG, who has spent many years involved in US canine rescue, the situations leading to a dog ending up in rescue can often be summed up in one phrase: 'Unrealistic expectations.'

She said: "In many situations, dog ownership was something that the family went into without fully understanding the time, money and commitment to exercise and training that it takes to raise a dog. While they may have spent hours on the internet pouring over cute puppy photos, they probably didn't read any puppy training books or look into actual costs of regular vet care, training and boarding."

That lack of thought was highlighted in a story that appeared last January in the Press in my Yorkshire home town. A woman went shopping on Christmas Eve in a local retail centre. She returned home £700 (over $900) poorer with a puppy she had bought on impulse. The pup was in a rescue centre two days later.

Common reasons for a dog being put into rescue include:

- A change in family circumstance, such as divorce or a new baby
- A change in work patterns
- Moving home

Often, the 'unrealistic expectations' come home to roost and the dog is given up for rescue because:

- He has too much energy, needs too much exercise, knocks the kids over and/or jumps on people
- He is growling and/or nipping
- He chews or eats things he shouldn't
- He makes a mess in the house
- He needs a lot more time and attention than the owner is able or prepared to give

There is, however, a ray of sunshine for some of these dogs. Every year many thousands of people in the UK, North America and countries all around the world adopt a rescue dog and the story often has a happy ending.

The Dog's Point of View...

But if you are serious about adopting a Boston, then you should do so with the right motives and with your eyes wide open. If you're expecting a perfect dog, you could be in for a shock. Rescue dogs can and do become wonderful companions, but much of it depends on you.

Bostons are people-loving dogs. Some of them in rescue centres are traumatised. They don't understand why they have been abandoned by their beloved owners and may arrive at your home with problems of their own until they adjust to being part of a loving family again.

Ask yourself a few questions before you take the plunge and fill in the adoption forms:

- Are you prepared to accept and deal with any problems - such as bad behaviour, chewing, aggression, timidity, jumping up or eliminating in the house - which a rescue dog may display when initially arriving in your home?
- How much time are you willing to spend with your new dog to help him integrate back into normal family life?
- Can you take time off work to be at home and help the dog settle in at the beginning?
- Are you prepared to take on a new addition to your family that may live for another 10 years?
- Are you prepared to stick with the dog even if he develops behavioural or health issues later?
- Think about the implications before taking on a rescue dog - try and look at it from the dog's point of view. What could be worse for the unlucky dog than to be abandoned again if things don't work out between you?

Other Considerations

Adopting a rescue dog is a big commitment for all involved. It is not a cheap way of getting a Boston and shouldn't be viewed as such. It could cost you several hundred pounds - or dollars. You'll have adoption fees to pay and often vaccination and veterinary bills as well as worm and flea medication and spaying or neutering. Make sure you're aware of the full cost before committing.

Some rescue Bostons have had difficult lives. You need plenty of time to help them rehabilitate.

Some may have initial problems with housetraining. Others may need socialisation with people and/or other dogs. If you are serious about adopting, you may have to wait a while until a suitable dog comes up.

One way of finding out if you, your family and home are suitable is to volunteer to become a foster home for one of the rescue centres. Fosters offer temporary homes until a forever home becomes available. It's a shorter term arrangement, but still requires commitment and patience.

And it's not just the dogs that are screened - you'll have to undergo a screening by the rescue organisation. Rescue groups and shelters have to make sure that prospective adopters are suitable and they have thought through everything very carefully before making such a big decision. It would be a tragedy for the dog if things did not work out.

In the US, The Boston Terrier Club of America (BTCA) runs a rescue service and there are a number of regional Boston rescue organisations. The main rescue charity in Britain is the UK Boston Terrier Rescue.

The UK group states: "There is no other dog like a Boston Terrier. They're playful, loving, energetic, adaptable - all in equal measures. There's never a dull day if you've a Boston in the house. However, before you go any further you have to ask yourself this one question: 'Is a rescue Boston Terrier right for you?'

"Rehoming a Boston that's lived somewhere else before is not the quick, easy or cheap way to get a dog. They might not be reliably housetrained (and may never be), they may have had behavioural issues such as separation anxiety and, whilst we assess the dogs that come into our care and try and address as many issues prior to rehoming, adopting a Boston with a history can sometimes prove a lifelong challenge. Are you ready for that and prepared to put the work in?

"Before any dogs leave our care, we make extra sure that they're going to the right home. That means lots of probing questions, one (or more) home visits and quite a bit of paperwork. And then we wait: you wait for someone to come out to your home and check that it's Boston proof... we wait for the vet to check the dog over and make sure there are no medical issues... you wait for us to assess the dog and discover what kind of home he or she is best suited to.

"Once a match has been made and you take on a dog from us, you'll be asked to pay an adoption fee to UK Boston Terrier Rescue. This goes towards the love and care that we've given your dog before finding them a new home with you and helps us to help other Bostons in need."

To try and combat this, most rescue groups will ask a raft of personal questions - some of which may seem intrusive. If you are serious about rescuing a Boston, you will have to answer them. Here are some of the details required on a typical adoption form:

- Name, address, age
- Details, including ages, of all people living in your home
- Size of your garden (if you have one) and height of the fence around it
- Extensive details of any other pets
- Your work hours and amount of time you spend away from the home each day
- Type of property you live in
- Whether you have any previous experience with Bostons
- Your reasons for wanting to adopt a Boston
- If you have ever previously given up a dog for adoption
- Whether you have any experience dealing with canine behaviour or health issues
- Details of your vet
- If you are prepared for aggression/destructive behaviour/chewing/fear and timidity/soiling inside the house/medical issues
- Whether you agree to insure your dog
- Whether you are prepared for the financial costs of dog ownership
- Whether you are willing to housetrain and obedience train the dog

- Your views on dog training methods classes
- Where your dog will sleep at night
- Whether you are prepared to accept a Boston cross
- Details of two personal referees

As a general rule of thumb, UK rescue organisations will not place dogs in homes where they will be left alone for more than four or five hours at a stretch.

After you've filled in the adoption form, a chat with a representative from the charity usually follows. There will also be an inspection visit to your home - and your vet may even be vetted! If all goes well, you will be approved to adopt and it's then just a question of waiting for the right match to come along. When he or she does, a meeting will be arranged with the dog for all family members, you pay the adoption fee and become the proud new owner of a Boston Terrier.

It might seem alike a lot of red tape, but the rescue groups have to be as sure as they can that you will provide a loving, forever home for the unfortunate dog. It would be terrible if things didn't work out and the dog had to be placed back in rescue again. If you are not prepared to go through all of this, you may have to reconsider whether rescuing a Boston is the right path for you.

All rescue organisations will neuter the dog or, if he or she is too young, specify in the adoption contract that the dog must be neutered and may not be used for breeding. UK Boston Terrier Rescue has a lifetime rescue back-up policy, which means that if things don't work out, the dog must be returned to them.

Rescue Organisations

Rescue organisations are often run by volunteers who give up their time to help dogs in distress. They often have a network of foster homes, where a Boston is placed until a permanent new home can be found. Foster homes are better than shelters, as Bostons thrive on human contact. Fostering helps to keep the dog socialised, and the people who foster are able to give sufficient attention to the individual dog in their care.

There are also online Boston forums where people sometimes post information about a dog that needs a new home. Even if you can't or don't want to offer a permanent home to a Boston Terrier, there are other ways in which you can help these worthy organisations, such as by short-term fostering or helping to raise money.

UK

The main Boston Terrier-specific rescue group is UK Boston Terrier Rescue
www.ukbostonterrierrescue.co.uk/

There are also some general websites:

www.dogsblog.com/category/boston-terrier

www.rspca.org.uk/findapet/rehomeapet

www.manytearsrescue.org

www.homes4dogs.co.uk

www.rainrescue.co.uk/rehoming/dog-rehoming

USA

BTCA rescue - www.bostonterrierclubofamerica.org/about-boston-terriers/boston-terrier-rescue.htm

American Boston Terrier Rescue, covers Texas, Louisiana, Southern Oklahoma and SW Arkansas - http://americanbostonterrierrescue.org/

Mid America Boston Terrier Rescue, covers Nebraska, Colorado, Iowa, Kansas, Missouri, North/South Dakota, Wyoming, Minnesota, Utah, Montana, Idaho, and Arkansas - www.adoptaboston.com/

North East Boston Terrier Rescue - Maine/Massachusetts/New Hampshire/New Jersey/New York/Pennsylvania/Vermont - http://nebostonrescue.com/

Alabama – see Alabama Boston Terrier Rescue on Facebook and www.bhambtr.org/

Arizona - www.azbtrescue.org/

California – Northern - http://awos.petfinder.com/shelters/ca192.html

Southern California Boston Terrier Rescue - see Facebook

Connecticut - www.bostonterrierclubct.com/Rescue.html

Delaware – Old Dominion covers VA, North-eastern NC, MD,DE and DC www.odbtr.org/

Florida - http://bostonrescueflorida.org/

Minnesota - www.mnbtc.com/rescue.php

Nebraska - www.rescueaboston.com

Nevada (Southern) - www.snbtr.com/ and Battle Born Boston Terrier Rescue on Facebook

New Mexico - www.nmbostonrescue.com/ and New Mexico Boston Terrier Rescue on Facebook

North Carolina - www.btrnc.org/

Rhode Island - http://fohari.org/#sthash.tcC2z8yf.dpbs

South Carolina (and North) www.bostonrescueteam.com/ and coastal: www.ccbtr.org/

Tennessee – covers the South, Florida and beyond - www.bostonterriertn.org

Texas - www.texasbostonrescue.org

North Texas - http://texasbostons.com/site/

Greater Houston, Texas - http://houstonbostonrescue.org/

Washington State, Seattle - www.spdrdogs.org/BreedInfo/BostonTerrier

Wisconsin - www.wisconsinbostonterrierrescue.com

Wyoming - www.wynotbostons.com

There are also general websites, such as www.petfinder.com, www.aspca.org/adopt-pet and www.adoptapet.com and Bostons and Boston mixes US-wide at http://bostonterrier.rescueme.org/, www.btrescue.org and www.adoptaboston.com

This is by no means an exhaustive list, but it does cover some of the main organisations involved. If you do visit these websites, you cannot presume that the descriptions are 100% accurate. They are given in good faith, but ideas of what constitutes a 'lively' dog may vary. Some dogs advertised may have other breeds in their genetic make-up. It does not mean that these are necessarily worse dogs, but if you are attracted to the breed for its temperament and other assets, make sure you are looking at a Boston.

DON'T get a dog from eBay, Craig's List, Gumtree or any of the other general advertising websites that sell golf clubs, second hand clothes, jewellery, old cars, bicycles, washing machines, etc. You might think you are getting a bargain Boston Terrier, but in the long run you will probably pay the price. If the dog had been well bred and properly cared for, he or she would not be advertised on such websites - or sold in pet shops. Good breeders do not let their dogs end up in these places. You may be storing up a whole load of trouble for yourselves in terms of health and/or behaviour issues, due to poor genes and environment.

....

If you haven't been put off with all of the above... Congratulations, you may be just the family or person that poor homeless Boston is looking for!

If you can't spare the time to adopt - and adoption means forever - you might want to consider fostering. Or you could help by becoming a fundraiser to generate cash to keep these very worthy rescue groups providing such a wonderful service. However you decide to get involved, Good Luck!

Saving one dog will not change the world,
But it will change the world for one dog

Useful Contacts

The Boston Terrier Club of America (BTCA) www.bostonterrierclubofamerica.org

The Boston Terrier Club UK http://thebostonterrierclub.co.uk

The Northern Boston Terrier Club of England www.northernbostonterrierclub.co.uk

The Boston Terrier Club of Scotland www.btcos.co.uk

American Kennel Club www.akc.org/dog-breeds/boston-terrier

Puppies via AKC marketplace http://marketplace.akc.org/search?breed=46&gender=&location=
(NOTE: Only Breeders of Merit and Club Members have been vetted by the AKC or breed club)

Kennel Club (UK) puppies available from breeders
www.thekennelclub.org.uk/services/public/breed/display.aspx?id=4083

Puppies currently available via Champdogs (UK) – not all are KC members, not all these breeders
health test; check details www.champdogs.co.uk/breeds/boston-terrier/puppies

Association of Pet Dog Trainers USA www.apdt.com

Association of Pet Dog Trainers UK www.apdt.co.uk

Canadian Association of Professional Pet Dog Trainers www.cappdt.ca

Useful information on grain-free and hypoallergenic dog foods www.dogfoodadvisor.com

UK dog food advice www.allaboutdogfood.co.uk

Helps find lost or stolen dogs in USA, register your dog's microchip www.akcreunite.org

There are also internet forums and Facebook groups that are a good source of information from
other owners, including:

www.bostonterrierforums.com/forum/

and on Facebook UK: https://en-gb.facebook.com/bostonterrierforums/

www.dogster.com/forums/Boston_Terrier

www.forum.breedia.com/dogs/boston-terrier/

List of Contributors

Jo Dalton, Mumuland Boston Terriers, Boston, Lincolnshire, UK
http://mumuland.org.uk

Pamela H. Preston, ChriMaso Boston Terriers, Shingle Springs, California, USA
www.ChriMasoBostons.com

Susan Maxwell, Maximum Companion Boston Terriers, California, USA,
www.maximumcompanion.com

Gwion and Lisa Williams, Wilarjan Boston Terriers, Bangor North Wales, UK

Bill and Anne Connor, Ringablok Boston Terriers, Carmarthen, South Wales, UK
www.ringablok.co.uk

Lindsey Scanlon, Fleurdelanne Boston Terriers, Mirfield, West Yorkshire, UK

Emily Little, Basildon, Essex

Michelle Courtney-Kaye, Huddersfield, West Yorkshire

Disclaimer

This book has been written to provide helpful information on Boston Terriers. It is not meant to be used, nor should it be used, to diagnose or treat any medical condition. For diagnosis or treatment of any animal medical problem, consult a qualified veterinarian. The author is not responsible for any specific health or allergy conditions that may require medical supervision and is not liable for any damages or negative consequences from any treatment, action, application or preparation, to any animal or to any person reading or following the information in this book. The views expressed by contributors to this book are solely personal and do not necessarily represent those of the author. References are provided for informational purposes only and do not constitute endorsement of any websites or other sources.

Author's Notes:

For ease of reading, the masculine pronoun 'he' is often used to represent both male and female dogs.

The Boston Terrier Handbook uses UK English, except where Americans have been quoted, when the original US English has been preserved.

Made in United States
Orlando, FL
13 March 2024